Readers Praise Jacqueline Marcell's *Elder Rage*

"A remarkable book! You have charted a relatively untrod field associated with the aging process. You deserve a great credit—congratulations!"
—Steve Allen, Television Personality, Best-selling Author

"Jacqueline's persistence and grace in the face of overwhelming obstacles is incredible. Delightfully written with wit and compassion, this firsthand drama is a primer for anyone with aging parents."
—Ed Asner, Actor

"As someone who has been through a similar journey with my own mother (for thirty-five years of dementia), I can relate to the sacrifice and reward, the horror and humor, and the evolution and eventual acceptance of circumstances that Jacqueline has gone through."
—Jacqueline Bisset, Actress

"Jacqueline has written a powerful and poignant story about the family devastation of dementia. This is a must-read for caregivers."
—Harold H. Bloomfield, M.D., Best-selling Author,
Making Peace With Your Parents **and** *Making Peace With Your Past*

"This powerful and rewarding daughter's story illustrates that it's never too late to conquer family secrets. Anyone struggling to manage an elderly loved one will be grateful for this heart-warming book."
—John Bradshaw, Best-selling Author, *Bradshaw: On the Family,*
Healing the Shame That Binds You, Homecoming, Family Secrets

"This amazing, moving book is a must-read for anyone who has an elder parent and everyone who may sometime be one."
—Hindi Brooks, Internationally produced and published
playwright and playwriting instructor at UCLA

"Jacqueline's heartfelt message is a gift to every Baby Boomer and professional managing a toxic elder. She illustrates that unconditional tough love, persistence, and creative behavior modification can work to turn around a seemingly impossible anomaly of aging."
—Gloria Davenport, Ph.D., Author,
Working With Toxic Older Adults: A Guide to Coping With Difficult Elders

"A poignant, humorous and entertaining roller coaster ride, laden with valuable and practical caregiving advice. Having survived being raised in a home shared by a demented grandmother, my hat is off to you. You should be canonized, my dear!"
—Pam Dawber, Actress

"Fascinating! Once you open it, you won't be able to close it—until you finish it."
—Fred de Cordova, Executive Producer
   The Tonight Show with Johnny Carson

"There's nothing like a real life story by someone who's been there—done that. This is a gripping true story that will make you cry and laugh."
—Phyllis Diller, Comedian

"This sharing of a caregiving experience, which reflects a journey of self discovery and perseverance in creativity, is a welcome addition to the shared journeys of adult children caring for their aging parents."
—Brian M. Duke, President, Children of Aging Parents

"As Frank McCourt did so poignantly in his best seller *Angela's Ashes*, so too has Jacqueline captured in *Elder Rage*. Both experienced devastating family tragedies, yet kept their sanity with touches of humor. As an elderly father, I would like to feel assured that there is someone as special in my family to play the role of caregiver with tough love and tender compassion as Jacqueline has done so avidly."
—Jerry Dunphy, Newscaster

"Fellow Baby Boomers listen up! With all the recent breakthroughs in medicine, you may find yourself caring for your parents for more years than they cared for you. *Elder Rage* will show you how to be an effective caregiver without ruining your own life in the process."
—Ken Dychtwald, Ph.D., Best-selling Author, *Age Wave* and
   Age Power: How The 21st Century Will Be Ruled By The New Old

"Jacqueline tackles that part of life that most think will never happen, and shocks us out of our denial with what it can really be like dealing with the personality and diseases of our elders."
—Dr. Dean Edell, Host of *The Dr. Dean Radio Show*
   Best-selling Author, *Eat, Drink, and Be Merry*

"An amazing success story! Jacqueline illustrates that determination and persistence are key to solving one of the most difficult aspects of aging."
—**Dennis Estabrook, Founder, Strive For Success, Inc.**

"A fascinating look at human behavior that illustrates the success of a daughter's devoted persistence. Written with the wit, compassion and integrity that you'll never forget."
—**Betty Friedan, Lecturer, Best-selling Author,** *The Feminine Mystique, It Changed My Life, The Fountain of Age, Life So Far*

"This is a touching book, full of valuable caregiving tips. Having worked with difficult and dementia patients as the administrator of an Alzheimer's clinic, I have met many families in crisis with their loved ones. *Elder Rage* is the first book that I have seen that so candidly describes and solves one of the most difficult aspects of elder care."
—**Cathy Galloway, LVN, Senior Healthcare Provider**

"Jacqueline's heart-warming account of the love she gives her parents touched my heart. This is must-reading for the Baby Boomers."
—**Leeza Gibbons, Host of** *EXTRA*

"I have consulted families with aging issues for over 25 years, and the problem of anger in dementia is one of the toughest. Jacqueline's story is a valuable resource that offers guidance and inspiration."
—**Dr. John W. Gibson, DSW, MSW, MS**
  The Institute For Successful Aging

"Jacqueline's ingenuity and her ultimate understanding will inspire and comfort anyone dealing with a parent's not-so-gentle decline. This true-life story of one of the ultimate family struggles will help everyone grow in emotional depth and understanding."
—**Barry Gordon, M.D., Ph. D., Professor of Neurology and**
  Cognitive Science. Director, The Memory Clinic,
  The Johns Hopkins Medical Institutions, Baltimore, MD.

"This devoted daughter's amazing journey will give you the skills and strength to manage your own elderly loved ones with humor and grace."
—**Dr. John Gray, Ph.D., Best-selling Author,**
  Men Are From Mars, Women Are From Venus

"Jacqueline's journey illustrates the power of wit, humor, and loving persistence that will keep you on the edge of your seat. You will laugh, you will cry—and you will never forget this daughter's story."
—**Lisa P. Gwyther, MSW, Duke University Center for Aging**

"Most Baby Boomers will spend more time and money on elder care than child care. This great insightful book will help you to know that you are not alone."
—**Mark Victor Hansen, Co-creator of the #1 *New York Times* Best-selling: *Chicken Soup for the Soul*® series**

"What a contribution—a true story told with compassion and humor!"
—**Julie Harris, Actress**

"Jacqueline has a story to tell that will engage anyone coping with the aging process in their own family."
—**Senator Tom Hayden of California**

"The reader will feel privileged to experience the challenges and eventual gratifying solutions that Jacqueline presents in this poignant narrative. Her courage, sensitive insights and excellent writing style will offer adult children a lifeline of hope and positive expectations."
—**Irene C. Kassorla, Ph.D., Best-selling Author, Lecturer**

"You'll learn, you'll laugh, you'll cry—what a wonderful combination of emotions—and you'll never forget this daughter's incredible journey."
—**Janet Leigh, Actress**

"Bravo! What an incredible learning adventure. Written with humor and wit, keeping you as spellbound as a riveting novel."
—**Art Linkletter, Television Personality, Best-selling Author**

"An emotional, moving story! Jacqueline shares a most difficult and amazing journey with humor, compassion and hope."
—**Nancy Logan, President, American Women In Radio & Television**

"Filled with humor and heart, Jacqueline's inspirational book delivers helpful life lessons for your own journey with elderly loved ones."
—**Dr. Ross D. Martin, MD, MHA, Harvard Medical School**

"How did Jacqueline come up with a 'fun-read' about such a difficult subject? Well, here it is—laughter amid the tears. And don't they always say that laughter is the best medicine of all?"
—Ed McMahon, Television Personality

"Congratulations! A very important subject that does not get enough attention, as more and more people are finding themselves having to cope with caring for their elderly parents."
—Hayley Mills, Actress

"I hear the frustration as Baby Boomers try to manage their own lives as well as the lives of their often times difficult elderly parents. I was moved by Jacqueline's informative, educational and entertaining book."
—Neil Neimark, M.D., Author, *The Handbook of Journaling: Tools for the Healing of Mind, Body & Spirit*

"Jacqueline has masterfully written a riveting true story, solving an issue that many adult children endure, but rarely speak about so openly—and illustrates the tremendous value of Adult Day Services in improving the lives of everyone involved with caring for an elder."
—Jan Nestler, Immediate Past Chair, National Adult Day Services Association, a unit of the National Council on the Aging

"Ms. Marcell has turned a tragedy into valuable guidelines for caregivers."
—Jane Powell, Actress

"This book provides great solace for anyone who has ever been through the pain of watching someone you love lose control and slowly become someone else entirely. I have lived through this nightmare and can attest to how difficult it is. *Elder Rage* is a thoughtful, personal story that will touch your heart and inspire you to keep going even in the most trying of circumstances."
—Senator John D. Rockefeller IV of West Virginia Founder of the Blanchette Rockefeller Neurosciences Institute Dedicated to research for finding cures for neurological disorders

"Dementia threatens the essence of our humanity. Jacqueline's book chronicles her struggle to effectively change her parents' brain chemistry and improve their lives."
—Lisa Routh, MD, Medical Director, Amen Clinic, Newport Beach

"There is no voice more honest and comforting than the voice of experience. This devoted daughter's hardships will become blessings for all those struggling to care for an elderly loved one who resists their care. If this must-read compelling story helps one person reach out for resources sooner than later, it will be a success."
**—Linda Scheck, Executive Director
The Alzheimer's Association of Orange County**

"Delightfully real, often funny, with twists and turns that will have you nodding in recognition, often laughing and sometimes crying. Jacqueline triumphs when she discovers that demented does *not* mean stupid (a concept that is not widely appreciated) and demonstrates that there can still be a good life after dementia, when it is properly managed medically and behaviorally."
**—Rodman Shankle, MS, MD, Neurologist Specialized in Dementia
Co-founder of the U.C. Irvine Alzheimer's Center**

"Jacqueline illustrates that love is always the most powerful medicine."
—Bernie S. Siegel, M.D., Best-selling Author
Love, Medicine & Miracles

"Jacqueline describes the extremes that a daughter must go through to save a father with dementia. She chooses the more difficult path of staying the course, a much tougher existence than just walking away, and brings honor to her parents and moves us to a world with insight."
—Nancy L. Snyderman, M.D., Medical Correspondent/ABC News

"*Elder Rage* works! First, as a riveting non-fiction novel about a daughter's unconditional love for her aging parents. Secondly, as an informational book on caring for the elderly—that solves the mystery of managing difficult elders. You will be helped and you will be touched by this amazing story's heart-line."
—Robert Stack, Actor

"Methinks you have a blockbuster on your hands. You deserve some sort of an award for producing a wonderful book like this—it's going to help so many people."
—Irwin Zucker, Founder, Book Publicists of Southern California

Elder

RAGE

—or—

Take My Father... Please!

How To Survive
Caring For Aging Parents

Jacqueline Marcell

**Impressive
press**

Elder Rage or, Take My Father... *Please!*
How To Survive Caring For Aging Parents

Impressive Press
25 Via Lucca, Suite J-333
Irvine, California 92612-0604
Phone: (949) 975-1012 Fax: (949) 975-1013
Website: www.ElderRage.com E-mail: impressivepress@home.com

Copyright © 2000 by Jacqueline Marcell
First Printing 2000
Printed in the United States of America

Publisher's Cataloging-in-Publication
(Provided by Quality Books, Inc.)

Marcell, Jacqueline
    Elder rage : or, take my father... please! : how to survive caring for aging parents : including A physician's guide to treating aggression in dementia by Rodman Shankle / Jacqueline Marcell. —1st ed.
    p. cm
    LCCN: 00-90875
    ISBN: 0-9679703-0-X

    1. Aging parents—Care. 2. Parent and adult child—Family relationships. 3. Adult children—Family relationships. 4. Aged—Care. 5. Aging parents—Psychology. 6. Adult children—Psychology. 7. Adjustment (Psychology) 8. Marcell, Jacqueline. I. Title.

HV1451.M37 2000   362.6
                              QBI00-352

Dedication

This book is lovingly dedicated to my parents,
without whose love and encouragement throughout my life
I could not have written this book.

♥♥♥

Special Thanks

I want to especially thank my dear friend, Linda Shea, for her encouraging words that kept me going, for her assistance in taking care of my home and mail forwarding during my long absence, and for her infinite patience during much needed computer lessons.

And to Linda's father, Mort Shea, a retired English teacher, for offering to take his red pen to the first draft and kindly refreshing me on long forgotten grammar and punctuation while giving me so much praise.

And to my dear cousin, motivational speaker, Judy Ness, for proofing the second draft and encouraging me by saying, "I can't put it down!"

And to my dear friend, writer/director, James Adams *(The US Air Force Fiftieth Anniversary Show* and *The Tribute to Bob Hope)* for getting tough with me on the third edit that cut *Elder War and Peace* in half.

And to writer/director, Susan Rohrer, *(About Sarah)* for proofing my manuscript and giving me so much praise and valuable advice.

And to my dear friend, writer/director, Don Roos *(Love Field, Single White Female, Diabolique, Boys on the Side, The Opposite of Sex, Bounce, M.Y.O.B.),* who proofed my manuscript and gave me so much loving encouragement by saying, "You wrote a wonderful book, you're a good daughter and an excellent writer—I hope you know that."

And especially to my life-long always supportive dear friend, Nancy Lewis, for so much help with the editing, advice on the layout, the subtitle, the logo and the cover design. Contact her for graphic design: (916) 451-3177 or e-mail: Thotovit@aol.com.

And to BigDevelopment.com for designing my www.ElderRage.com website. Contact them at (949) 645-6936 for all your website needs.

And to the nicest person I ever met in the entertainment business, Regis Philbin, for his wonderful quote and our enduring friendship.

And especially to my dear friends, Linda Flanagan, Kelly Greer, Herb Kalazair, Susan Lane Leonard, Nancy Logan, Bob Piedemonte, and Marla Zaslansky for their many years of loving support and encouragement.

Many Thanks

Kathy Aaronson, Debra Allen, Ken Allison, Bob Altenbach, Adonna Amoroso, Annie Atondo, Todd Ballard, Venay Beaulieu, Lisa Bemel, Jesse Bermudez, Rebecca Boe, Mark Branner, Candy Burton, John Burt, Craig Campbell, Carolyn Carlat, Hilary Carr, The Carrolls, Mario Casilli, Devon & Bree Chierighino, Thuy Chung, Joe & Marty Cisi, Mary Clements, Bill Clingen, Linda Combs, Rhonda Cook, Mike Corgnatti, Bob Cunniffe, The Cunninghams, John Darin, Terri Douglas, Kimberly Dubois, Rodine Durgin, Elliot Eisenberg, Elaine Farmer, Roxi Faircloth, The Fernandezes, Richard, Kathleen & Kevin Flanagan, Ruth Flores, Al & Terri Footnick, Eve Foussard, The Freids, Andy Gadd, Al Garcia, Margo & Ron Garton, The Gealers, Ed Goebel, Robert Goodman, Richard Gordon, Richard Greninger, Bill Groshelle, Randy Harabin, Ginny & Kathy Hayes, Ernie Hicks, The Hillbrands, Mike Hinkson, Liz Ingber, Floyd & Toni Ingram, The Italianes, Lorna Jangula, The Jencks, Herb Kalazair, Sr., Kalens Press: Ron James & Sherli Babakani, The Kanters, Catherine Kitcho, Bob & Jane Knudson, Stephina Knoll, Eric Kotowitz, Brian Kowalski, John Kremer, Jack Krozser, Michelle Kuster, Chris Larson & Hilary Poochigian, Carmen Leal, Stephen Liebes, Carol Lenoir, Ed Leonard, Roger Lovett, The Lutzkers, The MacAskills, Andy & Nicole Maisner, Anita, Mikey, Ashley, Gabriel & Gina, Jerry & Carolyn, All The Marcells, Chris Marshall, Dotty & Dick Marsh, Ron Matranga & Eddie Broussard, Bill & Annie Mauger, Norma McDaniel, Doug McKee, Kathie & Sylvain Melloul, Betty Munoz, Roberta Nadler, Barbara Nowak, Robin & Gabe Ornelas, Rachel Owens, The Packards, JoAnn Padgett, Clardy Paen, Bob Pearce, Nancy Peterson, Pete Peterson, Linda Pickrell, Shirley, Nancy, Bill & Diane Piedemonte, Susan Pike, John Pitkin, Judy Posnikoff, Randy Post, Dan Poynter, Clare Preis, Steve Pybrum, Forrest Quinn, Rollie Rankin, Tory Regan, Kevin Roberts, Tim & Judi Rook, Ester Ruenitz, Paul Ryan, Susan Scannell, MaryAnne & Michael Scheff, Al Schramm, Chuck Schuman, Michael Sederoff, Jeff Sessler, Rod & Junko Shankle, Lorraine Sharkey, The Shoops, Dixon Smith, The Stillwells, Marian & Doug Stone, Linda Stoppoloni, Jay Stubner, Tom & Mike Sullivan, Kathleen Tandle, Steve Thatcher, Virgil & Tess Thompson, Kimberly Thulin, The Vanfossens, Kathy Vankat, Rod & Dolores West, Joyce Wexler, Buzz Williams, Emerald Wu, Frank Wu, The Yanofskys, Philip Yee, and Sheldon & Hannah Zaslansky.

Table of Contents

Appendix

A True Story

The names and some situations have been changed
to protect the innocent—and the guilty!

♥ ♥ ♥

My grandmother always used to say:

"God makes teenagers and the elderly mean on purpose—
otherwise, their families would never be able to let them go."

♥ ♥ ♥

chapter♥one

IF IT ISN'T TEN THINGS—IT'S TWENTY

T he sweltering heat of this Southern California September day wasn't fazing me a bit. Nooo, the weather wasn't even *close* to being on David Letterman's "Top 10 List" or on my own "Top 20 List" of reasons my life had become the soap opera I now affectionately called: "9021-OH—MY—GOD!" It was just absolutely unbelievable—everything in my world was falling apart one by one. First, there was the much needed but still devastating breakup of my long-term relationship. That would have been bad enough, but then there was the sudden death of my only "child," Spunky, after sixteen unconditional cat-loving years. Then, working out, I caused myself two herniated discs in my neck and a torn rotator cuff in my shoulder. That'll teach me for trying to keep up with Jane Fonda and Richard Simmons. After that, my lower back started to intermittently ache, but all the doctors I went to couldn't find *anything* wrong with me and insisted it was just stress.

Then, there was the horrifying mugging by four coked-up gang members with knives at my throat, ready to kill me for thirty-six dollars. So, I had already earned bonus points on the stress test when another bombshell hit me. One minute I was Vice President of a respected television production facility, and the next minute I was canned, when the big client I had brought in four years earlier decided to buy the company.

"Thanks for the *millions* of dollars you've made for the company, but as of Friday (it was Wednesday) we won't be needing you or the General Manager. We're bringing in our own top executives from Denver." Yep, it was basically, "Good-bye, good luck, sayonara."

"Gee, don't sugar-coat it, Kid—give it to her straight." (Butch Cassidy to Sundance.) I should explain. I have this habit of always relating my reality to movies or grander fiction—it just helps

1

me feel better. Oh, and I always have to have a "theme song" to sing too, that summarizes what life has dished out for the moment. I better fill you in as to when all this started.

Yes, doctor, this obsession with movies and television began early in my childhood. Uh-huh, you see my parents (June and Ward Cleaver—with a twist) would take us to Disneyland and then to see all the live television shows like *Steve Allen* and *Lawrence Welk*. Lawrence was a distant cousin of my father's (not a claim-to-fame I tell everyone), so we watched Lawrence "turn off the bubble machine" every week. Dad would tell stories of Lawrence playing the accordion at the barn dance hootenannies back home, where the buffalo roamed on the range, and said it sounded like "the Heavens were opening up." My father and I took up the accordion, but there never was any parting of the big blue beyond. Anyway, the result of all these trips to fantasy land, seeing where they shot *77 Sunset Strip* and comparing my hands to Shirley Temple's at Grauman's, was that I always wanted to be in the entertainment business when I grew up. So, I did—and now I relate everything to show business.

But I digress—back to my back pain. Even that was dropping down on my "woe-is-me" list, as I started to have more flexibility after undergoing major spinal surgery recently. At least that horrible episode was quite literally behind me. Actually, nothing could ever be as high up on my list as what I was facing now. My beloved mother, Mariel (by now, kind of a frail Loretta Young type), was probably going to pass away soon. It had been eleven years already since her heart attack and coma, and she had never fully recovered. Now, when I talked to her by phone, she sounded like she was really going down hill fast.

My tears flowed as I recuperated alone in my bed from my back surgery, waiting for *the* phone call from her doctor. I laid there and thought about all the "elephants" in the road that I had maneuvered around these past couple of years, but somehow I knew that this next "senior safari" was going to be the ultimate challenge.

The back problem "elephant" had detoured me the farthest from the successful path I'd been on. The physical therapy the doctors insisted I endure just made it worse. I had tried everything anyone suggested, most of it not covered by my virtually worthless HMO health insurance plan. I had hundreds of chiropractic adjustments, numerous steroid injections, and twenty of the most unbearable Chinese nerve-block injections you can imagine.

The doctors kept telling me it was "just sciatica" and all I really needed was a good long rest. When I got so unceremoniously laid off, I thought, okay great, I'm going to take that rest. I hobbled into my massage-chair with my ice and heat packs and started my day at nine o'clock with *Regis and Kathie Lee* (I worked with "Reege" years ago and we have remained friends ever since), and finished up with Ted Koppel and Tom Snyder. Hey, I was resting!

The doctors were sure that I was "just fine" and refused my pleas for MRI's, as that would take money out of *their* pockets. They implied that it was all in my head—sending me to a worthless shrink-less who boasted she had more degrees than a thermometer. Okay, analyze this! After being stuck-on-stupid for far too long, one day I reached my limit. I called up my primary care physician, Dr. Quinn, Medicine Impersonator, and pleaded to get in to see her ASAP.

"Sorry, no appointments for several weeks."

I decided to go wait at her office but I was told again that I would not be able to see her. I broke down crying saying that I just couldn't take this constant pain anymore and that it was "driving me crazy."

"Sooo, are you going to hurt yourself?" the stepford nurse asked, peeking over her ever-so-attractive horn-rimmed pearly pink glasses. Hmmm—now there's an idea. I made a split second decision.

"Yes, I'm going to jump out of this window if I don't get to see the doctor right now!"

"Oh my, well um—I'll be right back." It wasn't long after that when Madame Killya showed up, very annoyed, saying what a drain on her day my death was going to be for her.

"Listen, you get a specialist to order MRI's on my back right now, or I'm going public with my friends in the media and I'm naming *you* as part of the problem with this ridiculous HMO." It was a great impromptu performance. "And the Emmy goes to..."

Well, you never saw anything happen so fast. Three days later the limping surgeon, with a cast on his leg, who had said I was "just fine," was looking at my MRI's. "Ohhh, I see the problem *now*. You have a tiny cyst *inside* your spinal canal pressing on the nerve. No wonder you have pain. It just never showed up on the (I shudda been glowing by then) x-rays. I'll be damned." Yeah, that would be good.

I wanted another opinion as my confidence level in Hop-along was pretty low. "So, how many of these types of surgeries have you done, doctor?" I asked the thick German-accented surgeon.

3

"Oh, what you havahere, very rare, yes, very rare indeed. I think maybe I seen two in my career." (And he was no spring chicken.) Geeeeese, I wouldn't let somebody cut my *hair* who's only done two haircuts. I doubt I'm gonna let Dr. Mengele here cut open my spine. And so began the long search to find the most experienced surgeon who had seen this rare condition. After an expensive, exhaustive search and numerous differences of opinion, I was back with the "third time is the charm" guy, as he was the only one covered by my worthless HMO, which I enjoyed referring to as *Fatal* Health Plan.

"Jacqueline, this is nothing for us here," he said very arrogantly. "We do the brain surgery much more complicated than you. On the scale of the one to ten, yours—maybe the three or the four. I told you, live with pain or get surgery. You just must to decide which opinion you trusta the most and just hope the best—that's it." I had a real problem with that "hope" part, not to mention his English and wondered if he could read the directions in the spinal surgery manual. Geeeeese, do they have a class in medical school to teach patient confidence? Maybe a basic sales class even? I had taught sales and marketing for years—they really needed a mandatory course.

"I'll bet if this was *your* spine that was being sliced open, you'd consider it a twelve! Have you seen the movie *The Doctor*, with William Hurt?" It had been on television the night before, about an arrogant doctor who gets cancer and has to become a patient himself, and gets *way* humbled in the process.

"Yes," he nodded in recognition.

"Well, see it again!" I said teary-eyed as I hobbled out.

Later, I was surprised when he phoned and sincerely apologized for his bad attitude, trying to assure me that *his* opinion was really the right one. I was still pretty leery as I'd even gotten a much different opinion from his own assisting surgeon about how much bone actually needed to be removed to get the cyst out. Greeeat.

Finally, I had to take a chance with Hans and Frans. Fortunately, they must have known something about what they were doing. At least I wasn't paralyzed, and I was starting to feel a bit better because it only hurt when I laughed—and when I didn't. Emotionally, however, I was going to need a frontal lobotomy, *or*—a bottle of "miracle tonic" in front of me.

♥ ♥ ♥

I've Seen Fire and I've Seen Rain Drops
Fallin' on My Head

My eighty-three year old father, Jake (by now, kind of an elderly Spencer Tracy type), is in *Who's Who* for being the most headstrong, obstinate man on the planet. Oh yeah, you'll find his picture next to STUBBORN in the dictionary. He's beyond belief. For eleven years he insisted on taking care of my ailing mother all by himself, refusing all suggestions to get help, preferring instead to call me long distance and complain daily. I finally just hired an agency to help him. As a favor to me the owner went to their house several times trying to convince him how helpful it would be to have someone come in to care for Mom, just for a couple hours a day. He would dictatorially stand over the caregivers and be so horribly mean to them—they'd quit.

"I'm sorry, Jacqueline, we just *can't* work with your father. I don't think you'll find anyone who will. He doesn't want anyone in that house and he's not going to allow it until he's on his knees himself."

Even though my mother needed quite a bit of care, she was still a good traveler and they would drive down from San Francisco to Southern California to visit me frequently. Things had changed quickly because it had only been a couple months since they had insisted on being with me for my spinal surgery. "Daaad, you can't see well enough to drive that far anymore—it's really too dangerous."

"Awhhh, we'll take it slow—three or four days maybe."

"We're going to be there with you, honey," Mom said adamantly. There was no way to stop them. I had tried many times in the past to get them to stay home, but they'd just show up whether I wanted them or not.

"Oh-k," I resigned myself, "but please drive slow, and only during the day for a couple hours and then get a room and rest."

"We will," they both said happily.

"Ding-dong," I heard faintly as I came out of a sound sleep, upset that someone was ringing my doorbell so early. I hobbled out of bed expecting someone selling *something*, but hoping for *The Millionaire*, or Dick and Ed giving me my check. Opening my door, I could *not* believe my eyes. I had just spoken to them the night before and here they were—my very old, very disheveled, barely able to stand themselves, devoted parents—proudly standing behind a wheelchair that they had hauled down for *me*, for after my surgery.

5

"Oh my gosh, what are you guys doing here already?" I exclaimed, embracing them both, as my heart sank to see how frail and weak Mom was and how much Dad had aged in a couple months. "You're not supposed to be here for three days yet. You could have been killed driving all that way at night. I'm so glad you're safe," I said, kissing them. "What time did you leave home, Dad?"

"Well, we went to bed at nine o'clock so we could get up at dawn to start driving, but we couldn't sleep. Mother kept asking me over and over what time we were getting up (no short-term memory left), so by about midnight I finally just said, now! So, we got up and started driving and here we are—ready to help ya."

"Oh my... you mean you drove all night, in the dark, for eight hours? Daaad, you aren't supposed to drive at night anymore."

"Awhhh, mother helped me, didn't you Mommy?" She nodded proudly. "Anyway, there really wasn't any traffic."

Shaking my head, "Yeah, but..." Huge inhale... and hold it... hold it... (oh there's no use)... and blow it out. Thank you, Jack La Lanne. I should explain again. You see, my mother and I always did our exercises and deep breathing with him and his white dog when I was little in front of the old RCA Victor television set. I have always practiced deep breathing exercises at times of stress ever since. Prepare yourself—lots of heavy breathing ahead.

"Mom, are you okay? Did you stay awake the entire night?" I asked, as I got some "sleep" out of her eyes, the way she always did for me when I was little.

"Oh yeah, he needed me. I could see real good for him. We made it just fine, but I'm awfully tired now, honey—can I lie down?"

"Of course, sure, let me help." I choked back my tears and turned away, not wanting them to see. I should have known. Never in my entire life had my parents not been there for me, and they weren't going to let a little problem like the fact that they shouldn't be driving four hundred miles, at night, with bad vision, stop them now. I fed them, kissed them, covered them up, and watched them, as they slept almost continuously for the next four days. My heart filled with so much love and then so much sorrow. I sadly realized that they were very close to the end of their lives, and I would never have anyone love me as much—ever again in mine.

Watching them sleep so hard, mouths open wide and snoring loudly with labored breaths, I remembered all the ill friends they had helped over the years. It seemed like they were always going to see someone in the hospital or to a funeral. Until very recently, they'd gone to all the cemeteries to keep up the graves and bring fresh flowers.

A childhood friend of Mom's and her husband had been very ill for years and my parents would frequently drive several hours to help them. Her friend had been so judgmental, making fun of fat people when she was young and beautiful, that Mom said she had to learn that lesson the hard way and have it happen to her when she developed diabetes and ballooned with her weight herself.

"Never make fun of anyone and their misfortunes. There but by the grace of God go I," she would always say when she saw someone less fortunate. "I want you to always remember the Golden Rule: *Do unto others as you would have them do unto you.* Make sure you never judge anyone until you walk a mile in their moccasins." I always pictured Pocahontas and Tonto crossing the shores of Gitche Gumee swinging tomahawks when she used that one. It took me a while to figure that lesson out, but when I did, it really stuck, and I have found it to be a very good rule to live by.

Now almost all their friends and relatives were sick themselves or gone. There would be no one to repay the favors and be there for them. The realization, that I knew deep-down for quite some time, was that there was *no* help coming for them—unless it was me. My only sibling, my older brother Jeremy (kind of a fifty-something, Arthur Fonzarelli type), wouldn't even speak to them for eleven years, let alone help me with them. (Don't worry—much more family dysfunction stuff later.) No, I was going to be the fall gal. It was all going to land right on top of me and I could see it coming like an avalanche—but I had no idea it would almost bury me alive.

But while they still had an ounce of strength left, they were going to be there for me. The day of my back surgery Dad got Mom up and dressed two hours before we even needed to get up. He hated being late and worried so much about how long it would take to get places. They insisted on waiting at the hospital during the long hours of my surgery and I worried it would be too much for them. I woke up to their relieved faces, as they could barely stand over me, smiling and assuring me that everything had gone well.

"The doctor said they got it out real good, honey. Don't you worry, okay, sweetheart?" Dad said as he patted my arm.

"The doctor is nice, very handsome too," Mom chimed in.

I had a flashback from the corner of my mind: I'm ten, having my tonsils out and they're the faces I woke up to then too, assuring me that I was okay. Even though my father was the source of all our family dysfunction, with his occasional explosive temper tantrums, I *never* questioned his or my mother's love for me.

Flash forward: Only two months later now, and it was pure torture waiting for the doctor to call and tell me if my mother was dying. Dr. Marie Kiljoy (kind of a fiery French, Hot Lips Houlihan type), my parents' cardiologist, had taken care of their health needs for almost twenty years. Ray Steer (kind of a forty-something, hunky Hungarian, Hawkeye type), Dr. Kiljoy's right-hand man, had been so much help to me the last three years as I learned that I could not trust what my father would tell me about their medical conditions. One day he'd say they were both "dying" and the next day they were driving through the Midwest to see the few relatives who were left. When he wanted more sympathy I'd get a laundry list of aches and pains. When he wanted me to butt out and not offer any suggestions he'd say they were "feeling great." Sometimes he would call and say that Mom was dying and I had to fly home. I fell for it a few times before I got wise. I'd call Ray behind my father's back and hear that they'd just been to the doctor's office and she was doing quite well. It was so frustrating, and my father was such a drama queen, okay king, "crying wolf" all the time, that I was never *really* sure what the actual truth was.

♥ ♥ ♥

Cries and Careless Whispers

When I noticed my mother's voice sounding so weak I phoned Ray at Dr. Kiljoy's. He said he didn't know how she was doing because my father had cancelled her last appointment. I got so upset with myself—being consumed with my own recovery, I hadn't kept up with Ray making sure Dad kept their appointments. Ray had so many patients that he hadn't let me know that they had cancelled and now Mom was probably paying the price—with her life.

I called my brother's ex-wife, Marina, to see if she could drop in on my parents and let me know what was really happening. She and her "new" husband of ten years, Don, were so helpful and went over right away to investigate for me.

"Mariel's asleep," Dad whispered. "I just had her up on the treadmill a few minutes ago so she's tired now but she's fine."

Marina was worried that Mom was dead in there and that Dad wouldn't part with her. "Oh, I'll just give her a quick kiss and then we'll go, Jake," giving him no time to stop her from opening the bedroom door. "Oh, Mariel!" she cried at the sight of my eighty-two pound mother wasting away in the bed. Mom, always concerned for others and barely able to whisper, reached out to her.

"Oh, Marina, how are *you*, honey?" Marina asked her if she wanted to go to the hospital, but she pleaded that no, she wanted to stay at home. She'd had quite enough of hospitals over the eleven years. Dad kept insisting she was fine, just tired from being on the treadmill and made them leave. Marina left in tears and called me.

"I don't want to alarm you, Jackie, but I think your mom is going to pass away very soon and your dad is really losing it. The house is *filthy* and there is no way she could have been on the treadmill. Can you travel yet? You probably should get up here right away."

I immediately called my parents and *pleaded* with them to go to the hospital, but they flatly refused. If she were going to pass away, she wanted to be at home with him. I finally convinced my father to take her to see Dr. Kiljoy in the morning.

After their appointment Ray reported back to me that she was extremely weak and he also thought she was at death's door. They did some blood tests and wanted to put her in the hospital, but both Mom and Dad adamantly refused.

Ray said, "Prepare yourself—we think her defective heart valve is finally going to take her. She's really outlived what any of us thought she would. All the blood tests will be in by late today and then we'll know what's going on so we can give you a better idea of how long she has left."

Tick, tick, tick, tick—that *60 Minutes* stop watch was echoing in my head. It looked like boulders were trying to get through the hour glass on my nightstand. Time is an amazing thing when you focus on it. Sometimes it can drag on sooo slowly, you swear the hands of the clock are moving backward. I called Mom a few times, to hear her barely able to answer me.

"Fine, honey, just feeling tired now. How are *you*, sweetheart?" Tears welled up in my eyes and I choked up trying to talk.

"I'm fine, Mom. Do you have any pain?"

"No, no pain. I've been very lucky never to have had any pain all these years. Don't worry about me, sweetheart. I want to go to sleep now. Bye, my darling—I love you."

"Bye Mom, I love you too." I shudda had stock in Kleenex. I guess I'd want to die at home with my husband of fifty-six years too. She had never been sick a day in her life or even spent a day in the hospital, except for the days Jeremy and I were born, until this sudden heart attack at sixty-eight, over a decade ago.

Then, Ray called excitedly, "We just got the blood tests back and it isn't your mother's heart at all. She has a serious liver and gallbladder infection and she's going to die without antibiotics and needs to be hospitalized immediately. I've been calling their house over and over but no one answers."

Oh my God. Why-why-why didn't he pick up? Just as I was about to call Clive, the next door neighbor, Dad finally answered the phone very nonchalant as I practically screamed at him.

"Dad, where *were* you? Ray has been trying to reach you."

"Oh, I just went to the store for about forty-five minutes is all."

"Listen to me. Mom's heart is fine. She has a terrible infection in her body and needs to go to the hospital right away."

"Well, what should I do?"

"Hang up the phone and dial 911. I'll get the next flight up and meet you at the hospital. She doesn't have to die yet, Dad. *Promise* me you'll call 911."

"OK, if you say so. I'll meet you there." Click.

I only had time to throw a few clothes in a suitcase and then I was airborne. Continuous waves of emotions consumed me as I felt them coming on, rising up, crashing into me, then subsiding and leveling off, over and over, as I thought about my mother. Many times I would find myself doing or saying something just like the way she would do it, and it would always please me so much. I loved that I had so many of her mannerisms. She was such a serene beauty with so much grace and poise. She had a soft-spoken classiness about her and I never heard her say a harsh word about anyone—and I never heard *anyone*, ever, say an unkind word about her, except that maybe her choice of a husband might have been a bit better. When she had her heart attack, so many people came to see her and said, "Why her? She's the sweetest, dearest person in the world."

The taxi ride seemed endless but I finally arrived at the hospital to find my mother in "critical" condition, emaciated beyond recognition, and hooked up to many ominous machines. As I looked at her once ravishingly beautiful face (`a-la Hedy Lamarr), now so gaunt and gravely ill, a tidal wave of tears consumed me. Dad shuffled in from getting some coffee, looking much older than he did when they had looked over my hospital bed just two months before. I hugged and kissed him, and realized that what I feared was coming to pass. She was going to go first, and then he would pass away very quickly without her. We held on to each other and cried as we watched Mom, who was by then unable to know we were even there.

♥ ♥ ♥

Reality Bites the Hell Outta Ya

During the drive home late that night I tried to talk to my father, but I was surprised that he wasn't making much sense. I helped him up the five wooden steps into their double-wide mobile home that they had retired to twenty years earlier when the senior citizen mobile home park was brand new. He'd had a quadruple by-pass and needed minimal stairs then, and I could see that very soon he was going to need *no* stairs.

Boy, things had really changed in twenty years. When they had moved in everyone was in their sixties and still in fairly good health. Now, they were all in their eighties and so many were sick and dying. My father graphically reported complete details of every person's illness I had ever met there, as well as all those I hadn't. Misery loves company and no one enjoyed sharing misery more than Dad. It had become very depressing for them there so they always wanted to spend time at my house. Consequently, it had been over six months since I'd been to their house and I was not prepared for what I saw next.

We walked in the back door, went through the little laundry area, and I was hit with a major dose of reality. This once perfectly neat and spotlessly clean home was in a ghastly state. I suddenly had Bette Davis eyes and had to bite my tongue from saying, "What a dump!" Everything

11

was out of place with piles of stuff absolutely everywhere. My mother's beloved dining-room table had become an abandoned workbench and was piled so high with junk that I worried it would be terribly scratched. The formal living room was filled—everything from the big box that the console television came in years ago to garden tools. You could barely walk from one room to the other. There were smudged black fingerprints on everything, dust was visibly thick and cobwebs were abundant in the corners. All the dusty drapes were closed and the lights had been left on, casting a musty eerie aura. The floors were sticky, the gold carpet had dark tracked-in dirt paths, and there was crusted-on food on everything. The kitchen table had so much food spilled on it that there were tiny little bugs feasting.

Nothing added up. After *years* of listening to him complain that he couldn't do everything himself, but continuously refusing to get a housekeeper, I finally figured out how to get him to accept help. I had Martie Sue, Dr. Kiljoy's receptionist say, "Jake, you are doing such a great job taking care of Mariel, but you poor man, you can't do all the housework too. I have a wonderful cleaning lady we call Dusty. I've known her for years and she cleans our offices here too. She'll keep your house clean so all you have to do is take care of Mariel."

Dad said, "Okay." I was in shock. A receptionist mentions getting a housekeeper *once* and he's willing to do it. Ten *years* from me, and he wouldn't hear of it. And, I wasn't going to get any of the utmost appreciation that she would continue to get, over and over, whenever he'd see her. Oh well—mission accomplished.

Dusty started cleaning their house twice a month and during our phone calls Dad would rave about the great job she was doing and then tell me every detail of her life. Sadly, I realized that he must have decided to let her go and that he'd been lying to me for quite sometime. I casually asked him when was the last time Dusty had been there. "Ohhh, just last week," said Pinocchio. I swallowed hard knowing I'd have to hire a cleaning crew to come in for at least two days because there was no way I could do it myself. I struggled to change the sheets on the guest bed in the back bedroom and sorrowfully went to bed with horrible remorse that I had not been able to be there sooner.

♥ ♥ ♥

12

Just a Little R-E-S-P-E-C-T When I Come Home

The next morning I heard Dad's alarm go off at a very dark and early five-thirty because he insisted on being at the hospital by six o'clock. I had to rest my back which meant I was stuck there without a car. Mom's vintage baby-blue Mustang, with only 65,000 miles on it (64,000 put on by me in high school), sat useless in the carport for eleven years. I rang everyone up and let them know that her passing was probably imminent. I decided I better put "call-waiting" on Dad's phone so I wouldn't miss a message from him or the doctor.

I called the mortuary where Dad had pre-paid for their funerals and plots when she had been in the coma a decade ago. I cried when they told me that he'd paid to have her casket lined with blue polka dot material because the day he met and fell in love with her in 1940, she was wearing a blue polka dot dress. Then I understood the sweet meaning of all the blue polka dot outfits she'd worn over the years.

I thought it might disorient him if I moved things, so after I got rid of the bugs I made a few piles of things I thought he'd let me throw away once we went over them together. That afternoon he came home exhausted so I got him to take a nap. I'd take his car to go see Mom and then pick up a few groceries, as the refrigerator was "breeding."

When I came back later that evening I was stunned when he raced into the kitchen looking like his evil twin, Horrible Hyde. He erupted into the most unbelievable rage at me for buying two little hand towels for the kitchen. I had thrown his disgustingly filthy ones away earlier and he pulled them out of the trash and threw them at me. I was so completely flabbergasted I could hardly speak. The barrage of verbal abuse that spewed forth was so unimaginable, so heartbreaking, that I couldn't believe that he was *my* father, talking to *me*. I'd been brought up on his hot-air temper tantrums, but *nothing* as irrational and illogical as this, and I was *not* used to being the target. For some reason, he'd *never* turned on me as he had everyone else.

"I've been taking care of Mother by myself for eleven years— eleven goddamn years. And now you come up here and start throwing out our things! Who the hell do you think you are? How would you like it if I came to your house and threw out your things?"

"Oh, Dad, I'm *so* sorry. The little hand towels were so dilapidated, I didn't think they'd even make it through the washing machine. I thought that it would be nice to get you some new ones—see how pretty? Were these special or something?" I asked as I desperately tried to brush the filthy ones off with my hand. The bulging veins sticking out of his neck and forehead really scared me. Wow, this must be the stress of Mom dying and I was the scapegoat. As Mom always said, "Just be patient and this too shall pass," but it didn't. He went on and on *screaming*, accusing me of throwing out all their things.

"Oh yeah, you're some big shot TV executive coming in here and changing *my* house. And where's my placemat?" He escalated his yelling as if this placemat was of extreme value.

"Dad, that was a padded mailing folder I sent you some papers in last year. It had so much food dripped on it, there were bugs—I *had* to throw it away. I gave you washable placemats last Christmas. I found them and put them out for you—see how nice?"

"I don't give a goddamn about *new* placemats. I want what I had!" My mind was in overdrive trying to make sense out of a completely non-sensical situation. He started shaking as he screamed at me, pounding the same metal kitchen table that I'd seen him pound on my whole life for emphasis and control.

"And you can't have our things!"

I tried hard to assure him that I did not want their things, but the yelling went to an even higher level. When he finally ran out of steam and went to lie down, I quietly closed his bedroom door. Then I tried to distract my broken heart with television. Suddenly he got up, threw the door open like a madman and started up again. I couldn't believe he'd gotten his second wind so fast. The hail of verbal abuse went to an even higher level.

"You've never helped me in eleven goddamn years and I don't need you to lift a finger for me now either." *Ouch*—that one really hurt so deeply. I had tried so hard to help him for *so* long, but his own stubborn resistance to any kind of change made him impossible to help. I really think he liked being a victim and playing the martyr role to the hilt. I bit my tongue hard and I was reaching my limit and, oh my gosh, it was only the first day. As Miss Davis so poignantly once said, "Fasten your seat belts, it's going to be a bumpy night."

All I wanted to do was escape but I didn't have a car and I felt beyond trapped. Now I knew how my mother must have felt for the last eleven years with him dictating her every move. I just couldn't get him to stop berating me. I begged, pleaded, cried, and tried the silent treatment, but nothing worked. I went into the back bedroom and closed the door, but he followed me, throwing open the door and hurling insults. When he went into the bathroom I rushed to the phone to call my best friend since first grade who lived forty-five minutes away.

"Linda," I whispered in desperation, "my Dad's just flipped out. Please, can you come get me?" It was already ten-thirty and she's usually asleep by then as she gets up early to teach high school, but for some reason she was still up and dressed.

"Don't worry—I'll be right there." Thank God for dear Linda.

"Where the hell are you going?" Dad shouted as I pulled my wheeled suitcase from the back bedroom into the little laundry area.

"I'm going to stay with Linda for a few days, Dad. It'll be less stress on you if I'm not here."

"Linda? Linda who?"

"Dad, you've known Linda Flannery and her family *forever*."

"What the hell did she ever do for you? She owes you two hundred dollars."

"Whaaat? For what?" I couldn't fathom for what.

"You took pictures at her wedding and she never paid you for them," he scowled. What was he talking about? Yeeesss, I had done some photos for her first wedding a couple *decades* ago, but it was my wedding gift to her as I was a professional photographer just out of film school at the time. There was no mention I could ever remember of her owing me any money. I politely corrected him and went out onto the back porch, overwhelmed with tears which started to flow full stream down my face.

"Get back in here right *now*," he demanded as if I were ten years old. "If you leave now, you'll *never* come back into this house!"

"I'll speak with you tomorrow. Try to get some rest now, okay?"

"You're grounded. I said to get back in here right *now*."

"I have to go now—I love you, Dad."

How on earth was I going to handle him and my mother's passing at the same time? I could barely see through my tears as I rushed down the five wooden steps as soon as I saw my dearest friend drive up. I hugged her hard, "Oh Linda, thank you *so* much for coming all the way over here to get me at this time of night—thank you, thank you." She was literally a sight for very sore eyes.

♥ ♥ ♥

15

Le Miserable

A rental car was a must because it was nearly an hour drive from Linda's house to the hospital. My father started calling, begging me to come home, but then he'd be nasty when I'd get to the hospital. He'd be there at the crack of dawn, sleep in a chair next to Mom's bed, feed her breakfast and lunch, and wait for me to arrive in the afternoon to feed her dinner so he could drive home before it got dark.

I immediately called Ray at Dr. Kiljoy's and told him about my father's irrational behavior, but whenever they saw him Dad was completely normal, an absolute *sweetheart*. I hoped that as Mom got better Dad's behavior would do the same.

Adding to my overwhelming plight came the sudden death of Princess Diana. I was beyond consolable, feeling consumed by all the injustices of life. I remembered my first time in Europe after attending the Cannes Film Festival. I just *had* to be an American in Paris before returning home so I pampered myself by staying at the wonderful Ritz Hotel. Now I watched Princess Diana come out of that circular glass doorway I knew so well. I wished I could rewind the tape and make her go back in, instead of dying so tragically in that tunnel. Why? Why? There just didn't seem to be any sense in anything now.

To cheer me up the Fabulous Flannerys (kind of an Irish Huxtable family type), dynamic Linda, her handsome husband Dick, and their two great kids, Kathleen (fourteen), and Kevin (ten), threw me a birthday party a few weeks early as I probably wouldn't be there for my actual birthday. Little did we know how many holidays we would be spending together.

I watched the *Emmys*, and had pangs of regret for my former exciting life. Normally I'd be a judge for them every year. No, I had a responsibility to take care of my parents now. Everything else had to go on hold. As Dad used to tell me when obstacles were placed in his path, "Okay, honey, watch—we'll go *this* way around the 'elephant' then." It seemed like I had been dodging an endless herd of 'elephants' for so long, but I had the confidence, instilled all my life by my parents, that I would not get trampled. I focused on a strong new theme song and sang it over and over. This week, all the way to number one, Casey Kasem, *"We Shall Ov-er-come."* Thank you so much, Joan Baez.

♥ ♥ ♥

chapter two

HYDE STRUNG IN PLAIN SIGHT

D ad started being nice again, trying to give me money for my birthday present—bribing with cash was always his way of apologizing. "Thanks, Dad, but all I really want for my birthday is for you to not yell at me anymore." He put his head down, nodded and solemnly swore that he wouldn't. But, as always, the promise was short-lived. Every time I suggested getting Dusty back in to clean the house the yelling would begin. I didn't want to go back to that hot, filthy house and fight with him, so I decided to wait and see if Mom would pull through. If so, there was no way I'd let her go home to that mess. I'd figure a way out then.

Startling news hit me next: the infection that almost took her life was caused by my father's inability to keep her clean. Her own waste had infected her and he had let it progress without taking her to the doctor—almost to her death. I dreaded the confrontations that I knew were ahead, but I was determined to do what had to be done if it meant saving my mother's life.

After an arduous month-long vigil, the hospital informed me that they had done all they could for her and she would have to go into a convalescent/nursing home for a while, if not permanently. I spent my days visiting nursing homes in the area, amazed that there were no openings, as I put her name on the long waiting lists.

I got another dose of reality as I visited these places and saw all the elderly people waiting to die. It was gut-wrenching to walk by and have them reach out to me from their wheelchairs begging for some attention. I tried to stop and give a little of myself but it just got too hard. It was so sad to see them sleeping, weary heads on chests, folded wrinkled hands in their laps, wearing baggy hospital gowns and drooling. The echoing of their screams for help, the buzzers above the doors flashing, the monotone chanting of one lost soul in the corner, and I was completely overwhelmed. Who were all these people when they were young and active with their careers and families? I cringed to think of my mother in one of these places. There wasn't much point to bringing her back to life to put her there. No, I committed to figuring out a way to bring her home.

To make matters worse, my Godmother, Shelly, had to go into a convalescent home and it was tearing my beloved Godfather, Bo (kind of a handsome, Italian, seventy-something, Blake Carrington type), apart. It hurt me so much to see her bed-ridden, covered by the beautiful blue afghan my mother had crocheted for them so many years before. Bo and I shared our similar sorrows regularly and it brought us even closer. When all the stress of caring for Shelly put him in the hospital with a fluttering heart, I sobbed all day. He had always been the salt of my earth. I went to see him and cried, "You can't get sick—I just can't take it if I lose you too."

It was very hard for Bo to imagine what I was telling him about my father's rages. He was even more shocked when I shared the dirty little family secret—my father had had horrible temper tantrums his whole life. In fifty-six years of knowing my dad he'd never seen anything close to it—my father *respected* him too much to ever show that side of himself.

Apparently, Dr. Kiljoy's office thought I was grossly exaggerating about Dad's temper tantrums. Whenever they saw "Jake Lemmon" he would be *so* darling and *so* loving to Mom that they couldn't imagine him being any other way. They all knew him for many years and just adored him and yes, his Jekyll side was wonderful, but unless you experienced the flip side of Hyde—you just couldn't comprehend it.

Linda wanted to see Mom (her second mother growing up) so she went with me to the hospital one day. When we walked in I was surprised to see that Hyde the Horrible was already very present— and in *public* even.

"Where in the hell is the doctor? He was supposed to be here this morning. They didn't feed Mother any breakfast and it's two o'clock and she hasn't had lunch." I went to investigate. Seems there was a *glitch* in the system, and I was placated by being told that the doctor had been pulled away on "an emergency." I made it pleasantly clear that my very frail mother had not eaten all day and that there was going to be big trouble with my father. Within five minutes, Dr. Tardie (kind of a Doogie Howser type—unmarried, but young enough to be my... never mind), finally showed up to check her pacemaker.

Harrowing Hyde flew into a rage, "Where the hell have you been? My wife hasn't eaten a thing all day." When Dr. Tardie tried to calm him down by putting his hand on Dad's shoulder, it got really ugly. "Don't you touch me—I'll knock your block off!" my eighty-three year old, very short father yelled up at the six-foot-two doctor. "Don't you tell me to calm down. I'll show you a thing or two. I don't care if you are a goddamn doctor—don't you *ever* touch her!"

My mother was lying there starving to death, but my father wouldn't let the doctor get near her. I took Dr. Tardie aside, explained what I had been going through, and asked him to please pass this incident on to Dr. Kiljoy's office. The rages that had been reserved for us "privileged" family members were manifesting themselves without boundary. Even though I knew Linda believed every detail of the rage stories, it gave me a great sense of credibility that she had actually experienced it. And since a doctor had witnessed it, maybe Dr. Kiljoy's office would believe what I was saying and start to give me some help with him.

Mom was finally moved to the "sub-acute unit" (the patient is still making some progress) of a nursing facility next door to Dr. Kiljoy's. Medicare would pay as long as she continued to improve—but once she plateaued she had to go home or into a long-term nursing home.

It was late Friday afternoon and Mom hadn't been in her new room for five minutes when a young social worker came in, eager to get going to a hot date, and started asking her questions very loudly, as if Mom's hearing was bad.

"Mariel, do you want to be revived if you expire here?" My mouth flew open as Mom shook her head emphatically *no*. "Could you sign here then, pah-leaze," she yelled, holding a clipboard over my frail mother, trying to hand her a pen that she could not possibly even grasp.

Dad yelled from the corner, "*Absolutely* she wants to be revived!"

"I'm sorry, we have to respect your wife's wishes and I believe that she is shaking her head no."

I quickly escorted Brainless Bambi out of the room and forward marched her in to see her supervisors. Quite an apology followed. "Look," I said, "if my father is here, you better revive my mother. I'll have a talk with her tonight and if she really does not want to be revived, I'll sign the paperwork. I've had Durable Power of Attorney for many years." After my father left for home, I had a heart-to-heart talk with my mother.

"Please don't revive me, please just let me go, honey," she begged with such a pleading look. She knew what she was saying and I sadly realized that I had to respect her wishes. She had been through quite enough in eleven years of being so ill. I had a hard time catching my breath as I tried to steady my hand to sign the documents behind my father's back—as my uncontrollable tears streaked down my face, fell onto the legal-looking paperwork, and smudged the stark black ink.

♥ ♥ ♥

What's It All About, Jackie

Very late one evening as I leaned over to kiss my mother and say good-night, she held onto me and asked me for the first time in these many months not to leave yet. "Okay, is something wrong, Mom?"

"I'm afraid," she finally whispered. I waited another hour, held her hand and tried to comfort her, and then I tried to leave again.

"Please don't go yet. I'm sorry, honey—I'm very scared tonight."

"Ohhh, no problem, Mom," I said as I carefully scooted her over in the hospital bed and climbed in with her, holding her for a long time. The stern night nurse came in and started to demand that I couldn't be in her bed, but after she saw my pleading look, relented, and kindly covered us up. Stroking my mother's once beautiful face, I tried to get her to talk to me about her life.

"What was the happiest time in your life, Mom?"

"When you were born, sweetheart," she whispered. I kissed her cheek, wetting it with the tears I could not stop from flowing. They had tried so hard to have another child for many years after my brother was born, but she had many horrible miscarriages, all boys. They desperately wanted a girl, and it was quite a surprise, I guess, when *I* finally showed up after a very difficult pregnancy and a terrible breech birth, as the blessed event.

"I saw my darling Belle today—I think she's coming for me," she said softly. I was taken aback. Belle was one of her dearest friends who had died of cancer many years before and she and my father had done so much to help her.

"*Really*, where'd you see her?"

"Outside my window right here."

"Uh… did she *say* anything to you?"

"Yes, she said not to worry—she would help me."

WOW, I got a chill up and down my altered spine. My mother was the most honest person I have ever known, so this really got to me.

"Well… that must be very comforting then. She's going to make it easy for you. Are you sure you're ready to go, Mom?"

"Yes, darling," she nodded, "I'm ready."

"Would you like me to stay with you tonight, so you won't be afraid?"

She nodded again, and I gathered all my strength to stay and help her die. I laid there holding her frail body and thought for hours about my own beliefs about life and death. The day she had come out of her coma over a decade before, she told us that she had gone down a long tunnel, following a bright light and then she arrived at the side of a beautiful stream. Her mother and one of her sisters were on the other side and she started to step across, but they told her not to because she had to go back. She told us that she was so disappointed and asked them why, since she was already there and it was so wonderfully peaceful. They told her that she had more to do in her life, but not to worry, they'd be there when she came the next time.

We were completely stunned because my mother *never* lied or made up stories like Dad did all the time, so it was quite a tingling revelation. I reminded her of her coma experience and she smiled and said, "Yes, it'll be good to see them again." Another chill shot through me and then a strange calm, as I contemplated my own beliefs and sadly accepted what was about to happen.

♥ ♥ ♥

Losing My Religion

We were not a religious family at all, but we did go to church most Sunday mornings when I was little. At a very young age I realized the hypocrisy and irony of the whole thing when Dad would swear a blue streak in the parking lot about one thing or another and then he'd throw down his cigarette and grind it in anger just before suddenly becoming holier than thou and walking into the church. After the sermon, it wouldn't take long before he'd be back to swearing Holy "goddamn its" about something or other.

I decided I just didn't know what I thought and as a result I called myself "Agnostic." Don't want to commit one way or the other, just in case. Like W.C. Fields, I started looking for "loopholes" in the Bible. The only thing I was sure of, was that no one ever got out of this world alive. If only I could have a *little* proof of something beyond it all, I'd feel so much better.

A few years ago, during a trying time, I was in bed and for some reason I began "talking" to a deceased friend, Reanne, who had passed away twelve years earlier. I had never tried this before, but she was the only person I knew well who had died and I thought well, just *maybe...*

"Reanne," I said, "you were such a good friend, I hope you can give me some divine guidance here." I told her the whole saga—this was a problem, what should I do here and there, on and on. I told her, "I need a sign though. I mean you're going to have to move the lamp across the room before I'm going to believe *anything*. So, if you could, please send me a really BIG sign that you hear me so I know that I should believe in something beyond myself." I went on to thank her for all the fun times we'd had and told her how much I missed her and then I fell asleep. Well... the next morning the phone rang really early.

"Hello," I said, angry that someone was waking me up.

"Hello, is this Jacqueline Marcell?" a southern voice asked.

"Yes, who's this?"

"Jackie, this is Grant Collinson."

OH—MY—GOD! I was instantly awake. I could *not* believe that I was hearing the voice of Reanne's husband! I had not spoken to him for over a decade, since the day I called to see if she wanted to go to lunch and he told me the sad news that she had just been killed in a terrible car accident. I was in shock then, and I was in very humbled shock now. OK, Reanne, that's a very good BIG sign. I believe, I believe, no need to move the lamp—I've got it. *("I'm a believer!")*

"Grant, *why* are you calling me?" I asked in awe as I bowed to the heavens.

"Well, it's the damnedest thing. I've been thinking about you all morning, just out of the blue. I went to look for your business card and I finally found it—I can't believe you're still at the same number. Say, did you ever marry that guy you were with for so long?"

"No, but we had a friendly break up," I said in total amazement.

"Oh, well that's always the best way. Say, I'll tell you why I'm calling today. You remember those beautiful photos you did of our penthouse for *Architectural Digest* magazine years ago?"

"Yeees," I was all ears.

"Well, I moved to Newport Beach a few years ago, and I have this gorgeous home and I just wondered if you'd like to photograph it for the magazine?"

"Oh, gee, I would have loved to, but I stopped doing professional photography and went into the television business many years ago. I sold all my professional equipment," I said as my mind reeled.

"Oh, good for you. Well, how the heck are ya? You know, you oughta get out of LA and move down this direction—I think you'd love it. I'll give you my number and if you want to come check it all out, you let me know and I'll give you a tour. I just love it down here and I bet you would too."

"Oh, thanks, that would be very nice of you." I could hardly talk.

"Okay then, good talkin' to ya again after all these years, Jackie."

"You too!" You have no idea how good.

OK-OK-OK, this is either the *biggest* coincidence of my entire life, or he picked up my brain waves that traveled an hour's drive south, down to Newport Beach overnight, *or* Reanne sent him the message to call me and show me a really BIG sign. WOW! I was definitely leaning toward the latter. I went to Newport Beach shortly thereafter and Grant showed me how beautiful it was. I took the message to mean that I should move there and I did after I was mugged at knife-point in the asphalt jungle of Los Angeles.

So now, I held onto my mother and remembered all the times she had lovingly taken care of me when I was a child, as I was always home from school with one thing or another. We'd giggle to the *Art Linkletter* radio show and play my own home-made version of Monopoly in my bed. Dad would call from work all day to see how I was and then come home and make me laugh.

I had ruined so many of their fun times when I was little. No matter where we'd go, I'd get sick or hurt. Once, a sewing needle that was in a skirt that we kids were playing dress-up in, broke off deep inside my leg. That stopped the party as they rushed me to the emergency room to have it removed. Then there were the piercing side pains that cut short a fancy party they were having as they had to rush me to the hospital again. Then there was the broken little toe that needed a cast up to my knee, in the middle of a big get together. Oh, and then there were all the disgusting bloody noses that ended many a camping trip—not to mention the mosquito bites from head to toe that needed Calamine Lotion on every single bite. It seemed like every time we took a vacation I got sick with *something*: a bad cold, flu, measles, bronchitis, a sprained body part or a sty in the eye.

It seemed like I was home more than I was in school until I had my tonsils out when I was ten. Accomplishing that, however, was one of the worst episodes of my young life. I remember vividly the look of terror on my parents' faces at seeing me so ill. After coming home from the hospital, I started hemorrhaging huge clots of blood. I still have total recall of that repulsive smell of the old-time anesthetic "ether" they used. My mother was cradling me in her arms as I laid on the cold tile floor of our bathroom as she tried to keep me conscious.

"Jackie, sweetheart, come on now—stay with me, Jackie!" she screamed frantically as she cried and washed my flushed face with a cool washcloth. "Hurry, honey!" she yelled for my father. As always, my father swooped in and took charge.

"OK, let's go," he said as he scooped me up in his arms and the next thing I knew they were rushing me back down to the hospital, cautiously weaving through red light after red light. "Never a goddamn cop when you need one," I remember him saying. I was rushed back into the operating room and then, when I awoke—there they were, standing over me with very relieved looks on their faces.

"You're going to be fine, sweetheart," Mom said holding my hand, with tears going down her gorgeous face. "You're our sweet girl— we'd never let anything happen to you, darling."

"You're darn right she is," Dad confirmed. "She's a fighter, aren't you, honey? That's our girl. Don't be afraid, we're right here. We won't ever leave you—I promise you that."

Yes, they were always right there, comforting me, through every accident and illness, every hang nail and paper cut, every event large or small, rain or shine, for my entire life. I never worried that they would not be there for me—ever.

Now, all that was about to change as I prepared myself for the final moments of my cherished mother's life. I asked Reanne to make it easy for her and to gather a welcoming committee, *or* just maybe… if she had some inside pull up there… she could give her back to me for a little while longer. I slept there that night, feeling her every breath so hard against me, and when I awoke I was surprised that she was still barely with me. Dad arrived at dawn and we stayed with her all day. We couldn't get her to respond to us at all anymore. Then she'd suddenly look up and point to the window and cry out, "Belle!" and then fall back practically unconscious and non-responsive to anything we'd do. The doctors told us that nothing else could be done. Dad sat on one side of her bed and I on the other, holding her hands, sobbing together, sure that this was really going to be it. I finally had to make him go home to rest before it got dark.

"I'll call you if there is any change, Dad. Please go get some rest. I don't want to have to put you in the hospital next." He left reluctantly and I heard him sobbing his heart out as he shuffled down the hall.

Hours and hours went by and then... suddenly Mom opened her eyes, smiled weakly and whispered, "Hello, darling." I was amazed and rushed to lean over her.

"Hi, Mom, what do you want?" I asked as I took her hand and a tear streaked down my face and fell onto hers.

"I want to get well," she was barely able to say.

"*Really*, you don't want to give up?"

"No, I want to get well and go home," she pleaded. "*Please*, honey, please take me home."

"Okay, Mom. I'll *make* it happen, I will—I promise."

The doctors were completely baffled by her miraculous change and I immediately went to tear up the documents and to sign new ones to make sure she would be revived. Thankfully, those orders were never executed. Thank you, God. Thank you, Reanne—you heard me again. Sounds like somebody up there likes us.

♥♥♥

As the Wounded Turn

The nurses all said the same thing that I loved to hear, "There's no doubt about who *your* mother is, you look just like her." I always said what a lovely compliment that was for *me*, but that I didn't hold a candle to her in her heyday. When I was a kid and she'd come to my school events, being our Camp Fire Girl leader, the kids would say,

"Wow, your mom is *so* beautiful—she looks just like a movie star." And more importantly, she was as sweet and kind as Snow White and they all adored her.

The head nurse said, "Your mother is the loveliest patient we've ever had. She never complains and she's always so grateful whenever we do anything for her. She always asks about us and how we are. We just love taking care of her." Yep, that's my mother—I never met anyone who didn't love her.

You have to supply your own television at these places so I bought one. Mom's roommate didn't have a television, so I made it easy for her to see ours. Poor thing, she was a huge woman with a dreadful skin condition all over her body. She had a hard time moving so I always helped her and I felt so bad that no one ever came to visit her. I was polite and didn't ask questions about her terrible skin lesions.

One evening I noticed a tiny sign outside Mom's room that warned that our roommate had a "contagious" condition. I pressed the night nurse and found out that this woman had open-wound herpes. *What?* All this time and they had never told us! I was sick to my furious stomach remembering that we all used the same bathroom. Here I was being Nurse Scratch-it, helping the poor woman, and I was being exposed to it. I was *seething*. Never in my wildest field of dreams could I have imagined this place putting us at risk.

I made it very clear to the night staff that I wanted a meeting with the administrators first thing in the morning. I'd spent my whole life being so paranoid about catching anything ("Hey, let's be careful out there"), like herpes from a *man*, and now I was at good risk of getting it from this *woman*. Shudder, goose bumps, nausea, yuck. All I wanted was a Silkwood scrub-down with Borax—twenty mule team if I could get it.

When I arrived the next day they jammed six people into a tiny room for a meeting immediately. "The bathrooms in the rooms are for the patients only," they announced. "We told you to get the key at the front desk and use the bathroom in the hall."

"Excuse me! No-no-no, I was never told about any key or any other bathroom for over a month now. We came in late on a Friday afternoon and no one told us anything. You've all seen us here, day after day, feeding my mother every bite of her meals and making sure she is comfortable. You know she is never left alone except very late at night. You're so understaffed that my father and I do much of your work everyday. I've never seen the caregivers put any tissue down before sitting her on that toilet without any protection. So, if my father and I aren't supposed to use that bathroom because it is contagious, how do you explain sitting my mother on it when she is so terribly ill already?"

"Well, the open sores are up a bit higher, not at the point of contact with the toilet seat, so you probably won't get it," the administrator said defensively. (Yeah, that's what they all say.)

"Oh, I see, so we'll only get herpes on our backs. My mother sits there and leans back all the time. I've never seen it being sterilized after each use."

"Uh, um," struggling to placate me, "you can't even get it as long as you've had chicken pox. I'm sure you've all had that." Wrong again, almighty amateur hour herpes breath.

"Nooo, I have never had chicken pox and I don't really know about my parents or all of our many guests who have come to visit, but if any of us get it, trust me on this, you are not going to like the outcome."

They explained that it was a little *glitch* in the system, and by the time I got back to Mom's room the herpes lady had been removed with a big "CONTAGIOUS" sign outside her door and we had a great big "DO NOT DISTURB" on ours. Suddenly there were toilet seat protectors in our bathroom and it had been scoured with Clorox. My gosh, what happens to all the patients who don't have a strong family member to keep all these things from happening to them?

All I had to say was that I knew the "Ombudsman" who monitors the area and I got anything I wanted. During my extensive research of the nursing homes, I learned my new favorite word that I loved to repeat again and again with popping penuche: "Ombudsman." That's the guy who investigates the nursing homes, complaints, and files reports rating them in terms of cleanliness, etc. If they get enough whistle blows they can be shut down. Suddenly Dad was getting free breakfasts, lunches and yummy snacks with Mom's meals, her room was kept private, and they all just couldn't do enough for us.

Luckily, Mom and I didn't catch herpes. I was afraid to plant the suggestion in Dad's head, he'd come down with it for sure, and I was too mortified to ask all of our many guests.

♥ ♥ ♥

One Life to Live–*or*–Two Minds to Lose

Somehow, my father confused a Medicare statement that said in big bold letters "THIS IS NOT A BILL" with an automotive survey that happened to come in his mailbox at the same time. He demanded that I stop by and take care of what he was leaving on the kitchen table for me. He had left his driver's license (and then drove several miles to the nursing home) and three hundred dollars for me to pay "the bill." Time for a new theme song: *"The lights are on, but you're not home—your mind, is not your own."* Thank you, Robert Palmer. Anyway, when I tried to explain, he went into a rage.

"Jesus Christ! I ask you to do *one* goddamn thing for me and you *won't* do it. I just can't trust you to do *anything* for me!" He worked himself into such a frenzy that I phoned Dr. Kiljoy's assistants, Ray and Martie Sue, and begged them to drop everything and take a two minute walk next door to the nursing home and see what I'd been talking about.

Ray said, "No, Jake, this isn't the bill for Mariel's ambulance. It won't be coming for quite a while yet."

Curtain up—okay, Larry Olivier, you're on in… five, four, three, two… "Ohhh, okay, my mistake—I'm sorry, no problem," he laughed apologetically. (Somebody, please… yell "CUT!" and stop this pitiful performance.)

I was aghast and looked like a complete idiot in front of them, as just minutes before I was describing a psychotic maniac, begging for them to rush over and calm him down. I gave them a pleading look of, "I promise you, cross my heart, I swear on my life—he was completely out of his mind just a moment ago." They gave me the most disparaging looks wondering what all the hoopla was about. (Tough crowd, tough crowd.)

I could just hear it. "Boy is she neurotic or what? Jake says she's pretty wacked-out." I was proud to have my new Simon and Garfunkle theme song ready to go though: *"In restless streams I walk alone."*

You know, it felt just like that classic *Twilight Zone*—the one where William Shatner is looking out the window of a plane, and he sees the gremlin guy in that terrible abominable snowman suit out on the wing but he can't get anyone to believe him? And then as soon as he gets anyone to look the creature magically disappears into thin air, remember? Well, that's *exactly* what this was like.

Soon, Mom would be coming home and everyday when I arrived at the hospital Dad started insisting that he could take care of her by himself again. I tried every tactic to assure him. "Dad, I understand that this is a big scary change for you. I promise I'll stay and find you a really nice person. All you have to do is relax, live *The Life of Riley* and enjoy being with Mom. Don't you trust me to do the right thing for you? Haven't I always been there for you and Mom? I'd never do anything that wasn't good for you—I love you."

He stood with his back to the wall and grabbed onto the wooden beam that runs in the corridors for the patients to hold on to. Pulling it with all his might, clenching his teeth and turning beet red with the veins in his neck and face pulsating, he erupted into an inconceivable rage. I was astonished at Mighty-Hyde's strength for eighty-three as he actually pulled the beam lose. Oh Dad, poor Dad, there just wasn't anything I could do to calm him, and I was afraid he might spontaneously combust so I just walked away—overwhelmed.

I was outwardly calm, but inside I was drowning in despair, wondering if I had enough time and patience to fight him. He hated change and he was *beyond* stubborn. I'd never tried to overrule him before because I knew it was against all odds to ever win. No one ever challenged my father and came out a winner. I could see that it was going to take a lot of courage and determination, but I committed to the task, having no idea that as I struggled to save my parents' lives—it would almost cost me my own.

Finally, Mom was ready to come home from the convalescent home. I organized a plot to have the administrators (who were very willing to help me after the herpes *glitch*) call Dad and me in for a serious meeting. I had them sternly inform us that they would not release Mom to his care without some in-home help and his house had to be cleaned too. They told him that they knew his negligence had caused her the infection and that they would be checking on her and if she wasn't being taken care of properly, they would have Adult Protective Services come take her away from him. I decided this was the best tactic because he usually had respect for authority. By this time I had everyone I knew helping promote the idea that he had to have a caregiver for Mom, and I thought it would eventually catch on with him and not be so scary.

One night he called me at the convalescent home, "Hey, can you stop by the house before you go back to Linda's tonight?" he asked, sweet as lemon meringue pie.

Oh boy, what now? Oh, I'm getting it. Here it comes—the sorrowful begging to let him bring Mom home and be by themselves again. Exhausted inhale... and hold it... (Edward G. Robinson was about to perform... see)... and blow it out.

Knock-knock. I was betting on Jekyll being home and that Hyde was hyding-out just around the corner. Yep, Jekyll answered the door in a jovial good mood. "Hi, honey!" The place was in even more disarray. "Hey, how about some frozen yogurt with almonds?" he offered. Yep, there's the bait, it was definitely coming. Frozen vanilla yogurt with almonds was our special treat we always enjoyed together. I carefully examined each spoonful for bugs as he made small talk. Then he started in, hands folded in prayer, like an altar boy with one eye on the wine. "Please, *please* let me take care of Mother by myself," he begged. "I'll give you a thousand dollars right now if you'll just tell all them people there that I can still take care of her." Uh, gee, Claus von Big-britches, that's not *quite* enough to let you kill Mom.

"Dad, I *promise* I'll find you someone real nice. I'll stay and train her until you're completely comfortable with her. Please give it a chance, you might really enjoy the company."

"I can do it, please, please, I *beg* of you. Get rid of those bastards who want to take Mother away from me," he said starting to cry.

Again, for the ump-teenth time, I went into a careful explanation of why he needed help, trying to calm his excessive fears and assuring him that Mom would not be taken away from him as long as he accepted help. "Dad, it's too much for you anymore, but that doesn't mean you haven't done a *great* job all these years. You'll really like having some help, just for a few hours everyday, for the hard stuff like bathing and cleaning her properly. I *promise* if you just have a little help they won't take her away from you."

Flash fire: "Goddamn it!" Hyde yelled as he came out swinging, pounding his fists on the fifty-six year old metal kitchen table with that familiar loud thud. "I'm going to take care of my own goddamn wife, and you're not going to stop me," he yelled right in my face.

Being nice was not getting through, so I decided to create my own backdraft and fight fire with fire. I took a deep breath and looked right

30

in his bulging eyes with renewed determination, pounded *my* fist on the table (*ouch*) and shrieked back at him.

"What part of NO, don't you understand?" Last bite, *crunch*, oh-oh, I hope that wasn't a bug, aaand... I'm outta here.

He practically foamed at the mouth as he yelled obscenities after me as I hurried to the door. "I was born at night, but I wasn't born *last* night. I know what you're trying to do. You just want my money. And I want this goddamn call-waiting thing off my phone too. I can't afford no three dollars and fifty cents a month!" Okay, I'm going to be stuck with an eccentric Howard Hughes. Whatever happened to Robert Young in *Father Knows Best*, waving good-bye to Kitten?

Thank goodness I could go back to the Flannery's and have some sanity. My hands shook uncontrollably on the steering wheel as I tried to sort out my dilemma: My father will never change—he's terrified of change. He needs medication to calm him down that I can't get from the doctors, because they don't believe that he can be so mean. He won't go to any other doctors, period. I have to get help in their home because he can't take care of Mom anymore. He'll alienate anyone I get because he doesn't want anyone in his house. They'll quit anyway when he gets mean and makes their life miserable. He can't be left alone with Mom—she'll just be back in the hospital from his inability to care for her. If I put her in a long-term care home, he'll act normal enough to be able to take her out. Inhale... and hold... hold... help... help... and exhale out.

I couldn't put both of them in a nursing home because he didn't qualify yet—nor would he go into an assisted-living situation where he would have his own apartment and a communal dining-room because she couldn't go with him. She needed full nursing care and he would *not* be separated from her—period. So now, I'm starting to feel like Jack Nicholson, ready to go berserk in that great restaurant scene from *Five Easy Pieces*. Okay, hold the walker... hold the bedpan... hold the Geritol... and somebody, please... bring me a respirator!

"This is *20/20*." (Don't you just love how Barbara says that? And don't you miss Hugh?) I remember being so thrilled to be hired by ABC News to photograph the four legends together when I was a young new photographer fresh out of film school. WOW: Frank Reynolds, Sam Robinson, Peter Jennings, and Barbara Walters! It was the first time a woman was a prime-time anchor and it was quite an event. Seems so silly now, huh? Anyway, I thought of that because that's *exactly* what I needed: An investigative news team to get to the root of this problem. Where's Woodward, Bernstein and Katie Couric when you need them?

Then a receptionist at the nursing home gave me a wonderful booklet called *New Lifestyles*: An area guide to senior residences and care options available in the county. Why hadn't anyone told me about this before? I found a few places that would take them as a couple and they could be together in their own room, *if* they both qualified for skilled nursing, meaning they both couldn't do much of anything for themselves. Dad just wasn't there yet. Gee, how can you get both parents to be at the same stage of ill health at the same time?

What about varying levels of care, where they *could* be together? There were only a few places that offered multi-level care, but they couldn't be together in the same room. The assisted-living area was across the street from the convalescent area in another building. Dad would never consent to that. After fifty-six years of marriage they would not be split up now. "Till death do us part" was the deal, and "a deal's a deal," Dad would always say.

When I told a nurse that my father had temper tantrums, she gave me a big tip. "When he finally does need a home, put him in one that has a 'lock-up dementia unit' because otherwise when he gets nasty, most places will call you to come pick him up and kick him out. If they have a lock-up dementia care area they will lock him up, away from bothering everyone else, until they can get him sedated." Well, wasn't *that* a good thing to know? "I did not know that, Ed." (I miss Johnny Carson so much, don't you?) Anyway, that narrowed my options down to just a couple places and I put their names on the long waiting lists.

I was sure that my father's temper had contributed to Mom's initial heart attack from all the stress he'd put her through. Apparently, he had been raging that day too. Then he almost kills her from neglect. I was not going to let him have a chance to accidentally kill her again. His need to dominate and control was going to be challenged like never before. OK, that's it—everyone get out of my way. Hey, I'm not my father's daughter for nothin'. You've seen the rest—I learned from the best.

♥ ♥ ♥

chapter♥three

MY LITTLE GANG OF RASCALS

Then I concocted another fabulous plot. "Just keep thinking, Butch—that's what you're good at." Sundance to Butch. (Sorry, I just can't help myself.) In front of the whole staff at Mom's nursing home, I told Dad that I was going to hire his "regular" cleaning lady to come clean up a bit (like a white tornado), so he *had* to consent to it. I hired Dusty, her sweet friend Camellia, and a professional rug cleaner friend of theirs. Then I got Marina and Don, and Linda's teenage daughter, Kathleen, to help me. When Dad left for the hospital early one morning, the magnificent seven swooped in like burglars at the Watergate, praying we wouldn't get caught.

Only seventy "people-hours" of labor later and it was looking pretty darn good. Every surface was scoured and Don hauled loads of junk to the dumps. We rearranged the furniture, making safer paths that would be easier for them to navigate. Marina got carried away scrubbing the kitchen cabinets (that hadn't been cleaned since they shot JR) and accidentally took all the finish off. Oh well, we figured Dad's eyesight was so bad he'd never notice anyway. I called her the next day and with a very serious, low voice, left a message. "Oh, Marina, um... I don't know how to tell you this, but Dad noticed the cabinets and went into a rage about the finish being removed, and I had to tell him that *you* did it. Now he's demanding that you immediately replace all the kitchen cabinets. (Long pause.) Just kidding! Get up off the floor, Marina. Are you still breathin'?" She said she almost had a heart attack.

We let the professionals take the bathrooms as they were beyond disgusting, and we did laundry for ten hours straight. My aching back kept me from doing any physical work, so my many years in business paid off as I claimed "executive privilege." They started calling me *Sgt. Bilko*. "Well, but what I *really* want to do is: Direct." It was like a bad episode of *Beat the Clock* as we tried to get the pigsty cleaned before he came home. Kathleen was brave to take on the refrigerator.

"Oh my gosh—Jackie, come quick!"

"What, honey?" I said as I hobbled over.

"There're ants frozen in the ice cubes!"

"Ewww!" we harmonized in disgust.

That was just the beginning. We found live creepy crawly bugs in the corn flakes and a flea circus in the dry goods. Most of the frozen food looked like road-kill he had wrapped up in aluminum foil. Expiration dates were a distant memory and *everything* had to be thrown out. Most of their medications were out of date, and his were all mixed up with hers in a little portable pill container.

There were so many fire hazards I was amazed that the house was still standing. The smoke detector didn't work and a knob on the stove wouldn't turn the flame off completely. The twenty-five watt sockets had one hundred watt bulbs in them and he left them on all day. The lint filter on the clothes dryer was completely clogged and apparently hadn't been cleaned for quite some time.

The carpet was so filthy the ugly plastic runners had to be pulled up and the entire carpet had to be shampooed twice to see the gold color. The toilets ran, the faucets didn't turn off, and the shower massager was so rusted on we just could not get it off. The bills and paperwork were all shoved into drawers, and the fifty-six year old mattress that my brother and I had been conceived in, had a broken spring coming up through the middle.

Dad called from the nursing home several times. "Hey, are you coming to feed Mother dinner so I can come home?"

"Oh, I'll be a little late, Dad. Dusty got a late start and I'm helping her finish up. Do you think maybe you could do it for me tonight?"

"What the hell are you doing there?"

"We've been working really hard. All I want to hear is *thank you* when you get here." He kept demanding to know what we were doing and I just kept repeating, "Dad, please be appreciative. We've worked very hard all day." He grumbled obscenities and hung up on me.

Helper Camellia mentioned that she takes care of elderly people and needed a new job. Dusty recommended her highly and we made arrangements to talk in detail the next day as the three of them left. Wow, maybe I had my caregiver lined up already. *"I feel good,"* James Brown. Exhausted with a sore back but *"Owh!"* very good.

Dad's car drove in. (Best if you play the theme to *Jaws* in your head here. "Just when you thought it was safe...") The car door slammed and the four of us looked like deer caught in the headlights. I swear I could hear our hearts pounding. Oh my God—what have we done? This didn't even look like the same house—we changed *everything*. Forget hand towels, we threw out major *furniture*. This is going to be horrible. What was I thinking would happen? He's going to *kill* us. Fe, Fi, Fo, Fum, I smell... Clorox. He walked in, stopped, surveyed the situation complete with hands on hips, and I could see that the dreaded moment of no return was about to return. He was just about ready to pop his cork when Maid Marina came out of hiding from the kitchen.

"Surprise! Hi, Jake. We came to help—doesn't it look great?"

He looked at me (at a safe distance on the couch) and I gave him a look that said, "What did I tell you to say?" He was trying hard to decide which way to go, weighing each option—raving lunatic vs. helpless victim. To be sane or not to be sane—that was the question. Finally, he burst into sympathetic tears, hugged Marina and started crying dramatically.

"Thank you, thank you so much. You know, it's just been so hard to take care of Mariel and the house too. I just can't do it anymore."

"I know, Jake," Marina said, hugging and patting him on the back, "we're glad we could help—you've been through so much."

"Thank you so much," he nodded to each of them, but of course, *I* was not thanked. "Gee, you guys really worked hard, huh?" he said as he looked down at the sparkling clean gold rug, missing those really attractive plastic runners. "Hey, where are the plastic runners?" he demanded. (Oh, somewhere at the dumps.) "You know, the rug is going to get very dirty without the plastic runners."

Somebody just shoot me. I couldn't believe it—*now* he's worried about dirtying the rug. I had to get outta there quick. It was a good thing I didn't drink (cheap date) or I'd have been drinking heavily by then. I said, "Oh-k then, gee it's getting late... time for us to get going... good to see ya... gotta go... bye-bye," as we all scurried outta there faster than you can sing, *"We gotta get outta this place."* Thank you, Eric Burdon.

♥ ♥ ♥

Phantom Menace of the Old Folk's Farm

While Dad was at the hospital during the day, I returned to Hydecliffe Manor so I could finish all the home improvements before Mom came home. When I showed her some pictures of her sparkling clean dining-room set that she loved so much, she exclaimed, "That's *mine*. I bought that with my own money. I took care of little kids while you were in high school and saved all my money and I bought it, all by myself." They had gone to a Hillsborough estate auction (like Beverly Hills), and bid on it and got a gorgeous carved antique dining-room set for four hundred dollars. It was so interesting to see how important it became for her. It was all hers, not given to her by my father—she had *accomplished* it. It reminded me of something Paul Newman said about not liking being complimented about his gorgeous blue eyes. "It's not an accomplishment." If the most satisfying things in life come from our accomplishments, I should be the happiest person on earth when I get all this straightened out.

I hired the resident handyman, Mick (kind of a sixty-something, Scottish, Al Bundy type), to fix things at the house and he practically had a full-time job. I had him install a remote doorbell on the back door that rang by their bedside because they often didn't hear the bell. Then he attached disabled grab-bars *everywhere*, even in the showers. He put together a portable closet with low rungs for easier access, and I put out fewer clothes to make choosing less stressful. I read that the glare from mirrors can cause elders confusion, so I removed all the portable ones. He leveled the raised thresholds so the dangerous lips were removed and wheelchair access was easier. I had him build a four-inch high platform for under the couch because it was so low they couldn't get out of it. Then he built a riser, slanted eight-inches in the back, to four-inches in the front, for under Dad's recliner to make it easier for him to use that. Then I had him slightly tilt the refrigerator a half inch higher in the front so the door would always automatically close.

We talked about building a ramp for Mom's wheelchair, but we were just a couple feet short of being legal for the slope, which is a minimum of a one inch rise per foot. He said that a foot and a half is safer and easier to push someone up. "We'd better not do it—the city comes out and makes people rip them out all the time. We also need a level landing at the turn-around and there's not enough room for it." I decided that if it got to that point I would buy them a hydraulic lift.

Several people in the park had them and I let them all know to call me if they wanted to sell theirs. I scoured the newspaper classifieds under "Medical Equipment" and "Senior/Elder Care Equipment." It didn't take up that much room and it would attach onto the back porch. You just wheel the person out onto the porch and then continue out a couple more feet onto the lift platform, push a button... and voilá, it lowers you safely to ground level—bada-boom, bada-bing.

Mick started to ask me how my father's disposition was. Oh-oh, he knew something I wanted to know. He said that he'd seen Dad's temper get progressively worse for years. Eventually the men wouldn't let him play poker or pool at the clubhouse anymore because he'd get in fights.

Between Mick, neighbor Helen at the corner, and Clive next door, I started to get a truer picture of what had been going on. It was not a *"beautiful day in the neighborhood"* anymore. It was sad because they used to have fun there. They had played bingo every Friday night and Dad had always been one of the cooks for Sunday brunch. They took care of each other's yards and had carport-patio barbecues all the time. But the camaraderie had gradually dissolved as he apparently alienated all the neighbors—one by one.

I ordered Mom's hospital bed and put it in the family room so she would be able see everything going on—out onto her front porch, into her kitchen, into her bedroom, the television set, and her guests seated on the couch. I was pleased, she had—"a room with a view."

To make it easier to pull herself up, I ordered a hanging triangle bar for over her hospital bed, and attached a dimmable reading lamp above it so she'd always have good light there. I put another clamp-on adjustable dimmer light on the headboard of their bed too. I read that shadows can be confusing for elders so I evened out all the lighting by using "daylight" bulbs to help reduce glare.

Since she was so little I ordered the smallest, fourteen-inch wide wheelchair, with a detachable tray table so it would be easier to navigate in such small quarters. To keep her from falling out I bought a snap-around bungee cord. I put whistles and little bells by the beds as sometimes Mom's voice was so low we couldn't hear her. By putting raised tables on both sides of her beds, everything was within arms reach. I also got a portable, battery operated radio/cassette player and tapes of all their favorite music which became very comforting.

Then I found a dual use porta-pottie commode. It had a closed bottom bucket, so it could be used next to her bed, for when it wasn't possible to get her to the bathroom. It also had an open bottom bucket attachment for use in the shower. This allows the caregiver to use the long shower massager to reach beneath her and spray her bottom thoroughly. I ordered raised toilet seats with hand rails, which made it easier for her to get on and off the pottie. I placed non-skid mats in the showers and also in front of the toilets. Then I put anti-bacterial handi-wipes and soap everywhere, and paper towel racks in the bathrooms to make it easier for the caregiver to clean up. I also found some amazing rinseless shampoo to keep her hair clean in-between showers. Just massage it in and that's it. I laughed when I found myself hanging out regularly at the medical supply store and reading the Sears medical supply catalog like a riveting novel.

My father's eyes were getting worse so I got him a large-dial alarm clock, several big display clocks, a large numbered weight scale, and a large easy-to-see address book. Then a friend gave us an adapter for the front of the television that magnifies the image making *it* easier to see. A wonderful invention for the elderly are the motion-sensing night lights, that come on when they get up at night. I put them all around and put night-lights in all the electrical sockets.

Another idea is to put glow-tape on things that they need to find at night, as well as around the perimeter of doors making them easier to find, and also on staircases. Putting colored tape on the edges of steps in a contrasting color, will help them navigate stairs better. Then, it's best to put a bigger piece of tape on the first and last steps so they know when they're at the end. Putting banisters on both sides of the stairs is important as well as very good lighting without glare, and a little bench for them to rest on at the top and bottom.

I got rid of all the throw rugs as they're a big hazard for the elderly who fall easily. That was another big fight with my father. I explained the danger over and over, and he'd nod in agreement, but as soon as I'd leave he'd roll them back out. It got to be a test of perseverance. Roll 'em up... roll 'em out... roll 'em up... roll 'em out—RawHyde! He finally gave up and put them away himself after he took a bad fall on one and had a heck of a time getting up.

Linda loaned me an egg-crate foam mattress for Mom's hospital bed. It really helps keep a patient's back from getting sore. I had learned so much from the nurses in the hospital and they always put a pillow between Mom's legs when she slept on her side to keep her knees from rubbing. When she was on her back they always put one under her calves, making sure her heels did not touch the bed as that was a common place for bed sores to form. Constant heel rubbing had cost my godmother half of her leg. A variety of pillow sizes and thicknesses were important to help the patient be comfortable. Then enough linens, blankets, water-proof incontinent pads and bibs had to be bought. As the time got closer for Mom to be released, Dad seemed to come home with supplies he said were "given" to him by the staff at the nursing home. Uh-huh—fell off the truck, you mean.

"I know *noth*-ing," Sergeant Schultz.

♥ ♥ ♥

Do Not Back Up: Severe *Life* Damage

I bought Dad a much needed new wallet, and as I transferred his things into it I noticed that the only picture he carried was one of my gorgeous mother holding me as I sat on her lap at age five. I had no idea he had carried this picture all these years, and as I stared at it, warm feelings filled me, direct express from my childhood.

As I sorted years and years of old clothes the lost memories of when they'd worn them instantly surfaced in living color, transporting me to another place in time. I loved feeling the exquisitely beautiful, embroidered blue silk Japanese robe, that had magically transformed Mom into a gorgeous geisha girl at a Halloween party so many years before. I could see Dad in his black coolie outfit, with the long black braid down his back and a black Fu-Man-Chu mustache. I could see them dancing in slow motion, laughing as he masterfully twirled her around the dance floor. I watched from the sidelines again, loving that they were the undisputed stars of the party. She was rhapsody in blue as she spun around and around, and then he carefully "dipped" her, brought her up for a kiss, and then put his palms together and slowly bowed to her. The room erupted in cheering applause. She was definitely the most beautiful, radiant woman in the room. I couldn't have been more proud then, or now as I recalled it.

So many lost memories kept flooding into me that I had to force myself back to reality to get the work done. I painstakingly sorted through years of tattered old clothes and sadly realized that my parents just didn't see dirt anymore. So many needed mending—a button here, a tear there. Since they were now the incredible shrinking couple, everything needed to be shortened several inches because I was worried about falls. Finally, I took a whole carload to the Goodwill and sorrowfully left a lifetime of stardust memories at their door.

Then I found myself somewhere in another time when I found Mom's beautiful silk lingerie, her long black opera gloves, fancy high heels and dressy beaded purses. I was struck by how new they still looked after all these years. There were so many beautiful things, now of no use to their aged, disabled bodies that *were* worn out from use. Isn't it interesting that we spend so much time struggling in life to get all the *stuff*, all the many *things*, that will always out-live us. It was so poignantly eerie when just then—one of my favorite songs came on the radio: *"And all your money won't another minute buy... dust in the wind... all we are is dust in the wind,"*—and it was never so true.

I wiped my tears and struggled to get back to virtual reality—there was too much work to do. Their mattress just had to go. When Dad had called 911 the paramedics broke the box spring getting Mom up. When the new mattress was delivered I asked the guys if they had ever seen a fifty-six year old mattress before. We only came in second place—one couple had slept on theirs for seventy-five years!

Every year my father would complain of allergies, but of course, he refused my constant pleading to go see an allergist. He'd just rather complain to me—daily. Gee, I wonder if there were any dust mites in that mattress? Operation "allergy" went into motion. I got rid of the old nappy electric blanket with the frayed cord, got an allergy-free, water proof mattress pad, and a Hepa air purifier. Then I had the heater vents cleaned and sprayed for mold for the first time in twenty years. I was betting that he was going to be allergy free for the first time ever.

As Plato once said... or, was it my mother? "Necessity is the mother of invention" and so, I became: The Velcro Queen. I had *everything* within arm's reach for them. I used Velcro on the new answering machine button so all Dad had to do was feel for the fuzz to get his messages. I used Velcro on the little flip phone to attach it to the side of the dresser, and on all the things that I wanted to secure but be able to easily move. I found a wrap-around at the waist half-robe, that secured easily with Velcro—making it easier for Dad to have something to put on quickly when he got up. Elderly arthritic fingers can't navigate zippers and buttons anymore, so Velcro is a wonderful solution for so many things.

Then, I noticed that the Polaroid camera that I'd given them years before was broken. As I packed it to send in for repair, I remembered the last time I had seen it. It was several years ago when I was having terrible problems with cracks appearing on the ceilings and walls of my house.

"Very high soil expansion index, Ma'am. The drought is drying up the water table down deep and the soil is contracting and all the houses around here are falling apart." Greeeat. I called an engineering company, who crawled under my house and reported back that my foundation was severely cracked every few feet. I'd need to retrofit the foundation, or the house could come down on my head. I called my insurance company and they came out, took pictures and also crawled under the house.

"You don't have *any* cracks in your foundation, but the cracks in the house and on the cement, well, unfortunately your policy does not cover earth *movement*—you are only covered for earth-*quakes*." Unbelievable. I made the mistake of telling my parents and my father was livid.

"Jesus Christ! What the hell is going on down there? Doesn't anybody know what the hell they're doing? We'll be down there tomorrow and I'll straighten this out."

The next thing I know, here they come. Mom, so frail, manning the passenger seat, helping him drive. I couldn't stop my father from putting on his coveralls, taking a light and the Polaroid camera, and crawling under my hot, fifty year-old house taking pictures. I yelled his position through the outside vents as he made his way around the very narrow crawlspace. He was nearly eighty years old, with a hip replacement, but by God he would not be stopped from crawling under his little girl's house to find out "what the hell" was going on.

The Polaroids showed the truth—only two small cracks, not worthy of worrying about. He hauled a hydraulic jack under there, propped up an area that needed extra support, and assured me that the house would not come down on my head. "Don't worry, honey. I'd never let anything happen to you or your house. We'll get this fixed." I loved him so much—my dad to the rescue. I should have known, he was always there to help me. Now, I was there to help him. The only difference was—he was *never* going to appreciate it.

♥ ♥ ♥

41

And Then Came Mom

With enough *"time, love and tenderness"* I was finally able to bring Mom home to her spotlessly clean home. To make sure she got the proper care, I moved back in that day. I had turned the Mobile Motel One into the Mobile Marriott Suites, and I was pretty darn proud of it. I told Dad that a nice lady named Camellia (kind of a sweet, southern, thirty-something, Suzanne Sugarbaker without any money type), who was a friend of Dusty's, was now Mom's caregiver. She'd work for two and a half hours in the morning and two and a half hours in the evening. He seemed to finally accept the idea, boasting to everyone that he had a "maid"—his personal servant and indentured slave.

"Umm, Dad, don't you think calling her your 'maid' is kind of demeaning? Why don't we all call her our Caregiver—Camellia." He'd never remember and we'd correct him thirty times a day after he'd call her his maid: Cammy, Candy or Catie Sue. It was like clockwork.

"Uh, um, Corrina?" he'd say.

"Camellia," Camellia and I would politely correct him together.

"Get me such and such," he'd demand. "Oh, thanks, Callie May."

"CAMELLIA!" we'd screech at him and look at each other and do gallows laughs that he just could *not* get her name right. Geeeese, it was worse than Chinese water torture all day.

Camellia prepared their meals and made sure they had their pills. She also gave Mom two Ensure Pluses a day, which at 365 calories for an eight ounce can would keep her weight up to a perfect one hundred and five pounds. Then, Metamucil (stirred, not shaken) daily to keep them regular. (FYI: Products like Metamucil should never be given at the same time as pills because it might bind with them and keep them from being completely digested.)

I strategized the perfect parent-care plan. I figured that if I got Camellia trained just right, he would come to enjoy her company and depend on her. Then he'd finally relax and enjoy being with Mom safely together in their own home until the end. I would be able to go home, monitor Camellia daily by phone, and feel secure knowing they were being taken care of properly having daily supervision. In "billions and billions" of light years (thank you, Carl Sagan) I would have never guessed all that was ahead of me.

♥ ♥ ♥

Penny Wise and Pounds of Foolish Fiddlers

As I organized about five feet of crinkled papers down to one little file drawer, I was astonished to find electric bills from the 1970's. I remember Mom saying if we left the lights on, "What-da-ya got—stock in the electric company?" Now, I can't turn off an unwanted light without saying that, even when I'm alone. As I sorted Dad made me ask him about each piece of paper before throwing it away. Then he started to sweepingly gesture with "throw it" even before telling him what it was. He was, however, unwavering about *how* it got thrown out. He made me finely tear up and soak everything in buckets of water for days before finally letting me throw it out. Shudda got a shredder.

"People could come into the carport and steal our trash and get all that information on us," he kept warning me.

"Oh, I know—Dow Jones could plummet if your 1970 gas bills get in the wrong hands, Dad."

The next big hurdle was to get him to consent to have their savings account transferred into a checking account, with all three of our names on it. Then I'd have all their bills sent directly to me for payment. My parents never wrote a check or used a credit card in their lives, so it was hard for him to understand. Dad had always made money the old fashioned way, he earned it—hour by hour. They always went in person to pay cash for their bills, or to the bank to buy a money order to send. Can you imagine? He always said that it was okay because it gave them something to do, and yes, it was an all day project to pay the phone bill.

Then I noticed that he was starting to confuse a twenty-dollar bill with a one-dollar bill and that he was losing his ability to add. I opened a Visa credit card account in my name, with a low credit limit, and got him a companion card so all he'd have to do was sign his name. I'd get the bill and there would be less chance of him being taken advantage of, or God forbid, knocked out and robbed in a parking lot. Getting him to use the credit card was completely impossible. I tried to explain it again and again, but alas, it was just too scary for him. He just didn't trust it, he had survived the Great Depression, and "goddamn it" he would not change how he did things *now!* Oy vey.

"Tra-di-tion... Tradition... TRA-DI-TION!"

♥ ♥ ♥

Grouch-*Ohhh!*

One morning Mom wanted to sleep longer, so Camellia went in the kitchen to make breakfast before getting her cleaned up. Dad was sitting at the kitchen table scrutinizing every move we made like a hungry hovering hawk.

"Jake, would you like to get Mariel up for breakfast for me, hon?" she asked sweetly in that charming southern draaawl. After his head spun around a couple times he got nasty.

"Jesus Christ! What the hell am I paying *you* for?"

"Oh, no problem then, I'll get her, hon." She brought Mom in the wheelchair to the kitchen table and proceeded to serve us all a lovely breakfast. As Dad started eating I could see him starting to stew. Oh boy, I could see a fully-loaded last freight train to Clarksville coming this time. Sure enough, Hyde threw down his fork and started yelling.

"She looks like hell! Why are you bringing her to the table looking like that? I want her fixed up *before* you bring her to the table." He looked at me. "You weren't brought up to come to the table looking like that. No, you bet your life you weren't."

"Daaad, Mom wanted to sleep a little longer. Camellia will clean her up now and then from now on, if you can ask her nicely, she'll remember that you prefer to have Mother cleaned up *before* breakfast."

"She looks like a goddamn imbecile," he went on unmercifully as Mom started to cry.

"Great Dad, real nice. I guess it's more important that she *looks* good rather than to have her *feel* good. You ought to be so ashamed."

"I'll take her to get cleaned up right now," Camellia said.

"You're goddamn right you will!" Hyde demanded as he threw his jelly toast smearing across the table, pounding his fist in it.

Camellia whispered, "It's okay, I can handle him. I just have to learn how he likes things done and then he should be fine."

"I'm so sorry, Camellia. He can be so horribly mean sometimes and then all of a sudden he'll be back to being a sweetheart again. You just never know what's going to set him off."

After he calmed down I got Camellia to role-play with me, so he could see how he should talk to her. "Now watch, Genghis, I'm you. 'Camellia, that was such a lovely breakfast. You know, in the future I'd appreciate it if you'd clean Mariel up before bringing her to the table. Would you mind doing it that way from now on, hon?'"

"Well, not at all—I'd be happy to," Camellia said, playing along.

"See, Dad? Now isn't that a lot nicer than screaming and yelling?" Hyde was not in the mood for my "Toni" Robbins seminar. He looked at us, grumbled obscenities and went back to his bed. Ba-hum-bug. Hey, I can do Dale Carnegie or Dr. Dean Edell if you'd prefer.

♥ ♥ ♥

Demented Times Require Desperate Measures

Mom had been on oxygen in the hospital and at the nursing home. When they released her they told us that she didn't need it anymore. Within a few days of coming home she was much less responsive and I was confident it was the lack of oxygen. I asked the doctor to send a nurse out to test her for it. "No, she's in the normal range," she said. They gave me the runaround every time I called until I had to get adamant that she was really going down hill and they'd have to come back out.

"I know she was better on the oxygen," I told nurse number two.

"Well, you can't get Medicare to pay for it unless her reading is at 89 or below so I'm sorry, but she's at 90. It's thousands of dollars for an oxygen machine and we've *told* you—she really doesn't need it."

I made their lives miserable until I got another company to come out and test her. I told Dad to take Mom to the back bedroom and when nurse number three rang the doorbell to get Mom up and walk around with her in there, so she would score low on oxygen and maybe we could get it. Seemed like a good idea at the time. Yeaaah, *"Desperado"* was my theme song. Anyway, she still scored just barely normal. I tried friendly crystal blue persuasion, but when that didn't work I *begged* for the nurse to help us.

"Tell you what," Nurse Nightingale said. "I'll tape a monitor to her hand and leave it on overnight and the computer will test her oxygen level. We'll pick it up tomorrow and get the readings. If it shows that she drops below the 90 point to 89, you'll be able to get Medicare to pay for it for three months. If she goes below that, you'll get it paid for a whole year."

We all went to bed but Dad and I couldn't sleep and we were up all night with a flashlight looking at the digital readout on the monitor on

Mom's hand. It was right at 90 every time we looked until about three o'clock in the morning. I whispered to Dad who was leaning over my shoulder straining to see the reading.

"It's down to 89!" I quietly exclaimed. "We got it!"

"All right, honey!"

Mom woke up and looked at us suspiciously, "What are you two up to now?"

"Nothin'," Dad and I said in unison. Then about five AM we were back together on our little mission whispering.

"Dad, it's down to 88... 87... 86... 85! Wow, we've got it for a whole year." We hugged and shared a moment of triumph as Mom was snoring away, unaware of our joy at her misfortune. Then the irony of it hit me and I looked at Dad and laughed. "Wait a minute. We shouldn't be *glad* that it's dropping. That means she needs oxygen, and she needs it real bad."

"Oh yeah, it's not such a good thing, huh?" I put my arm around him, we both took our deep breaths, and I walked him back to his side of the bed, tucked him in and kissed him good-night.

"Don't worry, Dad, we'll show them. We'll make her so well that she won't even need the darn oxygen machine anymore, won't we?"

"You're damn right we will, honey. We'll show them bastards."

The nurse called the next day apologetically saying that Mom had dropped so low, so many times in the very early morning hours, that we were approved for oxygen for a solid year. If I hadn't pushed and pushed, as with *everything*, we would have never gotten it.

Who goes to this much effort besides me? Not too many was my guess. Then the nurse told me to make sure I got the oxygen machine with a "humidifier" on it. Oh-kay. We had to sterilize all the parts with boiling water and vinegar after each use and make sure we only used distilled water in the humidifier. I figured I'd be getting a call to run *Chicago Hope* any minute.

Oh, and then months later I found out that we should be getting a credit off our electric bill because she was a disabled person on oxygen. Gee, I wish someone would have told me *that* before. You know I made them retro it and it took another nine whole months to get it straightened out with the electric company.

♥ ♥ ♥

chapter four

HONEY, I BLEW UP THE HOUSE

O ne absolutely "fabulous" day, Camellia was off and I'd gone shopping for several hours. I came back, opened the door, and the smell of gas was so strong it nearly knocked me out. Dad had left the stove on, without the burner coming on, and filled the house with gas fumes. He was obsessed with using the stove. Good thing I don't smoke. I rushed in aghast, threw open all the doors and windows and turned on all the fans. "Oh my God! Can't you guys smell the gas?"

"I don't smell nothin'," Dad whispered from his sleepy hollow bed.

Mom was in her hospital bed, looking drugged. She must have been looking at her *Life* magazine before almost being asphyxiated to *death*.

"Mom! Don't you smell the gas?"

She got renewed strength and threw down her magazine totally aggravated. "Yes, I smell gas. I've been telling him for hours now that I smell gas somewhere, but he just thinks he knows everything. You know it'll be the day when your father listens to me!" Oh my Looord.

The gas company came out right away and said that the stove top was a fire hazard and a death trap. One spark could have made an inferno and everything would have gone up in smoke. I had a new stove top put in with a safer, electric starter, and then I removed the knobs and hid them from Dad so he *couldn't* use it. I threw out his dented teapot and got him a big-numbered, very simple microwave, and put Velcro over the "On" button, so he could easily *feel* to use it. Luckily, I caught him just before he put a metal cup in it. All metal was removed and I bought microwave-safe everything.

"Dad, *please* don't try to use the stove anymore—you almost burned the house down. Here, use this cup—just fill it with water and push this little fuzzy thing and you'll have hot water, just at the right temperature every time." I put a BIG magnifying glass on top of the microwave so he could see the numbers and he finally learned how to use it. I decided to put oversized magnifying glasses all over the house for him—his eyes were getting as bad as his nose.

The next item I had to fight the insurance to get was the Nebulizer, a breathing treatment machine that uses a medicine called Albuterol. The medicine goes into a little cup and Mom inhales the mist through a mouthpiece. We also used small portable inhalers, but this machine gave her a full twenty minutes, four-times a day, super treatment that kept her lungs clear. All the parts had to be sterilized after every use with boiling hot water and vinegar. Whenever I'd hear any wheezing coming from Dad, I'd put him on it and it kept him clear too. After lots of red tape, I got the machine covered by the insurance.

The most embarrassing part for Mom was that she had to wear diapers because she was incontinent. I bought every kind to see which ones she liked best and which ones Dad could get on and off of her the easiest. His fingers weren't nimble enough to undo the buttons or use the peel-off-tape kind, so the slip-ons (just like padded underwear) turned out to be the best. We were using up some that were hard for Dad to manage, when one morning Camellia got Mom up and called to me. "Jacqueline, come look at this, hon—you're not going to believe it." Ohmigosh. There was Mom with her diapers *masking-taped* right to her body, around and around, just like a mummy. Well, we had to admit it—Master MacGyver was a resourceful little devil.

One day as I was changing her diaper, Mom started to cry. "This is so humiliating. I never thought I'd be like this, honey."

"Well, you'd do it for me wouldn't ya?" She nodded. "In fact, you *did* do it for me," I said, kissing her on the cheek. "Even June Allyson wears them so you're in good company. Hey, somebody will be doing it for me, and they won't even be my own daughter."

"Oh, honey, I'm so sorry to put you through this. I never wanted for you to have to take care of us."

"I know Mom, it's okay. You've always been there for me, and now it's my turn to be here for you. Payback's a pleasure—I consider it a privilege," I said, giving her another kiss and wiping her tears.

She had always said, "When we get old, just put us in a home, honey. Don't let us live with you, it'll ruin your marriage." (If only I had one.) It was so interesting that now that she was old, when I'd ask her where she wanted to go if Dad passed away first she'd say, "Well, with you to live at your house—of course."

The realization kept hitting me that we have to come up with a way for elderly couples to get every level of care as they go downhill, and still be together without ruining their children's lives in the process. I heard a frightening projection: With all the advances in medicine, children could be expected to take care of their elderly parents for as long as the parents took care of them! (Please do a Pee Wee Herman scream for me here: Ahhhhh!) Thank you so much.

Long-Term Care Insurance is going to be the answer, and I started to realize that it's going to be a huge business soon. It would pay for professional caregivers to come into the home so you wouldn't have to put your loved one in a nursing home. It was way too late for my parents to get it, but I started telling everyone I knew to look into it for their parents before they got sick. (Note: Once someone has been prescribed medication for dementia, they will be denied Long-Term Care Insurance.)

Camellia had Sundays off, so I made sure that Dad knew how to properly care for Mom, and figured he'd be real happy to see her back on Mondays if he had to do the work himself for a day. I spent a lot of time teaching him what had to be done and then I started to watch and not help at all to see if he could really handle it. I was quite encouraged that with the proper instruction he could really do it.

I had asked him frequently if he'd had her eye glasses checked, and he always said that he was right on top of it. Something didn't add up because the frames of her glasses were rusted. I took her to the eye doctor and discovered that he hadn't taken her in for an eye exam for almost *seven* years. They tested her eyes and I was stunned that she couldn't even see the BIG "E" at all out of her right eye, due to the cataract. I shuddered remembering that they had just driven all the way to Los Angeles just a few months before, with barely any vision between them. The blind leading the blind, with eyes wide shut, four hundred miles, at night, in a lethal weapon. OH—MY—GOD.

Time for cataract surgery. It went so flawlessly on her right eye, I had the left one done six weeks later. Amazingly, she could suddenly read the small print on her prescription bottles without glasses. We had to put eye drops in her eyes, four times a day, and use two different medicines. I made up a simple check-off chart to make sure that we never missed a dose, because Dad would forget if he didn't have something to check off.

If he hadn't taken her to the eye doctor, I was sure he had lied to me about the dentist. Yep, she had not had her teeth cleaned for many years and had numerous cavities. The dentist said he couldn't do anything for her and referred us to a Periodontist. After more X rays and evaluation he said, "Her teeth will out-live her. The nerve roots are so damaged that she doesn't have any pain. So unless she does, my recommendation is to do nothing. I'm afraid it would be too much for her to pull them or to try to fix them. The only thing you can do to slow the gum disease is to brush her teeth thoroughly with an electric tooth-brush and use a prescription mouth wash after every meal."

Dad had worn dentures for years, but I don't think he ever saw Jane Powell's Polident commercial. I finally convinced him to try it and pretty soon his dingy teeth were sparkling white—he was amazed.

Then came another major project for both of them—their feet. Mom's toes were so severely crossed we had to put rubber separators between her toes. They both had an awful foot fungus that made their toenails very thick and wood-like. I took them to a podiatrist.

Seems they were spreading this fungus to each other so they had to start wearing socks at all times. Then we had to spray the insides of their shoes with anti-fungal spray. Clorox had to be used in the shower or Camellia and I could catch it, and we were instructed to never go barefoot. There was a pill that could wipe out the fungus but they were too old and it could be damaging to their internal organs. All we could do was control the fungus, not eliminate it.

Then they needed custom orthopedic shoes. Instead of difficult laces, they used Velcro to fasten. Mom's had to be super-wide toed, and at one hundred and fifty dollars a pair, she got basic black and brown.

We had to soak their feet twice a day in warm water with regular salt to draw out the fungus and then apply a prescription fungoid tincture to the toenails to help control the fungus. Dad started to complain of jock itch so I got him Tenactin to spray on himself. The doctor said it probably came from the fungus on his toes that got on his underwear when he pulled them up. Inhale... and hold it... (solve one problem, get two more—somebody *please* save me)... and blow it out.

Then there was the heartburn (always a pending heart attack), that I solved with Tums. I gave up asking him how he felt because he'd always come up with *something* else that needed attention.

Next it was his legs that were always hurting him. Camellia would massage them everyday with lotion. Any water retention would show up in his legs first. This was crucial to check on both of them daily by pressing on the calves and seeing if the indention stayed there. If they retained water it could accumulate around the heart and be fatal.

His socks hurt his thick calves so I finally solved the problem with bootie socks that didn't come up on his calves at all. Then, the water pills weren't working all of a sudden. When he pressed on his calf the indent of his hand print would remain. Ray got us a stronger water pill. It helped for a while and then we had to get an even stronger one.

After breakfast one morning Camellia put Dad's pills in front of him in his little cup labeled "JAKE" that I had gotten to avoid confusion. Out of the corner of my eye I saw him put one of the pills in his pocket as he directed the attention toward Mom with his other hand. Pret-ty smooth, I must say.

"So, um, Dad... what's that in your pocket?"

"Nothin'." Uh-huh.

"Really? Oh, I think you might have one of your pills in there." He argued but sure enough, it was the water pill. I flashed on the time I put a mouthful of peas in my mouth, mumbled that I had to go to the bathroom, ran and spit them in the toilet but was caught by Miss Manners Mom. It seemed ingenious to me at the time and I was shocked she was wise to me. I chuckled as Dad defended himself, just like I had.

"I don't like having to go to the bathroom (eat vegetables) all the time. I don't wanna take it anymore."

"Daaad, please don't send us on wild-goose chases. Haven't we got enough to worry about? Your medicines require a very delicate balance, especially the water pill and the potassium. How can the doctor possibly know the correct dosages if you aren't taking it and we're reporting erroneous results?"

"OK! Give it to me, goddamn it." From this point on we watched *him* like a hawk. I got him a plastic portable bed-side urinal so he wouldn't have to get up as often. He *refused* to use it, preferring instead to get up in the middle of the night and pee-ing all over the floor of the bathroom. Bad aim. I finally solved the problem with a small bucket for him to go into.

Aaand... inhale... hold it... (I was sure I'd at *least* be running a wing of *General Hospital* soon)... aaand... slowly blow it out—again.

♥♥♥

Shock It to Me

One Sunday evening Camellia was off and I had rented the movie, *Die Hard With a Vengeance*, to entertain us. We hadn't even gotten past the first ten killings when I noticed that Dad couldn't grasp what was going on, asking me questions that didn't make sense. He got flustered and said he didn't want to watch anymore. Mom was dozing off anyway, so I asked him if he wanted to soak Mom's feet instead.

"Okay," he said, "I know how to do it now."

"Do you want me to help you?"

"No, I know how. You've shown me enough times." He got out the electric heat and massage foot tub I had bought for the "feet project," and took Mom in her wheelchair to the back bathroom. I laid on the couch, rooting for John McClane to capture the madman and free the hostages, but a battle started raging in my head. Should I go in and help him or let him struggle with it so tomorrow he'd *really* appreciate Camellia doing it again? I yelled in, asking if he wanted any help, but he yelled back, "NOOOOPE!" they were fine and dandy.

I must have had a premonition because I suddenly catapulted off the couch to go see how they were doing. As I entered the bathroom I was flabbergasted by what was happening. There was my mother, sitting with her feet in the portable tub filled with water, and next to her feet, also covered with *water*—was the *electrical* power-strip extension cord! My father had the other end of the cord in hand, casually headed for the outlet, less than three seconds away from plugging it in.

"What are you doing? That's electricity!" I shrieked, barely yanking the cord away from him. There was water all over the floor, he was in wet socks, and the realization that I had just saved them both from certain electrocution left me breathless. I lifted the huge foot-long power-strip, dripping out of the water and screamed at him, "This is an extension cord in the *water*. You almost killed her, and yourself!"

He had a look of (pardon the pun) shock on his face, as he begged me to believe him that he had not intentionally done it. He just didn't see the huge power-strip. Then I realized—I probably would have died too if I had rushed in there to help them not knowing what was happening. I'm sure it would have been the Hyde frequency surge of my life.

Ben Franklin, Jr. sat down on the edge of the bathtub, crying that he was so sorry. I started to shake uncontrollably from the adrenaline that short circuited through me. How he filled the bucket with water in the shower without seeing the enormous power strip was beyond me. I sadly realized that his mind just wasn't working right anymore.

"That's it!" I yelled as I threw the water splashing into the bathtub behind him. "You can *not* take care of Mother *or* yourself *anymore*. I have to have someone live here with you or you both have to go into a home."

"I want to stay in my own home. Please don't put us in a home, honey," Mom said as she started to cry and shake.

"I don't know, I don't know—I just didn't see it. I *beg* of you to believe me. I'd never hurt Mother," he said crying, shaking his head and imploring me to believe him. I was immovable by this point.

"I don't want to hear another word that you can do things for yourself. I'm the parent now and I'll do what's best for you. You're just going to have to trust my decisions that I'm doing what I think is right." I threw the power cord and bucket in the trash and cursed the day I bought them. Every time I thought about what had been such a few seconds away from happening, a chill would shoot up and down my shivering spine.

The irony was that when I was barely four years old, my father had been electrocuted when he accidentally picked up a fallen high voltage live-wire off the docks at the shipyards where he worked. To the amazement of all the workers, as the deadly current whipped him up and down on the dock, he broke the thick cable in half with his bare hands just before being knocked unconscious. Everyone was sure he was dead as his lifeless body was rushed to the hospital. The doctors were astonished that he survived and he had a very slow recovery. Since Mom didn't drive yet, we took a long bus ride to see him everyday in the hospital for many months. He endured numerous spinal fusion operations as well as a total body cast because of so many broken bones. I've often thought that maybe this accident fried some of his brain cells and contributed to his explosive temper. In those days no one sued anyone and he was a "company man" and would never do anything to hurt the company. All he wanted was to not lose his job for being out so long.

♥ ♥ ♥

Fred and Wilma Moved To Green Acres

As fate would have it, Camellia was having her own sordid soap opera: *All My Rotten Children*. Seems her adopted daughter (Bonnie) ran off with some young guy (Clyde) and together they had gotten into a little trouble as they began a crime spree at the local banks. Camellia had been living with them, but they weren't going to be contributing much rent now from jail.

Thank you—absolutely fabulous timing, for once. I really liked Camellia. She was strong enough to handle Dad's craziness and she was so great with Mom. I launched the campaign to have her move in. After days of Dad yelling, "absolutely not," he finally announced very proudly that he would pay her a whopping, "one hundred and twenty-five dollars a month, *plus* room and board!"

"Daaad, who can live on one hundred and twenty-five dollars a month?" Reasoning with Fred Flintstone about the cost of living was completely impossible because he was still living in the Stone Age. Wilma "tisked" from her bed, saying no one could tell him anything.

"Well, she's getting a free goddamn place to live isn't she?"

"Daaad, *ple-e-e-eease*, we need to pay her one thousand dollars a month *and* room and board. I promise you that it's an incredible deal. Then she'll be here most of the time in case you need help."

"Over my dead body!" (Now there's an idea.) Inhale... and hold it... (where's Vito Corleone when you need him?)... and blast it all the way out. Okay, so now I had *another* uphill battle trying to prove to Pa Kettle what a great deal it was. I had the social workers, nurses and the physical therapists who came to work with Mom tell him how reasonable Camellia's offer was, but he was stonewall immovable. Then, Diamond Jake Brady came up with a "great" solution.

"OK, *two* hundred and fifty dollars, but that's my final offer."

I was about to make *him* a final offer that involved a horse's head. I remember my mother lamenting that he expected her to get groceries in 1985 at 1945 prices. "Your father expects me to rub two nickels together and make a dollar. He thinks a penny saved is a dollar earned." Jake Benny was so tight with a buck we always had to lie about the cost of things so he wouldn't get mad, and God *forbid* if she lost her head and bought "retail." She'd try to sneak an extra buck here or there out of the grocery money he doled out to her. She'd always tell me, "You're going to have a good education, make your own money, and never have to rely on a *man* to give you what you want." Thanks my mom.

Anyway, I was just about to "agree" with him and pay Camellia behind his back, but I was afraid of bigger problems down the road. Better to get it solved and convince him that he was not getting a raw deal. Camellia had to know by the next day if she was moving in or not. I tactfully tried again to convince the very last tycoon.

He screamed at me as he threw a glass of milk in my face and pounded the table. "I said no!" OK... define "no." What am I gonna do? He just didn't have a clue—*but*, my fantasy life was alive in full bloom: Miss Jacqueline, with a lead pipe, in the family room. Finally, I flat-out told him that he was just going to have to accept it.

"Oh yeah? I'll throw her fat-ass outta here as soon as you leave, goddamn it. She is not going to live here, ever! This is my house, not yours, and I say who lives here. We don't need her anyway. I've always taken good care of Mother. And you're not telling me what to do!"

With a milk facial curdling on my face, I had to leave the room. I hate him, I hate him, I hate him. Let me count the ways. Somebody, please... bring me an asp. Wait, ah... a new film concept is coming to me: *Throw Daddy From the Train!*

Then I had a lightening bolt idea. I phoned my pillar of strength Godfather, Bo, begging for his help. He'd just gotten home from a very draining day with Shelly at the hospital, but he dropped everything and drove all the way up to see us and pretended to "drop in." He visited for a while and then he smoothly transitioned into asking about Camellia.

"Say, how's your caregiver working out, Jake?"

"She's pretty good, but she wants too damn much money. I just can't afford no thousand dollars a month *plus* room and board."

"Really, Jake? Wow, I pay over one hundred dollars a *day* for the gal I have to take care of Shelly and she's just so-so. I still have to pitch in and do quite a bit of the work. Is this Camellia good with Mariel?" Dad nodded. "And did I hear you say she cleans the whole house, does all the laundry, all the shopping and cooks great meals *too*?"

"Yep," Dad said proudly.

"Well, gee, if you don't want her, would you mind if I hired her? I'd love to get her at that price. That's an *amazing* price for all that work." I couldn't *stand* how perfect this was going.

"Well, I don't know, I, ah... ah... I think we'll probably just keep her," Dad finally spit out.

"Oh yeah, you really should grab her quick. I've been through six caregivers already. Half the time they don't show up, they don't speak English that well, they're late, they have car problems, family problems or some problem you have to spend all your time helping *them* with. As long as Mariel likes her, believe me, that's one helluva deal. Please let me have her if you decide not to hire her, but… do you think she'd want to live in Hillsborough?" I practically burst out laughing—ah, in a nano-second. *("Hyde-y I love you but give me Park Avenue.")*

"Um, no, no, her family ties are all up here in this area. I think we'll probably just keep her," Dad announced. "Yeah, I think we'll keep her."

I couldn't thank Bo enough as I beamed with so much love for my clever godfather. He had always been my most favorite person ever, my life-long hero, and once again he was there for me.

The next day we made Camellia a firm offer. The only thing she requested was HBO in her room. I talked to Dad about it being an extra few bucks a month and he was feeling like the "Grand Poopah" when he said, "Suuure, why the hell not?" Okay, I'd add HBO and for a few dollars more she'd be there most of the time, as she liked to stay home, watch movies and munch. She'd put in her own private phone line and pay for that herself. (I put 976 and International call-blocking on our phone, to be sure it wasn't used inappropriately.) I would be able to return home and feel confident that they were being supervised most of the day and all night long. Dad would do the minimum on Sundays when she was off, and if need be I'd get someone to come in that day. Yes, it was *finally* all going to work out perfectly and my mental health was just around the corner. I started doing the Watusi in 7th Heaven, singing a slightly modified version of my new theme song for the week: *"Southern California dreamin' … on such a winter's daaaaay."*

♥ ♥ ♥

The Man From U.N.Believable

The day came for Camellia to move in and as she was finishing soaking Dad's feet (in a *non*-electric bucket) she said, "I have a friend who works for a podiatrist and she'd be happy to make a house call to trim yours and Mariel's toenails for only fifteen dollars. She says that the tincture will soak in better if the nails are kept real short."

"How nice," I said as I turned to see Dad getting mad. He shook his head "no" at me. Oh great, what now? I'd gotten Camellia some extra midday work for the elderly couple next door and she left to go over there. She'd be back later to start moving in. I was so happy. "There's no place like home," I thought, as I clicked my ruby slippers together. The second she walked out, Wicked Hyde from the North started in.

"I'm not paying no *extra* fifteen dollars. What the hell are we paying *her* for? She's hired to take care of us and she better damn well do it!"

"Dad, it's no big deal. We don't have to hire her friend if we don't want to, but it's really not in Camellia's job description to be a trained podiatrist. Your nails are so thick, it's very hard to cut them unless you know what you're doing with the right clippers."

"Goddamn it! I'm always wrong and you think you just know everything. This is *my* house and if I say she is cutting our nails, she is cutting our nails! And I want this goddamn HBO taken off my television. If she wants it, she can pay for it herself—but I'm not paying for her to sit around all day on her fat-ass and watch TV. She's here to *work* and she better damn well work—*hard*—all day long."

Why couldn't I be Bewitched, wiggle my nose and have him disappear? Mom would love to be Endora. (Poof!) I should have just said, "fine," and he wouldn't have ever known that I was secretly paying for it. He couldn't find the *TV Guide*, let alone read it or recognize HBO if it hit him in the face. Instead, I said very nicely, I swear, that it was, "the least we could do for her, because then she'd be there the majority of the time to help them if need be."

Well… it was the wrong time to contradict Mussolini. He picked up a footstool and threw it towards me, screaming at the top of his lungs that he was, "ripping out the goddamn cable," before she could watch television on his nickel. Mom started screaming from her hospital bed for him to, "stop it right now!" Okay, here we go again—it's tantrum time. I was not going to egg him on. I decided to just ignore him as I sat quietly sketching a hangman. The phone rang and I calmly reached over and picked it up.

"Are you okay?" Camellia asked from next door. "We heard him yelling and then something crashing." Now… the *last* thing I wanted Camellia to see was Horrendous Hyde at his absolute worst, cancel moving in, and I wouldn't get to go home.

"Oh, don't worry, he's just having another little temper tantrum. I can handle it."

"Oh-k," she said nervously. As I hung up, he started going beyond ballistic. His strength astounded me as he picked up a heavy chair and effortlessly hurled it toward me.

"We were fine until you came up here and messed everything up. Get the hell out of my house! We don't need you *or* Cabrillo."

"Oh, Dad, please calm down. I asked you about adding HBO and you said it was fine, remember?" He took off his shoe and started pounding it as hard as he could on the table, inches from my face.

"You did *not*—goddamn-it!"

Wow, I wish I had this on his audition tape—he looks just like Nikita Khruschev at the U.N. Okay, let's call the KGB and get him *"back in the USSR."* God I wish I had a truth serum. Was this an act and he was just lying again as usual, or didn't he *really* remember? I was just looking at him, marveling that this maniac was actually related to me, my own flesh and blood. So, if men are from Mars, my father must be from—*The Andromeda Strain.* I just kept staring at him wondering where in the world he came from—aaand you aaaare?

"Stop that swearing, sit down and be quiet!" Mom commanded. Oh yeah. The phone rang again and he lunged for it.

"Don't you dare answer my phone. I'm going to rip out all the goddamn phones too!"

He picked up the large-button, volume-enhanced phone that I had just gotten for them (free from the phone company if you're disabled), that was to my right and slightly behind me, and smashed it down as hard as he could on the counter breaking off a part of it. I was so mad—now I was going to have to get *that* fixed. Little did I know that the telephone was going to be the *least* of my problems. Ranting and raving he walked away, back over to the couch as Mom continued yelling at him. I was really amazed that the phone still worked, continued ringing and would not stop. We always just ignored his temper tantrums and he'd eventually "take five" and calm down.

I turned my back on him and reached over to answer the phone, to hear Camellia yell in desperation, "What's going on over there?" Before I could answer her, I felt a set of very strong hands grasp my throat from behind. I didn't even see him coming. I tried to scream in horror and disbelief, but not too much would come out. *My* father, who had never laid a hand on me my whole life (no spankings, no swats, no slaps, nothing—*ever*), was trying to kill me over HBO! Oh-kay, point taken. I'll take this as a definite "NO" on the HBO. Hey, I can get

Showtime if you prefer. No? Ohh-K, maybe the *Delusional* Channel then? (Choke, gasp, ooouch, heeelp!) Oh boy, this was looking bad for the home team. But, always the consummate professional, I was thinking I really had a hot new series: *Home Sweet HBO Homicide.*

I just couldn't believe it—I was having the life choked out of me by my own father. I tried to hit him with the phone's receiver, still in my hand, but I couldn't even reach around to get him. He wouldn't let go and I was wondering how long it would be before I blacked out— or worse. Mom was completely traumatized, screaming for him to "STOP!—STOP!" as she started to climb out of her hospital bed to save me. Luckily Camellia rushed back over, frantically screaming at him until he finally let go. She was able to get between us and I was shaking so badly I could barely get my index finger to hit 9-1-1 for the first time in my life. Camellia was able to keep him from me, talking him down, as I kept thinking it all *had* to be a bad dream. What if Camellia hadn't been there? Gulp.

Finally, Hyde was spewed out and went to lie down. I was shaking in shock, feeling sweaty and nauseous, and I couldn't believe how long it was taking for the Boys in Blue to arrive. Okay, search the donut shops in Mayberry. This just couldn't be happening to *our* family. This happens to low-lifes. You see them all the time on *America's Dumbest Criminals.* Not *my* father trying to kill *me.* I'd always been the light of his life.

Then, *forty-five* minutes of disbelief later, I met Andy Taylor and Barney Fife look-alikes on the porch. Dad got up and came out when he saw the cops. "What the hell are they doing here?" he snarled.

"How can we help you, sir?" Sgt. Joe Friday asked, flashing his badge as he stepped in the family room.

"I've had it with her!" he yelled, pointing at me with a vile look. "She comes up here and cleans our house and makes us go to all these damn doctors and takes my wife to have cataract surgeries, and to the goddamn dentist, and to the goddamn foot doctor, and she keeps fixing *everything* in my goddamn house!" (OK, ya got me.) The cop looked at me and back at Dad.

"Well, that's *terrible.* Did you choke her for that?"

"Yes I did and I'll do it *again!*" he yelled as he lunged toward me, spewing with venom out of his beady little eyes. Friday saw the volatile situation and got between us. He looked at my neck with the red finger indention marks all around, looked at his partner and they nodded simultaneously in the affirmative.

"Sir, get your shoes on. We're going to take you someplace to get you some help." Dad resisted big time, but they made it very clear that he did not have a choice. They "5150'd" him (a police term I would become *real* familiar with), and hauled him off to a psychiatric hospital for a 72 hour hold to be evaluated.

"I'll *never* forgive you for this daughter, NEVER!" he yelled, spitting at me as many times as he could as they took him into custody in his white coveralls and slippers, locking him in their squad car.

Oh-kay, so now I'm stuck in a bad co-venture Peckinpah/Fellini film—it all seemed violently surreal. How could *my* Dad do this to me? I knew he was going down-hill, but the reality that he was losing touch with his reality, was really hard to swallow—literally. I'd have bet a million dollars my father would never do anything like this to me— *ever*. And right there is the reason I don't gamble.

"Are you okay?" Friday asked, examining my blood-drained neck.

"Yeah, I'm still breathin'. I'm just so stunned that my father would actually try to hurt me—he's always adored me," I said as I babbled on and on about all I'd been through.

"Just the facts, Ma'am," officer Bill Gannon interrupted. I recanted the power cord in the water incident and he said we would have all been electrocuted. "Well, what doesn't kill ya makes ya stronger," he said trying to make me laugh. Funny guy. "Actually, we see this kind of thing all the time when dominating elderly men rebel as they lose their control." I was so surprised to hear his nonchalant tone, but very comforted to know that my father wasn't the only nut case in town.

What to do now? Would Camellia still want to move in? Luckily she had no place to go and insisted she could handle him. "Are you *sure*, Camellia? I won't be mad if you back out, really." She assured me that she had no hesitation and I was so relieved to have her continued support. Thank God for sweet Camellia.

I had Hyde hopes that while Dad would be in the psychiatric hospital the doctors would finally take me seriously and give him some behavioral medication. I always wondered why I had gotten such bad vibes when I pleaded with Dr. Kiljoy for medication to help calm him down.

Well... you can imagine my furry when Camellia said that Dusty told her that the scuttlebutt around Kiljoy's office was that *I* was the completely neurotic daughter. Darling Jekyll had sadly told them all that I was going through "the change" (lie, not even close) and that

I was really the emotionally unstable one. He sadly told them that yes, I had lost my job, my long-time boyfriend, and I'd just been through spinal surgery, so I really wasn't myself anymore. He apologetically told them all that unfortunately I had gone—"a little wacky."

♥♥♥

Look Who's Talking Now

After Dad got hauled off we ordered a pizza and I was pleased that Mom sat up chatting with us, eating two big slices. She was having a ball. Dad would always demand that she lie down with him all day, and then as soon as dinner was over she'd have to go back to bed with him. Now she was wide awake, visiting with Camellia and me and even staying up enjoying a *Barbara Walters Special* until eleven o'clock—critiquing every detail of Barbara's beautiful outfits.

Camellia and I noticed how much more alert she was when Dad wasn't there, but she still asked us ten times a day, "Is Dad coming home today, honey?" I'd try to talk with her and she'd be right there, very coherent and then suddenly she'd look out on her front porch and be someplace else. "Oh look, my orchids are going to bloom!" The plants were more than half dead and were *never* going to bloom, but each time she'd notice them as if it were the very first time. She'd be just as excited the fifth time in the hour as the first. Then she'd suddenly switch subjects and say, "I used to be a teacher." She had taught kindergarten for a short time before she married my father at twenty-one. I noticed that being a teacher, even for that short time, was very important to her—it was one of her *accomplishments.*

I was really worried about how all this stress was affecting her. A couple of years before she began picking her face until it bled and the doctor didn't know why. I did, namely—my father. Once, when my parents came to visit I was shocked to see my mother's lovely face covered with bloody scabs. I trimmed her nails and put gloves on her at night, and she finally stopped the picking. Now, I saw that she was starting to pick at her face again, so I headed it off by filing her nails down and most importantly, I tried to calm her fears about Dad. Then, I was determined to give her some freedom while he was gone.

61

"Let's call everybody up and say hello, Mom. Dad never lets you talk on the phone without him dominating the entire conversation. Who would you like to have a good long talk with?" She thought for a moment and then her eyes lit up.

"Gineva!" Of course, her best friend.

"You got it." I called Gineva, gave Mom the phone and they had the best darn conversation they'd had in eleven years. I was delighted by how much more she was able to converse and comprehend as they chatted away. It was just that Dad never gave her a chance, as he always completed her every thought.

Everyday that Mom was lucid, I'd call someone and just let her chat away. I found out that her own sisters hadn't even been able to talk to her because my father had monopolized the conversations so completely. Then she got nervous. "We'd better not make anymore calls, honey. Dad's going to be mad when he gets the bill."

"I promise I'll intercept the bill, Mom, so let's take a walk on the wild side. Dad doesn't have to know a thing about it. You just talk as long as you damn well please."

"Really?" she grinned from ear to ear. The excitement on her face was priceless as we continued to call everyone in their phone book.

While Dad was in the psychiatric hospital that week I got a lot more accomplished. While organizing his two storage sheds I was horrified to find a Winchester rifle. Digging deeper I found the bullets. It was a farewell to arms as I removed them to a neighbor for safe keeping.

Then I organized all his tools. He had always been a fanatic about his huge workbench in our garage that had a large pegboard above it with an outline of each tool to make it impossible to put the tools back incorrectly. My brother would put them back wrong on purpose, just to piss him off. (Yeah, passive aggressive.) It was so unlike the father I knew to have all his tools in careless piles. He'd made me a beautiful custom desk when I was in the seventh grade that was so special, with so many secret compartments. He was always building something then. I organized his little work area and hoped he might eventually have a new project to work on. He had been on "Project Mom" for far too long and it had obviously flipped him out.

Then, I couldn't believe it—Dad was being a *model* patient. No outbursts, no rages, and just an all-around "great guy" to all the social workers. He was like an elder Eddie Haskell, "Oh hello, Mrs. Cleaver. My goodness gracious—you're looking exceptionally lovely today.

Do you think I could possibly have a word with Wally, the Beaver, and the psychiatrist?" Uh-huh, Dad knew where his Metamucil was mixed.

I talked to all these "professionals" daily, telling them about all of my father's bizarre behaviors. I told them that he was calling me and threatening my life for putting him in there. They said that they were waiting for him to act up, but he was completely "normal" as far as they could see. Nope, no problems of any kind and he really was "such a sweet and kind man" to everyone there. They loved him!

Oh-kay, so he must be a sociopath then and he *is* crazy—crazy like a frickin' fox! Yeees, Jekyll is a doll. Where in the heck is Hyde when you need him? Probably in a hyde-a-way with the Wolfman. I wonder if Robert Louis Stevenson would roll over in his grave if I wrote, *Jekyll & Hyde: The Sequel.* Can you get a Pulitzer Prize for a sequel?

After a few days, Dad had to go before a judge to see if he were sane enough to be released to come home. I was told to bring my mother and Camellia to the hospital that day and we walked into a large waiting room to see my father, dressed in baggy blue hospital "inmate" pajamas. He was talking to a weird man who looked *exactly* like an axe murderer, amid a room full of genuine psychos. I couldn't believe it—I was in *One Flew Over the Cuckoo's Nest* now.

Apparently, Dad had stubbed his big toe, lost the toenail, and it was bleeding and looked infected already. I was furious—what kind of care was going on here? Where's nurse Ratched when you need her? He jumped up crying, grabbed onto Mom and just *glared* at me. If looks could have killed, I'd have disintegrated. Under his enraged breath, Al Capone, Sr. whispered that I had double-crossed him, he would *never* forgive me and I was gonna be *real* sorry. I suddenly heard Walter Winchell. Okay, get Eliot Ness, The Untouchables and Linda Tripp over here right away with a wire.

A drooling "Jack Nicholson" took a liking to me and rushed over sidling up to me all goo-goo eyed, trying to pick me up. I started breaking out with hives. That's it, I'm taking a pill when I get old. Ohhh nooo, I have my father's blood chemistry running through my veins and I'm sure it *controls* all my mother's genes. I could end up wacko like this in a psycho ward when I get old, and I won't even have a devoted daughter to take care of me. They shoot horses, don't they?

Why was I going through this? I never thought I was a masochist. Who would go through three solid months of this living hell? I was trying to tap into the real answer: I was still devoted to my parents, especially my mother, for all they had done for me in my life. And since her heart attack she had been in a virtual prison with him and *no one* was ever able to stand up to him when he got out of hand. I wished I'd had the time and courage to stand up to him a long time ago, although I realized it had always been hopeless to fight him. The timing was finally right to take him on. I wasn't working because of the back surgery. I was completely single, no one even in the wings, well... except for this love-struck psycho next to me reading the personal ads. Nope, there wasn't anything I had to tend to—no job, no guy, no kids, no pets, not even an indoor plant. The only thing living back at my place was a little mold in the bathtub. Yes, I was ready to do what had to be done, and accomplish what no one had ever been able to do. I was boldly going where no one had *ever* dared to go before—and it was pretty darn scary.

To his credit, my father's method of encouragement was always to tell me to be strong, fight back when injustices came my way, and he instilled a "never let the bastards see you sweat" kind of attitude. (Actually, "glisten" in my case.) Winning wasn't everything, but losing was nothing. He was always right there cheering me on to overcome whatever got placed in my path. Well, I needed my Dad now because I was sweating bullets big-time (forget glistening) and all I had to draw on were my many memories of him always being there with that look of solid determination on his face *for* me, never *against* me, like it was now.

He'd always taught me that it was a dog-eat-dog, mad-mad world out there and only the strong survived—but then he was always right there protecting me from it. I had always been his beloved daughter, but now I was the accused, the one who had betrayed him. I sadly looked at my father's twisted, tortured face and tried to change him back into my "Burgess Meredith," rooting from *my* corner.

"Go on, go get 'em, honey! Don't give up, you can overcome this. Don't let them bastards get you down. You're the *best*, the *smartest*, the *prettiest*, and you can do *anything* you set your mind on. You'll figure this out soon. Listen to me now, this is very important. I want you to always remember—you're *strong*, sweetheart!"

Yes, I guess I am strong, Dad—because of you.

♥ ♥ ♥

Miss Judge What Your County Can Do For You

I was dazed to find out that my father was permitted to ban us from his hearing with the judge. What's up with that? The social worker said he was very rational in front of the lady judge and was released immediately. This was in the face of the psychiatrist's strong recommendation that he spend fourteen days there (called a "5250") because of his daily threats to kill me—unbelievable!

"So help me God, you are going to be sorry for putting me in here," he'd yell when he'd call me several times a day. What, he has his own private telephone in the psycho ward? Can't they hear him calling and threatening me?

"Dad, you *choked* me!"

"I did not! I'd never do that. I'll never forgive you for this—never!"

My gosh, did he really not remember or was he just lying again? Boy, I'd love to give him some sodium pentothal right about now. Maybe he was a split personality and Jekyll didn't know what Hyde was doing. Nooo, couldn't be. Maybe all those years of drinking destroyed some of his brain cells. So lets see now, just to keep score, we have—electrocuted *and* inebriated brain cells. And then on top of that, there was all the stress of Mom being so sick for eleven years, and then all the scary changes I was trying to make to help him, so maybe he was just completely, as Dana Carvey likes to imitate Regis, *"out-of-control!"*

Next they had us all in for a meeting with the psychiatrist and social workers before they'd release him. He was beyond charming to everyone, except me. We each had our turn to talk so Camellia told the choking story and then I added to it. Dad sat there shaking his head chanting, "no, no, no." Mom was sitting next to him and chimed in nodding emphatically, "Yes you *did*, honey. I saw you choke her."

"You shut up!" Hyde exploded, as he raised his fist an inch from Mom's face. "I've never laid a hand on anyone!" Then he pounded his fists so hard all the papers and pencils went flying. The therapists, who had been dealing with this "sweet man" for days, had a look of utter surprise on their faces. I was just sitting there, arms crossed, smugly looking at them with my favorite, "I told you so" look. They looked at each other in shock with the, "Houston, we have a problem" look, and quickly got up.

One of the social workers whispered in my ear that they were going to ask the judge to rescind her decision and keep him longer. With that, they left us sitting there staring at one another for forty-five minutes. Dad realized he had better zip-lock it and did a Mum's the word, taking "The Fifth." I was pretty sure he'd rather *have* a fifth at this point. When they came back, to my open jaw astonishment, they said that they *couldn't* do anything because, "Miss Judge doesn't want to have to re-do the paperwork." WHAT! Talk about obstruction of justice. It's a good thing I wasn't in the courtroom or I'd have been hauled off for contempt because I would have definitely been ruled— "Out of frickin' order!" (Where's Judge Judy when you need her?)

"So, we're supposed to take him home while he's this mad and threatening us?"

"I'm sorry, there's nothing more we can do. We can't legally hold him. If he hurts you again, have him brought in and we'll try to keep him longer." My mouth would not close. I was gonna be in the wacko ward myself soon. So now I'm in a Kafka novel, dealing with the epitome of the absurd. Okay fine, I'll be sure to bring him in right after he breaks my neck and I've had my private consultation with Quincy.

We went home and he wouldn't speak to me for days. Hmmm, not so bad. Every night he'd stand over Mom and they would fold their hands and recite the Lord's Prayer, make the sign of the cross, "In the name of The Father," and ask for God's grace to "forgive us our trespasses as we forgive those who trespass against us... and deliver us from evil, amen." Then in the morning he'd start in again calling me nasty names as he ate his daily bread. Oh yeah, his kingdom is gonna come all right. He kept saying how shocked he was that I'd had him taken away. I explained that *I* didn't put him away—SFPD Blue saw him threaten me, and *their* will was done.

Then, amazingly, he got really nice again. Camellia was moved in and Mom was starting to walk and communicate more. I had arranged for all the nurses and therapists to come regularly to work with her— so I thought that since he saw Mom getting so much better with the proper care, maybe he had finally learned his lesson and was ready to settle down, behave himself and accept help. Finally, I would be able to go *home* and jump-start my so-called stalled life.

Uh-huh, and Monica and Hillary are best friends now.

♥ ♥ ♥

chapter♥five

JACQUELINE, YOU IGNORANT SLUT

Camellia slept in the back bedroom, Dad demanded that Mom sleep with him, and I slept in her hospital bed. By splitting the phone jack, I ran an extension wire so a large-numbered phone could be at her hospital bedside in case something happened when Camellia wasn't there. Then I programmed all the phones for one-touch speed-dialing with a chart at each phone, and drilled Mom everyday how to dial 911 by hitting the number 9.

One morning as I was talking on this phone from her hospital bed, Hyde woke up and suddenly snapped into a full-blown rage that I was using his phone. He started calling me names that I have never been called in my entire life. "You're a goddamn slut!" he screamed. I was so completely flabbergasted I couldn't speak and quickly hung up, embarrassed to have my phone friend hear him. "Yeah, that's right—you heard me. Nothing but a goddamn whore and a *fucking* bitch!"

Well... isn't that special. I had *never* heard him use the "F word" in my whole life, but suddenly it was every other f-ing word to me, his cherished daughter. I had never done a f-ing thing for him, used up all his f-ing money, drained him f-ing dry, gave him nothing but f-ing grief my whole life, and... oh yeah, the worst... I was a *fucking* know-it-all. Uh... and your point is...?

Mom was traumatized again and started crying. "You drove off our son and you're not going to get rid of our daughter too."

"The hell I'm not! This is my goddamn house and I'm doing things the way I want to from now on. I'm not doing another thing that fucking whore says!" Mom started crying and shaking so Camellia rushed to try and calm her. He threatened me not to sleep in Mom's hospital bed again or I'd be sorry. "You just try it. Wait until dark and go ahead, fall asleep there. You won't even know what hit you. You'll never wake up—you *fucking* bitch."

I was in such shock, I couldn't even hate him, he was so pathetic. I went into Camellia's room completely frazzled, rested my back, watched HBO all day for spite, and *prayed* he would fall asleep. I left pleading messages for Dr. Kiljoy, but it was Saturday and she didn't call me back. Dice Clay, Sr. ranted and raved all day and I could hear him calling me every *f-ing* name he could *f-ing* think of. Ohh-kay, I'm in *Pulp Non-Fiction* now—and where's Travolta when you need him?

By evening, Camellia had served them dinner, cleaned up, and made us some chicken soup and sandwiches. On her way back into the bedroom to eat with me, the "Senior Soup Nazi" got up and physically blocked her from bringing it in to me with his outstretched arms in front of the door.

"Is that for her? You can't feed her *my* food—I forbid it."

"Uh, no, this is for me. Did you see me eat any dinner?"

"Then you sit out here and eat it," he demanded as he pointed for her to sit at hell's kitchen table.

My blood started coagulating. Camellia and I had just gone to the store a few nights before and bought five *hundred* dollars worth of food and supplies that I paid for with *my* money. I listened to the insanity through the door and then I was just completely fed up. I threw the door open, came out defiantly and went into the kitchen to get something to eat as he shot poison darts at me from the couch. He started yelling across the DMZ zone. "You'd better get out of here. I'm warning you. If you eat my food or sleep in Mother's hospital bed, you're not gonna wake up!"

Damian, the Demon Seed, continued his evil spewing until *my* head started to spin around. OK, where's his copy of *Satanic Verses*? I grabbed a handful of Animal Crackers and sat down at the table with Camellia. I was the defiant one, staring back at him as I angrily bit off each animal head with a loud crunching bite. "Hey, got milk?"

Then he started on the *"eleven years"* thing, repeating it over and over about how long he'd been taking care of Mom. I was so tempted to say, "Uh, Dad, let me ask you one question. Just *how* long has it been again?" But I was afraid he'd blow a gasket and his thick skull might actually explode. Too messy. Every time he looked away from me I did my best lizard impression, quickly sticking my tongue out at him like a rotten little eight-year-old. I realized I was starting to lose it but I enjoyed tickling Camellia's funny bone amid the absurdity.

He was really stewing and I was afraid he was capable of hurting me in my sleep—he was a man possessed. What in the world was I going to do with him? These stupid "professionals" he had conned were going to have to listen to me. I was going to have to get him committed one way or another. It was really getting too scary. I wondered how much of it was just his infuriation about my challenging his *control* and how much of it was organic uncontrollable dementia or Alzheimer's. God I wish I knew what was happening.

Mom cried and shook uncontrollably, wetting herself and all over the floor as Camellia got her away from him. I hated him so much for all this misery he had inflicted on us, and I was terribly worried that he might cause her to have a stroke. Why couldn't *he* have another heart attack and save us all this aggravation? Camellia was able to slip him an over-the-counter sleeping pill, but we were shocked to see that it didn't affect him at all. He was too mad for any drug to work on him. We couldn't believe that he didn't sleep, so that meant we weren't going to either. If anything, he was even more awake, and like Dracula, he was up all night. I decided I better go sleep with Camellia with a knife under my pillow. Geeeese.

We couldn't lock the Gestapo out because the lock was from the outside, preventing closing the door and locking yourself out of the bedroom—so we played *Hogan's Heroes* all night, taking turns lying on the floor, peeking under the door at the night stalker. I whispered over to Camellia as she's practically standing on her head trying to see him., "Hey, Anne Frank, Jr., what's Colonel Klink up to now?"

"This is unbelievable. He's sitting at the kitchen table swearing to himself... now he's pacing back and forth swearing... now he's playing solitaire, throwing all the cards down... swearing some more."

"Oh boy, well, it's only a good omen if it's 52 pickup—but unfortunately, I don't think he's playing with a full deck."

When he finally conked out the next day we felt like holocaust survivors on Schindler's List. I decided I better check his scalp for "666." Hmmm, just dandruff. Then I phoned Mick and had him quietly sneak in and turn the lock around so maybe we could relax and get some sleep the next night.

Exhausted inhale... (OK, I'm in *Nightmare on Elder Street* now) and blast it all the way out—again.

♥ ♥ ♥

Good Morning, Vietnam

I had *prayed* all night that Jolly Jekyll would be back in the morning. Au *contraire* almighty bitchy breath—Howling Hyde was even more "out-of-control" than the day before. He was so outraged that I was still there that *he* called 911 to have me removed from his house. The MP's came and I met them on the porch to clue them in as to what was happening. They stepped in, flashing badges, as Dad started in with his demands. "I want this bitch removed from my house right now. She is not welcome here!"

"Sir, what's your daughter done that's so bad?"

"She put me in the crazy hospital and I'll *never* forgive her for that—never! I'm not crazy like she thinks I am... and... and... I never attacked and choked her with my hands either."

"Yes you did! You choked her, honey—I saw you," Mom nodded.

"You shut up!" Hyde exploded as he whipped around and pounded his fists on the metal table so hard that the salt and pepper shakers bounced right off of it. They asked Mom if she wanted me to leave.

"No, this is our daughter—she's helping us." Thanks my Mom.

"She's no goddamn daughter of mine, that bitch!" Gee, Dad, if you can't scream anything nice...

They tried to talk some sense into him, counseled us all and then they informed him that I could stay since I'd been there so long I had established residency. We were all just going to have to try to get along, Rodney. The cops took me outside and said it might be best to leave and try to have an intervention later. (I'd rather have a court-martial.) They saw that he was exhibiting quite a bit of mental instability *(yeeah)* but they couldn't *do* anything until he actually *did* something.

"Okay, so I have to wait until he hurts one of us and we need a M*A*S*H unit before you can '5150' him again? That's exactly what he's so mad about now."

"Well, you'll just have to keep calling us and have him hauled off again and again until he realizes he can't be violent. We realize it's a Catch 22, but you can't lock someone up permanently for a screaming bad temper in their own home. It's not illegal to be a rageaholic jerk, unless he's violent enough to actually hurt someone. Our civil rights are very strong and it's actually a good thing (except of course in *my* case), otherwise any kid who gets mad at his parents could have them put away. He has to *do* something pretty serious first, to himself or someone else. If he doesn't have a record other than that one incident where you weren't really hurt, you don't have a chance of having him put in a home against his will unless you go to court. You have to build a case and even then it's going to be hard to accomplish. It's rough—we see this kind of thing all the time." Didn't I just hear this?

After they left, he got worse. The yelling continued and I was afraid he was going to clobber me over the head with the phone when he answered it behind me. I saw Camellia hold her breath and I quickly moved out of the way, not really wanting a concussion. Ohhh-kay... eeny-meeny-miney-mo... which one of us was going to get hurt before they helped me. Mom was so mad she wouldn't even look at him.

I had already called some of the Private Investigators in the yellow pages, looking for Magnum, P.I., to see about having a hidden video camera put in. It was six hundred dollars for one camera that had to run into a VCR close by, and it would only record for eight hours. Gee, how can I be sure he'll rage right then? If you wanted twenty-four hours, for a week, it was eleven hundred dollars to get the *Daddy Horror Picture Show* on tape. Where's Alan Funt and Suzanne Somers when you need them?

There were only a *few* problems I could see. Daddy Dearest would definitely find the hidden VCR, as he got into absolutely *everything* and it had to be accessible to change the tape. Only one camera would be a problem because he raged in the family room, at the kitchen table and in their bedroom. We'd definitely need the camera for several weeks to get enough of these episodes to do any good, if we were going to have, "Film at the Eleventh Hour." It was going to be very expensive and then I worried he'd probably smash all the equipment. And, the cops said the judge wouldn't even look at the tapes and surely wouldn't put him away just for screaming and yelling in his own house anyway.

The "professionals" were cavalier about it, "Well, if it's Mariel's choice to stay with him, what can you do? Just leave her with him, she'll dwindle back down to eighty-two pounds and then she'll be back in the hospital and either recover or die. You've tried everything already. She picked him, she married him and she chooses to stay with him, even if sometimes he is horrible to her. What more can you do?" Uh-huh, I'll be sure to remind you of all that when it's *your* mother we're talking about.

A few years ago I witnessed a heartbreaking scene. I was visiting my parents and I passed by their bedroom doorway just in time to see my father struggling with Mom to get her nightgown on. It was twisted with her arms over her head and he couldn't get it untangled.

He got so frustrated he took her by the shoulders and shook her tiny body very hard, and then he angrily pushed her backwards into a chair.

It was like a firestorm inside me. Throttle up—I *exploded* at him. It was the first time I had ever seen him be physically abusive to her. He went into a rage that she was "his wife" and he'd "do with her as he wished." We had a horrendous screaming match and I vowed to get some medication into him—*now*. I left early the next morning and went straight to Dr. Kiljoy's office and begged them to give him something for the stress of taking care of Mom. Ray called Dad in for an earlier appointment with Dr. Kiljoy, saying that she was going to be out of town and they needed to come in that day. As they were leaving the appointment, Ray was very clever. "Oh, Jake, I want to give you some free samples of something that might help you feel better." He was vague about what it was, but with *free* as the operative word, Dad started taking it and I noticed a big difference in his demeanor over the phone. The anti-anxiety/depressant drug had helped for quite a while, but obviously, it was not working anymore.

In the three months I had been there Ray had lobbied Dr. Kiljoy for a few medicines to help calm Dad, but I couldn't get him to take them and even when I did they didn't seem to work. Ray couldn't get Kiljoy to prescribe anything stronger because they never saw Joyful Jekyll be anything but terribly rational. I tried so hard to get my father to go to another doctor, but he adamantly refused to talk to *anyone* else. He hated Dr. Dolittle, the doctor from the psycho hospital, so there was no chance of him consenting to see him again. No, only if Kiljoy or Ray said so, would he take *any* medication—period.

Camellia called Dr. Kiljoy to tell her about Dad's Horrible Hyde side, but Kiljoy informed her that she was not a psychiatrist. Only a psychiatrist who saw him raging was going to prescribe any stronger anti-psychotic drugs and he'd have to be monitored regularly. How was I going to get him to see another doctor and be sure he'd be in a rage there? I guess I could bring up my brother at the appropriate moment.

And then there was getting Hyde to take his medications. He cupped pills in his hand, hid them under his tongue and threw them in my face. He poured the whole bottle of anti-anxiety medication that Dr. Dolittle had given him down the toilet before I could stop him. And then there were other days when he didn't mind taking the medications at all. One day Camellia noticed that there were at least thirty anti-depressant pills missing. I had color-coded the medicine bottles, red tops on Mom's and black tops on his, so they wouldn't get mixed up. Camellia was dolling them out, but he must have been getting up in the middle of the night and taking more behind our backs. Sometimes he was of the mind-set that if one worked well, many would work better.

Okay, time for a lock-box to keep all the medications in, and he was *incensed* that he no longer had control of his pills. I refused to give him a key to the box and had Camellia watch him swallow every pill. I put up a Monday to Sunday eraser-board outside their bedroom so that we could check off when they had their pills—morning, high noon and night. This made it fool-proof so we never missed a dose. Sometimes we ground his pills up in his food or told him they were his heart, blood pressure or water pills. I was sure that the answer to all this bad behavior was in some brain chemical altering medication, but how to *get* the medication was the problem.

How in the world does anyone figure out how to take care of their elderly parents? I knew my father was an extreme case... but *still*. Hey, I was a regular Diane Sawyer type, searching for all the answers and I was floundering. I bought all the books on elder care and they all made it sound so easy *if* you had a co-operative parent. So then, where's *Chicken Gumbo For the Raging Aging Soul*? Nope, I couldn't find anything about how to handle difficult elders—I was on my own.

Then I had *numerous* social workers and an experienced geriatric case manager come try to help me with him. He'd act charmingly adorable and totally agreeable to their faces, but then he wouldn't do *anything* they suggested. I spent hours surfing the internet and called every local, social, and government agency I could find, but no one had the answers of how to handle such a difficult elder.

Then I decided to try to diagnose my father myself by reading all the symptoms of the various diseases and psychological conditions I could find in the medical books. I remember when I was barely fifteen and had developed a strange skin rash. I went to the library, found a book on skin conditions, looked at all the pictures and read the symptoms. When Mom took me to the doctor I announced, "I have Pityriasis Rosea." Trapper John was floored, "How'd *you* know that?"

"Not so hard—that's the only thing that matches all my symptoms and looks just like what I have in the skin disease book at the library. Don't worry—it'll be gone in six weeks." See, I should have gone into medicine—a thorough doctor with a humorous bed-side manner. Now *there's* a rarity. Miss Patch-eline Adams, M.D., at your service?

So, I tried to diagnose my father, but this time there just wasn't an exact match. Was this a complex combination of ailments, or were they missing some simple little test that could tell us what was happening? I researched: Borderline Personality Disorder, Schizophrenia, Psychotic Behaviors, Bi-Polar Manic Depression, Multiple Personalities, Dementia and Alzheimer's and he actually fit *some* of the symptoms of every single one. Next I researched all the drugs, studied the side effects and became an amateur pharmacologist. Ughhh, maybe he's just an "out-of-control" grumpy old man. What good was it going to do to have a "label" for what was wrong with him? We still had to deal with the symptoms that changed every other day. I guess *I* needed a medical reason for what was happening to him—to help *me* cope.

One day he was having pain in his legs so I decided to try a little test. I said sympathetically, "Oh, I'm sorry, Dad—let me get you a pain pill." I substituted a similar looking vitamin pill and just quickly put it in his mouth aaand... presto, his pain went right away. Oh my gosh, he was completely psycho-somatic. We had to be so careful not to put the wrong suggestion in his head. If you casually asked him if something hurt, he'd say "no," but within ten minutes he'd say that it had started hurting. He'd be amazed too.

"Now isn't that something? It didn't hurt until you asked me about it—now it's killing me!" If you told him not to do something he was like a rotten kid who just *had* to do it. I had the perfect plan: The next time he was performing his crazy Captain Ahab act, I'd ask him if he was having a massive heart attack. But with my luck, he'd proceed to have one, and then I'd have to live with *that*. After all this work the *last* emotion I ever wanted to feel was—guilt. Then, I thought that what he needed was a hypnotist—no, probably just an exorcist!

During his stint in the "Cuckoo's Nest," I had to tell the psychiatrist all the drugs he had taken. I asked Ray to give me a list of drugs and duration of use. I was astonished to find out that he had been taking a strong narcotic pain killer for *nine* years! What? I couldn't believe Ray had never told me that he was taking this narcotic drug all this time.

"Well, you never asked what *pain* killer drugs he was taking." (Silly me—I coulda had a V8.) "We wanted to help him with the tremendous pain he was having." Okay, I get it. I could just see it—he went in dramatically crying of *so* much pain all the time that they felt so bad for sorrowful sweet Jekyll—they gave it to him. "Anyway, he's really not to an addictive level." Huh?

And to think, they could have been giving him a vitamin pill. My God, nine *years!* Okay, my father's addicted to a narcotic pain killer and we can't figure out why he's nuts? I had taken that same drug after my back surgery and a half a pill knocked me out for two days and turned me into a reasonable facsimile of Lizzie Borden. The psychiatrist at the hospital was stunned and told me to definitely take the pain pills away from him, cold turkey, right now. He felt certain that it could be causing some of the behavior problems. Ya think? Of course, this was easier said than done. Dad had some stashed away and wouldn't give them up, screaming at me that Dr. Kiljoy had prescribed them for his pain. Then I dreaded that his temperament would probably get worse as he went through withdrawal.

Dad left for his appointment with Dr. Kiljoy to ask her about his pain pills. I called Ray and begged him to make *sure* they backed up the psychiatrist and take the pills away from him right away.

While my father was at the doctor's I decided that the best thing was for me to leave again. He was not calming down and maybe I was just making things worse. As I started to pack, all of a sudden I broke down and had a crying jag that I could not stop. I couldn't catch my breath or stop the flood of sorrow coming out of me. I collapsed on the floor in a corner of the living room, out of view of Mom, curled up in the fetal position, and I actually felt myself losing control of my mind.

"Jacqueline, stop it now, hon, please!" I could hear poor Camellia pleading over me. "You have to be strong for your Mom. Don't you dare give up—you've come *this* far. Don't let him beat you! Oh my gosh, Jacqueline, *please* stop—you're scaring me to death." I just didn't have anymore left in me. The tears poured out of me from the depths of my soul. I could hear Mom calling from the other room.

"What's wrong? Jackie, honey, what's the matter?" She hurried to get out of her hospital bed to come help me but Camellia rushed to stop her. I realized that I was completely hysterical for the first time in my life. I wanted to stop, but I couldn't. I got scared that I had reached a point of no return. It was like there were two people in my head. One was completely hysterical and the other was sanely trying to talk her out of it. Is it me—or is it Memorex? Oh-oh, not good— I was becoming a split personality myself. *Nooooo.*

I finally wore myself out and started slowly coming back to my senses. What in the world was happening to me? The amount of stress I had endured was getting me to the breaking point. *I* was going to need major therapy after this, as well as an extended tropical vacation, and a great big bowl of Swiss Vanilla Almond with Prozac sprinkles. I was, however, very proud to still be able to come up with the appropriate new theme song: *"I heard it through the grapevine—and I'm just about to lose my mind—honey, honey... yeeeah."*

Then, Dad came home from Dr. Kiljoy's madder than a swarm of disturbed hornets, *screaming* at me that "Dr. Dingbat" said he could continue to take his pills for pain, as often as he needed to! He started swearing and spitting at me as he picked up some pillows off the couch and threw them at me as hard as he could. (Much better than furniture.)

Okay, welcome to HELL—endless frustration and torture. Fine, good practice because I was definitely headed there for strangling Ray and Kiljoy. I was *furious* that "Tweedel-dum" hadn't been *able* to catch "Tweedle-dee" to clue her in before Dad asked her about the pain pills. Or, was Dr. Kiljoy just snowed by the best, trying to help him, letting Jake ("you dirty rat") Cagney convince her with his famous poor-pitiful-pain-act, saying that he just *had* to have it for his pain? "I feel your pain." (Ohhh, so you want to be in pictures?) I loved it—*I* was still the horrible villain, taking his pain medicine away from him and making him suffer. What a shame, Dad could have gone far—he really should have been under contract with MGM.

I couldn't believe these stupid doctors. Why was I having to do this? One said this, the other said that. I tried to talk nicely to them but I was not getting anywhere. HELL-O! Okay, no more Ms. Nice Girl. I started *demanding* that they talk to each other and figure out what in the world was happening. For some reason, Dad loved Dr. Kiljoy—it must have been the french connection. No, probably just the fact that she *had* kept them alive with angioplasty after angioplasty for many years.

Ommmm, okay let's light some candles, have a séance, and try to get rid of this consuming curse. Mom always said, "Don't ever sell your soul to the devil." (Rock 'n' roll, OK, but the devil—no way.) I wonder what I did in my last life to deserve all this misery? Musta been that pyramid chain letter I ripped up. Maybe I need a past life regression to go back and cleanse my soul up a bit. And where's Shirley MacLaine when you need her? Life's a bitch, and then you die, and then you die, and then you die—and then you *die!*

♥ ♥ ♥

And Then Along Came Something About Mary Jo

Mom's occupational therapist, Mary Jo (kind of a pretty, Mary Richards type), was scheduled for her appointment to help Mom learn how to do some basic things for herself. Marina's husband, Don, and my nephew came over to give me some moral support. They had been suspiciously hearing about Horrible Hyde, but they had never *ever* experienced anything but Jolly Jekyll. At first, Dad was very cordial to everyone. Then, as Mary Jo probed further about why he had been in the hospital, he started to get angry. His buttons got pushed and well, let's just say—it was a Marty Feldman kind of eye-popping experience for all.

Let Jake introduce *himselves*. I can't tell you how satisfying it was to say, "I told you so," AGAIN. Mary Jo tried to calm him, but he became completely insane. (Hannibal, relax, we'll get you some Chianti and fava beans, I promise.) I realized that I had to start thinking of him as schizoid, not as my Dad anymore, if I was going to be able to hold on to my own sanity. Hey, even Van Gogh went a little wacky and cut his own ear off—happens to the best of 'em.

When Mary Jo got up to leave, Hyde put his raging fist in her face and threatened her. Then he threw me (the slut-bitch-whore) out again, so I followed her outside and thanked her so much for trying.

"Where are you going to go?" she asked.

"I guess I'll go back to Linda and Dick's again," I said crying.

"No you don't. Here are the keys to my house," she said as she wrote down the address and the alarm combination for me. "You go there and make yourself at home and I'll be there a little later."

Wow, I was blown away by her kindness. She really didn't know me very well, and I doubted I'd give some hysterical girl the keys to my house. I graciously accepted and was so glad I didn't have to let the Flannerys see me in such a bad emotional state and worry them that maybe my own mental health was slipping away.

I was barely able to hum, *"Stop draggin' my heart around"* as I got to Mary Jo's, absolutely exhausted emotionally and physically. I took a nap and when she came home she helped me sort everything out with her professional perspective. She would call Dr. Kiljoy and give her a full report of what she had experienced. "Jacqueline, I see this type of thing all the time with controlling elderly people, but your father may be the most difficult case I have ever encountered." She helped me so much and I will be forever indebted to Mary Jo for her kindness and compassion.

Then I got an awful call. Camellia was hiding in her closet, listening through the wall directly into Mom and Dad's bedroom. Hyde was in a rage with his fist in Mom's face. He had already thrown Camellia out of the room several times. I told her go back and get Mom out of there. She walked in just as he was about to slap Mom across the face.

"That's it!" I told her. "I'm calling Adult Protective Services to come out again to try to convince Mom to leave him." I had tried this before, but my mother never wanted to leave her own home to go into a nursing home, and I guess I couldn't blame her. How could I get *him* into a home? He would *never* leave her. They would never leave their home voluntarily, and if I went ahead and did it anyway, I found out I'd really have a big problem. An elder care attorney I spoke with said that all my father would have to say was that they were there against their will. The State would give them an attorney and I'd have a legal battle with him acting normal enough to make the judge let him take her home again. I'd be back to square one, and all I was getting was— *"another day older and deeper in debt."* Thank you, Tennessee Ernie Ford. I just *had* to get a psychiatrist to prescribe stronger drugs to sedate him so they could stay in their own home with Camellia taking care of them. I couldn't think of any other solution that was—*legal*.

Then, Camellia had to go see her father for a few days, who had suffered a serious leg injury playing baseball. She told Dad when she'd be returning but she was an hour late driving back in the rain. As soon as she walked in Hyde flew into a rage raising his fist to her face. With the stress of her father's fracture, her dopey daughter's dilemma, and Hyde's hysterics, she quit and walked out. She phoned and told me that she was staying with a friend until she figured out what to do. I assured her that I didn't blame her and thanked her for trying to help me. There was no joy in Mudville—or anywhere else.

I waited for my father to start calling me. Sure enough, he called Linda's, but I told them all to say that they hadn't seen me for weeks. Then I started getting messages on my phone in Southern California that "they" were coming to take Mother away from him and I had to come home and help him "right now!" I did not respond. I had to let him suffer alone for a few days so he'd realize what a tremendous help Camellia had been. It was hard to do—because it meant my poor mother was suffering too.

♥ ♥ ♥

I'm Steppin' Into the Third Dementia

Everything I did took me twice as long because I had to lie down and rest my aching back so often. I was getting physical therapy on it regularly from Red (kind of a handsome, Jonathan Hart type—married, I *checked!*), one of the physical therapists that came to work with Mom. I drove the fifty minutes from Linda's to see him as he was really good and he gave me a super deal. I had to pay for the treatments out of my own pocket as Fatal Health Plan would not continue coverage for physical therapy this whole time while I was living out of town—yet I was continuing to pay a two hundred dollar a month premium. Arghh!

So, after my treatment one day, I stopped by my parents' pharmacy to buy some ice and heat packs for my back. The pharmacists all knew me well because I'd had all my parents medications come from this one pharmacy to make sure any drug interactions would be caught by their computer. As I was making my purchases at the counter, I turned to see the long line of people waiting behind me, and I just could *not* believe my eyes and the amazing twist of fate. There was my *father*, three people behind me, waiting in line! What were the unbelievable odds? The timing was absolutely staggering since they seldom *ever* left the house. There was my precious mother sitting over in the corner waiting for him. He saw me, smiled and said, "Oh, hi!" My mind went into overdrive. He was probably starting to realize that he couldn't do all the work himself, so I had the upper hand. I nodded a very cold, "hell-o," finished my business, and went to sit with Mom, who started crying with joy when she saw me.

"Oh don't worry, Mom. You know I'd never leave you, don't you? Has he been treating you okay?"

"Well, yeah. Oh, honey, you know your father. Nobody has ever been able to tell him anything. He's the *boss* and things have to be done his way or else. I'm sorry he's being so mean to you. I don't know what's wrong with him—he's always loved you *so* much."

"I know, Mom, but believe me, things are going to change. Don't get upset with how I talk to him now, okay? I'm going to give him an ultimatum." We put our foreheads together, had a little laugh, kissed, and I remembered why I was going through all of this.

Dad finished getting his medicines and walked up to us smiling, "Hey, I need you to come home and fix the phone book and take care

79

of some paperwork—Calyla quit." It was all swept under that filthy carpet already as far as he was concerned.

"*Excuse* me! I don't hear an apology coming from you. I don't hear you *begging* for my forgiveness for throwing me out of the house again and again, choking me, and being so awful to all of us."

"Awhhh... c'mon," he motioned, trying to make light of it.

"Here are my conditions. *One*: you apologize and promise to never yell at us anymore. *Two*: you agree to let me take you to a doctor to get you some help with your 'mood swings.' *Three*: you let Mom talk to Jeremy, whenever she wants to." I took a deep breath, "*Or*... you can just figure everything out for yourself. I don't want to stay here any longer. I'm going home—I've had it."

"Well... tell you what," he started, sticking out his lower lip.

"Dad, there are no negotiations here whatsoever. I'm not playing *Let's Make a Deal,* so take it or leave it—period."

"OK-OK-OK, just come home and fix some things and I'll agree to all that you just said there," he said flustered.

Hold the phone. Did I hear right? Had his day of reckoning finally come? He was even going to let Mom *talk* to Jeremy! I should have thrown in that Mom gets to *see* Jeremy and that he'll jump off the Golden Gate if he rages at anyone again. Wait a minute, something's fishy here. Okay, where's Rod Serling? "Case in point and submitted for your approval... imagine if you will... a meglo-maniacal maniac and his desperate daughter... who finally have a meeting of the minds and see eye to eye... one last time in... *The Twilight Zone.*"

I followed them home on cloud nine, thrilled that he had *finally* gotten it—alternating my theme songs between, *"We Are The World"* and, *"What a Difference a Day Makes."* I fixed their telephone book, making all the numbers real big in thick black marker pen, and whistled as I worked paying all the many bills that had pilled up. Then I phoned Camellia and asked her to come over for an official apology. I made a nice dinner, and when Camellia arrived, Jekyll was his sweetest—*ever.*

He apologized to us very sincerely, begging for forgiveness, and for her to please stay and take care of them. My mushy heart went out to him and all the good things he had ever done for me in my life filled me with love. He *promised* that he would never raise his voice to any of us ever *ever* again. Talk about waiting to exhale. I was so *beyond* relieved, so very happy. Finally, finally, finally, everything was going to work out and fall into place.

Then, I saw what a difference a *minute* makes, when... he bombed Pearl Harbor. "Now, let's just get a few things straight," he started. "Camarillo, you have to be here whenever we want you, day and night, and you can't ever be gone to see your family." My heart sank as adrenaline coagulated and clogged my throat. No, no, no, noooooo.

"Jake, I'm terribly sorry, but my family is very important to me, and if they need me I'm going to have to go. I have a couple of very nice lady friends I'm sure you'd like that we can get as back-ups, if you're afraid to be alone occasionally."

"NO!" he shouted as he slammed his fist on the table and pointed his finger an inch from her nose. "I hired *you* and I don't want anyone else in this goddamn house, is that clear?" Huh? Okay, is anyone else experiencing a déjà vu?

Mom yelled for him to "shush up and stop that swearing right now!" He started in on her, screaming at her to "shut up!" Camellia rushed to get her away from him as she started crying and peeing all over the floor again. I was catching moths in my mouth—I was so stunned by the recent turn of events.

"Dad, *please* calm down. What's the matter with you? You just got done *promising* never to yell at us ever again, less than two minutes ago."

"I don't care. She's not going to take advantage of *me*. I'm paying her good money and she better damn well earn it!"

"Dad, you've got to trust me—you're really not well. I'm going to find a doctor for you tomorrow. We're going to get to the bottom of these incredible 'mood swings' you're having. I'm going to help you."

"The hell you are. I'm not going to any other goddamn doctor, *ever!* And get the hell out of here—right now. Don't let the door hit you in the ass on the way out either." Whaaaat? OK, God, take him, please take him *now*. I swear, if he were to have a heart attack right in front of me I would not call 911. The Hyde and The Mighty was back in full force. "And don't take anymore orders from *that* girl!" General Hyde ordered Camellia as he pointed at me. "Get the hell *out* I said," he yelled up close and personal in my face, "or you'll be sorry!"

What just happened? My world crumbled *again*. I sat there, stuck watching the sickest show on earth—as if someone turned a light switch, aaand... action! I felt my love turn to hate faster than you can say, "Meditated Murder, She Wrote." He was like the man with two brains. I was able to marginally maintain by visualizing him begging in that machine from *The Fly!* "Help me! Help me!"

Yeah, yeah… yada-yada-yada… and more yada. I've heard it all before: I'm no good… I'm just a goddamn slut… I'm nothin' but a bitch… I'm just a fuckin' whore. Same ol'—same ol'. Oh no, I had to be stuck in that Bill Murray movie, *Groundhog Day*, and no matter what I did I was back in the same darn mess being nothing but a— sluttybitchywhore. Fine. I bribed Camellia big time to stay and take care of Mom until I could figure out what to do. She was an angel and agreed, fearing for Mom's safety too.

Back to the Fabulous Flannerys, who earlier were so thrilled to hear the incredibly good news. "Oh my God, what happened now?" Linda gasped as I walked in, a defeated, beaten-down mess singing, *"Must be the season of the bitch."* Thank you, Donovan. "Not again!" she exclaimed as she rushed to comfort me. "Jackie, just remember, you're doing this for your mother. He's just not your father anymore. Keep your focus—you're trying to save your mother. I *promise* you that there's going to be a silver-lining to all of this. No one would have done what you've done to help their parents. I'm surprised the Vatican hasn't called yet to nominate you for sainthood. It's absolutely unbelievable—you should write a book!"

I cried in her arms all evening and continued sniffling the whole next day as I sat in their massage-chair *("I sit and watch… as tears go by")* with the phone book, calling every psychiatrist from A to Z within a ten mile radius. My research pointed me to several anti-psychotic drugs that can help calm aggressive bizarre behavior. I *begged* Dr. Kiljoy to try one of these drugs on Dad, just to see if they *might* work, but she refused. Even Ray, feeling bad about the last drug *glitch* tried on my behalf, but no chance. I begged and pleaded harder, but Kiljoy always gave me the same line about being a "cardiologist, not a psychiatrist." I'm going to recommend that she see a proctologist when this is all over with to remove the stick she has up her ass. She knew it was *impossible* for me to get Dad to go see any other doctor besides her.

Okay fine. Then could they *please* help me find a psychiatrist, and most importantly convince Dad to go see him? The few numbers they gave me were disconnected. I called Ray again and pleaded with him to really think if there could be *any* other psychiatrist they could possibly think of. "No, those were the only ones we know. We really don't deal with psychiatrists." Fine. I'll do it myself—just like everything else.

No one would take us—it was too close to the holidays. Finally after major phone groveling all day, I got a secretary to take pity on me.

She said that Dr. Peter Patetic would be on-call at the emergency room of another fairly close by hospital that night. If I could get Dad to go to the emergency room he would see him there. He was booked until way after the holidays just like everyone else. No other doctors even called me back so this was going to be my only hope. How in the world was I gonna get Dad to the emergency room that night? Hmmm—what could I do that didn't involve jail time for me?

Since I was not familiar with this hospital, I decided I better make a "dry-run" so I wouldn't get lost if I were lucky enough to get Dad in the car. Oh my God—I was becoming just like my father. Nooo! I hated it when I did something just like him. It was like creepy-crawly, tales from the crypt, icky-yucky-scary. He would *insist* on taking dry-runs everywhere. Once they drove all the way to Sacramento to know where to *park* for a wedding that was coming up in a few weeks. Dad hated to be late and would get to appointments two hours early and just sit in the car waiting anxiously. "Obsessive-compulsive" is the label we have for it now—or, as I liked to call him: "Chemically Challenged."

I found the hospital and then Dr. Patetic's office turned out to be right across the street. I decided to try to get a moment with him to fill him in about Dad and my goal of getting the drugs. I sat in the stark waiting room for an hour being told he was, "too busy" to see me. I could see by her body language that the receptionist was sorry she'd taken pity on me now.

"No problem, I'll wait." Another hour and then another, as my back started killing me. I couldn't sit that long—I had to constantly lie down. Finally the doctor stuck his very bald head out of the door.

"Look, I don't even *know* you. I'm very busy and my girl here has *told* you that I'll see your father if you bring him to the emergency room tonight—I'm on call there." He slammed the door, not letting me say a word, even though my mouth was wide open. My eyes were already swollen shut from crying and this rudeness pushed me right over the edge. I left sniffling down the hall, having a hard time catching my breath. This is just too hard. Why couldn't I find a really nice Dr. Frasier Crane kinda guy. I'm due some karma—I always voted for his Emmys. Somehow I had the perfect theme song ready though: *"How can people be so heartless? How can people be so cruel?"*

♥ ♥ ♥

I Remember Mama Said There'd Be Months Like This

I phoned Red, Mom's physical therapist, but he had already left his office for appointments. He was scheduled to come by to see Mom and I hoped I could catch him and elicit his help. I sat at Helen's, their neighbor, looking out her front window for two hours watching for him. If I could catch Red and clue him in maybe he'd help me get Dad in the car so I could take him to the emergency room and see the psychiatrist—and *maybe* get the drugs.

Helen brought me tea and homemade sugar cookies and couldn't be kinder. She knew all about Dad's horrific episodes and had been so sweet to take me to the clubhouse for dinner one evening to get me out of the house. I sat with several elderly widows and asked them about their lives.

"Would any of you ladies like to get married again?" I asked.

"NOOO!" they all immediately resonated loud and clear.

"Wow, why?" The responses were all the same. They didn't like the *control* they had lived under. They all enjoyed their new-found freedom to do whatever they wanted—and they didn't want to have to "cater to another man." Allll-righty then.

I dipped my sugar cookie in chamomile tea and dissolved into warm memories of my own long-term relationship. HB had been very supportive when my mother had her heart attack and he could make me laugh even in my darkest moments. We'd be driving to the hospital with Dad, and every time we'd get to this certain on-ramp, Dad would warn him about the cars that merged and didn't have their own lane, so there were frequent accidents there. "Watch out for those goddamn bastards—they just *shoot* right out of there," he'd say with the appropriate sweeping hand gesture, *every* single time. It got so that we would start cracking up as soon as we got within a mile of the on-ramp and would just look at each other and die. Dad was oblivious and we'd wait and sure enough, "Watch out for those goddamn bastards—they just keep *shootin'* right out of there!" We howled over it for years. Then after we broke up I would have such a giggle passing that on-ramp even all by myself. One time I egged Dad on as we approached the on-ramp. "Hey, have they ever fixed this on-ramp yet, Dad?"

"Hell no! Those goddamn bastards just keep *shootin'* right out of there," he emphatically told me, hand gesture and all. I loved it.

Then when I had my spine surgery my ex came to check on me and to say hello to my parents. He just couldn't help himself.

"So, did they ever fix that on-ramp you hated so much, Jake?" I was turning red holding my breath, pressing my lips together trying so hard not to laugh, waiting for the standard reply with the sweeping hand gesture as we exchanged anticipating glances ready to just burst.

"What ramp?" Dad asked. HB reminded him of the location but Dad looked puzzled. "Oh, did they have some kind of a problem there sometime?" Huhhh? We looked at each other completely dumbfounded and the sad fact that he was losing his memory smacked us square in the face. We were suddenly *so* melancholy, and we realized that we missed those goddamn bastards—more than ever.

I snapped back to reality when I finally saw Red drive up in his black Volvo. I rushed out and flagged him down to clue him in to my plight. He was a dear to help me and we stepped into the lion's den together.

"Hi, Jake, how are you doing?" Red asked.

"Fine, what's *she* doing here?" (Who me? What'd *I* do?)

"Jake, we have a serious situation here. We're going to have to take Mariel away from you unless you agree to go see a doctor and get some help with the stress you're under. I'd hate to see that happen to you because I know how much you love your wife and want to be with her."

I *loved* this guy. Dad put up a fight, but then he finally put his head down and listened as Red continued to try to get him to see the light. Twenty minutes of enlightenment later and he finally consented.

"Okay, I'll go. You make the appointment, Jackie, and I'll go."

Red said, "Well, it just so happens there's a doctor that can see you tonight, and he's recommended by Dr. Kiljoy (yeah right) and he's waiting for you." Dad protested but Red was *very* persuasive.

I gleefully cha-cha-cha'd to the back bedroom to phone Dr. Peter Personality to make sure he was still on call. They paged him for me, I waited *forever*, and then he finally came on the line.

"Okay, I'm ready to bring my father in," I said all excited. "I just wanted to make sure you were still available."

"Is he in a rage now?"

"No, he's actually being very nice right now," I said, assuring him that there wouldn't be any trouble.

"Well, Ma'am, I can't come running to the emergency room to see a man who's acting normally. Bring him in the *next* time he goes into a rage," he said nastily.

"Whaaat? But I can't get him in the car when he's in a rage."

"I'm sorry, Ma'am," he said very coldly.

"Doctor, *please* help me. *Please* listen for just a minute. You don't understand what's been going on. I waited for hours to talk to you today because I wanted to fill you in on what I've been going through to get my father to agree to even *see* a psychiatrist. I'm at my wit's end. This is serious because my mother has been very ill and I ha…"

"Ma'am, I don't have time for this call—I'm very busy." CLICK.

I was in *shock*. You want rage? I'll give you rage! I was so *appalled* that I felt like going there and exploding into a rage myself. Then they'd have to call him in to treat me and then I'd give him a bigger piece of my mind, but they'd probably put me in a strait-jacket when I'd try to strangle him. OK, *another* candidate for a copy of the movie *The Doctor*. Maybe I can get a discount for a bulk order. It was all so unbelievable—the whole day was worse than waiting to see Geraldo open Al Capone's vault.

I took several "village of the damned" deep breaths and went back to find my parents sitting on the sofa, waiting with their jackets on, finally resigned, all dressed up and no place to go.

"Ummm, the doctor just got called away to an emergency so we won't be able to see him tonight after all," I said with all the acting ability I could muster up. "We'll make an appointment soon."

Dad was thrilled he didn't have to go. I walked Red out and thanked him profusely for his great acting job—he was so great with them.

"You've got to find a psychiatrist tomorrow and get your father there before he has a chance to change his mind. I've really convinced him how helpful it is going to be for him and that we will take Mariel away from him soon if he doesn't go. You don't want him to find out we really can't do that if she doesn't want to leave him. He'll have to hurt her or you before they'll have a legal way of doing it. An explosive temper isn't enough to put someone away unless he's violent."

What an amazing day of roller coaster emotions I had had. From the highest high of hope and happiness to the lowest low of disdain and desperation. I knew that I was dangerously close to ruining my own physical and emotional health and I had to nurture myself. I decided to practice a little smile therapy with Stuart Smalley in the mirror: "You're a good person and you've done very good things for your parents. Gee, you're aging *terribly*, hon—but hey, I *still* like you."

♥ ♥ ♥

chapter♥six

IN A OH-MY-GODDADIVIDA, HONEY

E very night that I had to drag myself back to Linda and Dick's, I'd walk in announcing that it was just me, their wayward "child" returning home—singing the appropriate theme song which we got very good at adding clever naughty verses to:

> Hello Muddah, Hello Faddah
> Here I am at—Camp Ohmygodda
> Dad is very—In-furi-ating
> And they say I'll have a life when he stops raging

By the Friday before Christmas week, however, I was all outta theme songs as I sat at Linda's all day on her phone leaving *pleading*, detailed voice-mail messages for every psychiatrist in the entire San Francisco Bay Area. Again, none were available until way after the holidays. Most were out of town and not taking new patients. I prayed for just *one* doctor to call back who would see us. Late in the day I was elated when I actually got a call back from a Dr. Richard Endure himself. "I got your message and I can squeeze you in on Monday for a half hour at two-thirty."

"Oh, doctor, thank you so much, but is there *any* way we can see you for an hour?"

"No, and I don't think it's necessary. It sounds to me like your father might respond well to a small dose of an anti-psychotic drug that can help calm aggressive behaviors. It sounds like he's starting to get some dementia. I'm sure I can diagnose him fairly quickly and get him started on the right drug."

YES! YES! YES! I was so beyond ecstatic I couldn't stand it. (*"Everybody dance now!"*) I was running from room to room, flash dancing on the furniture, screaming in triumph like Roberto Benigni

87

accepting his Academy Award. *Finally* someone was going to help me! Suddenly I found myself on stage on the sofa singing with the Fifth Dimension: *"Let the sunshine—let the sunshine in—the sun shine in!"*

I had the best weekend ever with my friends because I had Hyde hopes that things would be better soon. Hope is a wonderful thing—if only we could bottle it. Even my back was better as I showed Kathleen how her mother and I used to watch *Hullabaloo* and dance The Jerk as we tried to figure out the dirty lyrics to *"Louie Louie."* Then I pretended that I was *Queen For A Decade.* My sob story had won the votes of the judges. Okay, where's my crown, cape, and carpet cleaner? Dad called three times wanting me to come help him over the weekend, but Linda kept telling him that I just wasn't there.

That evening he called again, "It's an emergency!" he dramatically begged Linda. I nodded in resigned responsibility.

"Hi, Dad, what's up?"

"Calilly left and wrote down on her time-sheet here that she left yesterday and she really left four days ago. Now I'll have to pay her. I need you to come here right *now* and straighten this out!"

"Dad, it'll be all right, really. I'll straighten it out before I pay her. Camellia knows that *I* know when she was there and when she wasn't. If she's been gone for four days, we just won't pay her, okay? I promise I'll take care of it—don't worry." I wondered what his Hyden-agenda was.

Sure enough, on stormy Monday morning, Camellia phoned very upset, "He's at it *again,* Jackie. He's raging that I've been gone for four days. You know I haven't—here, talk to him."

"Daaad, remember police woman, Sgt. Pepper, came to your house Friday evening (unannounced and sent by Adult Protective Services) and talked to all of us for hours and Camellia was still there with us?" The officer had been so great with him that by the time she left he invited her back anytime she was "in the neighborhood" for a lonely hearts club dinner. She talked to all of us together and then in private. As she was leaving she said that she, "sees this kind of thing all the time," and that I was really going to have an "uphill battle." Oh really?

Good, he's irritable. Hopefully he'll act up in front of Dr. Endure so I can get the drugs for sure. I arrived and tried to show him on the calendar when Camellia left but he just *couldn't* get it. When it was time for the appointment he ranted and raved that he would *not* go. I didn't care if I had to knock him out first—he was going. I was calm as I got Mom in the car and we sat there staring at each other shaking our heads waiting for him. Finally he got in the car grumbling and swearing up and down that there wasn't any "goddamn thing" wrong with him. Uh-huh, and Jeffrey Dahmer just had a little eating disorder.

I could *not* believe the odds—Dr. Endure's office turned out to be right across the street from Dr. Kiljoy's! When I told them that I had finally found a psychiatrist, and that it was Dr. Endure, their response absolutely floored me, "Oh yeah, he's great and he's right across the street. We should have referred you to him." Ughhh!

What a nice guy Dr. Endure turned out to be. (Kind of a very short, kinda geeky, curly-haired, Mr. Peepers type, unmarried—but who cares.) He was so great with Dad, getting him to relax and talk. I was getting nervous—fifteen minutes already and we were still on where he grew up. And then the line I'd heard all my life: "When I found out they had shoes in California, I left home and headed west." Jekyll was in his most charming mode again.

"So, how can I help you, Jake?" Dr. Endure finally asked.

"Well, I don't know—you're the shrink, aren't ya?" He looked at Mom and me, "*They* think there's something wrong with me."

"I used to be a teacher," Mom chimed in. Say good-night, Gracie.

"Well, what do you think, Jake?"

"Look, I'm going to tell you something," he said as he pointed to Mom. "She's a goddamn virgin and so am I."

Huhhh? Did I just hear what I thought I heard? I must have dozed off. Wait a minute. I'm not gonna find out I'm really adopted right here and now, am I? *("Love Child!")* I knew it! I knew I was switched at birth—I knew I was a Grimaldi... or a Kennedy... or *somethin'!*

"Is that a problem for you, Jake?" Endure asked, as I couldn't *fathom* that my father was discussing his *sex* life. I was about to be nauseous.

"Nooo, I just want you to know—eleven years!" he emphasized. "For eleven *long* years I haven't touched that woman. I've taken care of my wife for eleven years without any sex and without any help and I sure as hell don't need *her* coming up here and telling me how to take care of my own goddamn wife!" Um, thanks for sharing, Dad.

I couldn't believe the revelation and struggled to keep my jaw from hitting the floor with a loud thud. I had never even heard him use the word "sex" my whole life. He'd blush at any slightly risqué joke and was always extremely private about such matters. Now, the first thing out of his mouth is that he is mad about having to take care of her (just *how* long has it been again, Dad?) and he wasn't even getting laid for it. *Oh my God.* Eighty-three years old and *sex* was still the most important thing he had to relate.

The closest my mother and I ever got to discussing the facts of life was when I was starting to date and she said (best to say this with a Roseanne Conner impression), "Your father thinks he *invented* sex and nobody is supposed to enjoy it but him!" Once, as a young adult, I surprised myself when I asked her if Dad was a good lover. She gave me a *very* affirmative, slow, knowing nod. I said, "How do you know, if he's the only one you ever had?" She raised her eyebrows, sucked in her cheeks, slowly blinked and nodded with confirmed affirmation that meant, oh yes, he was quite the stud. Wow, how lucky is that? The first one she got was great in bed. My averages were not so good.

So back to Dr. Endure's psychoanalyzing. He said, "I have quite a few patients, like yourself, who have been under a lot of stress with family illness. I'm testing a new medication on them and they all tell me they feel a lot better on it. Would you be at all interested to take some free samples home and try them for me and then let me know if you're feeling any better?"

With *"free"* being the operative word here, "Suuure, I'll give them a try for you, Doc. Is that it? That's all there is to seeing a shrink?"

"That's it—not so bad, huh? I'd really like to hear more about your job at the shipyards the next time you come in."

"Suuure, I can tell you all about it."

As we left I silently mouthed to Dr. Endure, "Thank you—I'm *so* grateful." I could have kissed his geeky little cheek. I finally had the anti-psychotic drug in my hot little hand (I checked to make sure it was not Viagra) and he was going to take it one way or another—even if I had to jam it down his throat with a plunger. Luckily he didn't argue and took one as soon as we got home. I was dancing on cloud *ten* as I squealed a few high-pitched verses of my favorite Aerosmith ditty: *"Dream On... Dream On... Dream On... Ahhhhhhh!"* I couldn't remember *ever* being this happy and realized happiness only comes at these levels when you've just been in the pit of Hyde Hell for comparison. I was like a High Lama experiencing Shangri-La, but unfortunately, my new horizon was about to be—lost. (*Or,* as Mom would say, "Don't count your chickens before they're hatched.)

After we got home, Mary Jo came for her occupational therapy session with Mom, encouraging her to try harder with her ADL's, her "Activities of Daily Living" like: eating, dressing, walking, toileting, bathing, etc. She taught us how important it was to be more patient and not jump in to help Mom so fast so that she wouldn't give up trying to do things for herself. At first it was heart-wrenching to watch Mom struggle so hard to do some simple little thing and my instinct was to help her, but Mary Jo taught us to pull back and wait, and sure enough, Mom would eventually complete the task.

Then, Mary Jo casually asked Dad how everything was going with Camellia and he said cheerfully, "Real good." Camellia and I rolled our eyes at each other and when she told Mary Jo the truth, Hyde was suddenly the devil at four o'clock as he went on a rampage. Gee, I guess that new drug needs a little more time to work. I just sat there, happy that Mary Jo was there to experience Horrific Hyde again. Every time he looked away from me, I silently imitated him, like a sassy sixth grader trying to hold onto my sinking sanity.

Suddenly I was under siege again as he called me the endearing "bitch-whore-slut" names and demanded that I "get the hell out!" Exhausted, I started to leave, and for the first time Mom reached out and yelled that she wanted to go with me. She started to get up so I went to help her, but Dad forcefully ripped her hand out of mine. Mom was helpless, caught in the crossfire again. "I have no say about anything," she cried. He yelled at her so loudly and intimidated her so badly right in front of us that she was defenseless and sat back down and wept. I tried to get her to stand up to him and come with me but he defiantly stood in front of her with his hands on his hips, waiting for a physical fight. I was afraid that King Solomon might cut her in half, so I left again—completely overwhelmed.

I was starting not to care anymore—everything seemed so futile and hopeless. It just didn't seem worth this much time and effort. Maybe you just can't unwind someone this twisted. I wanted to go home, find a job, a new boyfriend, and a life of my own. After all, she married him, she's put up with him for over half a century, she's allowed his bad behavior, she won't fight hard enough to leave him—that's her choice. So what was *I* supposed to do? Hey, I'd made a valiant attempt to change him, hadn't I? Ohhhh, inhale… and hold it… (why did she have to be such a wonderful mother?)… and slow… resigned to my fate… exhale… all the way out—again. If she'd been a mean mom (I couldn't remember one time—damn it), I'd leave her Hyde and dry.

The next morning Camellia called and reported that Dad had been yelling at Mom again last night. When she asked Mom what he was yelling about, Mom told her that he threatened her, saying that if she ever tried to leave him again—she'd be sorry.

Then later, his tune suddenly took a drastic turn. Camellia called me again, "Wow, Jackie, maybe that medicine is working already. He's been in your Mom's hospital bed crying all day."

"Don't give into it. It's just a manipulation for sympathy."

"That's what I thought too but it's really going on for a long time and he's really *sobbing* uncontrollably now."

"Really?" I felt my compassionate side returning—but then I fought it. "Good! Let him cry himself to death. I'm sick of being stomped on and called every name in the book and thrown out every other day. Maybe the medication is starting to work and he's really going to be sorry for all he's done, but I'm not rushing over there to be abused some more. I don't care—let *him* suffer for a while."

♥ ♥ ♥

I'm Dreamin' of a Wishful Christmas

'Twas the nightmare before Christmas Eve and I couldn't believe that the Fabulous Flannery's were still welcoming Jackie Kato—as their permanent house guest. I laid next to Linda on their waterbed, teary-eyed, sniffling, holding onto her like a life-raft as we watched *The Grinch Who Stole Christmas* with the kids—oh how utterly appropriate. Then they tried to make me laugh with more lyrics to our favorite Ohmygodda camp song, but I was all outta kumbayahs.

By late that night I had used up all the Kleenex and the toilet tissue was in danger as I thought about all the sadness around me. In addition to my parental nightmare, an avalanche of bad news had been piling on top of me. I'd just gotten the awful call that my favorite former secretary, Rhonda (who I'd always buzz and sing *"Help me, Rhonda"* to), was in a horrible disfiguring car accident. Then another dear friend developed a tumor on her neck and had to go through surgery and radiation and her beautiful long hair was falling out. Then Aunt Dora's Alzheimer's had gotten worse and she'd fallen and lost a bunch of her teeth. Next I heard that my brother's girlfriend of thirteen years, Carrie, had colon cancer and would have to undergo surgery soon. I don't think my mental health would have survived without Linda and her family holding on tight to my lifeline.

Christmas Day I was with the Flannerys gathered around the tree. What would I do without them? Linda's Mom, Norma (my second mom growing up), related the horrors of taking care of her difficult father. "Jackie, he'd *count* the Tylenol pills every day and then wait for one to be missing so he could go into a *rage* that the caregivers were stealing from him!" Oh dear, send in the Marines. It was quite comforting to hear that my father wasn't *that* unique, and that braver souls had actually gone before me and survived.

Later—one ringy-dingy, two ringy-dingy, "Jackie, are you here if it's your father?" Kathleen yelled up to me as I sniffled in my room. After a long resigned sigh, I reluctantly yelled, "Oh-kay." Well, it *was* Christmas. Sure enough, Scrooge was calling, begging me to come home, pleading for my forgiveness and saying how much he loved me.

"*No!* You suckered me in the last time with your fake apology."

"Please, honey, come for Mother. It's Christmas and she misses you. You're all we have, sweetheart." I was so tempted to say, "Well, if you weren't such an *asshole* all your life you'd have lots of people around now, including your own son." But I didn't—why push it when I was finally getting an apology.

"I *beg* of you (one of his favorite phrases), I'll do anything you say. Just come be with us, honey." I just kept repeating "NO" *over* and *over* and he kept pleading and apologizing. It went on for a solid half an hour. "I promise you, I'll never yell again. Please, *please* come and see us. (Said the itsy bitsy spider to the fly.) Okay, just see Mother then. I'll go in the bedroom and close the door. You don't even have to look at me if you don't want to, but, um... maybe you could look at this bill that came—I can't figure it out."

"No! That's all you want. You just want me to come take care of more of your paperwork and I'm not doing it this time. You sit and think hard about all you've done and then write down what you're willing to do and sign it, and I *might* come over tomorrow if I feel like it." I drew upon an old family tradition we had, hoping it might make a difference.

Time warp: When I was a kid he'd have me write a "contract" for my report cards. Five dollars for every *A*. Four dollars for every *B*, etc. I negotiated a healthy bonus plan in third grade for all *A's*. He'd make a *very* big deal out of signing it and ceremoniously have Mom witness it. Then when I'd get my report card he'd make another very big deal about how smart I was and carry on and on that it was really starting to break him, but he *had* signed the contract so he *had* to honor it. I worked hard for those grades, not only for the money, but for the unforgettable praise of my devoted parents.

Kathleen came up to my room. "Oh, Kathleen, this is so hard. I hope you don't have to take care of us when we're old."

"Are you kidding—I'm calling Dr. Kevorkian for you guys!"

"*Very* good idea, honey. Don't put up with this lunacy."

"Oh, don't worry Aunt Jack—you know I'll always take care of you," she said as she hugged me and I instantly turned into milky marshmallow mush. Okay, I'll will you my complete collection of Avalon and Fillmore posters.

The next day Camellia reported that Dad would sign The Treaty of Versailles, *anything*—just please come home right *now*. I prayed that the medication was really starting to work and he was finally ready to abdicate his lofty throne. My disposition was colder than the Klondike as I drew up a long list of demands and told him to *sign* on the dotted line. Camellia and Mom witnessed it and I started feeling like Jimmy Carter at the Middle East Peace Accords. He shook Camellia's hand, I put my hand on top, and it was, *"signed sealed delivered—I'm done."*

The surrender at Appomattox had finally happened and he was being an *angel*. Could it be true? Was this drug working miracles on him? He said, "We're so lucky to have Cordilly and Jackie here to help us, aren't we Mommy?" My mouth dropped open and the perfect theme song came out: *"Devil or Angel?—I can't make up my mind."* Thank you, Bobby Vee.

He'd take Mom on their daily walks from the family room to the living room and encourage her to do "just one more, Mommy." They'd get such a kick out of my best Trevor Denman impression from the race track, as I talked into my cupped hands like a megaphone.

"Aaand they're off. It's Mariel and Jake, heading down the stretch. (Please make horse hooves sound effects here.) It's Mariel and Jake, neck and neck all the way. (More 'heeeee' horse effects.) And they're rounding the first turn and it's Mariel and Jake out in the lead. (Galloping sounds needed.) Now they're coming down the home stretch, ohhh, and Mariel takes the lead! It's going to be close, it's going to be a photo finish. Noooo, it's Mariel by a nose!" (CHEERS.)

♥ ♥ ♥

More Nonsense and Responsibilities

I was beyond astounded—just one tiny little milligram of the anti-psychotic drug seemed to produce such good behavior in my father. (Note to self: Buy stock in pharmaceutical company.) Used in combination with the anti-depressant, he was much less compulsive. *Or,* was he just *trying* to behave now? *Whatever*—I was just thrilled out of my mind and it was wonderful having him be so appreciative of everything we did for him and he was so loving to Mom again.

"Wow, you look so beautiful today, Mommy," he said as he kissed her, complimenting her blue polka dot outfit.

Camellia fixed her up so pretty everyday, doing her hair and make up real special and dressing her in her nicest clothes. I found out that the neighbors were just about to pitch in and buy her some new clothes because they only saw her in the same old tattered ones all the time before I had gotten there. Apparently, Dad had gotten so tired they slept in their same clothes—day after day. I'm sure they had started to look and smell a bit like the down-and-out-of-oil Beverly Hillbillies. *("Come listen to a story 'bout a man named, Jake.")* Sorry.

Mom loved flowers, especially gardenias with their wonderful aroma. I bought two beautiful blooming plants for her porch and the delectable scent would come in through the screen door. Not to be outdone, one morning Dad left to go to the store before Mom woke up and brought back two huge, gorgeous, blooming orchid plants.

"I want to surprise Mother," he said all excited as he instructed "Catilda" to take them out to the porch.

"But, Dad, don't you want to have them in here by her bed for a little while so she can enjoy them?"

"Nooo, I'm going to replace the old ones and she'll just think they finally bloomed."

"Oh-kay. Ummm, you don't think she'll notice the different pretty pots and the big red bow?"

"Naaaahhhh."

Camellia cleaned Mom up and then brought her out to the hospital bed to wait while she made us breakfast. Dad could hardly contain himself as we exchanged anticipation glances, anxiously waiting for Mom to notice her brilliant blooming violet orchids. Finally she did.

"Oh look," she exclaimed, "my orchids bloomed!"

Dad was right—she never noticed that they were different plants. He was so pleased that he had given her such joy and he grinned and giggled every time she said how much she loved them.

OK, truth or dare? Was all this good behavior attributable to the drugs or was he just finally ready to accept help and behave himself? *Or*, maybe the drugs made him feel better so he *wanted* to behave better. It was clear that *something* was working and I rushed around frantically trying to get everything done while he was in such a receptive mood—cautiously waiting for my Karma to crumble.

Their Durable Power of Attorneys for health and financial matters needed to be renewed as they were about to expire. Then I took them to the Social Security office to sign releases, allowing me to handle those matters for them. I increased their liability insurance to cover caregivers in the home, and I called my tax guy to find out how to set up paying employee taxes for having an caregiver in the home. Then I took pictures of everything, so I could monitor if things began to disappear, or if God forbid, there were a fire.

With the doctor's signature I got them approved to have the trash men come all the way into the carport and take the trash out to the truck. This is another service done for the disabled so they don't miss the trash pick up.

Dad was starting to lose everything, so for his keys I got a pet-tag engraved with the word "REWARD" and my phone number on the back. I sorted out a huge pile of keys and had duplicates made of those that worked and then gave them to the neighbors.

The two cataract surgeries were such a success Mom was able to read the newspaper I started having delivered. Then she would sit in her hospital bed with her little slanted reading table and sadly report Frank Sinatra's health to us day after day. When he passed away she wouldn't remember that part and tell us again, like it was the very first time she heard it—and then she'd *burst* into tears at the end.

Every time she'd take a loud inhale and exclaim, "Ohhh!" my heart would stop, wondering what horrible thing had just happened. Then she'd add with delight, "my orchids are blooming!" as adrenaline trickled down my throat at least twenty times a day.

As she got physically better she realized the mess she was in, unable to do much, and she began saying that she wanted to kill herself. "Please take me to the Golden Gate so I can jump off, honey." I tried so hard to cheer her up and make her laugh, but not until I got some Prozac into her did she become much clearer and more cheerful. Thank God, and the drug companies, for modern medicine.

Dad wouldn't be able to drive much longer and I dreaded the ultimate confrontation of taking away something he loved to do so much. I had his eyes checked by two doctors, as he kept hoping for a different diagnosis other than "Macular Degeneration" an untreatable disease. He had good peripheral vision but the blind spot in the middle would gradually get larger. They told me he was right on the edge of being able to drive and his eyes were getting worse fast.

I heard a statistic on *Oprah* that seniors have a "four times higher accident rate." Wow. I realized that the laws need to be changed to check senior citizens' eyes every year because their conditions can change so fast and they hate to give up the freedom of driving. I just hoped he wouldn't run over anyone, not see them, keep going, get sued and lose their house before I could tackle it. I added Camellia to the car insurance so she could drive their car to the Piggly Wiggly as needed. Then I got them approved for "Transportation for Seniors," another service for the elderly and disabled. In case of an emergency they could be taken where they needed to go locally for a small fee.

One day as I was following them in my rental car, I watched in horror as my father turned right in front of a car that had to slam on their brakes to avoid a head-on collision, and a poor pedestrian nearly had a heart attack as he barely got out of the way. (Where's Ponch and Jon when you need them?) I increased the car insurance to the max and started *begging* him to give up driving. He didn't believe me when I told him that he had just been on the Hydeway to Heaven.

In addition, his memory was going. It was like a tale of two cities when I took them to the neighborhood they had lived in for over thirty-seven years—where we'd had the best of times and the worst of times. As we drove through our town, past old familiar shops on main streets, it was like he was completely lost in some other space, giving me incorrect directions. We were in the exact same place, but somewhere else in time, and I had to dig deep to find the strength to hold back my sorrowful tears.

The next project was his ears. One day they were having free hearing checks at their clubhouse. "He has so much wax in his ears, I can't test him properly," the technician said. Down to Dr. Kiljoy's for a professional ear cleaning and then I took him to a hearing-aid clinic to be tested. "I'm sorry, there's so much wax in here, I can't possibly test him." Aye yi yi.

"Whaaat?" Dad kept saying, trying to be funny. Back to Dr. Kiljoy's and as you can imagine, I was just a little bit perturbed that we had to go through all this again.

"My goodness, we cleaned them really well and they're already full again," the nurse said as I watched her take more wax out."

"OK, so you're *sure* they're clean now?"

"Yes," she assured me. Back to the test. You guessed it—full of wax. Huhhh? Then they gave him a prescription for some "Drano-like" medicine to dissolve more wax. I couldn't believe that *more* wax kept coming out. Geeeese, maybe all this wax has been seeping upward and clogging his brain. He started to be able to hear fairly well after the reaming and cleaning. Who woulda thunk it? Finally they tested his ears and he definitely needed a hearing aid, particularly in his right ear. I bought him the best, paying over one thousand dollars for it—not covered by Medicare. It hurt him... I took him back to have it refitted... he didn't like it... he lost it leaning over the garbage disposal... I dug it out... he *refused* to wear it... I took it back... it's non-returnable. Say whaaat? OK, here we go... inhale... and hold it... (what'd ja saaaaay?)... and now drain every ounce of oxygen from your being... and blast it all the way out—again.

I kept Q-tips by his chair and reminded him to clean his ears daily and it was absolutely amazing that there was always more wax. Camellia and I finally decided that we actually preferred that he couldn't hear us plotting how to handle him under our breath because then—he could hear no evil.

♥♥♥

If This Table Could Talk

When I was a kid, dinner was the only time we all sat down together at the same metal kitchen table that Dad continued to pound on. (They sure don't build things like they used to.) Mom would take her bath and get beautified for Dad, who was always home from work by six o'clock. "Honey, I'm home!" He'd walk in expecting a little "Hail to the Chief" wanting our full attention. ("Sir, yes Sir!") She always put on a pretty dress (usually red, often velvet), nylons and high heels, fixed her beautiful thick dark hair, put just a dash of rouge on her peaches and cream ivory skin, and put bright red lipstick on her full lips. She was a knock-out by any standards and I could see that my father *really* loved her, but he was very possessive. He would make them each a "high-ball" as soon as he came home. They'd sit and talk a bit and then June Cleaver, pearls and all, would serve us a lovely dinner. Some topic of conversation would come up and you could always *feel* a sudden silence when he was expected to respond. Oh-oh, look up, hold your breath... oh thank goodness, he's just swallowing... *relieved* exhale as the adrenaline would drain down out of your throat again.

Then there were the times when you'd be sitting there, minding your own business, intent on winding your spaghetti, and there wouldn't even be a hint of it coming and BOOM—Hyde's fist pounded the table and all the plates went flying and your meat balls were nowhere in sight. Whaaa, what happened now? Instant adrenaline rush. Look up, who is *that?* Could it be... *Satan?* He didn't even look like my daddy. It was like *Invasion of the Body Snatchers.* Then disbelief, confusion and fear took over. Okay, who left the window open? Something flew in from Transylvania. Once Horrific Hyde got started, it was just like a tornado and the turbulence was impossible to stop. It was usually directed at my brother over something like eating the last drum stick—really, I kid you not.

"Oh for heaven sakes," Mom would say as she'd take a deep puff off her cigarette and pollute the already very thin air. She'd just sit there quietly staring at him, legs and arms crossed, shaking her head, "tisk-tisk-tisk"-ing, sighing in disgust, waiting to see if Old Faithful was going to stop spewing or not. I had learned from her that it was best to just give him the "Alice Kramden look of disgust," and not say a word. Arguing with The Great Santini just made it worse because there was no way to win a verbal argument with him. Couldn't live with him—couldn't kill him.

And then sometimes his impromptu performance hit like a sudden earthquake because it was: "Lights... camera... *action!*" and we'd be stuck shaking in front-row center seats, forced to watch his world premier one-man act as the facade of our "happy" family collapsed. He'd preface every other word with "goddamn" such and such, and punctuate with "Jesus Christ" that. Donna Reed would sit there and *demand* that he "stop that swearing," like *that* was the most important thing for us not to hear. I abhorred these episodes with my two dads. I'd be catatonic, afraid to move, except for my eyeballs that shot back and forth between my parents and my brother.

He never hit us, but I can remember him being so furious and standing over my mother as she'd sit there looking up at him with that ravishing face, repeating emphatically, "You better not ever hit me." He'd tremble and his whole body would shake with frustration. He'd work himself into such a frenzy, stomp his feet, look at her, and then pound his fist on the table some more, demanding control over something—telling us that father knew best about whatever it was. Finally she'd get up and just ignore him and start to do the dishes as he continued spewing. Why we were never sent to our rooms to avoid seeing all this behind the scenes reality is a mystery to me.

And then there was the time you could just *feel* it coming because it would have taken a Black and Decker buzz saw to cut the atmosphere at the dinner table. Suddenly the plate of meat loaf that had been sitting in front of Major Dad was flying across the room, shattering on the white wall and ooozing down. I jumped in fear and amazement, but I remember my mother didn't *flinch* an eyelash. She "tisked," sighed, put her cigarette out in her mashed potatoes, got up and disappeared into the bathroom for the rest of the evening.

The strange thing about these startling incidents was—they were *never* discussed later. Usually by the next day it was like the horror had never happened because everyone was back to acting completely normal. Ohhh-kay. Somehow I knew it was big time verboten to ever share these experiences with *anyone*, even Linda. No, just quickly sweep everything under that filthy carpet again, pretend there wasn't an elephant sitting under there, and push it further and further into the subconscious so at times I questioned if some of these episodes were real or not. Did I dream that one—or did it *really* happen?

But, I have to say that *most* of the time, thank goodness, it was more like Nick and Nora Charles from *The Thin Man* (or David and Maddie from *Moonlighting*) the way they'd tease and play off each other. He'd be silly and she'd laugh and do witty digs back at him and it was all in good fun. He'd reach over and eat some of my vegetables when Mom would get up to go to the stove, and it was our little secret. Mom would say, "Oh, you ate all your vegetables!" Dad and I would look at each other and then she'd say, "Okay you two, what are you up to now?" We'd look dumb and say, "Nothin'!"

After Mom had the kitchen spotless she'd come watch television with us and fall asleep on the couch. Dad and I had all our programs that we enjoyed together every night like clockwork. We loved watching *Red Skelton, Phyllis Diller* and *Lucy* and we thought *Alfred Hitchcock* ("Good eeevening") was sooo mysterious. Then we'd sneak back in the kitchen and make our ice cream creations (we didn't know about low-fat anything yet), and giggle about getting away with it while Mom slept. She'd open one eye, look at us and say, "What are you two up to now?" We'd be so serious and yell, "Nothin'!"

As long as we didn't cross him and just let Sarge have total control, his spirits were good, especially if we were having a party. We had our own *America's Funniest Super 8 Home Movies* of so many fun get-togethers where Dad would shine, telling stories, making us all laugh so much. He was always happiest with lots of people around who would give him attention, "Hail Caesar!" so most weekends we had a full house of friends and relatives. Mom would cook and bake up a storm, and he'd barbecue everything—*well* done.

It was a safe bet that he would not act up in front of guests, so you could let your guard down a little and relax, at least until the heavy drinking started. That could be the catalyst that I had seen so often turn the nice times into nightmares. Usually though, if he got mad when there were lots of people around he'd just get quiet and then put that person on his hit-list, and they'd be dropped from the party circuit sometimes for years and years for one innocent comment. My mother would not be allowed to have anything to do with them either, and so, one by one—he eliminated just about everyone.

My brother's mission was to get out of the house as soon as possible. Jeremy was extremely handsome (kind of an Elvis Presley type) and he and Marina (kind of a pretty, Annette Funicello type) fell madly in love in high school and soon got married. I was still very young and grew up virtually an only child after that, but I had learned very well not to rock the boat and bring on Dad's wrath as I had seen Jeremy do so often.

I think my father got some license for his bad behavior from some of the popular television shows of the time. I remember watching the *Honeymooners* and absolutely hating it. There was Jackie Gleason, another dominating man, raging and threatening to hit Alice and "send her to the moon." How funny was that supposed to be? Not a bit to me. I felt the same way about Yul Brenner in *The King and I*, and a raging Danny Thomas in *Make Room For Daddy*. I couldn't stand to watch any yelling, screaming, dominating character who used raging intimidation to control everyone. Give me *The Rifleman* or *Family Affair,* with a strong man who never had to scream or yell at anyone. I remember wishing my father would treat us the way Brian Keith treated his family on that show.

Mom and I felt the same way about Norman Lear's famous series, *All In The Family.* Mom laughed, "I can't believe it—they made a television show about us!"—and it was eerily true. There was my father, just like Archie, bigoted and throwing his ample weight around. There was Mom, a beautiful version of Edith, always trying to calm him down and walking on egg-shells trying to please him. And then it was really weird because my then boyfriend looked and acted exactly, I mean *exactly*, like Meathead. And, I really hate to admit this, but I had quite a few similarities to little Gloria, stirring things up. I'd watch it and just *cringe*. Was this supposed to be funny, little goirl?

Years later... I was at a lovely party at Norman Lear's home and I was so relieved that I didn't find myself in a conversation with him about his award-wining show, because I would have had to give quite an award-winning performance. Now *that* might have been entertainment. "Oh, I just loved your *All In The Family* program. How in the world did you come up with all those wild ideas and crazy off-beat characters? It was just *so* innovative, original and creative." (Other than the fact that I had already lived every single episode twice and could have written it in my sleep.) Hey, whatever happened to *Ozzie and Harriet?*

Now—*"Those were the days."*

♥ ♥ ♥

chapter seven

NURTURE *and* NATURE MESSED HIM UP

M y father's psychological problems must have begun in his early childhood. It really was an amazing story of survival. His parents were very wealthy French/Germans who had migrated to Russia. The Bolsheviks were just starting to organize and go after the rich and the politically-minded family was threatened. They already had a few young children when one night they had to escape with only a few belongings and barely made it to a small ship that they hoped would bring them to America.

Somewhere in the middle of the Atlantic Ocean, my grandmother gave birth to another baby. After a month on the stormy high seas they arrived at Ellis Island, but the ship was quarantined for another month because their eldest child had scarlet fever. They were turned away and made to set sail for *another* month to Canada. They had little kids, a new baby, a seriously ill child, very little money and were probably quite sea sick. Finally they came ashore and headed west by train. They had to become farmers, homestead the land and start all over. Wow, what am *I* complaining about? Like Cher in *Moonstruck* (SLAP), "Snap out of it!"

My grandmother proceeded to have a total of eighteen children. Apparently they took that "be fruitful and multiply" part a bit too far. Hey, it was cold, there wasn't much to do in the winter, and they needed more kids to tend the farm. Besides, birth control or refusing your husband wasn't an *option* for women then. My grandfather had been highly educated, speaking several languages, but with all the turmoil and loss of his wealth, was well on his way to alcoholism. He had his own repulsive "black rages" when he'd beat his wife and the children. My aunt told me that she and my father would cower together under the kitchen table while he beat their mother senseless around the room. (Light bulb moment: Maybe *that's* why Dad always pounded his fist so hard on the kitchen table!)

Then at only forty-seven years old, my grandmother suddenly died from a ruptured gallbladder on the operating table of a drunk doctor. (Where's Dr. Zhivago when you need him?) Rumors were that her alcoholic husband had beaten her just before she was rushed there. After that my grandfather's alcoholism was so bad Child Welfare took all the children away from him.

My father always told the sad story about being with many of his siblings in a car in front of a church. People were looking in, pointing, discussing which ones they might take. "It was like being a caged animal. I'll never forget the humiliation of that—never." Since none were babies, none were selected, so they were all placed in orphanages. They were outcasts, unwanted, unloved and abandoned. My father had lost his mother, his father, and his siblings were all scattered about. Suddenly he found himself enrolled in the school of even harder knocks—he was barely ten years old.

He was such a renegade that they put him in reform school, but he'd always escape and try to find his siblings. Once he ran away and kidnapped his little sister to go with him. They were half-way across a train trestle, fifty-feet up over a rushing river when the speeding train came. They ran but Dad could see they weren't going to make it. He jumped down onto a small landing, but it wasn't big enough for both of them. "Jump, Rosemary, jump—I'll catch you!" he pleaded, but she froze, starring up at the enormous puffing dragon coming at her. With seconds to spare, she screamed as she jumped and he barely caught her by her tattered coat—just as the roaring train sped by.

They had to steal food at night from the neighbors' farm fields to get enough to eat, and he was given soiled old clothes and worn-out shoes. When I was little I recall someone giving me some of their very nice, but outgrown clothes. He said, "Give them back. You'll *never* have to wear someone else's hand-me-downs, I promise you that—and you'll always have *new* shoes and a full stomach too."

All that abandonment as a child must have created a tremendous amount of fear within him. Having to survive alone by his wits and determination must have been brutal. I believe that he and his siblings inherited an obsessive-compulsive brain-chemical imbalance, as most of them matured into varying levels of rageaholic alcoholics. He had stopped drinking, cold-turkey, when he had his heart attack twenty years before, but by then the damage had already been done to his brain cells. Then he smoked so heavily for fifty years and I'm sure that didn't help either.

My father rode many a rail, jumped box cars, drove trucks and operated fork lifts. He was street-smart, always found work, and even had his own older brothers working under his authority at manual labor jobs. Dad would say, "I only had to work with my hands for a little while, then I learned to work with my head." He loved his 32 year career at the shipyards and rose high in the ranks because he was always using his head to come up with a better way of doing things. The funny thing was—he got so terribly sea-sick, he could never actually go out on a ship of any kind. (It must be an inherited trait because I also turn green just watching re-runs of *The Love Boat*.) After Mom had her heart attack, "the yard" would still call him to come look at a ship, but he'd always say, "No, thanks for thinking of me, but I can't leave my wife with anyone—she needs me now."

Being only five feet, four inches tall, he developed a huge chip on his Napoleonic shoulder. Shorty learned that he could get his way if he screamed and yelled loud and long enough because people would eventually back down. He used domination and intimidation to make up for his lack of stature and education, and it just became normal behavior for him. Rage was his survival tool, his armor, his defense mechanism, and it worked for him—*again* and *again*. The payoff was the "high" of power as he manipulated everything so he would be able to hold onto *control*. His internal programming was such an endless bad habit repetitive loop, such an ingrained pattern of how to cope with anger, that he didn't even realize the depth of the devastation he caused. He was addicted and trapped in his own bad behavior of a lifetime. Now we added very old age, a dash of dementia, and probably an ounce of Alzheimer's, and that's the volatile combination that I was trying to change at the ripe old age of eighty-three. No, I think I'd rather be responsible for moving Mount Rushmore to Vegas.

Could he possibly be a split-personality that had developed Hyde as a youngster to handle all the horrors he must have endured? According to the research I did, being subjected to physical and emotional abuse as a child is the main trigger for creating an alternate personality. His pain was probably buried so deep in him, so pushed down, that whenever he felt he was being wronged or threatened, it pushed that panic button and it triggered him back into that frightened ten-year-old. Hyde would *have* to surface and take control for *survival*. The research said that a true multiple-personality is an extremely rare condition and predominantly female, but I still preferred that scenario to explain my father's behaviors. I chose to believe that it was his terrible childhood and his inherited brain chemistry that had molded him with two distinct personalities. It was just so much more palatable and it made it easier to be compassionate and easier to forgive him.

♥ ♥ ♥

The Way They Were

My parents were harpooned with Cupid's arrow in 1940. It was love at first sight as she walked down the street in a small town in Montana and he saw her in her navy blue, polka-dot dress. Wow, an absolute 10! It was a whirlwind courtship of only a few weeks and then he left to find work out in the wild wild West of California. One day he showed up back at her door and asked her to marry him—and that was it. At the tender age of twenty-one, she was married and living in San Francisco, and then it wasn't that long before she was pregnant with my brother. He had picked a submissive wife whom he could manipulate so he would not be abandoned again—and she had picked a man who would take care of her, as her father never had, but whose temper tantrums sadly turned out to be just like her own father's. She was the sweetest, most beautiful woman he had ever met and they were blissfully happy for quite a while. She really loved him and I am *very* certain that she never looked at another man her entire life.

One time when I was trying to sort out my own love-life problems, I asked her, "Mom, how long were you *deeply* in-love with Dad, when every time you saw him, he just made your heart skip a beat?"

She smiled fondly recalling it, "Oh, he was just *so* handsome and charming—for about twenty years at that intense level I guess." My jaw dropped wide open. Then she added, "And then it only skipped a beat—every *other* time after that."

Mom always said that people would stop her on the street and say what a beautiful baby Jeremy was. Unfortunately, all that attention on

106

Jeremy created a constant source of jealousy for Dad. Mom's time was divided and he was in total competition with his own child. She always said that he was a bottomless pit for her affection and that she could never fill the void left by his dreadful childhood.

When the rages came, even though for some reason they were *never* directed at me, I was terrified at seeing his demeanor change so quickly. It seemed like the classic: "Better to be feared than loved," if it meant holding onto *control*, which was his tried and true method for security and survival. Sadly, since he always feared abandonment, he had never really learned how to trust or love.

Unfortunately, I learned that the line between love and hate was very thin indeed. The sad result was that my young free spirit lived in Hyde anxiety much of the time. I had a lifetime of balancing on that thin tightrope without a safety net, and like a cautious lion tamer I lived in constant fear that he would suddenly turn against me and bite my head off—like he had everyone else. I loved him… smack… I hated him… smack… I loved him… smack… I hated him—SMACK!

Unlike Dad, Mom never drank more than her one high-ball before dinner. I only saw her drunk once when I came home to visit them during college. They had obviously been fighting, Dad had just stormed out, so I asked Mom what had happened. I was so astonished that she was really looped with a very thick tongue, when she started in on me for the first time in my life.

"You're the *only* one he's never turned on, do you know that? Everyone else has borne the brunt of his rages except *you*. No, he's always had a blind spot when it came to *you*. You've always been his favorite. He loves *you* more than anyone. Anything *you* want, you can get out of him. *You're* just the apple of his eye—aren't *you!*"

I was so dazed I couldn't move. Never in my entire life had I heard my mother express any jealously toward me. The worst I ever got was when I'd be testing her patience a bit and then it was always, "Jacqueline!" and I'd hop-to real fast. So to hear these awful feelings come out of the deep recesses of her heart was completely devastating for me. I let her go on and on, not saying a word, just listening and trying to understand the pain that I had no idea even existed. Finally she went to sleep and I went to bed and cried for the loss of the complete love I'd always thought I had from my mother.

Early the next morning she came and sat on my bed, beside herself apologizing. "Oh, honey, I can't drink. You know I never drink. I'm afraid I was awfully nasty to you last night, wasn't I? Please try to forgive me. I don't know exactly what I was saying, but I don't think any of it was good. I'd never want to hurt you—can you ever forgive me, sweetheart?"

"Of course, don't worry about it, Mom. I know you love me and didn't mean anything. Alcohol makes people say silly things. Dad's been acting up again and I'm sure that's been upsetting you. I'm fine, don't worry—really," I said as I kissed her.

Poor Mom, she loved Dad so much, on some very deep level it made her jealous that I was never the recipient of his anger but she was. What an interesting dysfunctional family dynamic for our little glass menagerie. I wondered if now that he had turned on me, if there was some twisted satisfaction for her, but I'm sure that if there was, it was buried so deep—even Jim Beam couldn't get it out of her.

Since I was not the target, I always tried to create a diversion so my father's tirades would be drawn away from my mother or brother. Since I had taken "acting lessons" from my father for years, I was quite an accomplished performer myself. One time as we all sat in the kitchen, I could tell that something was rotten in Denmark—and putrefied there. Suddenly Mom cried, "But I still love you."

Dad yelled back, "Well I *hate* you!"

I had never heard him say anything like that to her *ever*. I only saw my mother cry a few times in her life, but this time she cried so hard my heart broke for her. I went into action and created my best diversion to date. I feigned fainting (`a-la Sarah Bernhardt plus) off the top of the step-stool, collapsing ever so dramatically to the floor.

"Now look what you've done," I remember her saying as they both rushed to my lifeless body sprawled out on the kitchen floor. It worked! Wow, was I brilliant or what? By the next day they made up and came into my room to assure me everything was going to be okay. Always the problem-solver, I presented them with a long list of things we could do together—as a family.

Things were calmer for quite a while after that. Of course, I couldn't use this fainting tactic too often so I had to constantly come up with new diversions to calm him down. One had to plan ahead and expect the unexpected. People always tell me that I am the most organized, prepared person on the planet. Hey—seems totally normal to me.

♥ ♥ ♥

Grumpy Old Men Was a Documentary

One of the worst scenes I can remember was on Thanksgiving when I was a teenager. Dad's older brother, Tommy, and his wife and three kids had just arrived after a very long out-of-town drive for the holiday. We were all dressed up and excitedly seated at Mother's pride and joy dining-room table waiting for the wonderful feast. Just as Mom set the steaming turkey down in front of Dad to start carving, all of a sudden he and Tommy started a heated argument. It was clear that Tommy had caught him in a silly little lie and wouldn't let him get away with it. It was a classic sibling power play and Dad was caught in the headlights in front of all of us.

"Are you calling me a liar?" Dad exploded.

"I'm just saying that you couldn't have done that because..."

"I'm no liar—*you're* the goddamn liar," he spewed and pounded, luckily dropping the knife and fork. Then Tommy spewed and pounded right back at him and their big disgusting noses were an inch apart as they tried to out-yell one another. We all just sat there watching in total amazement, wondering what in the world was going to happen. It was reaching a crescendo as the bulging veins in their foreheads pulsated back and forth at each other. All we wanted was a nice peaceful Thanksgiving dinner, not sour-Krauts—but nooooooo.

It ended up almost coming to blows, but rather than back down and just admit his little white-lie, my father ended up dramatically throwing them all out of the house, right then and there without so much as a single bite. Yep, it was Hyde's way or the highway. I was so *shocked*—his own brother's family, on *Thanksgiving!* Good grief. Mom was so disgusted with him as she apologized profusely to the relatives, "tisk-ing" up a storm and shaking her head in complete disbelief. They left and she silently wrapped up all the untouched food and put everything away in the refrigerator and we all went to bed without a bite. She didn't speak to him for weeks after that and would hardly look at him.

Dad never spoke to his brother again, but he'll proudly tell you that he's never held a grudge.

♥ ♥ ♥

It Shoulda, Coulda, Woulda Been a Wonderful Life

Thank goodness that *most* of the time, life with father was actually a lot of fun. I loved horses (being a regular National Velvet wannabe type) and my parents would take us riding, but all you could rent were these old, half-dead plugs. My Friend Flicka and Trigger were nowhere to be found. Dad would make us laugh so hard horsing-around, doing all the "Hi-O Silver" routines. He'd go, "I think I'm gonna have to carry this black beauty back to the barn myself, Keemosabe." Then he'd walk in his best John Wayne strut. "Well, Miss Kitty, I reckon' I'll be moseying over to the barn there now." Mom would laugh, "Okay, Marshal Dillon—we'll meet you there." We *loved* it.

Another fond memory: We were at a fancy restaurant that had these huge peppermills that my Aunt Dora admired.

"You'd like to have one of those?" Dad asked her.

"Oh yes, I wonder where you'd get one that big?" As we walked out, all of a sudden Dad was limping terribly.

"Are you all right, sir?" the maitre d' asked very concerned.

"Oh yeah, just an old war injury." We got outside and he pulled the three-foot long peppermill out from up his pant leg! My mother "tisk"-ingly shook her head in resigned disapproval, but everyone else howled and encouraged him. I was so happy when he was making us all laugh. If my father was laughing, he wasn't raging—and that meant things might be good again for a while.

My father had such iron will determination that if he'd had an education who knows what he might have become. I never saw him read a book or even a newspaper my whole life. It would surprise me when he'd call from work and ask me how to spell the simplest words. Mom would lay out all the voting information and read him every word before they cast their democratic votes. When they retired I got them a subscription to the *National Enquirer* and Mom loved it because he'd take it in the bathroom and be in there for hours and get out of her hair. Then he'd call and emphatically tell *me* the true Hollywood story about all the goings on in Tinsel Town, and who was dating and cheating on who. It cracked me up. His inquiring mind had finally learned how to read—by reading the rags.

One time just before I started college I asked him, "What would you like to have been if you'd had an education, Dad?"

"I think an inventor. I would have loved to have been an inventor."

"But you *are* an inventor. Look at all the neat things you've built over the years. You built that brick block-house in the garage and smoked your own home-made sausage in it every year. And what about the big train-set that you built for Jeremy, that folded up and down with counter-weights against the wall of the basement? Then you built Jeremy that beautiful knotty-pine bedroom and you remodeled Mom's kitchen and then practically the whole house. You're really a 'Jake of all trades' because you know how to do so many things."

"Yeah, but I would have done a lot more if I'd had some training." Then he looked at me and said, "That's why *you* are getting a good education—*I* never had the chance at one."

Mom whispered, "Yeah, get your education out of him while he wants to buy it for you. Don't get married and be under the control of a *man*."

I started my first year of college and suddenly I was at the heart of a tumultuous college campus riot. The Black Panthers were starting to demonstrate daily.

"Well, what the hell do the Pink Panthers want?" Dad asked.

"Daaad, not the *Pink* Panthers, the *Black* Panthers."

"Pink, black, blue, green, what the hell is the difference? I'm paying a lot of hard-earned money for *you* to get a goddamn college education, not watch the pink panthers or whatever the hell they call themselves get things done their way. Stay out of it!" Okay fine.

I had enough anyway after I watched the National Guard club all the protesters. I transferred to another college and fell in love with photography. I told my father the camera I wanted and to save money he went to a pawn shop and got me the exact top-of-the-line camera. He made the guy write on the receipt: "Good for a full refund if dissatisfied in any way." Sure enough, the film would jam. He took it back and the guy insisted there wasn't anything wrong with it and wouldn't give him his money back.

"Can I use your phone for a local call?" he said to the shop owner.

"I suppose so," the guy said. He called Mom.

"Hello, is the District Attorney in today? Uh-huh, okay... Hi, John, it's Jake. Say, can you meet me at this address, just a minute. What's your address here, buddy? Yeah, the corner, I'll be waiting outside for you. Oh, I've got a little problem with a guy here at this pawn shop. Yeah, okay that's great." You can just imagine my mother on the other end, shaking her head, "tisk-tisk-tisk"-ing and wondering what in tarnation he was up to *now*.

111

"OK-OK-OK, here's your money for the camera. I don't want no trouble," the guy begged.

Dad came home, cash in hand, and we howled at his brilliance. Then he took me to a real camera shop and let me pick out all the equipment I wanted. Soon after, he built me the most incredible color darkroom with all the best equipment. Then he beamed when I went on to graduate from a prestigious private college with a degree in cinematography and photography. I loved seeing him get so excited about building me many more wonderful darkrooms and studios over the years—each one more elaborate than the last.

♥♥♥

Merrily, Merrily, Life Is But a Scream

Then... life changed dramatically overnight for my parents when my father had to have a quadruple by-pass after a massive heart attack. He'd had so many operations over the years and Doctor Mom always took care of him, but this one forced him to retire early and it was devastating for him. He couldn't handle the stairs at their big house, so they retired to a new mobile home park. Without his work where he could boss everyone around at the shipyards, he started driving my mother crazy running *her* and her house. She couldn't have her own friends or go anywhere without him. I was in college and she wrote me letters that summed it up. "I'd better get this finished because as soon as your father gets up, he'll sit here and stare at me, wanting me to entertain him and I won't be able to concentrate."

When my father would lament about their illnesses and that they were going to die soon, I'd tell them, "Hey, you guys had pretty darn good lives when you add it all up. You both got to marry the love of your life, you had two great kids (one of whom brought you so much joy), you had nice homes, the picket fence, nice cars, good friends and you've lived longer than most people get to in your own home. That's life. *Everyone* is going to die, not just you. Life's a terminal illness and we all have eternity to be dead. That's just how it goes. Them's the rules... didn't make 'em... can't change 'em. So how about enjoying life while you're still here and stop sweating the dying part so much? You could both live to be a hundred (just shoot me) and

I can't listen to this worrying about dying until then. Now, let's sing a little, *'Don't worry... be happy,'* shall we?"

Then he started calling me *everyday*. After the national weather analysis, I'd ask about someone. "How's Aunt Gertie doing?"

It was always, "Oh, she's bad, *really* bad." Not wanting to hear the gory details, I'd change the subject.

"Well, how about Aunt Dora then?"

"Oh, her mind is really going. She tells you the same thing over and over and doesn't remember she just told you the day before. It's getting too hard to talk to her with all that repeating all the time."

"So... what are you guys doing today?" I'd *try* to be cheerful.

"Oh, not much—just waiting to die." Oh boy, my father's been dying for most of my life, and he doesn't want me to miss a minute of it.

"Well, I guess I better come up there and start getting rid of all your *stuff*, or are you having a U-Haul bring it all behind the hearse?"

"Yuuup, he's taking it *all* with him!" Mom piped in.

"Awhhh, cut it out you guys. Well, there's nothing to *do*." Stomp, stomp, whine, whine. "I'll tell you one goddamn thing. Don't wait for the goddamn golden years. Everyone is sick or dead and we don't have anyplace to go." Sigh, sigh. Oh boy, he's working overtime. Actually, I think he's on GOLDEN time. "I think we'll be down to see you next week. We won't bother ya though. We just *have* to get out of here for a couple days. It's just too damn depressing here by ourselves." Oh wonderful, come depress me in person. There would be no stopping him once he was on a mission. I hated it when I was the target of his missions, as I so frequently was.

The next day, after the *global* weather report (he was so thrilled when the *Weather Channel* debuted), I asked how uncle so and so was.

"Oh, he's bad, *real* bad too. But Aunt Dora is really the one I'm worried about now. She tells you something and then tells you again and again and again. No memory left anymore you know. She tells you the same story one day and repeats the whole thing again the next. It's just getting too hard to talk to her, you know what I mean?"

"Uh-huh, I really do." (Somebody, please... bring me a rope.)

OK, let's repeat again and again, my brain-dead inhaling technique here: Breathe in... and hold it... and out. In again... and hold it... and out. Now do that about twenty times until you're so light-headed— nothing bothers you.

"Umm, Dad, I'm feeling like I'm getting sick." (Not to mention, emotionally wacked with these poor-pitiful-me phone calls.) "I don't want you guys to catch it. You'd better not come down just yet."

Just like Louie Anderson imitates his father: "Naaaaah, we'll come down and take care of you, won't we Mommy? We won't get in your way, don't worry. We'll just be there a couple days and turn around and come home, promise." And they would come to take care of me for a week or more, whether I was sick or not. Then the next month he'd be pushing to come down again.

"I'm really busy right now, Dad—how about next month?"

"Naaaaaah. You just go about your business. We won't get in your way. You won't even know we're there, will she Mommy?"

They'd sleep in my big bed and then about three o'clock in the morning, after reprimanding them twice already, they'd get in a loud argument, wake me up and I'd go in to mediate. They'd be lost on opposite sides of my king-sized bed, tattling on each other. He did *this* and she did *that*. Mom was lying on her back and stretched her arm across to slap him, but she couldn't reach him all the way over there and her hand slapped the bed.

"See! She's trying to hit me!" Exhausted inhale... and hold it... (where's Doctor Spock when you need him?)... and blow it out.

"Listen you two rotten little rug-rats. Settle down right *now* and get to sleep or you're going to go home tomorrow without any Metamucil! Do you hear me? Knock it off! I have to get up and go to work in the morning, so don't make me come in here again—lights out!"

Then the next month he'd be pushing to come again. "Daaaad, I'm dating someone new now, so maybe you could come down next month when I'm ready to introduce you." (And I've had a chance to warn him without scaring him off.)

"Naaaaaah. We want to meet him, don't we Mommy? We won't get in your way. You'll have all the privacy you want." (Oh yeah, we're not talking Southfork at my house.) "Don't worry about us. We'll just stay overnight, maybe two, that's it—promise."

"Please, Dad, I really can't handle any company right now." I swear to *God*, hundred-dollar bills would start showing up in the mail, bribing me to let them come down. No more phone calls, the big chill treatment, and money that *begged* me to let them come. Geeeeese!

Then he'd call me up completely melodramatic. "We've just *gotta* get outta here now. We'll just be there overnight, promise—we've got some nice gifts for you too." I wouldn't have the energy or the heart to disappoint him any longer. The day after they'd arrive he'd always get sick and not feel well enough to drive the eight hours back home. Uh-huh. Cough, choke, sniffle, hack, wheeze. "I... I think I have a fever," he'd barely be able to whisper.

"Wow, we better take you to the emergency room. You don't look so good, Dad."

"Uh, no, no, I'll be okay. I just need to rest a few more days or *so*." (Or *weeks* if he could stretch it out.) Ya had to laugh. It was *kinda* cute that he would go to such extremes to stay longer to be with me. I'd shower him with the attention he wanted and he'd stretch it into a week plus every time. By the time they really were ready to leave, I'd just be getting used to them being there—and then cry my heart out and miss them terribly when they left.

Then one day the little freedom my mother had was gone for good. She had the audacity to have her childhood friend, Pearl, over for dinner and she wasn't giving Dad her full attention. How could she! He was pouting, sitting in the corner brooding by himself. Hmph! I'm sure it was another "cut the atmosphere with a sickle" situation as Pearl said, "Jake, are you going to play bingo with us down at the clubhouse?" He didn't respond. I'm sure he was thinking how awful they were, going to play bingo without *him* and he didn't want to play bing-o! Stomp, Stomp!

All of a sudden, Mom passed out in her plate without any warning. Dad jumped up and yelled for help from the neighbors and dialed 911. Clive and Edith came running from next door and Edith did the CPR that she'd learned forty years earlier on unconscious Mom. Rush-hour traffic delayed the paramedics from getting there quickly, but they finally arrived and took her to the hospital where she stayed in the ICU in a deep coma for many weeks. I had been at the *Music Video Awards* that night and when I got home and got the message, my boyfriend and I got the last flight out. Jeremy and Carrie were already there when we arrived, and we all cried our hearts out as we looked at Mom lying there so helplessly.

A few days later, a pathetic excuse for a "doctor" told us, "She can't hear you. There's no sense in you being here all the time. I'm sorry, but it's doubtful that she'll ever recover and if she does she'll be a vegetable. She was without oxygen for far too long and she'll have massive brain damage. You should all probably discuss disconnecting everything."

An intensive caring nurse came to comfort me with a Kleenex, put her arm around me and said, "You know, the nurses are here with these patients all day long. The doctors come in and out and don't really see what we see. We don't know why, but the patients whose families are here with them tend to come out of the comas more often. I think your mom *will* come out of the coma and be okay." What a kind thing for her to do. She gave me back my hope faster than an injection. After weeks of an around-the-clock vigil, Mom amazingly came out of the coma. It was straight out of a *Dr. Kildare* episode.

"If you can understand me, blink twice. If yes, move your right index finger, if no, move your left toe." She had a tracheotomy so she couldn't talk. Finally she was strong enough and we were all so excited, waiting to hear her first words: "I have to go to the bathroom," said Garbo.

One year later my father walked Mom into that Intensive Care Unit to a round of applause at her remarkable recovery—and specifically to see that grim doctor who would have had us end her life. I'll bet he never said anything like that to anyone again after Dad was done with him.

Suddenly the tables were turned and Dad had to take care of her for the first time in his life. Her illness gave him a new purpose, a new reason to live. He *poured* himself into taking care of her and no one could have any say about it at all, least of all her. She was in the gilded cage where he was finally secure and he could control every aspect of her life. No one could see her without getting past him. She couldn't handle dialing the phone, so he controlled all calls in and out. He kept elaborate Captain's logs of all phone calls (with star date and time), and a record of all the mail that came in. He even kept (I swear on my life) a record of every bowel movement she had for *ten* years. When I found these meticulous notebooks, I just couldn't believe it. *He* was the one who was sick, but he was happy. He was finally in total control—of her every movement.

♥♥♥

chapter eight

MENDING SHATTERED FENCES

O ne day as I was cleaning out my parents bottom dresser drawer, I couldn't believe what I discovered. There were all our family photo albums, but all the pictures of my brother had been removed. Fortunately, Dad's eyesight wasn't so good and many pages had stuck together and he missed whole pages of pictures. I quickly confiscated everything and sent them down to my place for safe keeping. With as furious as he was at me, I was sure *all* my baby photos would be mysteriously missing soon.

Then I was stunned when I found a cassette tape-recording that my father had made. He complained to my brother about all the things he had bought him, and all the things Jeremy did to cause him grief from the time he was born. I swear on my life, it started with the *tricycle* he bought him. It was so inconceivable that he was this warped about his own son. He itemized everything he had ever given Jeremy and then attached a price tag to it. Then he totaled it all up and said that *that* was what Jeremy owed him now. Then he recanted all the boyhood scrapes Jeremy had gotten into with Dobie Gillis and Maynard G. Krebs, none of which were really so bad. I thought, boy, good thing Dad doesn't have a teenager nowadays. I listened in complete shock as I realized that my father was just plain nuttier than a fruitcake.

And then there was the matter of all the dinners he'd paid for when they would all go out to eat after Jeremy was grown up. I'm sure Dad *insisted* on paying, like he always did, and Jeremy probably didn't argue with him long enough over the check. Then, he went on and on that they'd never even invited Mom and him over for dinner to their house. (Dad always wanted to go out.) He punctuated all the things he had done for Jeremy with, "and I never even got a goddamn dinner!" I just couldn't believe it—it was a Red Buttons routine!

117

Once Jeremy was married, they maintained an on again—off again superficial relationship. Then Mom had her heart attack. The tensions were at their highest when they got into an enraged argument in the hospital, had a blow-out and were kicked out. Jeremy washed his hands of Dad, and unfortunately that included Mom. I couldn't understand why his hatred for Dad had to also include never even phoning the mother he said he loved so much. He insisted that he couldn't call her because Dad controlled everything and if he tried to, Dad would make life even worse for her. It felt like a cop-out to me at the time.

It had been eleven years since Jeremy and I had stopped speaking. He'd said, "I *hate* him, Jackie. He's never done anything for me. I'll be happy when I can piss on his grave."

"But, Jeremy, Mom loves you and misses you *so* much. You're torturing her. Just call *her* once in a while. I know Dad was horrible to you. Just forget about him and call her every now and then."

He went *ballistic* yelling at me over and over, "You don't get it, you just don't get it!" I warned him that if he didn't stop screaming at me, I was hanging up. He continued yelling, I warned him again, he didn't, I did, and that was it. Irreconcilable differences, total impasse and—The Cold War began.

I decided to give up on Jeremy for a while, figuring that Dad would pass away soon and then we'd resume our relationship and he'd want to see Mom and me again, but it was many years later already and Dad didn't seem to have any intention of leaving for the Big Sleep without Mom—just wasn't gonna happen. I started to understand my brother's point when the mere mention of his name would cause Harrowing Hyde to surface immediately, spewing in every direction. It was the wrong thing to do, but easier on all of us, to just avoid bringing up Jeremy in any way. I never heard my brother's name mentioned, unless someone was whispering so my father couldn't hear, "Is the family feud still on? Have you heard anything from Jeremy?"

Whenever I got the chance to be with Mom alone (in the bathroom), she'd whisper, "Have you talked to Jeremy, honey? Is he okay? Please tell him I love him, sweetheart." I had spent a decade lying to Mom that he called me all the time asking how she was and to tell her that he loved her so much. It made her very happy and I couldn't bear to see her face if I'd said that he never called about her. I'd hear about things Jeremy was doing through the grapevine and pass it on to Mom when I'd see her. There was no way of telling her over the phone because

Dad never let her talk on the phone to anyone without him on the extension. Maybe Jeremy was right—why make her life even more miserable? I tried often to get Dad to make up but it was absolutely futile, so I just gave up. I was still trying to make peace. Maybe I should go work for the U.N. *("All I am say-ing—is give peace a chance.")*

No, there was not going to be any help coming from Jeremy, even though I knew he was getting reports from his son as to what I was going through. I had so many moments of intense anger at him as I spent month after month sitting there in the hospital with Mom. She was *his* mother too. He could have been sitting with her at night sometimes as Dad was never there then. I decided I needed to run a marathon in his moccasins and try to understand him. Okay, still waters ran deep and he had been so damaged by Dad when he was young, not getting the love that I had gotten, that he probably had to eliminate all of us to save his own sanity.

I realized that I couldn't change Jeremy—but what I *could* do was change the way *I* felt about it, or I'd have so much resentment Jeremy and I would never have a relationship again. I meditated to sort out the outcome I wanted and thought about how much I had always loved my big brother. I had to take the high-road, transcend my anger, forgive him completely, and keep my objective clear: I wanted a new relationship with my only brother, without any expectation of help from him in *any* way. It was New Year's Eve when I called him up, determined to set *myself* free of the resentment. He was quite argumentative but nothing could rile me. I listened calmly and let him rant and ramble on and on. Finally he was all spewed out.

"Well, I think we only have two choices, Jeremy. We can either continue being bitter or we can move past the past and look forward. We can't do anything about all that has happened, but we can make better decisions for the future." I expressed my desire for Mom and me to have some kind of a relationship with him again. He finally calmed down and then we talked for hours. It turned into *real* talking, real sharing, literally for the first time in our lives. I promised him that I would bring Mom over to see him before I went home. I hung up the phone and realized that I was instantly free of years of torment. Forgiveness had set me free and I had the perfect new theme song: *"Come on people now... smile on your brother, everybody get together, try to love one another right now... right now... right now!"*

I felt so incredibly mahvelous, I joined the Fabulous Flannerys at their friend's home for a New Year's Eve party, and we all laughed remembering when I'd said that I probably wouldn't be there for my birthday back in September. Oh yeah, many happy returns. "Well, if I'm still here for April *Fools* Day—please just shoot me."

A party guest, hearing only the gist my sordid saga said, "Why can't you move up here so you can take care of your parents?"

I looked over at grinning Linda and Dick and begged, "Please, just shoot me *now*."

Then the hostess asked, "Why can't your parents just move down there and live with you?"

I gasped on my eggnog. Linda and Dick burst out laughing and I begged, "Never mind, give me a gun—I'll do it myself!"

Then, another fly in the hemorrhoid ointment. I was so disappointed that Camellia started to be unreliable because of her own expanding soap opera: *Victim's Landing*. First, she lost her wallet with the five hundred bucks in it that I had just paid her. (Hmmm) Then, she was going to have to drive a close friend across several states for a funeral because the woman couldn't drive and she refused to fly. Okay. Then, her favorite aunt had to go into the hospital for heart surgery and she was going to be the only one who could take care of her for many days. Oh-k. Then, she was constantly going to Bonnie and Clyde's court hearings. Ohh-k. Then, she needed an advance in her pay for the attorney's fee for the daughter's defense. Ohhh-k. Then she bemoaned, "I didn't even have any Christmas presents for my nephews this year."

OK, call Dionne Warwick and tell her I'm sure I can save the psychic hot-line. I have a very strong sixth sense that an appeal for more money is coming. Oh yeah, and let's get the Amazing Kreskin and Nostradamus over here for a power lunch—*now*.

Since we missed Christmas and Dad was still being so nice on this new medication, I decided to throw an after-Christmas party. The Flannerys came and I had ten-year-old Kevin bring his Nintendo video game so he and my great-nephew could play together. The boys were having so much fun that I offered to drive them each home later after everyone else left. The next day Linda called.

"Jackie, did Kevin leave his Nintendo game there? He says he left it on the back step and forgot it when he got in the car." I looked everywhere, asked Camellia and Dad if they'd seen a non-descript brown cardboard box anywhere, and I checked all the trash bins.

"No, it's not here," I reported back. "Gee, this is really odd—we've never had anything stolen here."

"This is awful," Linda said. "He brought everything with him, about five hundred dollars worth of games. He's been crying all day and we're trying to teach him that he has to be responsible with his things, but he's just beside himself. It's breaking my heart but we don't want to rush out and get him another one—this is a big lesson."

I felt so *terrible*. After all the Flannerys had done for me and then this happens. Oh, I didn't like what I was thinking. Could Camellia have done a "finder's keepers" and picked it up for her "nephews who didn't get any Christmas gifts?" Nooo, she'd never do anything like that. I had no proof of what I kept trying to push out of my mind—as my heart broke for darling little Kevin.

♥♥♥

Too Good to Be True Lies–*or*–Dared Consequences

It was time for Dad's second appointment with Dr. Endure, his favorite "shrink." He went into the first rage we'd seen in quite a while and I realized that *fear* instantly translated into *anger* for him. Anger was his "cover" for deep-seated fear. I had an (as Oprah would say) "Ah-haaa" moment. It was clear that deep behind every rampage was a little boy in fear, who had to attack to protect himself. That life-time patterned button got pushed aaand—*sha-zaam.*

"He's going to put me away if I go there—I won't go!"

"No, no, he just wants to talk to you about the shipyards and maybe adjust the medication—that's all." He ranted for an hour but I finally got him calmed down and by the time we got to Dr. Endure's, Darling Jekyll was back in his most charming mode again. Endure said to keep him on the one milligram of the anti-psychotic, with the anti-depressant, as he felt sure that Dad was doing "just fine."

I dropped them off at home and said I was going to fill their car with gas and have it washed for them, and I'd be home in a couple hours. I came back thinking how happy he was going to be to see how nice his little Toyota looked. Wrong again, almighty Armorall breath.

Mount Vesuvius erupted the second I walked in, "Where in the hell did you go to get gas, Los Angeles?" Oh boy, here we go. What just happened? He had been such a sweetheart for weeks. "I get no respect from you—no goddamn respect at all." Oh *nooo*, he's not going to do Rodney Dangerfield now is he? Maybe he was losing all track of time and a couple hours seemed like a whole day to him. I had gotten him a bigger, brighter clock, as well as a huge wall calendar to cross the days off of, but of course he wouldn't use it.

"Pleeease, Dad, let's sit down and talk calmly about this. I'm sorry you're upset that it took me a couple hours to get your car detailed. Come see how nice it looks—just like sparkling brand new. Come on, what can I do to make you feel better?"

"You can get the hell out of my house—that's what you can do!"

It was no use, he just wouldn't be calmed down. Okay, that's it. "Hasta la vista, baby." I figured he'd calm down as soon as I'd leave. Thank God I had my little sanctuary and the voices of reason to go back to. I left for my permanent suite at the "Flannery Fairmont," belting out a combo of, *"BAD to the bone"* and *"BAAAD company!"*

I wanted to cheer Kevin up anyway, so I played hide and seek with him and his buddy. They were supposed to find me this time and I must have stayed in my hideaway for over a half hour before I finally came out, astonished to find them casually watching television.

"Hey, got a minute? You can't do that," I said genuinely mad.

"We gave up—we couldn't find you."

"There's no giving up in hide and seek! (Just like, 'There's no crying in baseball!') I didn't hear any olly-olly-oxen-free." They just looked at me pathetically like, "Geeeese, call a cop." I was incensed. How dare they break the rules. How double dare they! Wow, I suddenly realized that I was starting to lose it and I was going to have to get a life soon—I was becoming completely pathetic. I needed to Hyde or seek sanity for myself or next they'd find me standing in front of the microwave hysterically jumping up and down yelling, "HURRY!"

Then, Camellia called that night crying that Dad was screaming at her for washing three loads of wash in his machine and using his *water!* Oh dear—release the Hounds of the Baskervilles. I could hear him yelling in the background, accusing her of washing all the neighbors' and all her relatives' clothes in *his* machine.

"Jackie, I swear to you that I was doing their laundry. I don't do my laundry here because he stands over the machine like a madman."

"I know, Camellia—don't worry, really." I'd had the *twenty* year old washing machine fixed, and the repair man said they usually only lasted about ten years, so it was really on borrowed time. I knew how obsessed Dad was with it. When Hyde was on the washing machine detail he would bend over it, head down, with his out-stretched arms on top of it, I swear, encouraging it to make it through one more rinse cycle. (*"Madman across the waaa-ter."*) Thank you, Elton. And then, God *forbid* if it got off-balance and it started knocking, he'd really go berserk—yelling that we'd put too much in it. He'd start running amuck through the house screaming at us. Gee, I should have gotten him a calming Maytag repairman's job. Sometimes he'd insist on running it without any clothes in it at all, and other times he'd put his skid-marked underwear in it with all the other clothes. Ewww!

Camellia said, "Your mom stuck up for me and I swear I heard him slap her in the face."

"What! Is she OK?"

"Yes, she's fine, but now she denies that he hit her. She's afraid to stand up to him. I don't know, Jackie. This is just too much stress for me. I'm sorry, I really don't think I can do this anymore, hon."

I exhaled from the tips of my toenails and assured Camellia that I understood completely. She said she'd start looking for a place to move, but she'd stay and help me with them until she did.

The next morning Camellia had Mom call me secretly from her room and I asked, "Did Dad slap you last night, Mom?"

"Yes, he swatted me right in the face when I contradicted him and said that Camellia hadn't been doing laundry all night."

I was beyond livid and flew over there to confront my father, who just denied it while my mother was suddenly silent, completely intimidated and looked down quietly denying it had happened now.

Then Dad started yelling at Camellia again about the laundry and it escalated with Howling Hyde raising his fist to her face and nearly striking her. That was the last straw for her and she started moving out. Dad realized that he'd gone too far and tried to bribe her to stay by laying out hundred-dollar bills on the kitchen table. Camellia looked at him in disgust, "There isn't enough money in this world to make me stay livin' here with you, Jake—you're crazy!" Within an hour she was gone. Yep, it was *ov-er.* "Good-night, Chet." ... "Good-night, David."

I was outwardly calm, watching my four months of hard work go down the tubes, but inside I was *miles* past mad. The realization that I was not going home anytime soon, and that my salvation was walking out the door, was beyond infuriating. What was I going to do?

He was so stubborn and out of touch, he couldn't recognize how *perfect* the situation was that I had created for them. I didn't want to remember any of the good things he had done for me anymore. The bad was outweighing the good by megatons. Okay, I had to switch gears and go to Alternate Plan *B*. (Boy, I wish I had one.)

Camellia was gone without a trace and he continued to rant and rave about what a "goddamn bitch" she was and that he didn't like or need her anyway. I just watched and listened, completely catatonic and numb, squelching down the rage I felt simmering inside myself.

I tried to get him to take a pill, but he *refused* to take anymore medication or go to anymore "goddamn doctors." I called Sgt. Pepper and *begged* for her to please come back out and help me. Ohhh, no can do. She'd been moved out of our jurisdiction now. But of course, silly me—the *glitch*. Okay fine. Who's left at Police Academy? How about Charlie's Angels? No? What about Maxwell Smart and Agent 99? Noo? Well, was Cagney and Lacey available then? Nooo? Ohhhh-k. Well then how about just come gag me and frickin' rape me then! Beyond frustration and infuriation inhale… and hold it… hold it… (ohhh, I think I'll just keep holding it… until I just)… pass out!

Oh dear, seems we've erred again. Sgt. Pepper informed me that Camellia should have called the police the minute Dad slapped Mom, even though she didn't see it. If Mom said he slapped her, then they might have been able to "5150" him again. Now she wanted to "5150" Mom and take her to the hospital because she felt that Mom was incapable of taking care of herself. I said that my mother would never tell *them* that Dad had slapped her—she knew not to cross him and make things worse for herself. It would be too traumatic for her to be hauled off and my father would be charming and get to bring her home right away anyway. I'd just be right back where I was, except he'd be even madder and I'd have another expensive ambulance bill.

"Well, then I'm sorry to tell you that you have to promise to stay there and protect her, or we will come get her." WHAT? I was *boiling* over with anger at all I had been put through and realized I needed to stay away from sharp objects. Okay fine. I was trapped at the Hanoi Hilton, no helicopters in sight, and I had to sleep in the clothes I'd worn over from Linda's. The frustration was absolutely *unbearable*.

At-ti-ca!… At-ti-ca!

♥♥♥

I'm Mad as Hell and I'm Not...

The next day Hyde woke up raving nasty and insisted on dyeing his own three gray hairs with his Grecian Formula. Samson, Sr. pushed me to get out of his way as I tried to clean up his huge splattered mess before it stained the gold rug. He had used more than a little dab and I sighed when I noticed that he had mistakenly used Mom's prescription *mouthwash* to mix the dye. Amazingly it worked just fine so at least his hair smelled good. Only his hairdresser knew for sure. Dad was not only the President of Mouthwash Hair Formula, he was the only client.

Next he wouldn't take any of his pills and knocked a glass of juice out of my hand, breaking the glass. OK, time to pack up all the breakables and start looking for the Melmac. Then he yelled at me to, "get the hell out," screaming that I hadn't done anything to help him and they were fine until I came up and messed everything up. Yeah, I'd had a successful coup and destroyed Hyde Majesty's little dynasty. The man who would be king had lost his lofty throne—"tisk-tisk."

I called his doctors—of course, no return calls. What was I going to do with him? If I didn't love my mother so much, I'd have walked away. I was feeling *so* hopeless, *so* alone. There was no Camellia, no one was coming to help me. I felt like that lone protester in Tianamen Square facing a steel tank that could run over me at any minute. The trapped, frightful reality of being so alone overwhelmed me and hit me like a ton of bricks from the east side of the old Berlin Wall. (*"Nowhere to run to baby... nowhere to Hyde."*)

Ya know—it felt just like that *Twilight Zone* or was it *The Outer Limits*? where the guy plots his escape from prison and stows away in a coffin with a dead guy wrapped in a sheet. He gets buried alive and then his buddy, the caretaker, will come dig him up later to free him. He waits and waits. Finally he lights a match to look at his watch and the sheet slowly slides off the face of the dead guy lying next to him, and bummer of bummers—it's his buddy, the caretaker! AHHHH! Well, that was the exact feeling: NO ONE was coming.

So where's Superman with my deus ex machina? He always flew in at the last minute to save the damsel in distress. And what about Zorro with that gay blade of his? Nope, Little Joe and Hoss weren't coming... the A Team wasn't coming... F Troop wasn't even coming. Where's my *dad?* He always swooped in to save me, whether I wanted him or not. Then I realized: Dudley Do-Right wasn't going to charge in to save the day—and neither was my daddy.

I was trapped, having promised Sgt. Pepper that I would not leave my mother alone with him. Then he started in on me. Ohhh nooo, not again. "You're just a goddamn *slut*," he said with utter disdain. I just sat there trying to ignore him, dreading another episode. "That's right, you heard me." Please, *nooo*, he was getting all fired up again. Then he screamed right in my face, "A *fucking* whore, that's what you are. At least Elizabeth Taylor marries hers, you just *fuck* them!"

OK, THAT'S IT! The fact that I had never been married, only in long-term relationships, was directly attributable to *him*, as I saw him dominate my mother my whole life. I was terrified of being a POW and living unhappily ever after. When he'd rage Mom would sigh, "I can't believe I married my own father, tisk, tisk, tisk." She hated her father and Dad had been charming until way after they got married and then I guess she got the surprise of her life: "Ta-da," a rageaholic, just like her father. I was terrified of making the same mistake.

It made me *furious* that he was insulting me about my relationships, since *he* was the reason I had never married. *He* was the source for all our unhappiness growing up, and *he* was the cause of all this misery now. *He* was the reason my brother had left the family, and *he* was the reason they had so few friends left. *He* was the reason Mom had almost died several times, and *he* was the reason my life was going nowhere as I was trapped there month after month with—*him*.

I tried hard to "wag the dog" and create a diversion by focusing on Mom as I got her into her hospital bed, but he would not be distracted from his tirade. Then he started spewing insults at both of us as he paced back and forth pointing at us with the vilest of looks. "I've done everything for both of you and what have you two ever done for me, huh? You're both nothing but goddamn sluts! I earned all the goddamn money. You two never did *shit!*" I felt an *enormous* rage rising up inside me, expanding like a helium balloon inside my chest, bigger and BIGGER and then—it popped. I *exploded* with a torrent of fire and furry, firing back at him with everything I had in my arsenal, from a place I didn't even know existed within me.

"And what about you and your years of infidelity?" I screamed at him. He was visibly stunned that I knew about that. I started taunting him with, "Marsha—Marsha—Marsha," the woman he had supposedly carried on with behind my mother's back when I was a teenager. I was skeptical of my mother's suspicions because she had gotten a little wacky herself while she was going through "the change" and she was even accusing me of doing things I wasn't doing—*yet.* Hey, I was a regular Natalie Wood in *Splendor in the Grass* type. I had a hard time believing her because I just couldn't see my father with this weird woman at all. She was a foot taller than him, kinda crazy, and not at all pretty like Mom was. The problem was, we'd see her all the time at family functions because—she was Marina's aunt.

But *then*—I heard my father mistakenly say as he turned to my mother, "Right, Marsha?" loud and clear as he told a funny story, right in front of her mother and sisters in Montana. There was *no* mistaking it. Mom's face dropped a foot and I was blown away. Mom was right—*something* was going on. My heart shattered like glass for my mother, whose embarrassment in front of her family must have been overwhelming. She didn't speak to him, barely a "tisk," as we drove all the way back to California. (Now *there* was a fun trip.)

"That's not true! I did not have sexual relations with that woman!" Hmmm, it must have been an affair to forget.

"Bullshit, you didn't! You want the truth, you can't handle the truth! What about the part about 'forsaking all others?' And what about your first wife, whom you failed to mention to Mom until way after you married her and got her pregnant? And why, when I was a kid, did I hear you slam the phone down yelling, "I'm not your goddamn father!" to someone calling and saying they were your kid?" Hyde was astonished by the skeletons I was pulling out from under that filthy carpet now, as I did my own furious pacing, back and forth, as I yelled at him. He went into their bedroom, got into bed, rolled over and tried to ignore me.

I realized that I had turned into a John Belushi/Sam Kinison combo, as I screamed at the top of my lungs at him, "I had everything set up for you. All you needed to do was relax and enjoy being taken care of and not worry about *anything*, but nooooo! Camellia did three whole loads of wash and used your water! OH—MY—GOD! Oh, oh, oh, ohhhhhh! I haven't done *anything* for you because I'm just a goddamn whore! Oh, oh, oh, ohhhhhh!" I was right in his face. "You ungrateful bastard. No one would have done what I've done for you. Your own son won't even lift a finger to help you. You'd both be dead by now if it wasn't for me." He got up and turned off the light and got back into bed.

"I'm going to sleep, leave me alone—get out of my room."

"Oh no you don't." I yelled as I kept turning the light back on each time he got up and turned it off—*over* and *over*. I thought it was kinda funny amid the furry.

"What? You think I can't yell at you in the dark? Let's see how *you* like it," I screamed as I itemized all the things I'd done for them in the many months that I'd endured his raging wrath. "I've taken care of all your bills and finances, fixed your house (the money pit) and *everything* in it, fixed your car inside and out—and then I fixed both of you from head to toe, not to mention that I saved both of your lives a few times—but I guess I haven't done *anything* for you, because I'm just a fucking whore! Oh, oh, oh, ohhhh." I was really pumped up, but my throat was getting raw from screeching, so I went to get a drink of water in the kitchen. I heard a noise, turned around, and was caught off guard to see that he'd gotten up and followed me.

"I told you to get out!" Hyde screamed inches from my face as he pounded both fists on the kitchen table so hard I thought he'd shatter every bone in his hands. He gritted his teeth and made guttural growls as saliva came spewing out of his mouth. The purple veins in his forehead looked like they would have to burst. "You are not wanted here. How many times do I have to tell you? I can take care of Mother by myself. I always have and I always will. Nobody's going to tell me how to take care of my own goddamn wife, or my house, least of all—*you*. You've never done anything for me. Where the hell have you been the last eleven years while I've been taking care of her all by myself?"

"Where've I been?" I shrieked. "How *dare* you ask me where I've been. I've been working hard at a stressful full-time job and listening to you complain to me every single day for eleven years, refusing all my suggestions to get help for yourself and then watching you insult and fire every single caregiver I've hired to help you—that's where I've been!"

"Did I ever get any help from you? Nooo, you're too busy slutting around," Hyde continued, pushing me to the brink. "You're *nothing* to me, nothing—just like your goddamn brother! No one is taking care of Mother but *me* and that's final—DO YOU HEAR ME?"

I felt *hatred*, hatred like I have never felt before for *anyone* in my whole life. Please God, *please* take him. A massive stroke maybe, no? Okay a heart attack is good too. Okay, just a grand mal seizure, *fine*. Dial 9-1-what? Oops, sorry, wrong number. You say you can't breathe?

Oh, what a shame. What's that you're trying to say? Call who? What, Pork Chop? I can't *heeeear* you. Somebody please tell me why is he still living? I felt like I could have watched and been thrilled to see him go. Where's the Grim Reaper when you *need* him?—"I see a dead people."

"Now you read *my* lips. You are *not* going to take care of Mother by yourself, if it's the last thing I ever do. Do you understand *me?* You are not capable of taking care of her or yourself any longer. I'll take her away from you, and you'll *never* know where she is. I promise you, she will not be left alone here with you again—ever!" I quickly turned away and walked into the family room, knowing I had to get away from him or I was going to slap him across the face with the next insult. I turned around just in time to see him spontaneously *explode* with rabid rage.

Huffing Hyde came at me, charging like a wild raging bull across the family room with so much power and hatred in his eyes, he looked like the devil in the flesh. I was completely flabbergasted as I realized what was about to happen. Instant adrenaline rushed into my system and I was suddenly pumped up and ready for the very first physical fight of my entire life. I missed a great opportunity because if I would have moved slightly out of the way, he would have gone right out the window. (Oops!)

The physical altercation that followed was one of those scenes in your life you can't *imagine* could ever happen. I was so shocked that the father who had loved me so much, hated me so much now. Everything went into surreal slow motion, just like they say it does—two colliding explosions of frustration and hatred. In his demented mind, he could take care of her, and I was in the way of his total control. I had reached my limit and I released pent-up anger and frustration at a level I didn't even know I was capable of. It was a culmination of a lifetime full of domination and control that he was fighting to hold onto, and a lifetime of repressed rebellion that I was finally letting go of.

He weighed one hundred and eighty-five pounds and he was still *very* strong. Suddenly I had a panic thought that my little five-foot three inch body with a weakened backbone might be seriously hurt, but then I suddenly remembered my father's words when I came home from school crying about a bully who had pushed me off my bike. He brushed away my tears and got down on one knee and gave me a boxing lesson with true-grit teeth and clenched fists. "Remember now, always go for their weakest spot, honey," he said as he demonstrated the knee to the groin technique and encouraged me to retaliate and "hit 'em with everything" I had. I was shocked—it seemed *overly* dramatic to me then, and I was stunned that he'd *really* want me to get in a fist-fight with a *boy*. No, I walked away in third grade and I continued to walk away from physical conflicts my whole life—but now, so many decades later, his advice was of tremendous value to me. Suddenly I had the backbone, physically and emotionally, to take him on. *("C'mon and hit me with your best shot.")*

I instinctively put my arms up to cover my face and took a number of blows to my head, thinking he'd realize that he'd gone too far and stop himself. To my horror the blows got worse. I successfully blocked one after another and then I tried to lift my knee and get him in the groin, but he moved in the nick of time. I was impressed—pretty spry for eighty-three. I was *astounded* by what was happening, but I realized that I had to do *something* to get control of him. Okay then, let's see… where else was he the weakest? His arm! I finally got hold of his bad right arm as it pounded on my head and I gave it a little twist. There was complete shock on his face that I was actually going to defend myself. I could hear Howard Cosell, "The Champ delivers a sharp jab with a left, right, left. Baby-cakes blocks and tries to hit below the belt. The Champ blocks and counters with a blistering blow to her right." Boom, crash, bang, ouch-y. I just couldn't *believe* that he kept hitting me with all his might and that he wasn't ready to stop, but then again— *everything* was on the line.

He tried to get his hands around my throat again but I blocked his hands. Suddenly I had a clear shot and slapped him square across the face. "And that's for slapping Mother the other night." *Ouch*, that really hurt big time. I'd never even slapped anyone before. Gee, not like in the movies at all. It was reaching a feverish pitch and poor Mom was trying to referee from her hospital bed, traumatically screaming for us to, "STOP!—STOP!—STOP!"

Finally he backed away, but to my horror it was just to get more momentum to come at me even harder and we locked in a tug of war, back and forth, like two prize fighters afraid to break apart and get knocked out. I was finally able to get one hand around his throat and started to squeeze my long fingernails into him. "And this is for choking me!" With one hand on his throat, and my other hand trying to twist his arm, while *his* other arm was pounding on me as hard as he could, I was amazed that I had enough strength to maneuver him backward to in-front of his recliner that I'd just had raised up for him. With a surge of strength I pushed him backward so he fell into it, but he *still* wouldn't give up, lifting his legs and kicking me as hard as he could. I just couldn't believe it—he was about to get back up and come after me *again*. What can I do? What can I do? I grabbed hold of one of his frantically kicking legs and twisted *it* at the ankle. He kept kicking me with his other leg but I moved to the side so he couldn't reach me, and he was just about to slide off the recliner and fall on his butt onto the floor, when he finally threw in the towel pleading for tender mercy.

"OK-OK, stop!" he begged. I dropped his leg nodding victoriously.

"That's it?" I motioned with my hands for him to get up and finish it, "COME ON, MAKE MY YEAR!" (Sorry, way too many action movies.) I couldn't believe that *I* was suddenly completely fearless. "So, that's all you got?"

"Yeah," he said out of breath, panting.

I was thinking of making chicken noises, but decided I'd better not tempt fate. I was acting hecka-tough, standing over him with my fists on my hips. I suddenly realized I had a *Xena: Warrior Princess* kind of thing going on, and I was ready for round two, if I *had* to, but I was *sooo* relieved he couldn't go any further—and neither of us were hurt, except for his badly squished ego and oops, my broken nail. Wait a minute, oh my gosh, we've got another blockbuster on our hands: *Daddy Die Hardest: I'll Be Back—At Ya.*

Next I was looking right in the blood-shot eye of the tiger with my trembling index finger in his face. "If you *ever* come at me again, I'll really hurt you, so you'd better think twice before you ever try it again. And if you *ever* hit Mother again, consider it just like hitting me—you *will* regret it." He sat there, head down, defeated—for the moment.

I barely made it to the bathroom to splash cold water on my face as I shook uncontrollably with adrenaline. I could hardly stand up, my knees were knocking so badly. I was *astonished* at the depth of rage that had just come out of me. I would never have to fear his sinister threats again. What a breakthrough—and to think I could have saved all that therapy money. I just couldn't believe that *I* was capable of that much rage. *Moi?* It was suddenly crystal clear to me how a woman who is physically and verbally abused for years, could be capable of killing her abuser. *The Burning Bed* made total sense to me. Good reason to *never* have guns or gasoline in the house—ever—ever—*ever!*

As I held onto the counter to hold myself up, I marveled that I was living one of the most amazing days of my life, filled with every possible emotion. It was such a bittersweet triumph overshadowed by overwhelming sorrow at the depth that our relationship had sunk to—but at least I would never physically fear him again. "What I had to fear, was fear itself." (Thank you, President Roosevelt.) I felt certain he would never try to get physically abusive with me again because he knew that I had no hesitation of defending myself and big surprise (to me), I was quite capable of overpowering him.

He put his tail between his legs and slithered off to bed, and I went to the Flannerys' repeating something about, "Floating like a butterfly, but stinging like a bee." I had no idea what their reaction was going to be as I reenacted the blow by blow tumultuous tale, expressing my conflicting emotions of sorrow and triumph. Linda tried to comfort me, "I know you've always loved your father, Jackie, but I don't think you had a choice with this. You can't get any of the stupid "professionals" to help you. What are you supposed to do—let him hurt you—just so you can get some help? Unfortunately, it sounds like it was a necessary evil because maybe now he'll realize that he can't win by threatening or attacking you—hopefully he'll stop now."

Mild-mannered Dick piped up, "You know, I think it's actually the best thing you've tried yet—I just don't know what took you so long. Man, if he were *my* father—he'd be *real* sorry by now."

Once again my dearest friends were there for me, giving me the emotional support I needed. Yes, I had won the bitter battle, but I was devastated to be losing much more than the war. It was a "victory" that I never wanted to experience *ever* again in my life.

Then my theatrics got the best of me as I sprinted up to my room dramatically humming the theme to *Rocky*, jogging up and down those looong steps with my arms raised over my head in my dreams, and beating frozen carcasses—all night long.

"One small step for abused womankind—one giant leap for Ms. Jacqueline."

♥ ♥ ♥

That's Me in the Spotlight

The next morning I was back down to the scene of the crime at Hydebreak Hotel for an appointment with Eleanor (kind of a big, bold, by-the-book, Brunhilde type), from Adult Protective Services. I started telling her all about the heartbreaking altercation of the previous evening and I was *shocked* to suddenly be given the third-degree. I was told what a serious event that this was for *me*. OK, don't anybody move, round up the unusual suspects. She indicated that *I* was in very big trouble. Seems there is a law, Penal Code 368, that says you cannot hit an elderly disabled person, no matter what. "It's just like with little children, you can't hit them," she said, surprised that I didn't know that.

"Wait a minute! No-no-no, this was clearly *self defense* from a raging bully who attacked me *again*, and who is still very strong and *much* bigger. He is *not* some little ol' helpless disabled person!"

"Well, I don't think so. You still have to walk away—turn the other cheek. It's a crime to retaliate. I'm sorry, I'm going to have to report this abuse," she said very matter-of-factly, taking out her poison pen.

My heart stopped. What about *my* abuse? What about a lifetime of verbal abuse, four months of pure hell and now him physically attacking me for a *second* time? She whipped out a copy of the law faster than you can say, "*Con*-temporary insanity." I guessed that this happened quite frequently because she had quite a stack of them in her folder. I was scanning faster than Evelyn Wood. There had to be a loophole that would exonerate me. Where's the part about being attacked by a man possessed?

She acted like it was curtains for me and I had the right to remain silent because what I had just said was going to be used against me. I was guilty of Hyde crimes and misdemeanors. Hey, what ever happened to beyond a reasonable doubt and presumed innocent until proven guilty? Okay, no handcuffs, ooouch, please. I could hear the prison bars at Sing Sing lock in place: CA-LANK! I was pleading for immunity, okay "sanctuary—sanctuary," Esmerelda. "I coulda been somebody—I coulda been a contender." Thank you, Marlon. I could see that great big sledge hammer coming at me, pounding my criminal number on my forehead with that loud reverberating "CLINK," as I smiled for my mug shot, right hand under chin, poised for a formal portrait. How's my hair look? Wait, *this* is really my better side. OK, get me Johnny Cochran. He'll get me off, even with a mountain of forensic evidence and Dad's DNA under my fingernails. "If he throws a fit—you must acquit."

Back-peddle, back-peddle. Okay, ya got me, Mugsy—I'm scared straight. Greeeat, all I needed was for this to go on *my* spotless rap sheet. I was really kissing her penal code... you know what... and assuring her nothing was even bruised but his swollen ego. (I didn't mention that my hand still hurt from swatting him one or that I was missing a broken nail somewhere.) I assured her that it wouldn't happen again because *A)* He wouldn't *ever* try it again (if he knew what was good for him), and *B)* I'd call the SWAT team immediately and walk away, I promise!

She finally started to put her CIA pen down. That's right, put the pen down, nice and easy. Thank God it wasn't like Brodrick Crawford and the *Highway Patrol*. Once *they* start writing, it's all over. "10-4." Looked like my plea bargaining worked—I was freed on a technicality: no admissible evidence. Wow, I was really glad I didn't know about that law the night before—I hate not being a law abiding citizen.

Phew, that was heavy. Finally we got into what I was going to do next. Basically, their hands were tied (mine were clammy), until he hurt someone. Ohhh, I seeee, silly me—I shudda let him really hurt me! If I was in intensive care with a broken neck, *then* they could actually do something. Only if Mom got real bad could they step in to rescue her. She said it would be best if Mom said she *wanted* to leave him. I explained that she was completely codependent and that *that* was never going to happen. She said I should have called the police to come "5150" him again. I wasn't sure how I would have dialed 911 and blocked his blows at the same time. "Uh, could you, um... hold that right jab... right there for just a moment Sugar Ray while I try to get RoboCop on the line? Thanks, Lamb Chop."

Eleanor Rigby said, "There's nothing we can do but try to talk some sense into him." She was still living in a dream world.

"Oh yeah, that's been working sooo well. Fine, you try it then. *You* get tough and threaten him that he could lose Mom." Then we heard "Exhibit A" grumbling as he got out of bed to investigate who was there.

"Dad, this is Eleanor, from Adult Protective Services," I said, hoping that my broken nail wasn't sticking straight out of his neck.

"Jesus Christ! Can't you people just leave me and my wife alone?" he barked with the nastiest look.

"Jake, you are getting very close to having your wife taken away from you. If you cannot control your temper and take care of her properly, we will have to remove her from your home."

"What's *she* been telling you? Don't believe anything *she* says. She'll just lie to you. She's nothing but a goddamn liar. And I've never raised my fist to anyone, *almost* never. And I didn't attack her last night and I never choked her with my hands either." Eleanor looked at me, I did my favorite, "I told you so" look, grinning like a Cheshire cat, as my head finally came out of the guillotine for defending myself. "You ask my wife if I've ever raised my fist to anyone. Go ahead, I'll get her up so you can ask her yourself." (Oh boy, here we go—no *sex*, lotsa *lies* my father told me, and I wish I had this on *videotape*.)

Eleanor followed him into the bedroom and went over to Mom's side of the bed. "Hello, Mariel, how are you doing?"

"Fine," Mom said smiling, reaching out her hand to greet her.

"Mariel, we're very concerned for your safety. Do you think your husband is capable of taking proper care of you everyday?"

"Damn right I can—can't I, honey?"

Mom looked at Dad, who was *demanding* confirmation—then at me, *pleading* for her to tell the awful truth—then to judge and jury Eleanor. Just the facts, Mom. I could see total fear and loathing come over her as she realized that her answer could take her out of her home and back to the nursing home, and even *worse*—bring on the wrath of my father.

"Uh-huh, he does a pretty good job," she said softly as she looked down. My heart sank. The classic abused woman's syndrome. I just couldn't take much more. She could stay with him and dwindle back down to eighty-two pounds and he could burn the house down, electrocute her, feed her bug cereal, give her the wrong medication, and slap her silly—but she still wanted to be with him. Fine.

Dad looked at me and smirked victoriously. I knew he had drilled into her what to say and scared her to death about telling anyone the truth, or she'd be sorry.

Eleanor probed further, "But, do you think he needs some help here at home, a caregiver like Camellia to help him?"

"Oh yes, Camellia is so helpful to us. I don't know what we'd do without Camellia. It's way too much work for him without her."

Yippee! I gave Dad a nasty, "C'mon, ready for round two?" fake smile and batted my eyelashes.

"Jake, you will *have* to have some help here, Camellia or someone else. If your wife's condition starts to deteriorate because no one is here *every* day to properly care for her, we *will* take her away from you. *(Yes, yes, yes!)* We were appraised of your wife's condition when she was brought to the hospital several months ago, and we believe she almost died because of your inability to care for her any longer. Your daughter wants you to be able to stay in your own home together and has worked very hard to make that happen—but when she leaves, if there is no one here to take care of your wife properly every single day, we will have to step in and protect her. Do you understand the seriousness of this?" He put his head down, defeated for another moment, nodded and finally agreed. I was *loving* it and thanked Eleanor profusely as I walked her outside.

"Jacqueline, WOW, I feel real badly for you. I can see how hard he must be to deal with—my gosh, you poor thing, what a nightmare you're in. Promise me you'll walk away, run if you have to, but just get away from him, no matter how nasty he gets. You don't want to get yourself in trouble—he could say you hit him and act helpless."

"Yes, I will, I promise. I swear I had no idea there was a law against self defense—but I can *fantasize* about beating the crap out of him when he attacks me again can't I, or is that against the law too?"

She laughed, "Yeah, by all means if it helps your stress level. Just don't act on it—ever. Get away from him and call the police right away. The problem is that more and more we're seeing frustrated adult children cross the line and physically abuse their elderly parents. It's actually becoming quite an epidemic. You can understand that we have to be certain about what is going on. You'd be surprised that this is all a lot more common than you think, and it's so hard on an adult child when a parent gets old and combative. I see so many cases like this and it's really very sad. It's a terrible dilemma because they're right on the edge of having to go into a home and the controlling men put up the biggest fights. You really have your hands full, but unless she's willing to leave him or he ends up hurting her or someone else—*or,* you go to court and try to prove that he is severely demented, legally we can't do anything. It's a terrible situation for you, doing this all by yourself. The key is really going to be the psychiatrist and a diagnosis of dementia or mental illness. There's really nothing more I can do—I'm very sorry."

Outrageous frustration inhale… and hold it… (if you cannot afford an attorney, one will *not* be appointed for you—*and* if you cannot find professionals who'll listen to you, too damn bad.)… and explode it all the way out—again.

♥♥♥

chapter♥nine

FUGITIVES FROM INJUSTICE

tepping apprehensively back inside the house, I expected to face another exasperating episode with Horrible Hyde. I was *astonished* to see that Gentle Jekyll had magically reappeared, being very apologetic and up to his old tricks again. He wanted to offer "Catellie" money to come back. I blew off that idea, telling him that he and Alec Guinness had pretty much blown up the bridge over the troubled water of the River Kwai already. Then, I couldn't believe the absolutely uncanny timing when Camellia happened to call, wanting to pick up her homemade peach pie she'd forgotten in our freezer. I told her to come by and at least let repentant Jekyll try to bribe her and make some money off him. She liked that idea and came over right away. Dad pulled out a hundred-dollar bill, laying it on the table, apologizing to her, and *pleading* with her to reconsider.

"Casmelly, I *beg* of you to come back. So help me God, I'll *never* yell again." Uh-huh, "never say never," as Mom always says.

She looked at me with a "should I take it" look. I gave her a quick little shake of my head, no. I decided to inflict worse pain than rubbing Epsom Salts in his fingernail wounds.

"Dad, why don't you put your money where your (foul) mouth is. Just *how* sorry are you for being so mean to her?" Hitting Goldenfinger in the wallet was definitely *his* most sensitive spot. He pulled out another hundred-dollar bill. Camellia saw my signal and remained immovable. When *another* hundred-dollar bill came sliding out of his wallet—I started looking for his SAG card. Okay, get me Central Casting, this was going to be absolutely fabulous. Yep, three hundred bucks made the real award-winning performance begin.

"Calinda, I'm so sorry for all I've done. (SOB, SOB) Please, I *beg* of you to reconsider and come back and be a part of our family and take care of us."

137

Camellia looked for what to do—I blinked affirmatively.

"Well," she said as she picked up the money, "I'll have to think about it real hard. I'll let you know in a few days if I want to work for you anymore or not. I'm still very hurt about how you've treated me." He saw her pick up his money and I could see the panic start.

"Oh-kay, ah... think about it then," he said, realizing that he might be out the three hundred bucks for nothing but afraid to make matters worse and be out of the dough for sure. He went on and on delivering another oh-so-sincere apology and his one-take performance was really quite good. Camellia and I were *loving* it. Groveling, when you aren't the one down in the gravel, can be really satisfying.

The next morning darling Jekyll started to wheeze badly and he had greenish yellow phlegm coming up. I knew that meant antibiotic time so I hauled him off to Dr. Kiljoy's. Sure enough—bronchitis. Greeeeat, we needed this like a hole in the hernia. He was back in his lovey-dovey mode, all over Mom like cheap pajamas, feeding her bites off his fork and sips from his glass. I kept trying to stop him from exposing her each time when he'd "forget." I was trying to get him to wash his hands with anti-bacterial soap and not spread his germs, but as soon as he'd wash his hands he'd pick his Jimmy Durante sized nose. Lovely. I got him a dust and pollen mask to wear but he refused. Fine. *I* wore it. Talking in tunnel-tone, I calmly tried to explain that it might be best if Mom stayed in her hospital bed so she wouldn't catch it as she would have a hard time fighting it off. Valentino wouldn't allow it. Oh no, he wouldn't give her bronchitis. I started pumping mega-vitamins into all of us. He was hacking, coughing up phlegm, not covering his mouth. Ohhh yeah, it was just a matter of time before we all got it.

Sure enough, *I* started to get it and I was the only one washing my hands constantly, wearing a mask, and taking the Lysol out of my holster and spraying him and everything he touched every few minutes. Wonderful. Then Mom started coughing and I begged him to let her sleep in the hospital bed because it could be very dangerous for her.

"You just know everything, don't you? You're so goddamn smart." Oh nooo, pleeeease, Big Bang settle down—not *again!* Hyde was back again, yelling that he wasn't born yesterday and that he was sick of me knowing everything. Gee, Dad, you say that, like it's a *bad* thing. "You think I'm just some goddamn dummy, huh?" I tried to assure Quasimodo that he was brilliant and that Mensa wanted him. Then the familiar scene started up again. The insults, raging, yelling, pounding and throwing things, but I did not respond at all. I would remain calm at all costs. Eleanor would be proud, I would not retaliate in any way. I just walked away. I was, however, visualizing—"The Rack."

"We're getting the hell out of here today," he screamed in my face. "I'm taking Mother to get her nails polished." I had made the mistake of having her nails done professionally for the first time in her life a couple weeks before, when he was in such an agreeable mood.

"I want my nails done!" she'd insist, about twenty times a day now.

"Let's go, Mommy. I'm sick of this shit. And move that goddamn rental car or I'll *ram* it out of the way!" Cough, hack, choke 'til he turned purple and nearly passed out. God, if you can't fix him, can't you please just take him? Eighty-three is old enough. There's got to be an opening up there pretty soon. I put him on a waiting list months ago. He's going to kill my mother with all this stress, and I'm not feeling so great myself.

"Dad, ya know, it's raining and *very* cold outside. El Niño is really acting up today (just like someone else I know), you're really sick (understatement) and you shouldn't be going out in this dreadful weather—you could catch your death (hmmm). How about if I take Mother to get her nails done for you, so you don't get any sicker. I need to have mine done anyway, I have a broken nail." (By the way, have you seen it anywhere?)

I tried to ignore him and go about my business, translating all the screaming into background music to hold onto my slipping sanity. When he finally tuckered out and laid down he agreed to let me take her out, and I saw the first opportunity to do what I had thought about doing for quite some time—kidnapping my own mother.

I was thinking faster than a Pentium III on amphetamines. Byte me. It was the great escape from Devil's Island as I stuffed a few things into my coat pockets, grabbed her diaper bag, sneaked all her medicines into my purse and did a Papillon style quantum leap outta there before he could change his mind. I wasn't sure what my next move was going to be, but I was prepared to hold my mother ransom until I figured it out. We were suddenly fugitives, running from his ranting reign of terror. Where's Dr. Richard Kimble when you need him?

We had the perfect opportunity, so after the manicures I phoned my brother and asked if we could come over to visit them. As I drove the getaway car there my favorite Oldie's station played, *"It's been a looong time coming."* I looked at Mom and we smiled at each other because it had really been a *looong* time since she had seen her only son. He smiled as he opened the door to a new relationship and it was so satisfying to see the overwhelming joy on her face as she got to see Jeremy for the first time in eleven years. He only lived a half hour away—so near and yet so far. Then I called Camellia and told her about Mom's and my "mutiny off the balcony."

"Oh my Lordy, Jacqueline!"

I explained that if my father would not go check himself into the psychiatric hospital, I'd put us up in a hotel command post and I'd hire her to take care of Mom while I plotted my strategy. I was expecting a *huge* rage at this new double-cross and several weeks before Captain Bligh would cave in. I thought he'd have Lieutenant Gerard and Efrem Zimbalist, Jr. out looking for us, and that I'd be on *America's Most Wanted* with my picture at the Post Office as Public Enemy Number One, before he'd *ever* commit himself.

At my request, Camellia reluctantly went over to my parents' house but kept her jacket on and the back door open for a quick escape, just in case Hyde decided to shoot the messenger. She took my call at the appointed time, relayed the ultimatum, and I would have *never* guessed his willingness to cooperate.

"OK-OK, where do we go?" he said as he jumped up. Apparently he'd gotten so worried about us being gone all day, he thought we were in an accident. He was very receptive. Camellia drove him to the psychiatric ward of his regular hospital and stayed with him.

It happened to be Jeremy's son's birthday, so Jeremy took us all out to a fancy dinner. His girlfriend, Carrie, was scheduled to have colon cancer surgery very soon, so their tension was high too. I left Mom with my brother at the restaurant (diaper bag and all) and went to meet Camellia with Dad at the hospital. In front of the doctor Dad was very nice, saying he had absolutely no idea why he was there, but with Camellia and me privately he was really nasty and threatening. Infamous Jekyll & Hyde, back and forth like a light switch. Luckily a nurse overheard his raging threats and told the emergency room doctor. I spoke with the on-call doctor and explained what I had gone through to get my father to this point. Luck was finally on my side. Amazingly, Marcus Welby, Jr. had been through a similar circumstance with his own father and was very understanding. He was so persuasive and soothing that he convinced Dad to sign the paperwork and admit himself, assuring him of how much they would be able to help him. (At long last, a doctor who doesn't need a copy of the movie, *The Doctor*—married, I checked, big time.)

By the time I got back it was already one o'clock in the morning, but Mom was still sitting up just chatting away with Jeremy and Carrie. They were exhausted but she was wide awake—happy as a clam bake.

"Is Dad okay, honey?"

"Yes, don't worry, Mom. I'm going to figure him out and make him better."

"Oh, I don't know—I don't think he'll ever change. He's been like this for so many years you know. Nobody has ever been able to tell him anything. I tried to change him for years, but since I've been sick I haven't been able to fight him. I'm so sorry you have to deal with it now, honey. He's always loved you *so* much and he *never* raged at you before. I just don't know what's gotten into him—tisk-tisk."

I was taken aback by how clear thinking and articulate she was. I took her upstairs, got her ready for bed and slept with her in their spare bedroom. I spent the whole night trying to push her over on her side, as her snoring was reaching a damaging decibel level. I'd just get to sleep when she'd *s-l-o-w-l-y* roll back over on her back, and I'd bolt straight up out of a deep sound sleep with each of those attractive, intermittent snorts. OK, definitely time to get those little nose strips.

(Another idea I heard of is to sew a small rubber ball onto the back of their pajamas which makes it uncomfortable to be on their back so they will want to roll over onto their side in their sleep. Pretty smart!)

♥♥♥

He Ought to Be in Pictures Worth a Thousand Words

I was thrilled to find out that our own favorite shrink, Dr. Endure, was the head of psychiatry at the hospital. He did a CAT scan of Dad's brain as I hoped for a spontaneous, twenty-four hour brain tumor, a lesion, *any* organic reason to explain his nutty behavior, but nooooooo. I could *not* believe it—all Dad's tests were normal, completely *ordinary* for his age. "He's had a number of very tiny strokes and there's a normal amount of dementia for a man his age, but nothing out of the ordinary." Yep, Dad was being a plump peach again—totally "normal."

Four days later Dr. Endure had to work hard to convince me that Dad was ready to be released. He had been talking to him everyday and kept telling me what an absolutely "great guy" my father was and how much he liked him. I *begged* to try some Lithium on him, which I read helps manic depressives, but he said no—Dad was not manic depressive. "How about some Depakote then?" I'd been reading that it can smooth out bad moods. No, no need for any of that. "I've convinced him how important it is for him to get back on the small dose of the anti-psychotic drug and he's been taking it without a problem—so I'm sure he's going to be better now." No, there hadn't been anything even close to a rage and he felt sure that Dad had finally seen the light and the error of his ways. He was just an ordinary guy whose temper got the best of him occasionally.

Ohhh-kay, I get it—Dr. Endure must have studied under Dr. Seuss and Dad studied method acting inside the actors studio with Strasberg perfecting his motivation. My father was anything but *ordinary*. Poor gullible Dr. Endure had no idea that he'd just been snowed by the best, and that he'd never even met Jekyll's alter ego—Mr. Hyde.

Again we had to have the family meeting. Camellia had been such a dear to help me with Mom all week and came too. Dr. Endure's voice was very soothing and Dad really liked him. Seems they'd been having a whole lotta fun as they were both quite jovial, having quite a belly laugh when we got there. It felt more like we were picking up funnyman Mel Brooks from improv acting summer camp and we should be having a cast party. Okay fine—at least there was finally another doctor he'd listen to besides Kiljoy. Then Endure gave him a very stern warning about his temper, and that he didn't want to see him back in there. Dad shook his head back and forth solemnly *promising* that he had learned his lesson. Dr. Endure told me to keep him on the one milligram of the anti-psychotic drug, two milligrams if he got *real* irritable, and he was sure that he'd be "just fine."

We went home and Dad's had another epiphany, "hallelujah!" and he swore, "goddamn it," that he was reformed for good. (Best to clap and sing a little Gospel music here.) *"Oh Happy Days."* Yes in deedee, Elmer Gantry had seen the light and the error of his ways. Praise the Looord. Um-hmm. Let the first man who is without sin, cast the first stone. Oh yes, a repentant sinner has come home. Oh, happy, happy days! Uh-huh, and Jim Jones was running a Club Med in Guyana.

Mr. Magnanimous was back to being sugary syrup and old spice, and everything too darn nice, completely overboard pleasant. When he was *so* saccharine sweet it usually meant he was trying to hyde something. I decided to test it a bit. I could have bought a really nice used car for what I was paying for the rental car all these many months. "Gee, this rental car is really getting expensive for me, Dad."

"Why don't you take that thing back and use our car, honey? We hardly go out." OK, somebody, please… get me some shock absorbers.

"You won't get upset if I do errands or go see Linda with your car and I'm gone for several hours sometimes?"

"Naaaaaah, you deserve some fun. Tomorrow Mother and I will follow you over to the car rental place in our car so you can return it, and then you can drive us home in ours." Somebody, please… pinch me. Okay, Murphy, book him on *FYI* and *WKRP* and oh yeah, definitely on *CNN* for a live interview: "Maniac Miracles—Crazy Cures. Tune in for Larry King *Live!*—Altoona, go ahead."

I decided to go for broke. This should separate the men from the maniacs. Right in front of Dad, I not only *said* Jeremy's name out loud for the first time in a decade, but I also gave Mom an opportunity to assert herself.

"Mom, do you want to call *Jeremy* today and see how he is?"

"Ohhh, that would be just lovely, honey." I couldn't believe it— Dad didn't flinch a nostril hair.

"Okay, here Mom. All you have to do when you want to call him *anytime* is push the number 2 on the phone and it automatically dials his number. She still needed help doing it and then she just chatted away, a happy little camper. (*"A mother and child reunion."*)

"Hi, honey, it's Mother calling." Dad was sitting three feet away in his recliner, intently listening, but he didn't *dare* sigh a syllable. I was watching… waiting… wondering… how long he could hold out. Mom said, "Oh, not too much, honey. Well… my orchids are blooming! Uh-huh, and I had a vivid dream about Ronnie Wright last night." She had told him this story several times at dinner the other night, but to her it was brand new. "I was a little girl and he used to put me on top of his shoulders and parade me all around the one-room school house, calling me his 'sweet little Mariel' out there on the farm." They had a good ol' chat and then she did one more loud exclamation of, "*Ohhh,* my orchids are blooming!" and then she hung up on him in mid sentence.

Dad had not twitched a muscle. There was no perspiration on his brow and I thought I better check to make sure he had not had an aneurysm. I had visions of *Senior Weekend at Bernie's.* Nope, still breathin'. I knew we either had a major breakthrough or I was having the most implausible dream of my life. Okay, call *Meet The Press.*

Wait, I've got it—Time Life Books Presents: *Drugs Make Dreams Come True*. No, no, this is much bigger. Oh yeah, we've got ourselves another mega-hit. Where's Spielberg when you need him? Uh-huh, hold on... I'm getting the image: Disney's Dysfunctional Family Adventure Series Presents: *Loony Tunes Meets Drugzilla*. OK, so I'm mixing my moguls and we gotta work on the title—don't bother me with details.

I skipped to the back bedroom and phoned Jeremy back and told him all about the wonderful breakthrough we had with this new drug. It didn't matter a bit to him—he wouldn't talk to Dad if he was the last living lunatic alive. Okay fine. I switched to Mom's story.

He laughed, "When's that guy gonna stop putting her on his shoulders and get back to the little house on the prairie?"

"I know! Well, you know, Mom always said, 'No good deed goes unpunished.' I thought it would be fun to try to locate Ronnie for Mom and she said he had been a cop in Montana so I figured that it might be easy to find him. Aunt Agatha called and I asked if she knew Ronnie and she said he had died quite sometime ago and that Mom knew all about it. When I told Mom that he had passed away, she cried and cried. Some days she won't remember and go through the whole story and other days she'll remember right at the end and then cry her heart out. It's really hard. I don't know why she keeps telling that story." I could see that Jeremy was having more empathy for what I was going through. It was quite a bit different to experience it firsthand, and he had only experienced one day of it. That one day was worth ten thousand words.

Wow, Dad had passed the *ultimate* test. (Note to self: Buy *mass* quantity of stock in pharmaceutical company.) I was flitting around just so happy-happy-happy. *"I feel giddy, oh so giddy."* Everything was finally working out and Camellia had started working for us again. She was even thinking about moving back in if Dad continued to be so easy to get along with. She was having awful financial problems because of her daughter's predicament, so it would save her quite a bit of money to live in. I was all for it because I needed them to have overnight supervision before I could feel comfortable about going home.

It was the evening of Friday the 13th and Camellia was already gone, having asked for the weekend off. Dad had been so nice for so long, I decided to give him his birthday present early, because I was sure I'd be gone by his eighty-fourth birthday in a few weeks. He had collected quarters for years and had a huge jar of them hidden up in the kitchen cabinet. I got him an automatic coin separator so we could roll the quarters and cash them in. I didn't like having any cash in the house anyway. He opened his gift and was genuinely excited about it.

"Oh boy, let's get the quarters!" he said as he went to the cupboard and reached up and around to the back. "Hey, where'd you put them?"

"They're up there," I said. I'd just seen them the week before when Camellia and I were organizing all the cupboards. I got up on the step stool, reached around, and my heart sank to the pit of my stomach.

Dad asked me, "Are you *sure* you didn't move them someplace with all your rearranging?"

"No, I really didn't, Dad. Are you sure *you* didn't move them?"

"No, I always kept them hidden up there."

OK, who's minding the mint? Not another thing mysteriously missing! It was a Maalox moment as I got completely nauseated. We searched the house together all night. I begged him to think if he may have put them somewhere. He emphatically denied moving them, but he could be such a pathological liar I didn't trust him one bit. I searched Hyde and low, in the cars, the sheds, every nook and cranny that he could have possibly hidden them in. No one had been in the house and you'd really have to dig to find them. Perhaps Camellia "borrowed" them to help with the attorney fees for her dumb daughter and was planning on replacing them before anyone knew they were gone. I just couldn't believe it, but there wasn't any other explanation unless Dad had cashed them in. I called their little bank the next morning and talked to Carla, the manager, who knew me real well by then.

"Please ask all the tellers if my father brought in a really big jar of quarters to cash in." I was devastated when she called back saying that no one had seen him there for quite a while.

Why did *this* have to happen? I adored Camellia. If it was true, I couldn't leave her there if everything could end up mysteriously missing. I couldn't accuse her, I had no proof—but first Kevin's Nintendo and now the quarters. I'd been giving her bonuses for all her extra help and advances because she needed money so badly—so it made sense that she might have been tempted. Nooo, Dad must have done it. God, *please* let me find the quarters hidden somewhere.

I was a wreck all weekend with what to do. Manic Monday came and I gave Camellia the opportunity to admit her error without *any* repercussions, but she flatly denied it. If Dad were acting he really added some special touches to make me believe him. He declared, "Maybe I *did* put them somewhere and I just don't remember right now. I know my memory is getting bad, but I think I'd remember if I moved them—I've saved them for so many years."

"Pleeease, Dad, Camellia is crying really hard and *swears* she didn't do it. This is horrible for her after all she's done for us. Think again—could you have put them someplace for safe-keeping?"

"No, I wish I did! I don't want to have to get someone new *now*. Campabello already knows how to do everything. So help me God, why would I lie?" Hmmm, move away from him—there might be lightning.

I had no choice and it *killed* me to let Camellia go. Teary-eyed, I said, "Camellia, if you didn't do it, I am so *very* sorry. Please forgive me and don't hate me. I can't thank you enough for all you've done to help me. You have put up with so much and I am so grateful to you— but if you *did* do it, I hope you will never do anything like this again and you've learned your lesson. If the tables were turned and I was taking care of your parents, you'd be suspicious too if there were suddenly two things mysteriously missing. I suspect my father did it, but since we can't prove it either way, I'm sorry but I'm going to have to let you go. I wish you nothing but good luck." We hugged and cried, and I prayed harder that those darn quarters would somehow magically turn up.

♥♥♥

Star Searching For Sanity–*or*–All My Caregivers

Now, instead of going "home sweet home" as I *longed* to do, I had to start interviewing for a new caregiver. Maybe it was really for the best. A new person wouldn't have all that baggage of Dad's repulsive rages. I looked into Hospice care, but Mom was not terminally ill so she was not eligible. I put ads in all the papers, called all the elder care agencies, churches, nursing homes, senior centers, hospital discharge planners, and the managers of all the neighboring mobile home parks. I wasted so much time interviewing people in person, whom I had not asked enough questions of over the phone. A week went by and no new: "Camellia—Carinda—or Carmen Miranda."

Dad could see what I was going through and said, "Maybe if we put the silverware out, Camie Jane will come back. In fact, I'll even put out cash—ask her how much she needs." Hmmm, that's pretty clever if he really did it. Suddenly caring Jekyll was back and even trying to help me with the interview process. He'd be nice and meet each candidate and we'd discuss each one after they'd leave and we were pretty much in sync with our opinions. Hyde would come out for short little outbursts, but for the first time, I was consistently able to reason with him and he'd calm down and go back into his Hydeout.

I was determined to get a great caregiver this time. We made our list of non-negotiable qualities: They had to be geographically desirable (GD), a non-smoker (NS), English speaking (ES), have a valid driver's license (VDL), give out their social security number (SS#), have their own car (OC), have elder care experience (ECE), and be emotionally strong enough to stand up to Dad and physically strong enough to take care of Mom. So, what I really needed was a (WW/AB) Wonderwoman/Aunt Bee combo, because whoever I got, would probably end up in (AA) after the experience.

I must have trained twenty gals who either quit after a few days when Hyde popped up, or I let go after a few more. Runaround Sue worked for four days, and then got another offer and quit right after I had gotten her trained. Chrissy insisted her sister would drop her off and pick her up. That lasted three days. Barbarella wanted to take the bus and walk from there. It was winter—she lasted two days. Dirty Diana said she didn't smoke and then reeked when she arrived. The few teeth she had left were a lovely shade of brown. "I'm going to give it up," she wheezed, as I strummed a little *"Dueling Banjos"* in my head. Where's Burt Reynolds when ya need him?

"Get Back Loretta" had never done care-giving before but she wanted to make a career change. She quit after two days of training because it hurt her back. I asked Lavern if she drove her own car. "Oh yes, no problem driving at all," she assured me. She quit after four days because she was afraid to drive on the *freeway* and didn't realize that *that* could possibly be a pre-requisite. "Can I see your driver's license?" I asked li'l Lolita. "Oh, um, well, it's out of date. I had some bad accidents, so I'm not *supposed* to drive, but I do *have* a license."

Carmen had a cousin who would come for the interview. "Does she speak English well?" I inquired. "Ohh jes, berry berry good anglash." Uh-huh... not a *word*, saying "jesss" to all questions, and poor thing,

147

she had to be over three hundred and fifty pounds. She literally wouldn't be able to fit in the little bathroom at the same time with Mom. Gargantuan inhale... and hold it... (please, someone... take me away to Fantasy Island... okay, Gilligan's Island would be swell too)... and massive exhale... all the way out—again.

Layla worked on the weekends constantly crying to me about her horrible boyfriend, Spike, who controlled her every move with raging intimidation. My Dr. Laura-line counseling resonated more like Dr. Ruthless: "Dump him—run for your life!" She had already done nine of the stupid things women do to mess up their lives so I tried to help her get a new attitude about going for ten. I crooned her a few verses of Leslie Gore's, *"You don't own me,"* in-between frequent spontaneous outbursts of, *"Lay-la!"* (Thank you, Eric.) She quit with hurt feelings one morning because I didn't invite her to join us for breakfast.

I was having to do the work, the training, listen to all the sob stories in the naked city, *and* pay them to learn and then not work out. I had to lie on the floor frequently giving direction, my back was so bad. One night we had a power outage and I had to do everything by candlelight. Dad knocked a candle over while I was in the bathroom and we had a lovely bonfire. Yes, you're brilliant, *"Light My Fire"* was unfortunately the new theme song. It was really weird—he was like an obsessed pyromaniac. All candles and matches were removed and I bought more flashlights, rechargeable batteries and a charger, and several fire extinguishers. Okay, Atlas *had* to be standing on my head now, as I balanced on that looong staircase right in the path of *Elephant Walk.*

Then, as Dad's mood improved he showed me how well he could take care of Mom in-between the hard work that the caregivers needed to do. I really only needed someone for about two and a half hours in the morning and two and a half hours in the evening. The rest of the time they were both in bed and Dad could easily help Mom to the bathroom or get her something to eat or drink. Why couldn't we find this person? The split shift was one of the problems. Unless someone lived really close it was a waste of their day to go and come back. I told them, "I'm sure I can find you other work right here in the park." I put notices in the clubhouses of all the neighboring mobile home parks, thinking that would surely work. Nothing. Caregivers with families wanted to be home to be with their kids for dinner. I became *very* flexible. "My parents can eat breakfast between eight and noon. Dinner at eight is *not* required. We're easy!"—nothing.

Boy, I had really lucked out with Camellia when I was going through all that with Dad's rages. Where were those damn quarters! I wished I'd never given him that darn machine and I'd never have known they were missing and I'd been *home* by now. So maybe she'd steal a little here or there—hey, they didn't have that much and at least she'd *be* there. Then it hit me. Oh my gosh, this might be as good as it gets and this nightmare might actually be endless. I must be in *Midnight Express*, in a Turkish torture penal colony, and maybe nobody's *ever* gonna come to get me out.

♥ ♥ ♥

The Price of the Prejudice

I talked to a lady who sounded really nice, but when she came for the interview she was black, and I could see that Dad was not going to be congenial. *Diff'rent Strokes* was not his favorite show. I was so embarrassed when he told her that he'd *never* hire a "colored maid." My face turned scarlet red as I apologized, running after her as she quickly left. Archie Bunker's life-long prejudice sickened me.

"Daaad, that lady was so nice, so *perfect*." He was adamant that he'd just "throw her out on her black-ass," as soon as I went home. I was thinking of getting him a membership in the KKK and sending him and his sheet for a night in Harlem. *("In the Ghetto.")* Whenever he got in these racist modes, I always brought up Frankie, his black assistant, whom Dad thought the *world* of, and who worked with him for decades.

"He was different!"

"Yeah, he was a great guy. I'm sure there are lots of black people you'd think are great if you just gave them a chance and got to know them, and didn't judge them on the color of their skin." You could have moved The Rock of Gibraltar to Alcatraz much easier. Over the phone I interviewed several black women, but I didn't want to waste their time to come for an interview, to have them be insulted and thrown out. There was no way I was going to rid him of a lifetime of prejudice at his age, on top of everything else I was trying to change.

The problem with most of the caregivers, of any color, was that they didn't speak, read or write English very well. How was I going to talk to them long-distance and be sure they were doing things correctly?

Then most didn't drive which meant they couldn't do the errands. The best would be to find someone who *needed* a place to live, but how was I going to trust someone to move in so quickly? I started offering a finder's fee to everyone I spoke with to motivate them to find me the right person. It looked like I was going to have to hire two people, one for the morning and one for the evening shift, and back-ups for both. It became painfully clear how hard it is to get reliable home care. I was so mad that Dad had been so mean to poor Camellia. If she did take the quarters, I'm sure she felt she had earned them.

The problem with the caregiver agencies (I called every single one in the phone book) was that they had a four hour minimum, at sixteen dollars an hour (the women only made eight to ten), *each* time they came out, morning *and* evening. The time couldn't be split up, so I'd be paying a whopping one hundred and twenty-eight dollars A DAY to have someone watch them sleep! I just didn't trust Dad to handle either shift—they had to be checked on in the morning and again in the evening to see what he'd gotten into.

I finally decided that if the agencies could find me the right person it would be worth sixteen dollars an hour just so I could go home and start looking for a job so I could support the whole thing. They came out to interview us and I gave them detailed care instructions. I kept telling them how important English was, a car, that the person be geographically close by and have a strong enough personality not to be intimidated by my father. They sent people barely able to speak English, generally shy and withdrawn, being driven over by a relative from forty-five minutes away. I couldn't believe that they didn't have the person I needed in their databases—okay, file cabinet. These custodial care providers were not licensed so they were not allowed to give medications. A nurse would have to come out and pre-load the Mediset (weekly pill container) for them every week. With all the medication adjustments that we did with Dad, how in the world was that going to work smoothly?

Finally, they found me a gal who assured me that she could handle a difficult elder. She quit on the morning of her second day after seeing Hyde's raging temper as he pounded his fists on the table when she wouldn't give him a *huge* third bowl of cereal, yelling at her that she was *starving* him to death. I knew that none of the professional caregivers were going to put up with him when he got nasty. They did not need to work under adverse conditions because top-notch experienced caregivers are in such demand.

I ended up hiring four of the best agencies that had 24 hour, 7 day access, giving them advance money as retainers, just in case I needed someone in a pinch. That way, once I found my caregiver(s) and went home, if they couldn't come or quit on me, I could call any one of these agencies and they would have a caregiver to the house within one to four hours. I made sure they were bonded, members of state and national home care organizations, and that the caregivers would be supervised.

I ordered Meals on Wheels to cut down on the shopping and cooking a caregiver would have to do. The food was really *very* good, balanced and delivered fresh daily for a few dollars, on a sliding scale depending on their income. Just heat them up in the mini-oven. I showed Dad how to do it by putting a little fuzzy piece of Velcro on the little toaster oven so he knew right where to set the temperature and he was fine with it.

Dad was back to being on very good behavior and helping me again with the interview process. It must have been twenty-plus applicants and weeks later before our miracle worker, Bernadette, walked in. We all liked her instantly and she met every one of the non-negotiables. I was so tired of looking and we all thought she was just fabulous. She really wanted the job and she could even start the next day. Dad looked at me and I looked at him and in unison we looked at her and said, "You're hired!" We were so happy that night and I made my parents laugh as I did the Temptation Walk spontaneously belting out that great Four Tops song, *"Bernadette!"* I made us a special turkey dinner with all the trimmings and we all went to bed thrilled that we had finally found our ideal caregiver who was ready, willing and able. We just had to be patient—that was all.

The next morning it was nine, nine-thirty, ten, ten-thirty and then no answer at her number all day. Bernadette never did show up to sing any songs. Dad and I sadly sat across from each other at the kitchen table practically crying in our corn flakes. I held up a lovin' spoonful, "Flakes Dad, the world is filled with flakes. God I wish Camellia would bring back the Nintendo and the darn jar of quarters and we'd take her back right now. No, even just the quarters."

"Really? I think I'd tell Cookie to keep everything—and *take* the goddamn television!" Barumpbump.

"Good one, Dad."

♥♥♥

The Old and the Restless

One night Mom wouldn't sit still for a minute. She was able to walk a bit now without our help and she'd figured out a way to escape the imprisonment of the side rails by scooting out the bottom of the beds.

"Where's my lipstick? I want my lipstick," she kept repeating.

"I just put some on you, Mom—what's the matter?"

"I want to be in here with you," she said as she climbed in my bed.

"Okay, is Dad being mean or something?"

"No, I just want my lipstick! Do I have any lipstick on?" I kept re-applying it for her and then within two minutes she wanted more and she was ready to get up again. We couldn't leave the lipstick where she could get it because it would end up all over her face.

"Your lipstick is on beautifully, Mom. You... look... mahvelous. You're ready for your close-up with Cecil B. DeMille over on Sunset Boulevard."

"Nooo, I gotta have my lipstick!" she shrieked.

"Mom, what's the matter? Come sit and tell me." I tried hard to get her to calm down, but all she wanted was to go from her hospital bed, to their bed, to my bed, playing musical beds.

Dad woke up and started to get mad at her. I could see his frustration level being pushed over the top and he was just about to blow-up.

"Dad, come talk with me," I said as I sat down with him on the couch and we watched Mom hunched over, slowly darting back and forth like an elder Road Runner. "Remember that day in the nursing home when you sat on one side of Mother holding her hand and I sat on the other?" He nodded. "And she didn't respond to us all day and we cried thinking that she was dying and then she'd see her dead friend, Belle, in the window?" He continued nodding, acknowledging that sad day. "Well, wouldn't we have given *everything* we have, just to see her darting from room to room like she is right now, only wanting her lipstick on?" He thought real hard for a minute.

"You know—you're absolutely right, honey." He lovingly smiled as he watched her now, nodded, patted my knee, and then got up and took her hand. "Come on, sweetheart—let's get your lipstick and go to bed."

It was so amazing to see their love among the ruins. He carefully applied some bright red lipstick to her quivering puckered lips, kissed her, told her she was *so* beautiful and that he loved her more than anything in the whole world. She calmed down immediately, smiled contentedly, and then they held hands and shuffled, side-by-side, back into their bedroom. She went to bed and slept peacefully through the night cuddling with him. It was truly wondrous to see. That old law of, everything is relative (and in my case—everything *is* a relative), was really slapping me in the face again. Yes, it's so true—how you *perceive* a situation, can completely change how you feel about it.

I had taught this concept to my father many years before when he would have terrible road rage at other drivers, thinking everyone on the road was an idiot but him. Then, he'd swear up and down that there was a "goddamn conspiracy" against *him* every time a light would turn red and he'd pound the steering wheel, point, look at me and say, "See!" (The brain serotonin's been a quart low for years.) I always reminded him of a little story to help him to *perceive* the situation differently:

A father and his two young children were at an outdoor café having lunch. The children started running around bothering a couple who were seated at the next table. The father did not discipline them and sat reading his newspaper, oblivious to the noise of his children. Finally the woman got so annoyed she asked her husband to say something to the father. "Excuse me, sir, but could you possibly control your children? They're very noisy and we're trying to have a relaxing lunch here." The father looked up and snapped back to reality. "Oh, of course. I'm terribly sorry—I didn't realize. We've just come from their mother's funeral, and I guess I didn't have the heart to reprimand them. I guess I'm kinda numb." He called for his children to come sit and be still as the couple's attitude changed immediately. "Oh, no, no, that's quite all right. Please let them play—*please* don't stop them," they begged. Yes, they instantly had a new perspective of the exact same situation.

It had worked for a while on my father, at least when I was with him. Every time he started to get irritable when someone cut in front of him, he'd look at me and say, "I know—they just came from their mother's funeral and they aren't concentrating on what they're doing right now, so I'm just going to ignore the bastards and let them go."

"Very good! Now doesn't that help your blood pressure?"

"Yeah... but how in the hell did all these people get on the goddamn freeway at the same damn time, coming from so many goddamn funerals?" No one could make me laugh or cry more than my Dad.

I tried to practice what I preached, knowing that *I* was the only one capable of turning my emotions around. I just needed to *perceive* things differently and take one day at a time. Some days I was very successful at it, and other times I was not. When my father was being deplorable I'd chant over and over, "hate the sickness, not the sicko." Then I'd try to visualize his brain cells short circuiting, trying to talk to each other and connect, but unable to jump over the gapping synapses. "Hey, we can't make it that far anymore—we're too old. Don't get mad at us, we're trying." Then I'd visualize him as a little boy, being beaten and abandoned with no one to turn to. I'd picture him alone and unloved, struggling to survive. Then I'd run through the *long* list of good things he had done for me in my life and remember the love I had always felt. By focusing on the places in the heart that were filled with love, my compassion would return and I'd be able to cope again.

However... one of the times that I couldn't find compassion in any of my organs, happened over a relative-ly insignificant incident. I had taken some clothes to the cleaners and Dad insisted on picking them up late Saturday afternoon. He brought them in and laid them on the couch. I threw the plastic, tags and receipt in the garbage. A little while later I took the garbage out to the big trash bin and dumped it in. After dinner I began putting the clothes away.

"Where's your little jacket, Dad? Did you forget to pick it up?"

"What? I paid for it—it isn't there?"

"No problem. It'll be at the cleaners. You probably left it hanging there when you walked out. They'll hold it for you until Monday."

"Where's the goddamn receipt?"

"I threw it away, but don't worry about it, Dad. I promise you, they'll know you paid for it already."

"Goddamn it! Can't you do anything right?" Oh greeeat, here we go. He would not be calmed now. He became *obsessed* with finding the receipt, dragging the huge filthy trash bin into the house as well as another big trash can to sort it into. Then he scavenged through a week's worth of disgusting garbage looking for this little wadded-up receipt with a flashlight.

"Dad, it's okay, really. Oh all right, here, at least put on some rubber gloves. Let me call and see if someone is still there." Inhale... and hold it... (ring... ring... ring... of course not)... and exhale out.

"NO, NO, NO!" he screamed with tunnel-vision and I knew there would be no stopping his manic mission. "It's not in here! Goddamn it, where'd you put it?"

"Oh my dear God, here, let me look." I painstakingly transferred everything back into the original bin, tiny bit by bit, looking for this miniscule piece of paper. I was covered with goop from practically getting into this horridly filthy trash bin, filled with dirty diapers from Mom. My back was killing me from bending over. Finally, I found the needle in the haystack, but it was also the last straw that broke the caregiver's already weakened back. *He* was thrilled—I'd just saved him four bucks.

"Wait a minute," he said suddenly. "I'll be right back." He shuffled out to the car and came back in swearing a blue streak. "Jesus Christ, son-of-a-bitch! I *am* losing my goddamn mind. My jacket was on the floor of the backseat. It fell off the little hook somehow and it was out there all along," he laughed apologetically.

I feigned a *little* laughter. Mom's jaw dropped open and she shook her head doing continuous "tisks" in disbelief. This was really getting too close for comfort. I didn't like getting this much of a glimpse of my own *Back to the Future*. Oh no, I had to get out of there before I went stark raving mad. Pleeease God, find me the right caregiver who can deal with this insanity. I'm one step beyond my *"Nineteenth Nervous Breakdown."* I'd like to buy a vowel, Pat: Ohhhhhhhh! No, maybe just a stairway to *"knock, knock, knock on Heaven's door."* I must be in Purgatory, waiting sentencing for past sins. Hey, maybe I can get a part in: *Women on the Verge of a Nervous Breakdown—The Sequel*.

Then… another wrenching week of entrapment went by and I just could not believe that after at least twenty more interviews there was still no Alice, Hazel or Maude Frickert. We couldn't even find a quirky cross-dressing Mrs. Doubtfire. Then… out of the blue Dad announced with complete conviction, "You know, I think I'd actually prefer a colored maid." I got such a whiplash turning to look at him.

"Black *Caregiver*, Kunta, not slave. You told me that you wouldn't allow me to hire a black lady." He looked at me totally insulted.

"I *never* said that!" Oh—My—LOOORD. What free-spirit from "The Hood" was homeboy Jake channeling now? I thought that if he started rapping in Ebonics and weaving back and forth singing, *"Ebony and Ivory"* I'd pass out. OK, alert the media. Call up Jane Pauley and Connie Chung—I'm sure they'll scratch each others eyes out to get the exclusive on this one. And get the Eyewitness News Team out here right away. Okay, let's roll that videotape.

"Say it loud—I'm black and I'm proud." Thank you, James.

♥ ♥ ♥

Midsummer's Nightmare at the Alamo

Late one night my father leaned over my bed, softly rocking me and waking me up at four o'clock in the morning. "Are those two guys still here?" he whispered.

"Huh? Oh, Dad, I think you've been dreaming. I'm sure there's no one else in the house." He looked so lost so I got up to walk him back to their bedroom, just as he had walked me back to mine after I had seen the Bogeyman so many years before.

"Yes they were! They were sitting with me right there at the kitchen table and I even gave one of them a cookie—see for yourself."

"Oh, I think you probably just had a really vivid dream. I know they can seem so real sometimes, huh?" I said as I put my arm around him. "So then... what did they look like?" I asked, practicing my psychoanalysis.

"Well, one had on a coons-skin hat!" he said, surprising himself.

"You mean like Davy Crockett?" I was thinking that I'd check the *TV Guide* in the morning and see if ol' Davy had been on the tube.

"Yeah, and the other guy was from the government—maybe even the FBI!"

"Oh-oh, not J. Edgar Hoover in drag I hope."

"No... I'm not sure who he was or what he wanted."

I was diagnosing: Okay, he's contrasting the free-spirited Davy with an authority figure. It's obvious that he's in emotional conflict with a deep-seated desire for... Thank you, Dr. Freudeline.

"Well, let's go see if Mom saw them. She'll tell us if they were real or if you just had a vivid dream." We walked into their bedroom and when I turned on the light he got very excited.

"There! There's one of those guys right there," he said, pointing to Mom in their bed, who's looking at him, arms crossed, shaking her head, "tisk-ing" up a storm in complete disbelief.

"Are you *sure* about that? Let's get a little closer so you can see who it is better," I said as I led him over to Mom's side of the bed.

"Oh, that's no guy, that's my *wife*. Well then... where'd that *guy* go?"

I thought I'd *die* when Mom piped up indignantly, "Well... he most *certainly* isn't in *here* with *me!*"

"Mommy! There were two guys right here. I know what I saw!"

She rolled her eyes. "Next he'll be telling us he saw Harvey with the Easter Bunny." I put him to bed, kissed him good-night and tried to calm his fears. He held onto me like a frightened child, begging me to believe him with such a tortured look, I couldn't bear to leave him.

Instant replay: I'm nine—my new white Persian cat had gotten out and I was so afraid something would happen to him. As Dad leaned over my bed at midnight, I held onto him and *begged* him to let me go look for my cat. After hearing my case, I was *so* grateful when he said we could go look for him. I remember Mom saying, "Oh, for heaven sakes you two, it's dark outside, you can't find him. He'll come home when he's good and ready." Dad whispered to me that we'd go take a look anyway, and that Mom just didn't understand how important it was to me. He bundled me up, gave me a flashlight, and we went outside waking up all the neighbors calling, "Cindy, come here, Cindy!" (We thought Cindy was a girl when we first got him. We had to officially change his name to "Cinderfella" for formal affairs.)

Dad said, "I've got an idea. Let's open the kitchen window and turn on the electric can opener like we're opening him a can of food. Maybe he'll hear it and come home to eat." Wow, what a great idea—my daddy was a genius. I'm sure the cat was evaluating. Let's see: sex? ... food? ... sex? ... food? Hmmm. Finally, we saw him take a big leap over the fence as he came running home, and I was so overjoyed that my cat was safe. We quickly locked the doors together and I saw my dad's face beaming that I was so grateful to him. He was my hero.

It had been many years since I remembered that feeling of being so *relieved* that he had believed me. Now it was like it was yesterday. The tables were now turned as I leaned over my father's bed, and the love in my heart overflowed. "Okay then, Dad—let's get up and look for them, just in case." I helped him up and took him on a thorough search of the house, turning on all the lights and giving him a flashlight.

Mom shook her head as she "tisked" us. "Oh, for heaven sakes you two—there's no one else in the house."

"We'll just make sure that Davy and J. Edgar left, okay? Mom doesn't really understand how important it is to you," I whispered.

He looked at me *so* relieved. "Thanks, honey. You know, I think they must have left now, but they *were* here. Please, you gotta believe me, sweetheart."

"You know, Dad, I think you're absolutely right—I think there *is* a cookie missing here! It looks like those guys are gone now though, and nothing else seems to be missing. They must have been nice guys, not thieves or anything. Let's lock all the doors together so you know that no one can get in and you can sleep better, okay?"

"Okay, yeah, that's good," he whispered. I finally got him back into bed and kissed him good-night as Mom shook her head. I went back to my bed and intensely studied the texture of the ceiling as tears streamed down the sides of my face and clogged my ears. I'd have never guessed that I'd have to be my parents' parent, and wasn't it amazing that I was an absolute natural at it… but then again—I had very good teachers.

As I soaked my pillow, I marveled that there were so many things that I found myself knowing that I should do for my parents because they had done them for me. An early childhood memory surfaced about the first night I went from my crib to a regular bed. Dad got lots of pillows and put them all around me so I would feel more secure. "There you go, don't be afraid," he said as he adoringly kissed me good-night. "Call us right away if you get scared, honey."

Now, Dad was the one rolling out of bed, so I put pillows all around him—but he'd just toss them on the floor. I put big pillows on the floor to soften his landings. That didn't work because he'd trip over them when he got up. I thought I had the answer with children's side-rails that secured between the mattresses. They easily folded up and down, which would prevent them from accidentally rolling out in their sleep. Wrong again, almighty ka-blam breath.

One night I was sound asleep and BOOM, I thought the "Big One" had hit. No, he had forgotten to pull up the side rail after he'd gotten back into bed and he rolled right out. I rushed in, he was okay, nothing broken but his pride. I finally got him back into bed and he crawled over to cuddle Mom. He looked up at me and asked, "What time is it?"

"Two-thirty in the morning, Dad."

"Oh, good, I'll get a few more hours of sleep before I have to get up to go to work at the yard." Mom and I raised our eyebrows at each other and then we looked at him—and then we all burst out laughing.

"Where'd *that* come from, Dad? You haven't worked for years."

"Hell, don't ask me," he giggled, as he hugged Mom close and we all had a belly laugh. I smiled as I covered them up and went back to my own bed humming, *"Memories… like the corners of our mind,"* as moisture started to cloud my vision again—and I realized how absolutely true that sweet song was.

♥ ♥ ♥

chapter♥ten

ENTER TERRI

Finally, we hit the jackpot when we hired a young gal we were all just wild about instantly. Terri (kind of a very thin, very blonde, twenty-something, Annie Hall type) was really fun, with a fantastic sense of humor. She lived fifteen minutes away, had a valid driver's license, had her own car, didn't smoke, was an English speaking American girl, who had experience doing elder care work. BINGO! She seemed strong enough to handle Dad if he got out of hand and physically capable of lifting Mom. She turned down another job to take ours and was even able to start immediately. She was very loving, hugging and kissing them, calling them, "Mom and Dad" right away. She did a fantastic job of taking care of them and after what we had been through to find her, I could not believe that we'd finally won the lottery.

Terri made wonderful dinners and fun desserts and then did so much to entertain us all. She'd put on fashion shows of her latest "finds" from the thrift stores and we were all so tickled with her antics. I overlooked the fact that she was *never* on time and would completely "forget" to do the simplest things I asked. I created a buffer so Dad wouldn't know and figured that when she got into the swing of things she'd get more reliable.

We all got so attached to her that we couldn't wait for her to come over to lighten up our days. Then, after a few weeks she started to dim down and not feel well with terrible piercing migraines. She looked so wiped-out that we all got very worried about her. She'd feel so bad she'd have to lie down and sleep all day. I'd wait on her hand and foot, bringing her food as I did her work, really concerned about her, and never docking her pay. She didn't have any health insurance so I checked into the cheapest ones and pushed her to get something as soon as possible. Then suddenly, Sleepy Beauty would be just fine, up and bubbly, making us all laugh again. She said there was a lot of diabetes in her family, so I warned her that she was going to ruin her health because she nibbled on so much candy all day long. "You're driving your blood sugar through the roof and then you're coming down faster than the Hindenburg." (She didn't get the reference.)

Then... one day I heard Dad screaming in pure agony. I rushed into the kitchen to find him bent over with his index finger jammed inside the bottom center hole of the dishwasher, trying to clean it out. It was really stuck and he was trapped in terrible pain. I quickly squirted some dishwashing liquid on it and he yelled as he pulled his bleeding finger free, tearing it to shreds. As I bandaged him up I was back to the sad realization that someone needed to live there with them. Who knew what he was capable of getting into if someone wasn't there all night when he was up the most. Finally, "Terri-The-Tool-Time-Taylor" arrived and they worked on the dishwasher together and soon got it working right. They hugged and laughed in triumph over their accomplishment, and I was encouraged again. Maybe the medication was really going to work long-term and he would *try* to behave himself because he liked bubbly Terri so much.

I must have earned some good karma because the timing that happened next couldn't have been more perfect. Terri was living with her father, but she was not wanted there any longer. She said, "Wow, you've been here for five whole months taking care of your parents? I wouldn't take care of my father for five minutes."

Seems she was cramping the seventy year old's love-life with his three rotating girlfriends that he used up faster than Kleenex. One morning, arriving late as usual, Terri was crying at being thrown out with no place to go. Opportunity was finally knocking. *("I hear you knockin'.")* I talked to my folks and they were all for having her move in.

She lit up our lives so much and I was so happy at how great everything was finally working out. Oh, so *this* was the reason I never found those darn quarters. I had the perfect new theme song ready too: *"One of God's greatest gifts, is unanswered prayers."* Thank you, Garth.

Late every night *Jake And The Thin Woman* would rendezvous in the kitchen to eat more dessert and giggle about it together. She was like a Martha Stewart Mata Hari, keeping him happy with goodies. Then I started snacking with them and Dad and I began to gain weight, but it didn't look like Ally McBeal gained an ounce.

Things were going pretty well and then one day I saw Terri crying in the corner. Before living with her father she had been living in a small trailer that had been given to her by her grandfather after her abusive boyfriend, Pierce (not even close to Brosnan), threw her out again. Then the grandfather up and died without making the trailer legally hers. Her selfish aunt came and threw her out, and put all her stuff in storage. Well, she'd been unable to pay the eight hundred dollar bill and *today*, all her earthly stuff, was going to be auctioned off to the highest bidder, unless she came up with the money—now. ("Oh Rhett-etta-line, I've just got to have the money to pay the taxes on Tara.") I felt so bad for her and all the horrible things that had happened to her, I decided to loan skinny Scarlett O'Hara the money. I know, I know.

I talked to the storage place to make sure I got the story straight and made sure she got a "paid-in-full" receipt. I hoped that it would make her more indebted to us so I could go *home*. I told her I'd take one hundred dollars a month out of her pay, and when I got eight hundred dollars, I'd save it and give it back to her as a bonus if she worked for us for one year. I could see she was a little miffed that she wasn't getting it with no-strings-attached. I was trying to establish trust because she said she never trusted anyone her whole life because everyone ended up taking advantage of her. I told her that she could trust me, but not to ask me for *anymore* extra money. "What do I look like—Bank of Bolivia?"

♥♥♥

May the Driving Force Be With You

Dad insisted on driving back from Dr. Kiljoy's one day and I sat in the backseat shuttering as Mom gave him directions. "Okay, honey, get ready to turn right... almost... almost... OK—now!" Then, as he backed the car into the carport his foot slipped off the brake, onto the gas, and we went *flying* backward toward Mom's pride and joy sitting duck Mustang. I screamed, "Braaake!" and held my breath as he fumbled to get his foot to the brake. We all got a whiplash when he pulled on the emergency brake inches from a collision. "Oh my gosh, Daaad, your reflexes are just too slow to drive anymore. Please don't

161

argue with me about it any longer and please—you *have* to give up driving." He silently nodded and let me drive everywhere after that.

It was really hard on him because he loved to drive more than anything. When I was a kid we'd go for Sunday drives around the freeway's cloverleaf for fun. Usually every other summer we would take a three week driving trip back to see all the relatives throughout the Midwest. When Mom would fall asleep I'd climb over the seat and he'd let me steer the car as we'd whisper about pulling a fast one over on Mom. She'd open one eye and say, "Be careful you two!"

"We will!" we'd say and have a good ol' time laughing together, stopping for our almonds and then at the Frosty Freezes for our ice cream. Then, on a very regular basis I'd ask, "Are we there yet?"

Dad would hurry, hurry, hurry to get us someplace, and then hurry, hurry, hurry to get us home. And God *forbid* if we wanted to stop and actually *see* something. Oh no, he was on a mission. He had a terrible sense of direction and we would go miles and miles out of our way taking one of his infamous short-cuts. Mom would politely try to tell him that he was turned around again, way East of Eden, but of course, he wouldn't believe her. (Why did Moses wander in the desert for forty years?... He wouldn't stop and ask for directions. Precisely.)

One time we passed some guys on a rocky mountain high road with the hood of their car up and a big sign that read, "Need Water!" Dad was always more prepared than a Boy Scout, so after he drove way past them he put a big container of water out on the roadside and then hollered at the guys, pointed to the container, and drove off.

"Why'd ya do that, Dad?"

"It could be a set up to rob us, honey. I'm not taking any chances, but I hate to leave them there if they really just need water."

"Wow, pretty smart, Dad." Months later, we got a phone call.

"By any chance were you travelling in the mountains a couple of months ago, and did you leave some water for some guys who were stranded up there?"

"Maybe, why?" Dad answered bluntly.

"Well, I'm the guy you left it for and I just want to thank you. We were stranded there for a long time. We had some field glasses so when you drove off, we got your license number and we've been trying to find you ever since. I just wanted to thank you for what you did for us."

"Ohhh, well, I'm glad we were there to help ya," Dad finally acknowledged. He always went out of his way to help people.

162

Then one time, we almost became the Donner Party. We got snowed in overnight somewhere in the High Sierras on our way to Lake Tahoe for Christmas. Jeremy and Marina were following us with their two babies when we got trapped in a blizzard. The heater couldn't be kept on so Dad got out all our clothes and made us put on as many layers as possible. After he was sure we were all okay, he took extra supplies to the other stranded cars. He was always prepared with water but he shared it and we ran out. No problem, he melted snow for us. Lewis and Clark would have been proud. (Lois and Clark too.)

He was a real hero, taking charge, keeping us all calm as he went out in the blizzard from car to car making sure the other people were okay as he coordinated efforts for meeting everyone's needs until he couldn't go out anymore. This was way before cell phones so we had to wait for the snow plows to come dig us out the next day. It was pretty scary and beyond cold, but I had complete confidence in my father—there was no way he'd let anything happen to us. We were finally rescued and so many people came to thank him for his bravery in helping everyone. I was very proud. He always took charge in a crisis—which was the most positive aspect of his need to control.

Then one Christmas we went to visit all the relatives in the Midwest and it was one of those forty-below *Ice Station Zebra* type winters. I've never been as cold since. We got caught in another blizzard somewhere across the Great Divide, on a highway to hell, and were forced to travel at maybe two miles an hour. It was becoming a complete white-out and the road was virtually ice. We started down a long grade and suddenly started skidding into a surreal *s-l-o-w* motion slide, gliding down, down, down, gaining momentum and heading straight for an enormous cement overpass. Dad yelled, "everybody down!" as he frantically maneuvered the steering wheel just right, and we miraculously slid right through the tunnel side-ways, narrowly missing both sides.

As we finally came to a stop, we could barely see a car that had slid off the road and turned almost upside down in the big ditch right in front of us. Dad carefully got our car out of harm's way and then got out in the blinding blizzard. We could hear lots of people groaning—it must have just happened. The car was a convertible so he got his knife and carefully slit the top and we just couldn't *believe* it—a tiny baby fell right into his arms. He brought the freezing child to Mom to warm up and then went back to get the others out. The father's leg was broken and he was wrenched in so badly that he couldn't be pulled free. Dad safely lifted the rest of the family, a mother and five more children, out through the roof. Finally, he was able to get the bleeding father out and we took all of them safely into the next town to get help. What he did was so heroic because those people really could have died—I was very, very proud of him.

Then there was the time at Grammy's (best to play a little Sergio Leone's theme from *The Good, The Bad, and The Ugly* here), when Dad went to the store by himself and some red-necks boxed him in with their cars as he tried to drive off. One punk got out of his car and came sauntering over, but the original Dirty Harry didn't even give him time to talk. He rolled down his window part way and said, "Now look, you *son-of-a bitch,* you don't think I'm travelling cross-country without any protection on me—do ya? I've got a loaded pistol right *here,*" he threatened as he patted the little console box between the seats, that had nothing in it but the maps he never consulted. "Now I may not be able to get all you *bastards,* but I'll tell you one goddamn thing—I'm sure as *hell* gonna get *you!* So, you gotta ask yourself one goddamn question: Do I feel lucky? Well, do ya—do ya punk? Now I'm gonna give you until the count of *three* to get out of my way." I could just see the "look of death" he was giving the guy. "ONE... TWO..." he went for the "gun" and the guy started running and screaming to the rest of the wild bunch to get the hell out of Dodge or Wyatt Earp was gonna blow their heads off. They all laid reams o' rubber getting the hell outta there. We heard Dad's car screech into Grammy's driveway and we ran out to see him white as a sheet as he told us what had just happened. I remember being so impressed and *very* proud of his quick thinking.

There was another time when his quick thinking came to the rescue. He had stopped at a store after work and came out to find several punks with the hood of his new Buick open, trying to remove the battery. He walked by and didn't say a word, went around the corner and then yelled, "The cops are coming! The cops are coming!" The guys all scattered, and he hurried into the car and got the hell outta there. He came home and shocked us with what had happened. I never imagined that many years later I would be saved by using his methods myself.

I had gone to meet some friends for dessert and dancing at a nice restaurant one evening. I got there a little late and I didn't want to valet park and then have to wait for my car at the end of the evening, so I found a spot down the street, around the corner, under a lamp post.

As we were all leaving my six-foot, three-inches tall, two hundred and fifteen pound friend said, "You didn't use the valet? Let me walk you out to your car then—to be safe." We were walking and chatting when all of a sudden, four guys in a convertible came screeching down the street, stopped, jumped out and started running toward us. I didn't even *get* it as I looked around to see what in the world they could be running after. I had no idea that it was *us* they wanted. After all, I had the Marlboro Man with me.

They grabbed us and it seemed like there were knives everywhere. I froze with a sharp blade at my throat and I kept thinking that this just couldn't be happening to me. Two of the thugs started fighting with my friend and they tried to stab him. He narrowly got away and they chased him down the long street. Okay, so I was left alone with Charlie Manson wannabees and they were taunting me, obviously coked-up and higher than kites.

"We're gonna cut you pretty girl—we're gonna cut your face up real good."

I was thinking—what'd *I* do? I had my right hand free and reached into my pocket and pulled out a fistful of dollars (actually only thirty-six bucks) and it fell out of my shaking hand onto the sidewalk. It couldn't have been more perfect if I had planned it. I felt the cold sharp blade move away from my jugular and the thug's grasp on my body loosen. I flashed on Dad's method from the corner of my mind and it was a split second decision as I yelled at the top of my lungs, "The cops are coming! The cops are coming!" I started to sprint, expecting a switchblade in my back. Instead, they frantically picked up the loot as I did the hundred-yard dash in three inch high-heels faster than you can say, *"Helter Skelter."* My heart was pounding through my chest as I made it back to the closed restaurant at the same time as my exhausted friend did from the opposite direction. It was 2 AM as we both yelled "bloody mugging" frantically pounding on the door for help.

The desperados sped off and it was so unbelievable that our eye witness reports did not match at all. My friend saw them as taller middle-aged thugs while I saw them as much shorter, younger punks. Then I realized that I had absolutely no idea what they looked like and I would never be able to identify them, even though I had looked right into each of their faces—as I pleaded and begged for my life.

♥ ♥ ♥

Long Day's Journey Into Nightmares

Dad wasn't trying as hard to behave now that the psycho ward experience was becoming a distant memory. He started having temper tantrums about Terri being late *all* the time, and about her going out and coming home at three in the morning. I was trying to buffer it, not wanting her to experience his wrath and then quit. I hoped that when she got her own sordid soap opera, *Lays of Our Lives*, better organized, she'd be on time and ready to work.

She informed me that she was taking a few days off to go see her new boyfriend, Chip, who was on a construction job in Viva Las Vegas. She told Dad she was going to see her grandmother who was very ill. He was trying to control everything she did and he was becoming completely possessive of her. He yelled, "You mean your grandmother is more important to you than *we* are?" Well, um, actually. Yeah, it got really ugly, a full blown rage, and Terri left for her call of the wild weekend while I was left to deal with his ranting.

I was back to begging Dr. Endure for help. He said, "OK, try going up to *two* milligrams of the anti-psychotic drug now. It sounds like he might be developing a tolerance to it."

Dad was a "Sundowner," which meant he was like a nocturnal vampire bat and his inner clock was set to sleep all day. Then by nightfall he'd be Sleepless in San Francisco, working the graveyard shift, reeking havoc for moonlight madness. I tried so hard to turn him around but I just could *not* get him to stay awake during the day so he'd sleep through the night. I tried turning on the television real loud, blasting Rap music next to his good ear, opening all the drapes and windows, slamming doors, but he could sleep through a nuclear blast during the day. At night, however, his antennae was scanning and he could hear the *slightest* creak in the floor from tiptoeing Terri trying to sneak in every time.

Ray suggested we try some Melatonin to help him sleep at night. Oh-kay. Then his leg cramps were so bad, Dr. Kiljoy recommended we try some Quinine. Ohh-kay. I was so exhausted from trying to fix all his health problems (I'm only one woman), but I went to bed that night so happy, thinking he was going to be just *great* by the morning. Wrong again, almighty mixed pharmaceutical breath.

The next morning when Dad tried to get up he couldn't walk and he was drooling out of one side of his mouth and couldn't talk. I thought for sure he'd had a stroke and called Ray immediately. He said Kiljoy said it was probably just the combination of all the new medications and not to worry about it, it would wear off. After a day and night of pure hell, he wasn't getting much better. By the next day I *begged* Ray to get Dr. Kiljoy to squeeze us into her appointments to take a look at him. I hobbled in with an invalid on each arm and it must have been a pathetic sight. Kiljoy rushed in and barely examined him.

"He'll be fine by tomorrow—just stop the medications for now," she said as she started to rush out. Wait, wait, but I *had* stopped the medications. I was terribly concerned that he couldn't talk, not even one word, and he drooled continuously out of one side of his mouth.

"But... but... do you think he could have possibly had a stroke, doctor?" I asked *totally* concerned.

Kiljoy looked up from her clipboard like she was so exhausted, sighed, and said nastily, "Why do I have to repeat everything *twice* to you?"

Hold on. Is she talkin' to me? Let me get this straight. Is *she* talkin' to *me?* I was so completely *stunned* by her grumpy inappropriate reply that my blood was on instant boil after all I'd been through. I didn't have a second thought about letting her have it. "Well, I guess I'm just a frickin' idiot!" (Oops, did that slip out?)

"Well, *you* want to be the doctor," she retorted. Look out—system overload. ABORT! ABORT! Can't do it.

"Well, *somebody's* got to be!" (Oh my, did I really say that out loud? I guess I'll never eat lunch in their cafeteria again.) Geeese, what a crab. Or, as Mom would say, "Looks like somebody got up on the wrong side of the bed this morning—tisk, tisk." She must have gotten mixed up and taken the Hypocrite Oath today. I was way past livid and gave her the "evil eye" *and* the "look of death" as she walked out. OK, *another* candidate for the movie, *The Doctor*. I swear I'm gonna buy a whole case. Luckily Ray, not a doctor but more help than anyone, came in and calmed me down saying that Kiljoy was not known for her bedside manner with anyone. NO! Really? Ray actually spent some time with Dad and assured me it was *probably* just a little too much medicine. By morning, all of Chewbaca's saliva on the floor should be dried up.

That night Hyde was impossible to handle, getting into *everything*. He took a terrible fall, was completely disoriented, and he pee'd all over the carpet. OK, I'm in *Night of The Living Dead* now. Terri missed her plane and *might* be home tomorrow. She'd gotten a terrible ear infection and might have to delay further. Huhhh? Well isn't that conveeenient? OK, do not pass GO—rather, find yourself right smack dab in the solitary confinement of HELL now.

The next day, I was out of my mind trying to take care of him. I called Dr. Endure and left a pleading voice mail of the situation. He called back promptly for once. "Take him to the emergency room immediately for a shot to counteract the reaction to the combination of drugs and I'll meet you there a little later." Oh my Looord.

I packed up both parents *again* and had to walk each one separately into the emergency room as there were no wheelchairs left and no one came to help us. We waited in the ER all day. They finally gave him a shot and he seemed to get a bit better. They *assured* me that they didn't need to, it was the drugs, but at my adamant, repeated *insistence*, they finally did a CAT scan of his brain to make sure he hadn't had a stroke. I asked to speak with the neurologist, who turned out to be Dr. Dolittle from the psycho hospital. I looked with him on the light box as he compared the new CAT scans to the old ones. We could see several *new* lesions so it seemed he'd had some more strokes. Then, he floored me. Seems these *new* strokes could really just be *old* lesions that showed up better on the *new* CAT scan machine they'd just gotten. *Or,* maybe they really were new lesions, which would mean he'd had some more strokes and it wasn't the drugs at all. So basically, they really didn't have a clue. Welcome to *glitch* gulch and Murphy's Law—*again.*

"Doctor, *please,* are there *any* other tests that could *possibly* tell us what's happening." He thought for a moment and then suggested that perhaps they should do a "Doppler study" of the carotid arteries in Dad's neck to see if there were any blockages. I had never heard the term so I began to do research. It was an ultrasound and the best non-invasive test to see if the arteries in his neck were blocked. Lo and behold, Dad had gone from thirty percent blocked, to *one hundred* percent blocked on the right side, and from forty percent blocked, to *seventy* percent blocked on the left side, in just a year and a half.

"Yes, this would clearly effect his behavior," Dolittle said calmly as he looked at the results. No kidding—who woulda thunk it? So *that* was why he was so nuts—he wasn't getting any blood to his demented brain. I was *furious*—if I hadn't pushed and pushed, they would have never found it. I wanted an honorary degree from Harvard Medical School *and* the Daughter of the Century Award, and I wanted them—yesterday.

♥ ♥ ♥

Clear and Present Danger: The Hospital

Dad needed to have an arteriogram on his neck to see where the blockages were that showed up in the Doppler studies. Terri finally came back from her "sabbatical" so I left Mom with her and went to see Dad the night before his procedure, bringing him some non-fat frozen yogurt and almonds. He was scared and held my hand, and for the first time he thanked me for all I had done for them. I had waited so long to hear that, so of course, I was putty and cried all the way home. It's *really* time to give up on the mascara, Tammy Faye.

When I got home Mom caught me off guard when she anxiously asked, like an infatuated high school girl, "Did he... did he ask about me? Did he say anything about *me*, honey?"

"Well, yes, Mom, of course he did. He loves you and misses you *very* much. He's doing fine and he'll be home real soon." She calmed down immediately, smiling contentedly.

The next day after the procedure, Dad had to be strapped down to prevent hemorrhaging. He had to lie still for six hours and the minutes were going by like hours for him. I sat with him the whole time trying to distract him with my entire repertoire of, "funny things that happened to me on my way to growing up." That took about ten minutes and then I tried to distract him with his favorite—the weather station, but he complained that his eyes were suddenly out of focus. His surgeon, Dr. Ridgly (kind of a dorky Dr. Strangelove type—unmarried, but trust me, way too weird), came in and I privately asked him about Dad's vision.

"The loss of vision is usually permanent. This happens sometimes when a little piece of plaque breaks lose and goes up to the ocular nerve and affects the vision." He was so nonchalant, so casual, as if the ramifications were a splinter. There was no, "Gee, I'm so sorry that your father will never be able to watch television or see your mother's lovely face clearly ever again." It was just the attitude of "shit happens." (You know the long list I was adding *his* name to.)

"His arteries are clogging up at an alarming rate. If we'd caught the right side before it filled up completely, we could have done something, but once it's completely blocked, there's nothing we can do. Sorry about that. We need to schedule surgery on the left side right away."

The next morning the hospital couldn't release him until the doctor saw him on his morning rounds. I waited by the phone all day to get the call to go pick him up and it was already very late in the afternoon.

169

He was calling me every half hour *begging* me to come get him. "Please come get me, honey. I can't take it—please hurry."

I phoned Ray to hear, "He's Dolittle's patient. He has to release him, not us." I called Dr. Dolittle and couldn't believe it.

"He's Dr. Endure's patient—he has to release him." I couldn't figure out why he wasn't Ridgly's patient, he did the procedure! I called *his* office. "Nope, we're not supposed to release him." There appeared to be a gaping *glitch* in the release orders. Terri was nowhere to be found, so I had to pack up my mother again and go down to the hospital with the legal Durable Power of Attorney in my furious hand.

Dad cried when he saw me, reaching out from his bed and begging me to take him home. Flashback Rewind: I was the one in the hospital after the tonsil fiasco, and they had put a thick net over the top of my bed as they probably often did to prevent children from climbing out. I remember being so upset to be in a covered cage that I reached up and tore it—and the nurse was mad about it, being very mean to me.

"Daddy, take me out of this cage—please!" I cried as I frantically reached through the black netting when I saw him.

"You get the goddamn doctor here right now," he said to the nurse. "This child will *never* be in a cage—do you hear me—never!" The next thing I knew he was lovingly covering me up in the backseat of our car, wiping my tears, and assuring me that he would never let anything happen to me, and that he and Mom would never leave me.

Fast Forward: "Don't worry, Dad. I'll take care of this. Are all his vital signs okay?" I asked the nurse.

"Yes, he's fine. It's just a formality. Legally we have to have the doctor release him—we can't do it." I called Ray *again*.

"Unless you can give me a really good reason why he can't go home, I'm using the Durable Power of Attorney to take him out of here. We've waited all day, this is ridiculous."

"Well, you might not want to do that because then the insurance can deny the whole bill."

"Whaaat?" OK, that's it! I told Ray to page Dr. Kiljoy and *someone* had better release my father *now!* (OK, where's Annette and Bobby? I swear I must be at the M-I-C…K-E-Y mouse hospital.) Ray put me on hold as he paged Dr. Kiljoy, and in less than two minutes, glory hallelujah, we were released. Ughhh! I signed the paperwork while they helped Dad get dressed.

We *finally* made it home and Dad went into the bathroom as I got Mom ready for bed. He came out asking, "What should I do about this thing, honey?" He pulled up his sleeve and there, still in his vein, was the entire heplock they had failed to take out of his arm. Oh—My—GOD! The *glitch* is back. I called Ray *again* and even *he* was appalled by this one. He proceeded to instruct me how to remove it. OK, if I had known that hands-on nursing with needles was going to be on the final exam, I would have studied a whole lot harder. Oh-kay, I was now expecting an Honorary Nursing Degree from St. Mary's or at least—*St. Elsewhere.*

The next day Dad was back to being a raving lunatic. OK, I'm in *Dante's Inferno* now. I called all four of his doctors and left pleading messages for help on the weekend. Not one of them called back.

Finally, Ray called in a prescription for a drug that should help calm him down. I ran down to the pharmacy and was told I had a two hour wait. I *begged* the pharmacist to fill the prescription ahead of everyone else as I was so worried about them being alone. Terri was gone, who knew when she'd stroll back in. By the time I got back Dad was hanging from the rafters. I got the medicine into him but it didn't calm him at all. To my horror it had the opposite effect and he was even more agitated. I frantically read over the little sheet of paper that came with the prescription and found that on a small percentage of patients this drug could actually have the *opposite* effect. Inhale... exhale... inhale... exhale... yeah, yeah—you know the routine already.

Then the Academy Awards were on—I never missed it. *Titanic* walked away with all the awards and oh-oh, not good, I had a sinking feeling that I might like to be on it. When I was a kid we always went to the movies, so I had taken my parents to see the much awaited *Titanic.* What a project to get them to the theatre. The second it was over my King of the World father gave it a big "thumbs down" rating. Siskel Senior said (loud enough for everyone in the theatre to hear), "Ahhh, it was real phony looking. The original movie was so much more realistic." Okay, S.O.S. (Save Our Sanity.) Yep, iceberg dead ahead. (Note to self: Do *not* take Dad to parties at Leonardo DiCaprio's.)

I couldn't really enjoy the movie because I spent the whole time repeating to Mom as she cried, the words she had said to me so many years earlier. "Don't be scared, it's just a movie. The camera and the director are over there, and that's actually a miniature." I related all the special effects that I had read about but she still sobbed so hard that I *had* to reach over and cover her eyes for most of it. It was still upsetting her terribly after we got home and she wouldn't stop crying.

Flashback: I had been so frightened by a cheap horror film that Linda and I had gone to see when we were kids that I was having nightmares. I crawled into bed next to my mother and her voice was so soothing, "Imagine yourself standing next to a beautiful waterfall and there's a brilliant rainbow in the sky over a lovely green meadow filled with blooming flowers." She was able to get my mind off Godzilla and taught me how to use visualization that very day. I tried to return the favor and use that lesson from another place in time.

"That was just a movie, Mom. All those people were just actors. Let's visualize a beautiful green meadow, a pretty rainbow and..." (I threw in a leaping leprechaun and a small pot of gold to keep it interesting.) She looked at me, smiled sweetly in recognition and tried to comfort *me*.

"Oh, honey, I'm okay—don't worry," she said as she patted me. "I know it was just a movie—but it made me so sad to see how all those people *really* drowned on that unsinkable ship so long ago." Ohhh.

Time for the pre-op day with Dr. Ridgly for the carotid artery surgery. I hauled the walking wounded there, one invalid on each arm and me hobbling in the middle. Ridgly came in and cheerfully asked how we were. Oh, just *peachy!* I commented that I was upset because when I had called in such desperate need of help he did not call back and his service had promised me that they would have him call. He said that he had gotten the message, but that Dad's agitation did not fall under *his* responsibility and he made a conscious decision *not* to call.

"Gee, I wish you'd had her call me back and let me know that. I had an unbelievably hard day with him. I felt so alone and not one doctor called me back to help me with him."

"I'm sorry, I'm afraid I will not be able to do this surgery. You are not happy with how I do business and I believe I should not do this surgery now—you'll have to get someone else." Well... you know the begging that followed. I would have to kiss his "you know what" to get his help now. Ray told me that he was the only surgeon under our insurance that he'd trust to do the surgery, so I really didn't have any other option that wouldn't keep me there for another month or more. Okay, okay, just give me the darn humble pie and I'll eat crow.

"Oh, I'm *so* sorry doctor, *please* forgive me. I'm just so frustrated trying to fix all his medical problems all by myself for so many months now. *Please* do his surgery—I wouldn't trust *anyone* else. I've checked you out and I've been told that you are by far the most gifted surgeon in the entire Bay Area, maybe even in the whole state." (NOT!) After I had stroked his huge ego and groveled in the dirt long and hard enough, he finally consented to do Dad's surgery—and I was practicing my acceptance speech. "I'd like to thank all the little people, and you, the esteemed members of the Academy for this Best Actress Award. 'You like me, you really-really like me!'" Thank you, Sally.

Next we went to the hospital to do the pre-op blood work. I pushed both parents, side by side in wheelchairs to the admitting office to sign the papers. Suddenly Dad started to get confused and said he couldn't breathe. It looked like a terrible panic attack or a damn good acting job himself to get out of this surgery. He became *so* hysterical that the administrator *insisted* we wheel him over to the emergency room, and looked shocked by my seemingly "uncaring" reluctance. She pushed Dad and I pushed Mom over to the ER. No George Clooney anywhere. After two hours (they didn't do *anything* for him), *I* was the one who talked Dad out of his "panic" attack. Aaaand now everyone inhale... and hold it... (beam me up, Scotty, *please* beam me up—*now*)... and *try* to release the tension... all the way out—again.

After the longest day we finally made it back home and as I put them to bed Dad looked up at me and asked, "What's your name?"

"Dad, it's me, your daughter. Now, what's my name?" I asked him softly as my compassion returned and I took hold of his hand, turned up the night light and put my face closer so he could see me.

"Jenny?"

"No, that was one of your sisters."

"Rosemary?"

"No, that's another one of your many sisters. Dad, you had two kids: *Jeremy* (I thought that would work) and..." He got frustrated.

"I don't know, I don't know—*please* tell me."

"Jackie, Dad. It's me, Jackie, your only daughter."

"Oh yeah, that's right, yeah," he said as he calmed down. My eyes filled with tears, I covered him up, kissed him, and I then went over to Mom's side of the bed to assure her that he was okay, as she had been watching, sadly "tisking" and shaking her head.

Finally it was surgery day. Terri stayed with Mom and I took Dad to the hospital and waited with him for several hours. He got so paranoid that he did a swan dive off the end of the bed, begging me to back-out. "I don't want to go through with it. I have a bad feeling about this!"

The nurses were getting very perturbed as I kept trying to procure their sympathy, but they were at their absolute limit with him already.

"Dad, you only have a thirty percent blood flow to your brain. This surgery will open that up so you'll think better. Please trust me—I love you." I kissed him and as they wheeled him down the hall he *screamed* that he knew it was the wrong thing to do. Inhale... and hold it... (God, *please* let this help him)... and anxious exhale out. I was on needles and pins waiting for him to come through the surgery. If he died now, I'd kill him, because his words would haunt me forever.

Yeees, he made it through the surgery just fine and now the left carotid artery, instead of being seventy percent blocked, was ninety percent open. They told me he would be thinking clearer as soon as the blood started to flow again. I couldn't believe that this hadn't been suggested *months* ago as I reported all his nutty behavior. I made them test Mom's Dopplers right away and hers were about the same. I was back to feeling so much empathy for him as I realized that all his deranged behavior could be because of blocked arteries.

I flashed back to Mom sitting on the edge of our bathtub, crying her eyes out into her monogrammed lace handkerchief when I was eleven. I was trying to console her because Papa's *latest* delicate condition was his gallbladder and he was in the hospital having it out.

"That's why he's been so mean," she sobbed, "he's sick." Then the same scene years later after his open-heart surgery. "So this is why he's been so irritable—he's sick." This went on for hip replacements, numerous angioplasties, vein replacements, etcetera, etcetera.

My father's like the Six Million Dollar Bionic Man, wired with fiber-optic cable and all new parts. He's going to out-live all of us! I wondered if maybe we could get him a brain transplant. I begged God, "Please let *this* be the reason he's been so deplorable. We're running out of things to fix on the 'King of Mean.'"

Additionally, I was struggling with whether I could fix Terri. On the one hand, she was so great when she was awake and with them, and they just adored her—but then, I couldn't believe how messy, ignorant of basic things, and irresponsible she was. I rationalized that it was just because I was there pitching in and doing so much of her work. I kept telling myself that I wasn't in *The Odd Couple* with her and once I went home she'd rise to the occasion—wouldn't she?

Maybe it was just me. No one was going to do things the way that I would. So she'd be late—big deal, they weren't going anywhere.

So she was messy and didn't understand Organization 101. So what? For sure they'd be much better off with her there than they were before I came up and straightened things out. Dad would be getting blood flow to his brain so maybe he'd be much better, and if she didn't get back home on time he could handle the simple things—couldn't he?

Dad was home from the hospital now but he started complaining of *severe* pain in his neck—saying he *knew* it was the wrong thing to do and he just couldn't go on. He claimed hourly that he might even *die* it was so bad. (Promises, promises.) We *loved* it when Mom called him a "big ol' sissy!" Dr. Ridgly said that he couldn't be having *that* much pain—they hadn't cut through any muscles and his other patients were fine in a week. Oh no, Dad would milk this one for a couple months. The moaning and groaning for sympathy escalated if we didn't rush to his side, but then when he didn't think anyone was watching he was up and spry as a free-range rooster. He was always so overly dramatic you never knew for sure what his pain level really was. Mom had spoiled him for fifty-six years, being his enabler, letting him get away with his bad behaviors, so he'd learned that if he complained loud and long enough he'd get a pay-off in attention and sympathy. If we ignored him he'd just keep *pushing* and *pushing* so it was just easier to give him the darn sympathy. I guess he had to have huge amounts of pampering to feel loved—to make up for that damn childhood again. Thank you, Dr. Spock-eline, for that astute analysis.

Flashback: I remember once when I was little the doctor came to our house to treat Dad. (Yes, they still made house calls back in the "olden" days.) Dad screamed so loud in pure *agony* that I was completely traumatized and locked myself in the bathroom crying, thinking the doctor was killing my daddy. Mom had to get a knife and jiggle the lock to get in to calm me. "Jackie, honey, he's just getting a penicillin shot, that's all—I promise!"

Then one time he came frantically running out of the bathroom completely hysterical, *screaming* at us to call an ambulance because he was dying. "My urine is blue!" he shrieked. Mom started to giggle, enjoying torturing him for a moment, and then she informed him that she had put this new product in the back of the toilet tank that made the water turn blue and he was actually going to live a while longer.

Oh yeah—we *really* enjoyed never letting him live that one down.

♥ ♥ ♥

Joined at the Hip

One day Mom floored me when she looked down at her naked hand that didn't have her wedding ring on (it was in the safety deposit box) and cried, "I look like a *slut*. People are going to think we're just shacking up!" I covered my mouth, trying so hard not to laugh—she was *so* serious about it being such a scandal. So when I decided to throw them a party for their fifty-seventh wedding anniversary, Dad loved it when I suggested that we get Mom a new wedding ring. I bought her a simple gold band, but with cubic zirconias, as she tended to lose things down the toilet. It really warmed my heart to see how much joy this little ring brought her. When Dad put it on her finger, "With this ring," kissed her and told her he loved her so much, the vows they took fifty-seven years before hit me hard: "For better, for worse... for richer, for poorer... in sickness and in health... until death..." I *prayed* I would not have to part them.

I invited everyone in their phone book over for an open house. Terri complained that she hated meeting new people and after she did Mom's hair she was leaving. I wanted her to meet everyone so she'd know who they were if they called or came over. Finally she got on the glamour-detail and did Mom's hair and make-up real special, and we put a lovely dress on her and she looked so beautiful. It took an act of the Independent Council but we actually got Dad out of his stinky, stained white coveralls, into the shower, and into a pair of slacks and a nice shirt, literally for the first time in years. Oh yeah, he was a fashion emergency—even on one of Mr. Blackwell's lists.

Terri needed a long nap after fixing Mom up—poor baby, she was just exhausted. She finally came out at the end of the party to met the three people who were left. I was so disappointed in her, but I was afraid to go back to square one and have to try to find someone else after the horrendous "in search of" that we'd gone through before.

The party turned out so nice and friends they hadn't seen in years came to see them, well, Mom anyway. They all marveled at how wonderful she looked and how clear thinking she was. Mom and I had a lovely time, but all Dad could grumble about was that someone had stolen his new glasses (that had been sitting on top of his head all day) and that they had been *purposely* switched on him.

♥ ♥ ♥

chapter eleven

AMAZING ARIANA

Terri and I were so happy to find a great gal for the weekend shift. Ariana was a cheerful young woman (kind of a spirited, Laura Ingalls type) and all of our non-negotiables were met. She was very bright and caught on quickly. I felt really good about her, but after all I'd been through I was beyond cautious. After her first day of training, Terri casually announced that she was going away for the weekend leaving Ariana in charge.

"Terri, you know I'm going home any day now. Ariana's only had a couple hours of training. Are you telling me that you'd leave my parents alone with her and not even be close by to check in on them?"

"Ariana can handle it, and *I'm* going out of town to see Chip in Los Angeles," she informed me as she sashayed out.

Well… she better know Peggy Fleming, because she was skating on very thin ice. I wrote her a letter, listing all of her responsibilities and ample compensation. If we could not agree or reasonably negotiate, she'd have to move out ASAP and I'd have to find someone else. I was not going home to be this frustrated with her during long-distance phone calls everyday. I left the letter in her room and waited. She finally came home, went in her room, and shortly thereafter came out screaming at me—calling me a "bitch" and that she'd be moving out.

Resigned inhale… and hold it… (at least I hadn't pre-paid my airline ticket)… and blow it out—again. Okay fine. I was going to be stuck at *Buzzard's Crest* for a few more months. I'd have to get her moved out, find someone else, get them trained, get them moved in, have a nervous breakdown, and *then* maybe I could go back home. No, I was going to have to come up with Alternate half-baked Plan *C*. Calgon, take me away—*ple-e-e-ase*.

Bright and early the next morning perky Pollyanna came skipping out of her room, sprinkling pixie dust and being ohhh-so charmingly cooperative. She acted like *nothing* had happened. "How about if I help train Ariana tomorrow and the next day so she'll know enough, so that I can take the weekend off to go see Chip?" I just looked at her, wondering how many more Psycho Sybils were in there. No wonder she related so well to Dad. She went on and on about how she could make it all work and then she said the magic words about my being able to "go *home*." Toto help!

I stuffed down the nasty comments and heard myself say, "That's sounding more reasonable." She phoned Ariana—no problem for her. Okay fine, *maybe* I would be able to go home soon. I was probably making a huge mistake, but I just didn't have anymore time, patience and stamina left in me. Mom and Dad loved her so much. It would be fine once I went home—wouldn't it?

♥ ♥ ♥

Oh What a Mangled Web We Weave

Thank goodness my basic instinct told me not to go home yet. Apparently, Terri of Sunny Brook Funny-Farm had not gotten the time-off memo, and had been AWOL since early Friday morning— and it was already Tuesday at three o'clock in the afternoon when she happily strolled in telling me all about Universal Studios, fiddle-de-de, and all the fun they'd had. Uh, frankly Scarlett. She was trying *really* hard to divert the attention away from the fact that her two days off had somehow turned into four and a half, without even calling me. She was just happy-go-lightly and I was completely furious-go-figure.

"Terri, all this is just *teetering* on being interesting, but we need to talk—now!" Ohmigod, no time to talk *now*. She had to go pick up The Chipster who was back in town with her.

"Apple Annie, this is a *job*. You can either do the job as I need it done, or you can't."

She called me a "fat ass" and with that, she was gone with the wind. Well, isn't that special. I'd finally had enough. Being called a "bitch" is one thing, but a "fat-ass?" OK—*now* I'm mad. I phoned Ariana and asked if she'd be interested in a full-time job. To my delight, she was. I phoned Mary Jo and hired her to be the case manager, checking on Ariana. As always, Terri cooled off and called later.

"Oh, you know I didn't mean any of that," she laughed.

"Terri, you have no boundaries, appreciation or respect, aaand big surprise, YOU'RE FIRED!" (Adios to my eight hundred bucks.)

"Fine, *bitch*—then take this job and shove it!" CLICK.

Yeeaah, she had spunk—I *hated* spunk... but, I *loved* the fact that we now had a *real* cliff hanger.

♥ ♥ ♥

The Hardest Working Maniac in Show Business

Ariana began full-time work the next day and I was pleased to see how efficient she was at getting Dad into the car to take him to the doctor's. When I heard them drive up I went to the back porch, so happy to see him really laughing hard about something with Ariana. I went down the steps to help him get out of the car.

"How are you feeling, Dad?"

"Ohhh... not so good, honey." Ariana's head spun around, her mouth fell wide open and she burst out laughing.

"That's not what you said five minutes ago, Jake!" Oh, she nailed him good. He could *barely* get out of the car, grunting and groaning and carrying on. She looked at me shaking her head in total disbelief. "Jaaake, this is pathetic! You were able to get in and out of the car just fine a few minutes ago at Dr. Kiljoy's. Now all of a sudden you're acting like you're about to keel over and die right here."

We looked at each other rolling our eyes. I *loved* her! She was not going to let him get away with his "poor-pitiful-me act," *ever*. Oh, he was going to *hate* that. How absolutely perfect.

"And now without further adieu, right here on our stage, ladies and gentlemen—step right up for the really-big-show. Jake, the human chameleon, will instantaneously change into someone else right before your very eyes. Now you see him—now you don't."

(You'll want to play a little James Brown departing from the stage music here.) *"Please, please, please."* Dad shuffled stage right, doing a *great* Helen Keller impersonation with outstretched arms, playing blindman's bluff, barely able to find the steps and embellishing his performance with major grunting and panting sound effects. "Thank you, thank you very much." Ohhh yeah, Elvis is gonna leave the

179

building all right. When he didn't think anyone was watching, he was up and down those steps like Jake up the proverbial beanstalk. Then he looked back at us like he was expecting a piggyback ride up the steps. Okay, time to get him a rhinestone cape for these performances and sell tickets for P.T. Barnham.

Ariana looked at me in shock, shaking her head in total disbelief. "WOW, he's a *great* actor!" she said, still having trouble closing her mouth. "But then... how can you tell when he's lying?"

"Oh, real easy—his lips are moving."

OK, get me Opie on the phone. Oh yeah, I'm sure he'll want Dad for a big part in his next blockbuster: *Cocoon Deux: Metamorphosis.*

♥♥♥

Pros and Cons

"I'm so glad you got rid of Terri," Ariana nodded, as we sat at the kitchen table discussing the details of her new job.

"Yeah, I know, she was driving me nuts. I hope she moves out ASAP."

"What I mean is... you really made the right decision."

"Yeah, why, what are you trying to say?"

"Well... uh... you didn't know she's on drugs?" she said totally surprised. I looked at her stupefied. "Oh yeah, I'm positive she's on speed. I thought you knew."

"WHAT! You mean meth-amphetamines? Is that the same thing?" I asked, looking around for the *Candid Camera* crew. OK, it *had* to be sweeps week.

"Uh-huh, I left my husband because he got into speed and I'm an expert at spotting people who are on it. I knew it the first day I met her."

"OH—MY—GODDD! Are you sure? If that's true, I'm *furious* about all this time I've wasted on her. Why didn't you tell me?"

"I'm sorry, I *really* thought you knew. It seemed obvious to me and I was just part-time and she was going to be my boss. She always talked really fast and would be buzzing around and then she'd crash and sleep all day. You told me she ate sweets all the time but she never gained any weight and she was so thin. She was always feeling sick and would have to lie down and then miraculously she'd be up and bubbly. All the crazy logic, the mood swings, and then you told me that she'd disappear real late at night. It just all fits the pattern of what they do. Oh, and then you said that she protested that she didn't want to meet anyone at the anniversary party. That's because they're afraid someone will spot it and figure them out."

"I just *cannot* believe this is happening," I sighed as I sat there in catatonic silence—the wind had been knocked right out of me. Finally I said, "Do you know what speed looks like?"

"Oh, yeah, and what it smells like too," she said proudly.

We looked at each other, paparazzi strobe lights went off, and suddenly we were racing each other for Terri's room for search and seizure. Dickless Tracy found some right away on the nightstand— a crumpled up cellophane wrapper from a pack of cigarettes.

"Here! This is what they like to use a lot," she said as she carefully unwrapped it, holding it up to the light so we could see all the powder residue. Then she took a little sniff. "Yup, there you go—crank!" she announced, as she held it for me to get a whiff. OK, we have a loser!

"Nice work, Shirleylock." Wow, I was learning how to be a D.E.A. agent in the valley of the dolls. Suddenly we became a mini Miami vice squad. We rejoiced in triumph as we found her drugs and then each piece of drug paraphernalia: the baggies to store it, the mirrors to cut it, the straws to snort it, the papers to smoke it. And the final answer is: things that can completely destroy your life.

Then the worst. She had all the pictures I had taken of everything in the house in her drawer. I shuddered as I remembered she always talked about her pawnbroker friend. Thank God all this happened and I fired her. Who knows what she would have hocked to feed her habit.

I immediately phoned our local Hyde Street Blues and to my delight, San Francisco's *finest*, Officer Toffee (kind of a really cute, T. J. Hooker type—and even seemingly single!) responded, ready to protect and serve. Mmmm good. He confirmed what Emma Peale had already ascertained: "Crank." He went to his squad car and came back nodding, "She has a Felony warrant out for her arrest for defrauding welfare." HUGE con-artist inhale... and hold it... (why?... someone please tell me... why me?)... and shout it out-out-out!

"What! A felon?" I was ninja fighting mad. Officer Toffee said to block the doors so she couldn't get in if she came back that night and to have the locks changed. "What about all her stuff? She owes me eight hundred bucks and she's not getting a thing until I get paid back." Columbo and Nancy Drew stood there shaking their heads.

"She's a *drug* addict," Toffee said. "She doesn't have any money or it would be up her nose. Forget about the money and just threaten to turn her in if she doesn't come get her stuff out of here right away. All you want is to get rid of her without any problems. We'll pick her up later."

Ariana saw that I was not going to give up. "How are you gonna get money out of her? She doesn't have a dime—she's a drug *addict*. You just don't understand. They'll sell their soul, their families, everything they have, *anything* for a high. I know, I was married to one."

I was way past infuriated about this recent episode of: *Lifestyles of the Ignorant and Infamous*. I said, "Well, I'm gonna make her an offer she can't refuse." *("Watch me now, hey!")* I just wanted a *little* revenge. Was that so wroooong? They laughed at me but I was not deterred. "Go ahead and laugh you two, but don't touch that dial and just stay tuned."

Mom and Dad woke up wondering what a cop was doing there again. I showed them what we had found and Mom started to cry. "Oh no, not our darling Terri on drugs. We loved her *so* much."

Dad sadly shook his head. "Don't show me anymore. I feel sick seeing it. I can't bear to think of what could have happened after you went home. Just do what you have to do to get rid of her, honey. I don't ever want to see her again." I assured them that I was gonna take real good care of Terri, and once again we were a united family front. Yep, blood's thicker than crank.

Luckily, Terri did not try to tiptoe in that night. Lucky for *her*—I was an experienced street fighter. ("Yo, Ariana!") Hey, it could have been better than Joan Collins and Linda Evans in that little wading pool.

The next day Terri called up, like ya know, with a real nasty bad Valley attitude—totally. "I will be ov-er to get my things to-mor-row."

"Weeell, I've got some good news and some bad news for you, Terri. You're welcome to all your *stuff* as soon as you bring me eight hundred bucks—*cash*." I heard her mouth drop open.

"What? You can't do that! That's my *stuff!* How dare you... you fucking bitch! You're going to be just like the storage place and hold my property ransom?"

"For once in your pathetic life—you are correct."

"I knew you were nothing but a bitch! I *knew* I couldn't trust you!" Blah, blah, blah, she ranted on and on, but I was beyond immune to raging insults. Slings and arrows, tisk-tisk. "Anyway, you *can't* blackmail me—I'll call the police!" Oh my-my, goody goody gum drops. I started dancing a little Mashed Potato Time.

"Oh *really?* Well, they'd just love to hear from you. In fact, they were just here and there's a felony warrant out for your arrest for welfare fraud *and* they'd love to discuss your little amphetamine drug habit with you, YOU LITTLE SPEED FREAK!"

Ya coulda heard a heroin needle drop. There was stunned silence on the other end of the line and for the first time in her disgusting low-life, Terri was completely speechless. I did, however, hear her stomach turn over a couple times in the deafening silence and then—CLICK.

Terri's boyfriend, Chip, the chump, called me looking for her, crying that he'd lost his job for taking the four days off to be with her. The night before last they were *so* "in looove" and planning on moving in together. *("Wild thing, I think I luv you.")* But, alas, last night she didn't come back to the Motel Six where they were staying. *("Suspicion!")* So, early this morning he called her ex, Pierce's number (it was on his motel bill), to hear Terri answer, obviously in bed with Pierce. (Don't ya just hate when that happens?) Terri proceeded to drop Chip like a hot hash pipe *("the thrill is gone")* and told him she was going back with Pierce. *("Heart-breaker!")* Now, Chippy was drunk as a skunk *("I've been cheated, been mistreated")* trying to drown his sorrow, lamenting to *me* that she had used him.

"Well, join the club! (*Or*, as Mom would say, 'That's the way the cookie crumbles—tisk!') Chip, she's been playing you for what she could get out of you for months now. *("Everybody plays the fool.")* Get over it and move on." Wow, I cannot believe this—we have another perfect spin-off: *The Bold And The Brainless.*

To make the never ending story a tiny bit shorter (aren't you glad?), I did get all of my money back when Terri showed up with The Chip Dip (now that's what you call a glutton for punishment) and his twin brothers—Bud Wiser and Bud Light. She tried hard to get me to sign a receipt but I pointed out that the exits were clearly marked. ("Show me the money!") "I guess crime doesn't pay... YOU," I said as I carefully counted the bills, holding each one up to the light making sure they were real. (She had bragged once that she knew where to get fake bills.) I grabbed Ariana and did a little Tango and cash singing my favorite, *"Gypsies, tramps and thieves,"* as they drove off.

Yeah, she had hustled me good. As Dad always said, "I never met a con artist I didn't like." And what happened to the two suckers in her life—Dumb and Dumber? History. She burned Pierce and then torched

Chip's heart again. Her references turned out to be bogus and I heard that most of the affection she gave my parents was a complete act.

Well... I had worked for a prestigious private detective agency while I was in college, and I'd handled all the top-secret, undercover, espionage, sting work. (Okay *fine*—I was a Rent-a-Serpico at the drive-in theatre, busting kids for putting Milk Duds in their pockets before they got to the cashier.) But hey, I had forgotten how much I enjoyed my moonlighting. The name is Bond, Jacqueline Bond. I think we can wrap this case up and safely say: "Case closed."

I was delighted that the adorable Officer Toffee returned frequently to the scene of the crime to check on me, uh... us. He and Ariana were so impressed with me as I fanned myself with my eight hundred bucks and cited my favorite line from Faye Dunaway's, *Mommie Dearest*: "Don't FUCK with me!" I had Perry Mason and Inspectress Clouseau roaring. After Ariana left I rambled on to Officer Toffee about all I'd been through with caregivers and begged him to run a check on Ariana for me. He was kind to help and I was so relieved to find out that she was squeaky felony-free. One time, shame on Camellia. Two times, shame on Terri. But *three* times—shame and just shoot me!

Ariana was finally the angel I had asked for. Please God, let her be *"The One."* (Oh boy, I used to say that about men, now I was saying it about caregivers—sad, really sad.) She was available to move in but I made it very clear that this was my last crusade to try to keep my parents together. If I had *any* problems with her, I would be back to put my parents in a home, one way or another. I told her it was nothing personal, but once she heard all I had been through she tried hard to get me to relax and not worry about anything.

Ariana had lived a lot for a twenty-six year old gal and she was very bright with a great sense of humor. She called the doctors and she was strong enough to get what she wanted out of them. She brought her mom, Tina, over to be her back-up and she was a doll too. Ariana had a darling little five-year-old boy, Gary, and I could see that she was a wonderful mother. She'd gotten rid of the dead-beat husband and had a new man now, her boyfriend, Lee. Dad wouldn't let him in the house—slamming the door right in his face. I was back to heavy breathing as I worried that this would be the next straw to break caregiver number 41's back.

♥♥♥

chapter twelve

ONCE AN ADULT, TWICE A CHILD

Grammy always used to say, "God makes teenagers and the elderly mean on purpose—otherwise, their families would never be able to let them go." What a calming, insightful perspective and how absolutely true it was. Yet, I realized that even with as mean as my father had been to me, it was still so hard to face that one day I'd have to let him go—forever. Because of all the good things he had done for me in my life, and for whom he had helped mold me to be, I just couldn't give up trying to help him—until I had to.

I asked Mary Jo if there was anything *else* I needed to do before I went home. "You really should have DNR's posted by their beds."

"Oh-k—what are they?"

"**Do Not R**esuscitate. You need to have a talk with your parents and ask them if they are not breathing or don't have a heart beat, if they want to be resuscitated. Ariana has to be instructed to call 911, you can't put that decision on her. Once 911 is called and the paramedics come out, the law says that they must resuscitate them unless posted by their bed is a formal DNR for each of them. That's the only way the paramedics can peacefully let them go. Resuscitation can be awful, their ribs can be broken and I've had so many patients who wake up absolutely furious that they were brought back for another round of horrors in the hospital, begging to be let go. You can get the forms from their doctor."

Tortured responsibility inhale… (how was I gonna approach this?) and exhausted exhale all the way out—again. I waited until they both seemed clear-headed and then I swallowed hard and forged ahead one morning at breakfast.

"Ummm, Mom, Dad, I need to ask you both something."

"What, honey?" Mom said, and Dad looked up inquisitively from his Ben Gay rubbing ritual.

"After I go back home and you're here with Ariana, if something happens and one of you passes out, Ariana will call the paramedics. If you're not breathing or you don't have a heart beat, do you want them to bring you back? I mean, do you want them to resuscitate you if you're already gone?" Whew, I got it out—maintain, maintain.

"HELL NO!" Dad yelled, and Mom shook her head emphatically.

"Oh-kay, well… then we need papers signed by both of you and Dr. Kiljoy, and we'll tack them on each side of your bed. If you'd like to be revived, put them in the drawer that day—if you don't, leave them up. It's your decisions and you can change your minds. I'll have Ariana ask you what you want everyday."

"We won't change our minds, will we Mommy?" Dad said, as he gently took her hand.

"No," Mom said as she sadly shook her head.

I looked at them, looking into each other's eyes, holding on to each other as they kissed tenderly, and I was filled with so much love and then, so much overwhelming sorrow. I hurried to get up. "OK then, that's settled. Umm, I have to go to the bathroom," I said as I turned away not wanting them to see. More precisely—I needed another *box* of Kleenex.

"I'm fahklempt—talk amongst yourselves."

♥ ♥ ♥

Old Age Is Not For Cry Babies

Dad would say over and over, "Don't wait for the goddamn golden years, I'll tell you that!" He got such a kick out of a little poem that a neighbor gave us and he loved sharing it with our visitors—and then they'd all have a good old golden-age giggle.

> The Golden Years have come at last
> I cannot see, I cannot pee
> I cannot chew, I cannot screw
> My memory shrinks, my hearing stinks
> No sense of smell, I look like hell
> My body's drooping, got trouble pooping
> Yes, the Golden Years have come at last
> The Golden Years can kiss my ASS! (Author unknown)

186

A few days later the golden pond years were kicking Dad's behind again. He wasn't looking at all good to me, kinda gray, so I had Ariana take him to see Dr. Kiljoy. Sure enough, he needed to have *another* angiogram, this time on his heart. They found a seventy-five percent blockage and he would have to have angioplasty the following week. I was planning on going home, but then I was torn because if something happened to him I'd just have to turn around and go back. I finally decided that there'd always be *something* else to fix until the day he died. Ariana was working out great, every detail seemed to be resolved, and I was finally ready to go home, and by Jake, I was going.

I could not believe it—late one night, after nine months of pure HELL, I finally made it back to home sweet home. I eagerly opened my front door and stepped from the outer limits of sanity, into my brave new world. I did a midnight run to the balcony and exclaimed, "Free at last! Free at last! Thank God Almighty—I'm free at last!" Thank you, MLK, Jr.

Yes, both Jekyll & Hyde made it through one more angioplasty just fine. Well, they did fall out of bed at the hospital because they hadn't put the side rail up. Must have been a *glitch*, but what else was new? Ariana and I got cell phones and she reported to me at *least* twice a day long-distance. Managing their care continued to be a consuming and costly job as I did it, *"From a distance."* Thank you, Bette Midler.

I had installed an baby monitor when I was there so that Ariana could hear everything going on in my parents' room from her room. (Note: audio plus *video* baby monitors are now very affordable.) One day Ariana heard a sad pillow-talk conversation as Dad comforted Mom. "Don't worry, honey, we'll be together. We're getting closer now and it'll all be over soon."

"Oh, Ariana, it must be awful to lie there, day after day, just waiting to die. I know it's virtually impossible to get them up, but is there *anything* you can think of to get them to do something?"

"I'll try harder to get them interested in things. Jackie, if your father passes away first, I'll take care of your mother always."

"That's so comforting to know. I sure hope that's the way it happens."

"Oh, guess what? I've figured out a way to get Mom to stay up longer in the morning. I do her hair and make-up in front of the television now and we watch *The Golden Girls* together and laugh."

"That's a great idea."

"And then we watch the *Jerry Springer* show and she loves it."

"Oh my gosh, *Apocalypse Now*. You've got to be kidding. Not *my* mother—I can't believe it," I said laughing.

"Yeah, and yesterday these two girls and this guy were on and Mom said, 'What are those two girls talking about? Oh my, look how short her skirt is, Ariana, tisk, tisk, tisk!'"

"Jackie, I whispered to her, 'Mom, they're *lesbians*. They're lovers and they don't want that guy around anymore, and he's in love with the one with the short skirt!' Her eyebrows went up and her eyes got real big and her mouth opened wide and she said, 'Oh my Looord! Well, no wonder, he looks like a scum-bum. They're real cute girls, but *her* skirt is just too darn short, if you ask me.' Jackie, it was such a crack-up, I was just dying. Then the girls got in a big ol' fist fight with the guy, and Mom was completely glued to the TV. You should have seen her, rooting for the girls to beat up the guy and yelling for them to 'let the scum-bum have it.' Now she can't *wait* to watch that show with me every morning. She'll whisper to me so your father can't hear, 'Ariana, let's turn on that show before Jake gets up and wants all our attention.' I'm telling you—you'd get such a kick out of her, Jackie!"

"Oh Ariana, you're doing such a *fantastic* job. I'm forever grateful that you're there with them. Without you they'd have to be in a home and they'd probably be dead now. Isn't it funny that you have the world's easiest and hardest patients to take care of at the very same time? And just think, you have complete job security because as soon as you're done with them—you can come here and take care of *me*."

"Oh, don't worry about that—you know I would."

♥ ♥ ♥

Still Crazy After All These Years

Ariana and I charted our calendars with Dad's behaviors daily so we learned to expect about seven days of Jovial Jekyll before Horrible Hyde would pop up to reek more havoc. I said, "Hyde's due back from his hyde-atus in Purgatory any minute now, Ariana."

"Yep, I'm all ready for him," she laughed.

Sure enough, the next day as Ariana was doing their laundry, Dad came of out the bathroom screaming, doing a complete *Full Monty*. He took all the wet towels out of the washing machine and chased Ariana around the house naked, throwing them at her, yelling that she was doing *her* laundry in *his* machine. I was really astounded by that one because he had always been *sooo* modest his whole life. "Oh Ariana, I'm so sorry you had to see the family jewels," I said, starting to laugh.

"No, I didn't—I refused to look down. I didn't want *that* image etched in my head!"

"Oh, good thinking, honey."

The craziness continued with him unplugging the vacuum every time she tried to use it and then taking off Mom's diaper the minute she put a new one on her. Then he kept stripping all the bedding off the bed right after she'd make it. That night he tried to break into her room with a screwdriver in the lock. "He was trying to be so quiet but then he finally gave up and went back to bed." A chill shot through me as I flashed on a story about a man who had never been violent in his whole life and then one day killed his sleeping wife with a hammer.

"That really scares me, Ariana. If he hurts you I'll never forgive myself. Please lock up all the sharp objects. You know to dial 911 at the slightest danger don't you? Don't wait to see the cataracts in his eyes."

"Oh yeah, I will—don't worry." She was a pretty strong young gal so I knew she could handle herself, but what if he busted down her door ("heeeere's Jake!") and then bludgeoned her to death like Janet Leigh in the shower and then went after Mom?

I could just hear his attorney. "But your Honor, he's never done anything like this *before*." Not to worry, Judge Wapner gets tough and throws the book at him: Two counts of first degree murder—life in prison without the possibility of parole. Uh-huh. He'd pull out a "Get Out of Jail Free" card and be released after three days because of *exemplary* good behavior.

♥ ♥ ♥

Liar Liar, Pants on Fire

Dad had not tried to drive since his foot "slipped" off the brake taking us on Mr. Toad's Wild Ride in the carport. Once I was gone, however, he started telling Ariana that he wanted to drive again. I told her to keep the car keys with her at all times and to just evade his pleas with distractions. One day she saw him going out the back door with his jacket on. "Where ya going, Jake?" she called after him.

"Ohhh, I'm gonna take a little ride. Please give me my keys and please move your car."

"It's too dangerous for you to drive because you don't see that well anymore. I'd be happy to take you wherever you'd like to go."

"I'm the *boss* here and I say move your goddamn car!"

"Well, I'm sorry. I know it must be hard on you but I can't let you hurt yourself or some innocent person now can I?"

"*Goddamn it!* I was driving Model T's before your grandmother was born. You work for me and you do what I say, or else!" he yelled inches from her face, pounding his fists on the kitchen table again. (It's really amazing that it's not concave by now.) Ariana didn't flinch—she'd learned my mother's technique already.

Later that day—Ariana came back from the store, threw her purse in her room and got Mom up to go to the pottie. Dad sprinted out of bed, doing the ten yard shuffle racing into her room. Ariana's little Gary yelled, "Mommy, Mommy, he took the keys out of your purse!"

"Jaaake," she said to her other child, "give me the keys. It's too dangerous for you to drive. Where would you like to go? Come on, let's go out for a nice ride. I'd be happy to take you if you give me the keys."

His wrinkled up nose started to grow. "I don't have 'em." She tried every which way to persuade him into giving her the keys on his own. No luck all day. Nope, he just didn't have them. I tried to talk some sense into him.

"Daaad, I'm sorry you can't drive anymore. I know how much you love driving but we can't risk an accident. What if you hurt someone? Wouldn't you feel just awful? Please give Ariana the car keys."

"I don't know where they are—I swear to God."

"If you won't give her the keys on your own, you're forcing me to have to get them away from you forcefully. You don't want to go through *that* do you?" He went into a rambling rage calling me every nasty name he could think of and then hung up on me. Yeah, yeah, I know—I'm a bitch, I'm a sleazy whore again. Gee, no *new* terms of endearment?

Mom got so upset with his screaming rampage she passed out at the table, head-first, right into her mashed potatoes. Ariana rushed to the phone, but Dad physically blocked her attempt to reach it with his outstretched arms and wouldn't let her call 911.

"You let her *go*," he commanded. "That's what she wants!"

She must have just fainted because she came to quickly and Ariana asked her if she wanted to go to the hospital. "No! I just want to go to my bed and go to sleep, and I *hope* I *don't* wake up to this living hellhole." My poor Mom.

When I checked my answering machine that evening my father had left me several nasty messages saying that if I took his car keys away he'd, "Put a curse on me, so help me God!" Perfect, a new theme song for the week: *"I put a spell on you."* Um, gee, could you possibly remove the *existing* curse, prior to putting on the *new* curse, Mr. Hocus Pocus Voodoo Maniac?

I told Ariana to wait until he went to sleep and then she could find the keys. She was up all night trying to find them and then called me exasperated when nothing turned up. "Did you check in his shoes?"

"Jackie, I swear to you, I have looked absolutely *everywhere* and they are not here," she said in total exhaustion.

"They're on his body then, I'm sure of it. Did you check inside little Napoleon's jacket? He kept his hand in there for a reason."

"Yes, I patted him down and they weren't in his pockets. I can't *imagine* what he did with them." Hmmm, tricky little dictator.

The next morning clever Boris Badenov tried to get her to go to the store for some milk for his cereal. "Not until you give me your keys, Jake. I'm not moving my car out of the way."

"I told you, I *swear* I don't know where they are. I wouldn't *lie* to you. Maybe you lost them." ("Yeah, that's the ticket!")

Ariana called with a brilliant plan. "Once I finally get the keys away from him, I'll get a copy made, and then I'll go buy The Club, and put *that* on his steering wheel. That way he can keep his darn keys and he still won't be able to go anywhere."

"Wow, I'm ashamed I didn't think of that myself, Ms. Einstein-ela. You're a genius. Maybe try secretly asking Mom where he hid them."

Ariana got Mom up and took her in the back bathroom and tried to get her to rat on Dad, and for the first time ever Mom was mean to Ariana. "He's a good driver and that's *our* car and you can't have it, and you can't have *my* dining-room set either!"

Ariana called again, "Jackie, I found the baby monitor covered with a blanket so I couldn't hear them last night. It appears he's brain-washed her all night because now, she sounds just like him! You won't believe the words coming out of your mother. Here, you try to talk to her."

"Hi, Mom. You know, Dad's eyes aren't good enough to drive anymore. You don't want him to accidentally hurt someone do you?"

"No, of course not, honey, but Dad's never had an accident and that's *our* car and he's a good driver and I can drive *too*. And that's *my* Mustang out there and I can still drive her if I want. And that's *my* dining-room set and nobody's gettin' it!" Alllll-righty-then.

Ariana took Mom to the kitchen table and waited for Dad to get up. All of a sudden she heard, "clink, clink, clink" as he walked to the table. "Jaaake, what's that clinking noise I hear?"

"I don't hear nothin'." Uh, General Stockdale, turn up your hearing aid. Dad *refused* to wear his hearing aid, so, he really didn't hear nothin'.

"Jaaaake, lift up your pant leg, on the double!" He finally complied, and there, *masking-taped* to his calf, were the car keys. "Okay, so you lied to me, huh? You've had the keys all along. I'm very disappointed in you, Jake. Are you going to hand them over?"

"NO, they're mine!"

"Okay, then I'm not going to speak to you today." She made breakfast and fed Mom her last few bites and didn't acknowledge him.

Eventually he couldn't stand it. "You're a traitor. You're supposed to be on *my* team. You called Jackie and tattled on me."

"Jake, there are no teams or sides here. We're all working together to keep you and Mariel together in your own home as long as possible. You've lied to me for days about the keys—you had them all along."

"I don't give a goddamn about the keys. You're a traitor!" he yelled across the kitchen table as he pounded his fists.

"And you're a liar," she told him.

"Traitor, traitor, traitor!" he started chanting and pounding.

"Liar!"

"TRAITOR!"

"LIAR!" Nah-nah-nah-nah-nahhhh. Poor Ariana realized that she was starting to lose it. She retreated into the "cone of silence" and ignored him for hours.

Finally he gave up. "OK! Will *this* make you happy?" he said as he untaped the keys from his leg, which by then was losing all circulation.

"Yes, very happy indeed. Thank you very much. You will not be getting dessert tonight for lying to me." (Major exhaling required here.)

Then... he started harping that he *had* to have his eyes tested again. We learned that if she just ignored these demands, usually by the next day he would forget all about them. This time he wouldn't let up and made her absolutely miserable for days on end. Back to the optometrist, Dr. Cei. I had her call ahead and explain the situation. Even if his eyes were somehow better, he shouldn't be driving with such slow reflexes. Next door to Dr. Cei's was the hair dresser who colored Mom's hair, so she made appointments for the same time. Dad insisted that Ariana stay with Mom during her hair treatment while he went next door to Dr. Cei's. In a half hour he came back to the beauty salon wearing a big smile. "Guess what? I have great news—my eyes are much better and I can drive!"

"Reeeally? That's great," Ariana told him as she smelled a skunk. "Stay here with Mom and I'll go get a written report from Dr. Cei."

Ariana said Dad sounded just like an elderly Mr. Bill getting smashed. "No, no, no, nooooooo."

Dr. Cei protested, "I *never* said that. His eyes are *terrible*. He barely has any vision left out of one eye and the other one isn't much better. I told him his eyes were quite bad and he should *not* drive at all."

Ariana walked back to the beauty shop to find Sorry Cyclops with his head down like a bratty school boy waiting for his detention. "What am I going to do with you?" she scolded one-eyed Jake.

"Well... it was worth a try," he sighed heavily in the agony of defeat. "I'm a very good driver," said Rainman.

A few days later he called me practically crying, "Dr. Cei doesn't know *anything*. I know I can still drive. Why are you doing this to me?"

"Oh, Dad, tell you what—Ariana will take you to the DMV and you can take the eye test. If you pass it you can drive home, no questions asked, okay?" (And be sure to drive past the grassy knoll.) I had Ariana talk to the supervisor at the DMV and if by some fluke Mr. Magoo passed the eye test, they'd make him take the written test too. She had it all lined up and they were dressed and ready to walk out the door when suddenly he had a change of heart.

"Awhhh, you just take us wherever we want to go, Ariana. I don't really feel like driving anymore."

Okay, all together now: let's inhale and hold it... and breathe out. And another deep inhale in... and hold it... and out. And *again*... hold it... that's right, continue hyperventilating until you just don't give a—you know what!

♥ ♥ ♥

Unsolved Maniac Mysteries

Mom loved Ariana's little boy, Gary. Every morning he'd run to Mom's side of the bed and yell, "Good morning, Mariel! Can I get you some milk, Mariel?" Then he'd whisper very apprehensively, "Good morning, Jake." He'd watch Dad like a baby hawk and then squawk to his mom if Dad was doing something he shouldn't. Jekyll nor Hyde could get away with *anything* with Gary on the tattle-tale detail.

Gary loved to play "peek-a-boo" with Mom and he'd insist on holding her hand at the kitchen table. "I used to teach kindergarten," she'd tell him. Then he'd love to hear all about her horse, Nellie, that she rode bareback to the one-room school house when she was five.

Gary had been staying with his grandmother for several months and he couldn't wait to tell Mom all about the camping trip they'd gone on and the big fish he'd caught.

"You did—how wonderful, Gary!" Mom said delighted.

Dad yelled from bed, "What the hell are *you* doing here again? You woke me up."

"It's one o'clock already, Jake, way past time to get up," Ariana said, "and don't talk to him like that. He's just a little boy and he's not hurting you. Mom loves having him here."

"Well, goddamn it, this is *my* house and *I* say who can be here, not *you*." She took Gary to her room and explained that the old man was really sick, and even though he looked grown up, his mind wasn't even as old as Gary's. From then on when Dad would be mean, Gary would look at Ariana and say, "His mind is only three years old, huh, Mommy?"

I felt *terrible* about it. Not another "Jeremy" in the making. I made Ariana promise me she'd get Gary out of the way of Dad's verbal abuse immediately and give The Abominable Hulk more drugs. I'd rather have him chasing windmills and drooling from too much medication, than to have this sweet child psychologically damaged as Jeremy and I were.

As always, Repentant Jekyll would return. Later that evening Ariana couldn't believe it when Dad said, "Hey there, Gary, so good to see you again. I understand you caught a big fish—come tell me all about it!"

♥ ♥ ♥

Gentle, Dependable, Overnight Disbelief

Ariana started jogging at night for some much needed stress relief. Dad told her she couldn't leave the house and had to stay in their room and watch them sleep. "You better read your contract and stay here and clean the goddamn kitchen."

"The kitchen is spotless and I don't know if you've heard yet, but slavery was outlawed quite a long time ago, Jake."

"You better not leave, goddamn it—I'm warning you."

"I'll be right back. I've just *got* to get a little exercise." When she came back something smelled terrible. "What's that repulsive smell?" she gagged as she searched through the house to find the source. "It's coming from in *here*, in your room. Do you guys have gas? Mariel, do you need to go to the pottie again?"

"No," they shook their heads, "we're fine."

"Well, let's go to the pottie anyway, Mariel." She pulled down the sheets, and there, was diarrhea absolutely everywhere. Mom couldn't feel it and they both couldn't smell it. Mom was so embarrassed.

"Oh, Ariana, I'm so sorry—honey, I didn't know I did this." The diaper couldn't hold it all and it went all over her nightie and on the carpet as Ariana helped her to the bathroom.

"Oh, don't worry about it, Mariel—that's why I'm here." It was a huge job to clean up and then she said, "Okay, Jake, it's shower time, and then I'll change the bed and scour the bathroom."

"Nahhh, I don't need a shower *tonight*."

"I said get up right *now* and get in the shower! And don't just run the water and wet the towels trying to trick me again either. If you don't pass the smell test, you're going right back in."

She scoured everything, having to wear a mask and wishing she had a rubber suit. She finally got them back in bed and couldn't believe what Dad asked her, "Did Mariel have a BM yet?"

Please God, don't let Ariana quit. She handles these crises with such an uncanny ability to know what to do. She has more patience than anyone I've ever known. Who would put up with this? Without her, I'll be up a clogged-up creek without any Kaopectate.

A week went by and then Ariana reported that Mom had diarrhea *again*, completely all over everything. "Jackie, it smelled putrid, like something died in there. I was just *gagging*."

"Oh, Ariana, I'm so sorry you have to clean that disgusting mess up *again*. Did you notice any link with what she ate?" She said no, there didn't seem to be any correlation. She had to give Mom a shower, change all the bedding, clean the bathroom and carpet, and put everything through the washing machine. She finally got it all cleaned up again but it took hours. Thank goodness she was making more money than she ever had in her life—she was sure earning it.

The very next day she called beyond FURIOUS. "Jackie, Mom had diarrhea again *today* all over everything that I just cleaned up yesterday. It went absolutely everywhere and it was so *gross*. I just couldn't believe it and I asked her what she thought might be causing it, if she's upset with Dad or something. She felt so bad and kept apologizing and then you won't *believe* what she told me. She said, 'I'm so sorry, Ariana—maybe it's that little pill that Dad gave me.'"

"Jackie, I went through the *roof* at your father. I shrieked, '*What* pill? Dad's not allowed to give you any pills!' He just denied he'd given her anything as I started tearing the entire bedroom apart right in front of him, until I finally found his private little hidden stash of Ex-lax pills! Jackie, he's been giving her Ex-lax! I've never been so mad in my entire life, but he just laid there denying it. Then, I nearly had a fist fight with him trying to take the pills away from him, and then he almost busted down my door kicking it as hard as he could while he *screamed* at me to give them back. I was *so* upset because everything had diarrhea on it and I had that disgusting mess to clean up *again*. I told him to get up and help me but he refused. *Then*, he asks me in all seriousness if Mom had a BM yet!"

"Oh my *gosh*. I'm *so* sorry, Ariana. Well, at least we know what's causing it. Take everything out of their bathroom. Next he'll be pouring Drano down her throat to get her to go pottie. Honey, I'm so sorry you had to go through all that *again*. You really are amazing to continue working for us. I am *so* indebted to you for hanging in there. He would have accidentally killed her again if it wasn't for you."

As I hung up I realized that I was completely exhausted and I wasn't even there. I wondered how much more patience Amazing Ariana had to put up with such insanity. How was I ever going repay her? All my bonuses, gifts, cards and raving words of praise seemed so insignificant compared to what she did for me and my parents—every single day.

♥ ♥ ♥

Even Ripley Won't Believe It

My phone rang one morning. "Hi, Jackie, it's me, Ariana. I'm sorry to call so early, but I just *have* to ask you something," she said giggling.

"Uh-huh, it's okay, what, honey?" I said waking up.

"Ummm... did you ever call your father a 'fucking cock-sucker?'"

"Whaaaat?" I couldn't believe I heard the question correctly.

"Well, Mom's been so mad at Dad this morning and she wouldn't tell me why. Finally I got it out of her. Apparently he's been ranting and raving about you and Jeremy, calling you both nasty names while I ran to the store. She finally got so furious that she yelled at him that he had gotten rid of Jeremy but he wasn't going to get rid of you too."

"Yeaaah," I was waiting for the *interesting* punchline.

"She said that you were sitting at the kitchen table and that he attacked and choked you with his bare hands... and you couldn't breathe... and then Camellia came running from next door... and she barely got him to let go of your neck... and you screamed... and then you called him a 'f---ing c-ck s--ker!' Jackie, my jaw hit the *floor* to have your sweet mother use that kind of language. She *never* uses foul language like your father does all the time. I said, '*Mariel*, are you *sure* you didn't dream that?' She said, 'No I didn't!' and then she repeated it *again*. I've been just dying all morning and I just had to call and ask you if it were true or if she dreamed it."

OH—MY—G'. My mind instantly went into auto-search of "All Files" trying to remember the gory details of that terrible day when my own father tried to choke me to death over HBO. "This is absolutely unbelievable, Ariana—I'm living one of my life's most embarrassing moments. I swear, I honestly don't remember saying *anything* remotely even close to that, but maybe as I was getting close to death without oxygen I snapped into premature Turret's Syndrome and who knows *what* I said. Geeese, it's like having little kids that pick up your bad words!"

"Oh my Loord. Well, Mom's the maddest I've *ever* seen her. Then she said, 'Jackie called him *that* and you know what, Ariana? He *is* a f---ing c-ck s--ker!' Jackie, I thought I'd die trying not to laugh, she was *so* serious. Now, every time your father goes into the bedroom to lie down with her, she yells at him to 'get out!' Now he's sitting on the sofa, arms crossed over his chest, head down, like a scolded little boy being made to take a time-out. (How about a *knock*-out?) He's been sitting there for a really long time and looks *really* sad.

Wait... oh my gosh, he just tried to go in to see your mother again, *begging* for her forgiveness, and she yelled at him, 'Get out of my room, you... you... *fucking cock-sucker!*' Jackie, I don't know how much more of this I can take—my sides are *killing* me."

Oh my dear GOD! Okay, that's it—get me a meeting with Bill Cosby right away. Oh yeah, tell him I've got a hot new summer replacement series for him: *Seniors Say The Silliest Things.*

Later that day Ariana called to let me know that Mom's foul language had finally let up, and I decided to tell her the secret I had been keeping for several days. "I have some bad news, Ariana. I'm very upset—my brother blacked out and fell down the stairs, having a heart attack several days ago. I warned him that he was a heart attack waiting to happen. I'm terribly worried about him."

"Oh no, is he okay? Are you going to tell Mom and Dad?"

"He's home now but very lucky. They had to do angioplasty on a ninety-eight percent blockage in his heart. I debated telling you, but now he's home from the hospital and hopefully he'll be okay. What I need to know is—do you think Mom can handle knowing about it? Dad won't care a bit, he hates him so much, but I'm worried about Mom being so upset that it would cause her a stroke or something."

"I don't know. She's still so mad at your father for saying all those bad things about you and Jeremy all day. Let me check it out at dinner and I'll call you back, okey-dokey artichokey?" It tickled me pink—she'd picked up one of Mom's favorite sayings.

Later that evening she phoned, "Jackie, you *won't* believe this one. I sat with them at dinner and Mom wouldn't speak to your father and when he'd try to touch her she'd give him the sternest evil-eye you ever saw and he'd look *so* sad and finally give up. I told them I had something important to tell them but that they shouldn't worry. I said that Jeremy was home now but that he'd had a very mild heart attack and he had to have a little angioplasty. Your mother handled it great. She calmly asked lots of questions, but then, I just couldn't *believe* it—your father started to *cry*, really hard. I was so stunned. I think he still *really* loves your brother. I know it was real too—I'm getting to know him pretty well."

After I could close my mouth I said, "Ariana, I just can't believe it. He's hated him so much—you just have no idea."

"Well, all that anger they had earlier just went away and they held hands and talked about Jeremy, their little boy, their son. Dad wants to call him and go see him right away and wants to talk to you too. I told him, 'See, Jake, what if your son had died and you didn't get a chance to ever talk to him or ever see him again.' He *burst* out crying and just sobbed, 'Yeah, I never thought about that. Too much time has gone by—I *have* to see him tomorrow.'"

"Wow, Ariana. I *never* expected a reaction like that after all these years. I'm so happy he is finally ready to make up. Let me talk to him before you let him call Jeremy though. I need to prepare him that Jeremy probably won't talk to him right away—if ever."

Ariana took the phone to Dad and suddenly he talked to me like the father I wished was always there. "How's Jeremy, honey? Is he going to be okay? Please tell me what's happened. Please tell me he's okay." I should have known, Dad was always there if we *needed* him. It was so interesting how he was able to be completely normal when he really needed to be. Then I realized—if he was needed, he felt loved.

"Well, he's home now but he's going to need lots of rest. He can't have any stress and he can't be upset by anyone."

"I want to call him. I really need to tell him something."

"I'm *so* happy to hear you say that, but I don't want you to be mad if he doesn't want to talk to you. You have to understand that he's going through a lot right now and he may not be ready to talk to you."

"Oh, yeah, no, I won't get mad. I just want to tell him how sorry I am about all this lost time and… and that I love him very much."

I might as well get electro shock therapy. After I got up off the floor I said, "That's *wonderful*, Dad! Ariana can call his number for you and you can tell him that." I decided to confront his temper while he sounded receptive. "I need to talk to you about your bad temper."

"What? I've been good."

"You know, if Ariana quits, I can't come back up there to take care of you or interview forty more people. You're gonna be real sorry when I have to put you both in a home. There isn't going to be any discussion about it once I get there. I was there for over nine months, I'm done. You better decide which is better—Ariana, or going into a home?" I threatened him real good with Shady Pines and then I asked, "Does Ariana keep the house clean?"

"Yeah, real nice."

"And what about her great meals, and keeping Mother so beautiful, and giving you your medications, and taking you to the doctor's and staying there even after you've been so horribly mean to her?"

"Yeah," he acknowledged softly.

"Well, then I think you better start thanking your lucky stars that she stays and puts up with you. She could quit and you're going to be real sorry, because I'm not going to be able to keep you in your home any longer. Do you understand? She can get lots of jobs with less stress than what you're giving her. Please behave and treat her nicely."

"OK-OK, I'll try—I will. I just want to call Jeremy now, that's all I'm worried about right now. I have to tell him how much I love him." I couldn't believe it. I thought that if they made up, Ariana and I should split the Nobel, finally some, *Peace* Prize.

Dad phoned, but Carrie said Jeremy wouldn't talk to him. It was going to take a while, if ever, for that to happen. As the story went, they'd had a huge blowup the last time they had seen him. Dad had locked all the doors and wouldn't let them out as he proceeded to tell Carrie all the "horrible" things Jeremy had done during his growing pain years. It must have been pathetic. He ran from one door to the next like a madman, blocking them from getting out with his outstretched arms. Then he caught Carrie's fingers in the door as she tried to escape. She was begging Jeremy to call the police and it almost came to blows and basically—that was the last straw for them.

Unfortunately, they had gone there because I had urged Jeremy to make up after the previous fight they'd had in the hospital, for Mom's sake. She'd just come home and missed Jeremy so much. I was so upset that my "plot" for a reconciliation hadn't really gone as well as I had planned. I hoped that these fights would eventually blow over, but they never did. I prayed that they'd both realize what a waste it all was and make up before anyone died, but I decided I better not interfere again and I'd support whatever decision Jeremy made. *Our* relationship was back on track and I would not run the risk of losing that again. Every time I caught myself starting to concoct another ingenious "scheme" of how I could maybe fix it all, I immediately practiced my new theme song over and over like a melodic mantra: *"Let it be... let it be... let it be... let it be."*

♥ ♥ ♥

chapter thirteen

FRIENDS AND FAMILY MATTERS MOST

M y savings were really dwindling, and then I got hit with capital gains tax because I had not been able to reinvest in a new home—having been stuck with my parents for so long and I *just* missed the deadline. Of course, the new law was not retroactive to me. I had tried so hard to get an extension from the IRS, but you know how that went. Sorry, death and taxes. Thank goodness my parents had always taught me to save for a rainy day. Who knew it would turn out to be—The Flood? Where's Noah when you need him? It seemed like every time I tried to pull myself up, get stronger, and started to get going again—something else pulled me right back down.

In addition to my brother's heart attack, I was devastated by the unbelievable news that a very dear scriptwriter friend, MaryAnne, was diagnosed with a brain tumor. She had encouraged me to write for twenty years, and the last thing she said to me as I stood next to her hospital bed, making her laugh with the details of my father's antics, was that she wanted to proof my manuscript for me. A few days later, I was inconsolable when she was gone, but I know I have her valuable guidance—even as I write this.

Then, another friend had to have a grapefruit-sized tumor removed and a hysterectomy at only thirty-nine years old. I was the face she woke up to after her surgery, assuring her that she would be okay.

Then, a week later, another dear friend stepped on a sewing needle and it went so deep into her foot she had to have surgery. Being the only one of our friends not working, I volunteered to go be her feet for several days.

I just got home from that when I was hit with the shocking news that one of my most favorite people on the planet just barely made it to the hospital after a freak accident and was rushed in for emergency brain surgery, hemorrhaging, and almost died.

The very next day, another dear friend needed a place to stay after her eye surgery and I just couldn't say no after all she had done for me. I just couldn't believe the non-stop string of woe that was happening around me. I thought maybe it was time to officially start "Jacqueline's Caregiving Service." (*"That's what friends are for."*)

I realized that it's a good thing that we can't see our future shock. Your mission, should you choose to accept it: Become a successful executive, travel the world and meet interesting people, fall in love, feel great, lose job, outgrow guy, wear out *"Unbreak My Heart"* CD, have terrible undiagnosed back pain for years, endure spinal surgery, and then experience a seemingly endless nightmare taking care of your disabled elderly parents while draining your bank account and gaining weight. *But*, on the brighter side, you'll be a lot stronger, fatter, and impoverished at the end of it all. Uh, gee, no thanks—gotta go. Got any good old-fashioned Black Plague out there? Oh good, I'll take that *and* The Day of the Locust.

Amid the many sorrows, the only good thing happening was that my brother and I were finally communicating regularly for the very first time in our lives. I had completely let go of my anger at being the sole caretaker for our parents (you can't make anyone do anything they don't want to do, so get over it—bygones), which allowed me to truly enjoy the sharing we were finally able to do.

"Do you think that Dad really had an affair with Marina's aunt, Marsha, Jeremy?"

"Nahhh, that woman was completely crazy and she flirted with every man she could find. I think Dad got a little flattered by it and I think Mom just got jealous."

"Hmmm, that's very interesting because Marina said the same thing. What about violence? Did you ever see Dad be physically abusive to Mom? I never did."

"No, I never did either. It was all just a lot of hot air."

"Did Dad ever hit you?"

"Well, I got 'the belt' spankings over his knee a few times when I was a kid."

"You did! Wow, Rawhyde, I didn't know that!"

"You mean you never got the belt?"

"No, never! Dad never laid a hand on me, not even a swat, well... until the Bay Area Strangler tried to choke me to death over HBO— but other than *that*. So, did you ever spank your kids with a belt?"

"You know, I did a few times—I'm sorry to say. You can't do that nowadays, they'd put you in jail for child abuse."

"See, you just passed down how you were taught. The sins of the father—like father, like son. I'm sure his father did the same thing to his kids and probably even his father before him."

"Yeah, you know, that's probably true."

"I never got any physical affection from Mom and Dad, did you?"

"*You* didn't either? I thought for sure that *you* did."

"No, I *felt* loved, but they were never demonstrative at all. I always said my back itched so I could lie on Mom's lap to get some physical contact with her. I guess that's the way they were raised too. You know, I don't ever remember Grammy being affectionate either. And then Mom's father was a compulsive gambler who lost all the money they'd get from their yearly crops at the poker tables in town. Mom told me that he'd beat Grammy real bad, pull her hair, and throw his eggs on the floor if they weren't done just right. He burned all of Grammy's family photos and wouldn't even allow her to write to her own parents. I heard that Mom was really the only one of the seven sisters who ever stood up to him. One time she hit him with a broom and jumped on his back when he was beating the hell outta Grammy."

"Wow—really?"

"Yeah, and then on Dad's side, his mom died when he was ten, and the father beat the kids and was a raving alcoholic out there on the Ponderosa. The kids were all put in orphanages and probably abused there too. So neither Mom nor Dad saw much loving interaction when they were growing up. It's sad, no one ever taught them how to really love. Then, they both struggled to survive through the ten years of the Great Depression, actually living *The Grapes of Wrath*, and then the war, and then Dad's near-fatal electrocution at work. When you add it all up, it's pretty amazing that they held it all together to raise us as well as they did."

"Wow, you know... I never thought about any of that. And you're right—they just passed down how they were taught. And you know what? I've passed the same damn thing down to my own sons. I've really been trying to correct that too. For the first time, just a week before my heart attack, I was able to hug them and tell them that I loved them. I was worried that they wouldn't be able to say it back to me because we've never said it before. I was so happy when they hugged me back and said they loved me too. I gotta tell ya—it really felt great."

"Oh, Jeremy, I'm so glad to hear that," I said as I teared up. "How wonderful! Congratulations for being able to do that, and thank you so much for sharing it with *me*. Maybe you can turn this awful family history around and your children will be able to be more loving to their children, and so on... and so on... and so on."

"Yeah, that's really my hope."

We continued to eagerly share so many more childhood memories and emotions and then at the end of our conversation, for the first time in my life, my brother said, "I love you." I effortlessly repeated it back to him, and it felt absolutely wonderful. I hung up the phone and shed a tear of happiness for all the future times we would have, and several tears of sorrow for all the lost years—we'd never *ever* get back.

♥ ♥ ♥

Desperately Seeking Sanity

Ariana and I were thrilled to get ten good days out of Dad after he was told about Jeremy's heart attack. She said, "Dad's being so nice to us now. He's really a pleasure to take care of when he's like this. He's so cooperative and makes Mom and me laugh all the time."

"Oh I know. If it wasn't for Joker Jekyll being there the majority of the time, I'd have left Hyde Hitler in the dust long ago. I think it's also partly due to my telling him he'd better be nice to you or he's going into a home. Well, it's ten whole days of good behavior now. Tomorrow he'll break the record. Time to break out the champagne. Too bad I don't drink—but I think this may make me start."

Early the next morning the phone rang and I was so upset to hear Ariana's voice so down. "Don't look now but—heeee's baaack. I guess we shouldn't have tempted fate. I knew it was too good to be true. He's been up all night ranting and raving at Mom and me again."

"Oh nooo—what now?"

"I'm not sure exactly, but at three in the morning they woke me up yelling at each other. I rushed in there and tried to find out what in the world was going on. I gave them a long disciplinary talk about getting along and told them they *had* to go to sleep. An hour later there was more yelling and I heard her say over the baby monitor, 'Don't you hit me. You better not ever hit me—I'll slap you silly!' I charged in there and they were really yelling at the top of their lungs at each other."

"Did he hit her?" I asked as my blood started to curdle and I could see the whole ugly scene in Imax living color in my head.

"No, but he had his fist in her face and it was really close. I tried to get her to come into my bedroom with me, but she absolutely refused to get up. I just couldn't budge her. Then she got mad and yelled at *me*, 'This is *my* bed, let *him* get the hell out!' I gave them a stronger lecture, calmed them down and said, 'If I hear one more peep out of this room—Mariel, you're getting up and coming to bed with me.' I went back to my bed and I couldn't believe it—a couple hours later they started in *again*. Now he's really being a monster, calling her all kinds of nasty names. She's been crying and yelling back at him and I'm worried because it's too much stress for her. I've been scolding and shaming him but it doesn't seem to matter to him at all—he just won't stop it this time."

"Drugs, Ariana, drugs—*now*. Will he take anything if you try to slip him something?"

"No, he refuses—I tried that already. I have to wait a couple hours until his regular pill time with lunch to sneak some in there. If I give him something now that puts him out, I know he'll *never* let me put any pills in his mouth ever again."

I was thinking: Okay, how about a frying pan? No, a frozen leg of lamb, like in that great *Hitchcock* episode, where they can't find the murder weapon because it thawed out and they ate it. OK-OK, not a good idea to give her the wrong impression. "Oh, honey, do the best you can to get the drugs into Raging Rambo sooner than later. Maybe change the clocks ahead on him so he thinks it's time to eat. Leave messages for all the doctors and get Mom out of harm's way. Don't hesitate to call Officer Toffee to help you if you can't take it and get him outta there. I'll be anxiously waiting to hear the next segment of *General Geriatrics* so call me soon and we'll figure out the next step."

Jeremy called to get the update on our *Not-So Little Shop of Horrors*. I said, "Dad's being such a nightmare now and we just had quite a few good days with him too. We just never know what's going to set him off. When he's like this I'm sorry I had all those life-lengthening surgeries done on him—only to have him live longer so he has more time to torment us. I kept thinking I was doing the right thing and that the surgeries would make him better and he could live happily with

Mom until the end—but he's making everyone's life, including his own, so miserable. I think he's studying the seven deadly sins and I'm pretty sure he's mastered six already. You'd think he'd be all out of lifelines by now, but I swear, he's like the Energizer Bunny—he just keeps going and going and going."

"Oh boy—what's he up to now?"

"Oh, let's see. Well, he raised his fist to Mom and Ariana—calling them nasty names. Then he yelled at sweet little Gary. Then he stole the car keys out of Ariana's purse, demanding to drive. Then he refused to take a shower and chased Ariana naked while he threw wet towels at her. Then he gave laxatives to Mom and you don't *even* want to know the details of that one. And *then* The Incredible Bulk refused to eat anything but ice cream for days on end—but other than *that...*"

"Ice cream? He's not supposed to eat ice cream, is he?"

"Oh, I meant fat-free frozen yogurt. *Everything* is fat-free."

"Hmm, maybe *real* ice cream isn't such a bad idea!" Jeremy laughed.

"Yeah, maybe some real rich Haagen Dazs is exactly what the 'Bad Humor' man needs, or some Ben and Jer... (light bulb)... no, I know what we should get him: A gallon of Jackie and Jeremy's Select Killer Ice Cream—only 99.9 % butterfat!"

We *howled*—and I realized how much I had missed my brother.

♥ ♥ ♥

The Three Faces of Jacqueline

Later... Ariana called again, "Dad finally spewed himself out and took a long nap. Then when he woke up he started ranting and raving about *you* again, calling you every nasty name he could think of, saying he never wants to speak to you again. He went out to the car and threw a terrible temper tantrum nearly ripping the steering wheel out, trying to get The Club off. He's all tuckered out again now and back in bed. My gosh, what a day."

"Oh dear, I'm so sorry he's being so difficult again. What are we going to do with him? None of the nursing homes are going to put up with his raving. I wish he could understand how lucky he is to be at home yet and not in a lock-up unit of some institution. Please point out all the things I've done for him and Mom, Ariana."

"Of course, I always do that for you. I know it must hurt you, huh?" Deep breath, "Yeah, it does. Raising parents is a thankless job—probably just like raising kids, I guess. At least when you raise kids, you get to see the fruit of your labor, but when you raise elderly, disabled parents—you only get to see the fruit rot."

I sadly hung up and put on REM's, *"Every-body Hurts"*—wanting to wallow for a while. It's amazing that it's not worn out by now. Okay, I had to be PMS-ing big time. I knew I'd done one *helluva* job and my father would have been so proud of me if it hadn't been *him* that I had conquered—but it was such a bitter-sweet, dark victory. I had so much anguish that he was so frustrated about getting old. Everything I did to try and make him better, just made him hate me. I was so afraid that he would die hating me and that brought me great sorrow. *("I haven't got time for the pain.")* Thanks, Carly.

I really needed to get to the bottom of the complex emotions I was having, but I kept pushing them away, not wanting to deal with them yet—they were going to be too painful to examine. I was sweeping everything under the carpet again and there was an "elephant" sitting under there now and darn it, I was gonna have to let him out. I know, I know, Socrates, "An unexamined life is not worth living." What about an intimidated life? Hey, I had been in therapy—enough already with the ninety dollars an hour to reiterate what I already knew: I was an adult child of an alien invader. "Na nu, Na nu."

Deep within my conflicting aching head, my Adult, Parent and Child (me, myself and I) were having a free-for-all fighting for position about whose pain was worse. I decided I better stop avoiding everyone so I laid down to listen, trying to understand what was going on within me.

Parent Jacqueline's anger rose up immediately, "I want my life back! I don't want to have to be a responsible parent to my parents anymore. If I had wanted to have children I would have had them. Thank goodness I've never seen that 'ooga-chucking' dancing baby that Ally McBeal is tortured with all the time. I've never heard my biological clock *'ticking, ticking, ticking.'* Elder parenthood is a parent trap. I might have years and years of this nightmare ahead of me!" She started singing her theme song: *"I wanna be freeee."*

Adult Jacqueline interrupted her, "And I want a love-life again. I'm so consumed with this full-time job of managing paperwork, bills and every little crisis for Mom and Dad, talking to Ariana three or four times a day, that I haven't even felt like getting out and trying to meet anyone new. Who would want to hear about this ordeal all the time?" She started singing her theme song: *"Only the lonely."*

Then, Little Jackie started crying and the other two stopped bickering and turned their attention to her. Parent Jacqueline said, "Just let it flow, it's okay to cry. This is all too much for a little girl like you to have to deal with. Tell us what's wrong—can you, sweetheart?"

Barely able to get the words out, Little Jackie stuttered and then blurted out that she felt abandoned and missed her daddy. "I've worked *s-so* hard—where's my daddy's praise? He doesn't appreciate *anything* I've done to help him. In fact, he *hates* me," she sobbed.

Adult Jacqueline tried to comfort her, "Oh my gosh. We didn't realize how much you hurt. You miss being the apple of his eye, don't you?" That ball went straight over the goal post and then, that sweet little girl, the one inside his wallet, burst into confirming tears.

"Yes! I want him to love me again, just like he *always* did. Why doesn't he love me after all I've done for him?"

The Adults tenderly cuddled their little girl. "He loves you so much, honey. There isn't anything he wouldn't do for you. He'll always be there, in your heart, forever. You have to forgive him for getting old and unable to understand all you've done to try to help him."

"I'm trying to, but it's just too hard," Little Jackie whimpered. "I... I want him to be there and watch over me again." The Adults nodded and sadly realized what was happening. They held her close, rocked her back and forth, and started singing softly to calm her: *"Someone to watch over me."*

Finally, with enough comfort and assurance Little Jackie began to quiet down. It was suddenly very clear to the Adults that they would have to work together and help each other deal with their numerous responsibilities, but more importantly, they had to help Little Jackie cope with the profound loss of her daddy. The realization that they knew all along, but didn't want to face, was that...

"The Wonder Years had passed and the old days were gone, and things were never going to be the same... again."

❤ ❤ ❤

The Outer Limits of Suspected Belief

The next morning I got an awful call from Ariana. "Jackie, he's at it again! When I tried to get Mom up she said that her ribs hurt her, so I looked to see if she had a bruise or something. Dad took his cane from the side of the bed and brought it up and hit me over the head with it, yelling at me to 'leave her alone!' He said that *I* dropped her and that *that* was how she hurt her ribs. Jackie, I swear to you—I *never* dropped your mother."

"Ariana, I trust you completely. I know you'd never drop her."

"Then I asked your mother and she looked right in my eyes and then back at your father and she shook her head and said, 'NO, I'm not going to lie. Ariana didn't drop me—you hit me!' He started yelling that he, 'DID NOT!' and then *she* actually slapped *him*. He got so furious he tried to push her off the bed. Luckily I got there in the nick of time to catch her because she could have really gotten hurt breaking something if she hit the floor. I got her up and brought her into my room, but now he's just ranting and raving, throwing things all over the house. I can't control him. I think I'm going to have to call the police to come take him to the hospital."

"Call 911 right now, Ariana, don't wait. Call Officer Toffee to come help you—he knows what's going on."

"I did already, but he's been moved out of our jurisdiction now."

"Well of course he has—that would ruin our batting average with the *glitch* otherwise."

She dialed 911 and when she thought she heard the cavalry coming she opened the back door. Dad pushed her out as hard as he could and tried to close the door on her arm as she struggled to get back in. It only took *three* phone calls and over an hour and a half later before the final insult of Lieutenant Frank Drebin and Police Squad showed up. (You have to be gushing from an artery before they come quicker.)

Jubilant Jekyll was back in his most charming mode already—acting very sane and cordial to them saying he had absolutely no idea what Ariana had called them about. Ariana *insisted* they take him, but they were skeptical and wouldn't without talking to Dad's doctors first. Endure didn't return any of Ariana's *pleading* pages. Kiljoy was in a "meeting of the mindless" so they had to wait *forever* to speak to her. Finally she broke away and confirmed that yeah, yeah, Dad should be taken to the psychiatric hospital.

While the officer was on interminable hold with Kiljoy's office, they heard Dad sternly whisper to Mom over the baby monitor, *demanding* that she tell the cops that *Ariana* had dropped her and that she hurt her ribs *that* way. He told her not to say that *he* had hit her or they'd take him away to jail—but Mom finally said loud and clear for them all to hear, "Well, it serves you right if they take you away—you hit me!" Excellent Mom, we need more of that.

"How long have you been married, sir?" the cop asked.

"Huh? What are you trying to say? You mean I had a baby out of wedlock?" Now there was a sideways demented Freudian slip for ya. Okay, great—if I have some extra brothers or sisters somewhere out there, ah... wish you were here. (There's got to be a Shakespearean play in here somewhere.) Luckily the Rookies barely had enough to "5150" Freddie Kreuger *again*. Ariana instructed them to take him to the psychiatric division of his regular hospital where Dr. Endure was the head of psychiatry. This was a huge problem because it was out of their jurisdiction. Ariana called me so I could help shed some light on the situation and I explained that it meant two expensive ambulance rides and lots of unnecessary time and red tape with the transfer. Finally they took pity on us and agreed to take him directly there.

When they got him there he acted *so* normal, *so* darling, that the nurse phoned Ariana and said they were going to release him. Ariana called me in an absolute panic and I called and *demanded* that they hold him for Dr. Endure to see. Of course, Endure was not expected in until the following day. Ariana paged Endure *over* and *over* to get his help. Late that night he finally returned the pages and assured her that he'd call her immediately after evaluating Dad first thing the next morning. I tried to calm Mom.

"Hi, Mom, are you okay? Did Dad hit you in the ribs?"

"Yes, he poked me real hard—I'm so sore that I can hardly move." My *infuriated* blood was boiling that he had hurt her, but I was so glad that she was finally speaking up and telling me what had happened.

The next day, Ariana called me several times while we were waiting for Dr. Endure to call. "He *promised* he'd call me as soon as he examines Dad, so I hate to call and bug him, but it's really getting late now." By the end of the day Ariana decided to call the hospital to see if Dr. Endure had been in to see Dad yet.

"Jackie, you *won't* believe this—Dad's not there. They transferred him late last night to another nearby hospital where Dr. Endure has no authority. Nobody even called to tell us!"

Huhhh? I was so beyond outraged, I wanted NAMES, Ranks and Serial Numbers. Greeeat, so a new psychiatrist would be charmed to death and lovable Jekyll would be released again—presto.

I instructed Ariana to call Ray, Dr. Endure and the hospital and to start screaming foul play at all of them and I'd do the same. "Jackie, if they release him, I swear I'll pick him up and drop him off right in Dr. Endure's private office myself. Dad's not coming home and making Mom so nervous that she pee's all over herself again. He's going to cause her a stroke with all of this stress. Her ribs are still really hurting her too. I can barely move her to get her to the pottie. He's getting dangerous now—he could have seriously hurt her."

Boingggg! "What's *wrong* with me? Call Ray and tell him we want x-rays on Mom's ribs right away. If Dad cracked her ribs, that'll help us keep him there for quite a while."

♥♥♥

I'm All Outta Whole Lotta Love

The next day Dr. Endure finally called me back. "We don't know why your father was transferred to the other hospital, some *glitch* in the system," he said like it happened all the time. "The psychiatrist there said he seemed totally normal. He's been complaining of chest pains so they transferred him back to his regular hospital. If he's okay, he'll be back here in my psychiatric division and then I'll have jurisdiction over him again."

I experienced about five guiltiseconds of compassion and then it hit me. Oh brother, he's feigning chest pains to get out of the Funny Farm and get back to Dr. Kiljoy, who he thinks will help him. Believe me, he's not as dumb as he looks. I told Dr. Endure, "I *guarantee* you, he'll be absolutely fine."

Later in the day Dr. Endure finally called me back again, "I've just finished talking to your father and he's fine, although he did take a bad fall. He's totally rational and calm and we've had a good long talk and he tells a *very* different, *very* convincing story than what Ariana is saying. (Oh boy—here comes the greatest story ever told.) Now, he freely admits that he lost his temper a little bit and he's sorry about that, but he absolutely *insists*, swears on his *life*, that the only reason he got so upset was because *Ariana* dropped your mother and *that's* how she hurt her ribs. I can understand how that would make him awfully mad—I know how much he loves your mother." Huhh? I had lock-jaw, in the open position.

Beyond stop the insanity inhale… (okay, the inmates are running the asylum) and blast it out—like Mount St. Helens. I'd *had* it with being nice, waiting for them to do something. Grace under pressure was no longer working. Mom always said, "Don't say or do things in anger… you'll always regret it later—tisk." I took a deep breath… made my fateful decision… and then I released *months* of frustration at all the medical incompetency I had experienced.

"What's *wrong* with you? You can't be serious! My mother *told* me he hit her—she does not lie. Ariana does not lie. Didn't you even read the police report? You've just been snowed—hook, line and sinker, by the greatest living actor since Olivier. I'm telling you—he's in a league of his own. I can't believe you believe *him*. Would you like to go over there and look for the invisible people he's seeing too? You've been hearing every week for over *nine* months now about all the demented crap he's been pulling, and you're telling me you believe *him* and not us? You've never even met Horrible Hyde!"

"Jacqueline, I'm sorry, but there's just no judge in the world who's going to hold him any longer. He's *very* pleasant and completely rational. What he says and how he says it is totally believable. He may have a bad temper once in a while but you can't lock him up in a hospital for that." ("This isn't a hospital—this is an *insane* asylum!")

"Well, guess what? We're not going to pick him up, so you need to figure out a way to hold him or Ariana is going to pick him up and dump him off in *your* office—and then she's gonna go home and take the phone off the hook. Ariana and I, and even Ray Steer, have had to call you five or six times before you return our calls. The *only* reason I have continued to try to make this work with you is that Dad likes you so much and will consent to see you. He's never let any other doctor but Kiljoy near him. I've asked you if you want to bill me per call, if you want to see him more often so you can get paid more, but you always say no, there's no need for any of that. You don't even see him once every few *months*. You haven't spent any time with him to see who he really is. I know you have many patients to deal with, but either do your job right or get me a psychiatrist who gives a damn about their patients."

"Well, I'm not really sure what can be done. I'm just not going to be able to legally hold him any longer," he protested.

Why doesn't he *hear* me—I can hear my voice. I'm now relentless, madder than Holyfield with a real bad earache. ("What we have here is failure to communicate.") "Wait a minute! *You're* the professional. *You're* supposed to know how to work the system. *You* have to be the one to figure this out and help me. If you will spend some time with him, you're going to see that he does not think rationally at all. And if he gets mad, you'll get to meet Horrific Hyde, I guarantee it."

"But..."

"Look, I understand that you cannot put him away permanently for a bad temper, but please, you have to believe me—he's dangerous. I'm not waiting for him to hurt my mother, Ariana or her child. I'm not sure what he's capable of anymore. I'd never have believed he could choke *me*. If you can't lock him up long enough to figure him out, then you better come up with a drug to put him *'out'* when he gets nasty."

"B-b-but..."

"I swear to you—if he hurts *anyone*, I'm naming *you* in a lawsuit for negligence. I've had a solid year of this. You've heard it from Camellia, Terri, Ariana, and me, but I guess we're all just making it up for the sheer fun of it. And I've asked you to call Mary Jo, the case manager, and hear it from another professional."

"I don't need to call her. I *believe* you, I really believe you!"

Somebody stop me! I started to realize that I was sounding just like H. Ross Parrot with out-of-sequence bar charts. "You're not listening to me. Are you through? Can I finish? CAN... I... FINISH? See, here's the thing. I'm not *asking* you to call Mary Jo, I'm *demanding* you call her. I've told you that she has experienced my father's rages several times when he's threatened her. She fears for my mother's safety too. So, how many danger signals do you have to get? Either drug him or place him, because he is not going to stop the raging—he's been raging and apologizing for it his whole life. My mother packed us up and left him many times because of it, but he'd always be *so* apologetic, we'd eventually go back. He'd be really good for quite a while and then it would happen again. She had no

213

education, no money of her own, two little kids, no place to go, and he knew he could get away with it. He's always been just a lot of hot spewing air, but now it's become illogical and irrational raging that's turning into demented violence. And it's going to be on *your* head when he actually does something that hurts someone, and I'm going to make sure *your* name is in all the papers and that the Psychiatric Board knows all about it. And how are you going to face yourself after he really hurts someone? Now, I'm going to ask you one more time—are you going to help me or not?"

"OK! OK! Calm down—I'll call her. I will call Mary Jo, I promise! (Had I finally penetrated Dr. No's inner sanctum?) I'll have to think about a drug that will help him sleep, that won't make him hallucinate, but you don't want him asleep twenty-four hours a day, do you?"

"Why not? If he's being unbearable, yes, that's exactly what I want. My mother will be happy as long as he's there with her, asleep. If he's being Jovial Jekyll, great—no need to give him anything, but as soon as he turns into Daddy the Menace, I want something to knock him out immediately, not two hours later after he's pushed my mother off the bed and broken her neck, or he's hit Ariana over the head with a half of watermelon and knocked her out cold—both of which he has tried to do. Even if I could get a nursing home to take both of them, when he rages, they're just going to kick him out or sedate him. I want to sedate him—now!"

"OK-OK, gee, I'll figure something out—I will, I will!"

Well, well, well… by Jove—I think Sigmund has finally got it!

"The strain on the brain in driving me insane." Thank you, Henry Higgins.

♥ ♥ ♥

I'd Rather Donate a Kidney… To Oprah

My frustration level had reached another all-time-Hyde. Okay, get Swifty, my agent on the line—it's time for another spectacular spin off: *Who Shot JM?* No, Dad would be so mad, he'd come back as my own private poltergeist and I'd have to hire the Ghostbusters. I was so fried out of my mind that I just couldn't see the big picture anymore. I could feel my heart palpitating and I was having strange chest pains. Oh-kay, I had to get a grip on myself, get centered, calm down and do the deep breathing. *"Breathe deep, the gathering gloom, watchlight fades on..."* (Moody Blues: *Nights in White Satin.*) Sorry.

It had been over a year already that my life had been totally absorbed with my parents, not to mention the eleven years before that. I wanted freedom from all the responsibility and emotional torture before *my* life was over. I needed primal SCREEEAMM therapy! Tremendous inhale... and hold it... (the mind is a terrible thing to be tormented by)... turn blue... and blast it all the way out—again.

Ohhh, thank GOD, a little oasis—time for *Oprah*. Don't you just LOVE her! I had a television in my office and everyone knew not to bother me *too* much while *Oprah* was on. I always taped it anyway so I don't think I've *ever* missed a show. I remember once when I gave her charming beau, Stedman, a ride in San Francisco when we both came out of a television convention at the same time and there were no taxis to be found. Finally my friend drove by to pick me up and I yelled, "Hey, Stedman, can we give you a lift?" He was so darling and cordial, and of course we felt like we knew him. "We just *love* your girlfriend! So when are you going to marry her?"

"Oh, we're real happy just the way we are," he said. Oh my *gosh*, what a stupid-stupid-stupid thing to say. Poor guy, like he never heard *that* before. I turned red and apologized profusely.

"I'm *so* sorry for teasing you. You must go nuts hearing that from people you don't even know. I guess it's because we see how much she beams when she talks about you. I think that the 'adoring public' just wants to live vicariously through the celebrities we feel like we know." He assured us he wasn't offended at all and then we had a good old chat, we were all staying at the same hotel, and then he gave us his card and invited us to come see the show if we were ever in Chicago. What a great guy, not to mention gorgeous. It was easy to see why Oprah loved him so much.

I've always identified with Oprah on so many levels. We both didn't want children, had never taken those life-long wedding vows, and had long-term relationships. (Well, I used to have one.) We're both strong career women, very independent and in the television business. (Well, I used to be.) We both love to talk, value the written word, and have kept our personal journals religiously since we were fifteen. We're both active searchers for all the answers in life and love helping others find theirs too. I always feel so in-tune with her programs on simple abundance (appreciating what you have right now—or, as Mom would put it, "count your blessings!") and we understand the amazing life-changing power of gratitude and forgiveness. And then, we were both always fighting the dreaded battle of the bulge. (But then again... who isn't?) She is truly a hero for so many of us—dedicating her life to helping millions of people that she will never even meet.

I had been to a party recently where a woman said she didn't care for Oprah. I went off on her pretty bad. "Hey, don't anybody be dissin' my Oprah, girlfriend!" Then she went on to make some statements about her own reincarnation beliefs. "We keep coming back, life after life with the same people until we get it right. So, unless you resolve all this with your father, you may have to come back and he could be your *husband* next time." (Please play *Psycho* music here.) I jumped up, screamed, and threatened to jump out the window—but then they reminded me that it was only a one-story home. It's always something.

Back to Oprah. She quotes the writer, Alice Walker: "Suffering is the soul of the spirit." SLAP! Wow, that really hit me hard and then I realized—this whole unbelievable experience had paradoxically *enriched* my spirit beyond anything I had ever had to do previously in my life. Through adversity, I had been forced to grow immeasurably, finding a part myself I didn't even know I had. Even though I had tackled lots of hurdles in my time and knew I was strong, none of them—not college, not the stressful executive jobs, not spinal surgery, and not the devastating relationship break ups COMBINED had made me grow as much as this heart-wrenching saga had.

Yes, yes, here we go—that's so right. I needed to remember my spirit and change my perspective again—and be *grateful* that I had been forced to learn so many things about myself and my family that I may have never learned otherwise. Suddenly I had a strange appreciation for the amazing never-ending adventure that had forced me to dig down to the depths of my heart and soul, and reach a level of understanding and enlightenment within myself that I had no idea I was capable of reaching. What a marvelous gift to be able to *clearly* see it this way.

Thank you so much, Oprah—right on, right on!

♥♥♥

chapter fourteen

GULLIBLE'S TRAVELS–*or*–SMALL BALLS OF FIRE

Ariana called very excited, "Good news! Mom's ribs aren't broken, just badly bruised, so she'll be fine. Oh, Jackie, you really scared the heck outta Dr. Endure yesterday."

"Good! He really deserved it. I've had it with him believing Dad's pack of lies. Tell me everything—I can't wait to hear this."

"He said he would *not* release Dad yet because he's afraid that if he really does do something violent and hurts one of us, you'll sue him and he can't afford to take that chance. So he's keeping him in there a lot longer for observation."

"YES! Gee, how interesting—looks like a frightened psychiatrist really does have some power to convince the judge to hold him longer after all."

"Then you won't believe what he said next. He said, 'I'm afraid if I don't keep him, she's going to come up here and cut off my testicles!' Jackie, I burst out laughing. What in the world did you say to him?"

"Wow, I swear I never mentioned his private parts, but isn't it interesting that he translated my message into what's most important to him. Like Dad always said—hit 'em in their most vulnerable spot."

"Then I told him absolutely everything that's happened again and it was like he had never heard most of it before. I couldn't believe some of the basic questions he asked me because I've been leaving him messages all about Dad's bad behavior for months now."

"I'm so furious, Ariana. What's he been doing for nine months, fast-forwarding through our messages when he gets them? I know doctors are very busy, but my gosh—this is unbelievable."

Later on—Mary Jo called. "Dr. Endure just called and WOW did you ever scare him into action. He said, 'I *have* to call you or I'm going to lose my testicles.' Jackie, I started laughing so hard and then I said, 'You mean you still *have* them? I'm very surprised she hasn't cut them off yet! You really have to help her with this nightmare she's in.' I told him that if Jake were my father there'd be no way I'd leave him alone with my mother ever. He's a danger to himself and everyone else. I told him that I had been physically threatened with his fist in my face a few times myself. Then I phoned Larry, the social worker and I told him everything *again*, and then I called Dr. Marie Kiljoy and told her everything *again* too. I think we may actually have a breakthrough."

"Oh, thank you so much, Mary Jo. So now let's see if Marie, Larry and Curly finally believe me and come up with something."

The next day Dr. Endure called. "Gee, you really gave me a tongue lashing the other day, Jacqueline."

"Well, I'm sorry doctor but you really deserved it. I'm at my wit's end here. I'm glad you're finally starting to listen to me. Isn't it a shame what extremes I had to go to just to get your attention? So, let's move past it now—what's the game plan with my father?"

"Well, he's been apologizing and crying really hard all week. He refuses to get out of bed and he solemnly *promises* that he'll never yell at anyone *ever-ever* again. He misses your mother terribly and he's really one sad puppy. In all my years I've never seen anyone this remorseful, *ever*. I feel real badly for him. I'm sure he's learned his lesson and I think you'll see a big change in him now."

My eyes glazed over and rolled back in my head as I knew every word verbatim. "Did you hear him say, 'I *beg* of you,' and 'so help me *God*,' about a hundred times?" I heard his jaw drop open.

I tried to be nice, really I did. "Doctor, I'm glad to know that you're a compassionate person, but you just have no idea who he really is—because he's an *incredible* actor. Yes, he's very sorry he got caught, but I promise you—he is not going to stop the raging. He will say *anything* to manipulate you to get what he wants for the moment. You're not alone though, he's always been able to pull the wool over everyone's eyes. He's been raging and apologizing for it his whole life and getting away with it *again* and *again*. He has learned how to get forgiveness by being very, I mean, *very* dramatic. The problem is, he's now adding demented violence to these performances, and I can't afford to forgive him any longer. If he hurts Ariana or her child, I'm looking at a lawsuit—and so are you."

"Well… oh-kay, I'll guess I'll keep him here several more days to observe him. You know, the good thing is that your father admitted that he knows he has a bad temper once in a while, but he doesn't know what causes him to erupt like that. I'm threatening him that just one more violent action and he's going away for good—without your mother. But... you'd just have to see that he's *so* distraught and *so* remorseful that I really think he's finally understanding how serious his bad behavior is now, and I'm *sure* that if you'll just give him *one* more chance he'll behave much better from now on."

I hung up and exhaled from the seat of my soul. This had to be such a huge problem for so many elderly people whose controlling partners had added demented violence to their warped personalities in their advanced years—but who were smart and clever enough not to let their doctors see it.

♥♥♥

Bound and Gagged By Honor

Ariana had me talk to Mom because she was worrying about Dad. "Mom, he's with Dr. Endure and Dr. Kiljoy—they're trying to figure out what's wrong with him. Can you be strong and wait a couple of weeks while they try to help him?"

"Oh, I'll try, honey. I know you're trying to help him, but he's old now and just not himself anymore. Don't hate him, sweetheart—he's always loved you *so* much. I hope you find a man who loves you as much as he always has, but who doesn't have that awful temper. It's time for you to find a good man now—I want you to have some happiness and I don't want you to be alone when you're old. It would be much too hard. You know how to work, I've instilled that in you, but I don't want you to be alone when we're gone. I'm real tired now my darling—I need to go to sleep. I don't know why I'm so tired all the time. I wish Dad were here with me. I know it's silly after all he's done, but your father has been a good husband *most* of the time. He has that bad temper sometimes, but after all these years, I still love him, in spite of his faults—you know?"

"I know, Mom, I know you do. Too bad love can't conquer all, huh?" Sadly, I inhaled... *("what's love got to do, got to do with it")* and as I slowly exhaled... I felt so much sorrow that we were in such a sad no-win American tragedy. I started to choke up again, tears flooded my heart, and my tough exterior dissolved right off. I'd been through

Hell and Hyde water and I sorrowfully hummed a new theme song that came to me: *"Imagine all the people."*

Maybe I should have just stayed out of it and let happen whatever was going to happen—but how could I stand by and let him bring Mom home to accidentally kill her again. My mission was becoming impossible. I had tried so hard to "Honor Thy Father and Mother," but I was damned if I did—and I was damned if I didn't.

If I hadn't interfered from the very beginning and insisted that he take her to the hospital, they'd both be gone now, where they'd prefer to be anyway, and I'd be moving on living my own life instead of theirs. He would have gone to his grave loving me instead of hating me, and they'd be out of this torture of living twenty-three hours a day in bed, just waiting to die. I had upset the balance of how it was supposed to end, creating my own nightmare. My fears of being alone in the world without them—had made me a virtual prisoner of them.

I was having those dreams where you want to scream but nothing comes out. Then the one where you're being chased and you try to fly, but you're like lead and you can't get off the ground. Next I was being suffocated in quick-sand that was slowly taking me under as I struggled to keep my head up. I woke up with a sore jaw from gritting my teeth—more exhausted than when I went to sleep. Every night I'd get into bed and wonder what the torturous coming attractions were going to be. OK, call Webster's. I'm sure they'll want my picture to illustrate the F word: FRUSTRATION!

Then I had an amazingly clear dream. I was in that incredible scene from *Sophie's Choice*, where the mother is forced to choose between her little girl or her little boy, and has to hand one over to be killed by the Nazi's. I think it is the most powerful scene I have *ever* seen on film—I screamed in horror when I saw it in the theatre. How ironic that in my dream *I* was the mother now, with my two "children"—my parents, whom I wouldn't let go of. I held on to them with all my might as the soldier of death tried to rip them from my grasp. I woke up with deep fingernail indentions in the palms of my clenched fists, in a cold sweat trying to scream, beyond relieved to be in my own little bed. My heart pounded as I laid there completely astounded that the mind is so amazing to put all that symbolism together. Then I grinned, surprised by the fact that I hadn't said, "Here, please—take them both!" and... I marveled at how interesting it was, that I still wasn't ready to let go of—my father.

All I ever wanted was for them to be together until the end, but the stress on me to do that was becoming unbearable. I tried so hard to change my perspective again and rise above it, but I just couldn't find it this time and wallowed in despair instead. Even my closest friends were fried out of their minds with my endless nightmare, helpless to do anything to really solve the situation. Where's Oprah when you *need* her? Deep under the covers I cried me a river, and then I laughed at the irony of my human bondage. My parents had each other and full time care while I was all alone. Who's going to call Rescue 911 for me? The chest pains were not going away—I got an EKG and treadmill test. DeBakey, Jr. said, "You're fine—but you really *have* to take it easy and relax. I'm sure it's probably just all the stress you've been through."

Ya think?

♥ ♥ ♥

Two, Two, Two Minds in One

Dr. Endure called me after Dad had been in the psychiatric hospital for nine whole days without a rage. "Well, I finally see the dementia you're talking about. Legally we have to let him go soon, he's not psychotic, but I now see that he is much worse than the last time he was here. (So, he finally talked to him for more than twenty minutes.) He doesn't remember things and he can't learn very well. He's quite a difficult case to diagnose." Now there's an understatement. Gee, I guess I should have threatened to change Dr. Endure "from a rooster to a hen" a long time ago, Dolly. "He's been able to control his temper since he's been here, so he does have some control left. We'll just have to see if he can control his impulses and remember what's going to happen if he doesn't. I have *drilled* into him that this is his last chance and that if he acts up again he's going away for good, and your mother isn't going with him. If he can't control himself and he gets violent again, I'll help you place him in a home."

"Oh, thank you so much, doctor."

"I'm going to give Ariana a new medication to try on him if he acts up. I don't know if it will work or not, we'll just have to see. The bottom line is that he's not going to get better, he's just going to get

221

worse, and we'll probably have to put him in a home fairly soon. He probably has vascular dementia from all the clogged arteries."

"Holy diagnosis, Batman!" Gigantic inhale... aaand hold it... hold it... (and begin the exhale I've been waiting to do for over a year now)... and blow it all the way out—again. I could *not* believe what I had been through to get to this point. Had I not been strong enough to threaten Dr. Endure with a lawsuit (in his most sensitive spot), my father would have been released after a few days, before the dementia surfaced again and he wouldn't have seen what I was talking about. I kept thinking that if Dr. Endure *really* helped me, I should figure out a way to send him to Vienna for a refresher course to see why he equated everything to his tiny tormented testicles. Poor baby, *he* needed help.

I listened intently to everything Dr. Endure said and then I asked him apprehensively, "Does my father hate me?"

He hesitated, "Well... he's *afraid* of you."

My heart broke in two as I hung up. Not again! Toughen up, don't get sucked in again—you'll just get stomped on! I even tried a verse of, *"Big girls don't cry,"* but I couldn't help it. After all I'd done for him, he *feared* me. I knew he hated me, he'd told me that dozens of times. In his mind I was a defector, the unforgiven, and I must be exiled. I'd committed Hyde Treason and no, I would not be pardoned.

It helped to buy all the books about elder care and read that many times "the primary caregiver is the most hated." I called Dr. Endure back and left him a message asking him to *please* also try to make my father understand that all I had done, had been out of love and honor for him and Mom.

♥♥♥

Abbott and Costello Meet Jekyll & Hyde

It was time for Dad to come home from the psychiatric hospital again. At the family meeting Dad grabbed Ariana and cried profusely, apologizing with real Jimmy Swaggart tears. When they got home Ariana went over how things were going to be. "Do you know how much Jackie loves you to go through all this for a whole year now, trying to keep you both at home? She takes care of all your bills, talks to us several times a day, makes sure you are being cared for properly, fed properly, taken to the doctors, and oversees everything for you. Do you realize what a huge job that is for her? She's made sure you have a chauffeur, a cook and a maid at all times." Dad nodded, put his head down and cried all evening.

Then, after only five days since his stint in *Knuts Landing* he had his first rage about wanting the car keys *again*. I instructed Ariana how to handle it. "He's three years old. Don't raise your voice to him. Be as calm as you possibly can and try to talk him through the impulse to rage." She was able to sit calmly with him as he pounded his fist and spewed in her face. She kept repeating that it was too dangerous for him to drive and reminded him of his promise to control his temper and what would happen if he didn't. She'd earned her advanced degree in psychology by the time he calmed down and went to lie down.

"Are you going to call the cops on me?" he asked her softly.

"No, you were able to calm down before it went too far. Why do you think you blew up like that?"

"I don't know. I really don't know. I'm sorry, Ariana."

"You did real good stopping yourself. I'm going to keep reminding you when you get mad, and we'll just keep working on it, okay?"

"Okay, Ariana. I'm going to try really hard to control myself."

The next night Ariana told me that she'd be back within the hour. "They're sound asleep, sawing redwoods in there, and I need to buy a few groceries at the corner store for the morning." I never questioned her judgment as she always told me every move she made. So, when the phone rang shortly after speaking with her, I was surprised to hear my father's voice.

"Hey, where are those diapers you had?"

"Um, what diapers, Dad? We used up all those extra ones months ago. Ariana buys new ones all the time—do you need one for Mom?"

"No, no! *Those* diapers—are they in a home?"

"Are they there in *your* home, you mean?"

"Goddamn it, where are they? Are you paying for two goddamn homes?" Oh my gosh, he was really agitated and Ariana wasn't there.

"Dad, please try to listen to me, okay? You're almost eighty-five years old and you have some dementia now. Sometimes you can't think as clearly as usual. I know you *think* you're thinking clearly, but please believe me that you really aren't right now. Calm down and Ariana will be right back to find you a diaper for Mom."

"I don't need a goddamn diaper! Listen to me—*you* aren't getting it. *You're* not thinking clearly, not me. Now, for the last time. Where are those goddamn diapers—in a home?"

Oh-kay, Who's on First? "No, Dad, they're not in a home. I'm not paying for two homes. Everything is going to be okay. Please go lie down with Mom and let me call Ariana to come help you, okay?"

"OK, but I just want to know *where* in the hell they are!"

"Don't worry about them, Dad—they're doing fine, I promise."

I called Ariana on her cell phone and she dropped everything to rush back and play, "What's on Second" about the diapers. "Wow, Jackie, the dementia is really bad all of a sudden. He was so clear a few hours ago. Mom is lying there shaking her head and she's even trying to figure out what he's talking about. She said, 'Honey, you're really wacky tonight.' Then Dad buried his head next to hers and said, 'I'm sorry, I guess I am wacky. *I* don't even know what I'm talking about.' Then we all just laughed about it. He keeps apologizing and I tell him it's okay if he gets confused as long as he doesn't yell or get violent. I think he might just be a little scared tonight so I'll sit and talk with him and try to soothe him until he goes to sleep. Don't worry about him, Jackie, he'll be okay—I have it handled."

"Oh, thank you so much again, Ariana. I can't tell you how much comfort it gives me to know that you're there with them and that he's actually starting to listen to you. We'd all be so lost without you— you're simply beyond the best."

Inhale... and hold it... (note to self: investigate technology to have Ariana cloned)... and exhale all the way out—again.

♥♥♥

In the Heat of the Day For Night

Ariana and I constantly brainstormed to improve upon things. I had her get Dad an ID bracelet with his name, address and all our phone numbers engraved on it. It could only be removed with pliers so he couldn't get it off. If he started to wander off, maybe someone would return him before we had to put out an APB. (Gee, maybe we should re-think that one.) The Alzheimer's Association has a great program called "Safe Return," that uses a bracelet registered with the local police to help with this problem.

Then, we got my parents approved for physical therapy at the hospital twice a week to improve their strength so they wouldn't end up completely bed-ridden. They went and Mom enjoyed it, but Dad couldn't stand to have her out of his sight. "Where's Mariel?" he'd ask Ariana in a panic over and over.

"I'm watching her, Jake," Ariana told him, as she went back and forth to each of their little exercise areas. "Jackie, Mom works so much harder for the physical therapists when Dad's not in there with her. I think it's good for her to be able to get away from him for a while. When he's with her she just wants to sit down, afraid to do anything that will upset him."

"Ughh! He's got so much control over her. Try to keep them apart during the session. It'll probably do her a lot of good." Just as they started to enjoy going, after only five sessions, of course, the insurance *glitch* would not pay for anymore physical therapy.

Ariana noticed that the practice bed they had at the physical therapy was lower to the floor than their own bed and much easier for them to get in and out of. She took their fifty-seven year old bed apart, and with a lot of ingenuity and several bricks made it the same height as the practice bed. The side rails could still fold down and just miss the floor. Now, if they fell (or got pushed) out of bed, it wasn't as far to the floor anymore.

Dad was always cold but he refused to put on more clothes or wear a jacket when he went outside. If we put extra blankets on his side of the bed, he'd cover up Mom, up to her nose, so she'd practically suffocate. We tried to get him to drink warm liquids but he'd only drink cold milk. Then he'd get up in the middle of the night and quietly turn the heater up to ninety degrees, even in the sweltering heat of the long hot summer. He wouldn't allow a window to be kept open so it was like a sauna most of the time. (It was a dry heat though.) I had Ariana buy a dual-control electric blanket, thinking that was the solution. He could be nice and roasty on his side and Mom could be comfortably toasty on hers. Wrong again, almighty sweat breath. He'd turn his *and* hers on HIGH as soon as Ariana would leave the room. Poor Mom would be ringing wet the next time Ariana would go in to check on them. "Jaaake! Mariel is sweating to death over here. Leave *her* side of the electric blanket alone!"

"I didn't touch it—honest to God."

Ariana tried to hide the controls from him by Velcroing them under each side of the bed. Being the rotten little kid that he was, he fell out of bed (then pretended he couldn't get up) and got under there to turn the dials with hog-wild abandon. She tried to tape them into position but he was so obsessed with the dials it was like they were forbidden fruit and he just *had* to take the tape off. We finally had to retire the electric blanket. If he was cold, then everyone must be cold, and he and Ariana played the "dialing for the heater control" game all night long, every night. She taped the thermostat in position, but it was no use—she finally had to have a lock box put on it.

Can't live with him, can't commit him... yet.

♥♥♥

Relative Relativity–*or*–Tommy Can You Hear Me?

Dad kept talking about his older brother, Tommy, whom he hadn't spoken to since he threw him and his family out on that Thanksgiving day many decades earlier. We all thought he had passed away a long time ago. I did some detective work and found out that Tommy was still very much alive and kicking hard in an assisted-living home in Oregon. He and Dad were the only two left from that huge family. I located his son, Gaven, who said that at eighty-seven, his father still drank heavily and would get horribly mean and raving nasty just like Dad. He'd tried to have Tommy live with him, but it was impossible for him to handle the rages. I assured him, "Don't feel bad—you have no idea how much I *completely* understand that."

We arranged to do a conference call one day when Gaven brought Tommy over to his house. I talked to Tommy first, and even though he mumbled a lot and was difficult to understand, it was so eerie that his voice sounded *exactly* like Dad's. Then there was the familiar "Goddamn" this and "Jesus Christ" that, and general negativity that made me realize that their related genes were much thicker than the different environments they'd been in all their lives.

Then I phoned Dad and surprised him with Tommy already on the line. It was so interesting to hear them, sounding *so* much alike, comparing their situations and trying to out-do each other with their

226

various ailments, pensions and memories. It was good for them both, they sounded happy to finally talk to each other, and I was glad that I'd arranged it before either one had died. Yep, it's never too late to mend a mangled fence, and it gave me some very valuable insight: it doesn't matter how old we get, we're still who we were in terms of our life-long relationships. That baggage of a lifetime just keeps tagging along—*"like a ball and chain."* Thank you, Janis.

Then, I was caught off guard when my father called me the next day. He rarely wanted to actually talk to me, so I was pleased to hear him sounding so coherent. "Gee, thanks for arranging that phone call with Tommy yesterday," he said cheerfully. "What'd that *cost* ya?"

"Oh, not too much. I'm glad you two could finally talk to each after all these years."

"Yeah, that was real nice. So when are you coming home, honey?"

Shock wave. "Oh, I don't know when I can again. You know I was there for nine months, so I have a lot to do to get caught up, but you can call me anytime you want to talk, okay?" Wow, he was right there: no sign of dementia, no rage, normal and missing *me*. Why can't we figure out a way to freeze-frame him this way? What in the world happens to him? I realized it was my job to learn how to grab on to these times when he was lucid, cement them in my brain for future use, and just let go of the pain that his rages caused.

Then, after five good days of loving behavior, he got furious about wanting cereal for dinner and put his fist in Ariana's face threatening to hit her.

"OK, that's it, Jake. I'm calling Dr. Endure." She went into her room and called me with the latest antics.

"Oh my gosh, Jackie, he suddenly looked like a spitting, spewing piranha and I thought his false teeth were going to fly out of his head and bite me. I did what you said and talked calmly, warning him of the consequences if he didn't stop raging. Then I gave him three warnings and when he wouldn't stop I walked away."

As we spoke we were amazed that he was at her door apologizing already. He was able to stop raging as soon as she disappeared. It was proof that he could stop it if he really wanted to.

Knock, knock, "Ariana? I'm sorry." Knock, knock. "Please don't call the doctor. I'm sorry, I didn't mean it."

"It's too late. You threatened to hit me so I'm calling Dr. Endure," Ariana yelled back through the door.

"I *beg* of you," he cried.

She let him go on believing that she had called Dr. Endure and wouldn't talk to him. We were wondering how long he would apologize before he'd go into another rage if she didn't come out. We decided she'd tortured him long enough and when she went out he was beside himself. "Please, Ariana, don't put me away."

"You're really Mr. Lucky this time. Dr. Endure wasn't in." She sat down with him and discussed his impulse to rage. "You're supposed to tell me if you feel like you want to explode so I can help you."

"I know, I know—I don't know why I did that. What's wrong with me, Ariana? Why do I do that?"

"Well, you have a little dementia so you don't always think clearly, but you can stop yourself if you really want to. You have to let me help you before it gets too far out of control. Trust me that I just want to help you, Jake." He finally settled down and went to lie down.

"Who are you?" he asked Mom as he looked right at her.

"It's me, Mariel."

"No you're not! Mariel's out there on the couch." Ariana heard it all over the baby monitor and rushed in to straighten him out. Mom started a crying jag that he didn't even know her anymore.

"He thinks I'm Elaine," she sobbed. Ariana rushed to call me to ask who in the world Elaine was. OK, somebody... please, bring me some nitroglycerin.

"Oh boy, there's a sore spot. That's the girl he left behind, his first wife, who he was married to for a short time before he met Mom. I've only heard her name mentioned a couple times in my whole life. She died of alcoholism when I was little and Mom said he always 'carried a torch' for her. I think Mom's real jealous of her."

"Ohh, no wonder she's so sad. Don't worry, Jackie. I'll whisper to her that we're trying some new medication on Dad for his dementia, and that's why he doesn't know her right now. I'll assure her that he'll be back to smothering her with love again real soon."

"Oh, thanks *again*, Ariana—thank you so much." I hung up and realized that we'd been touched by an angel to have Amazing Ariana in our lives and that there wasn't enough money in the world to buy this kind of compassion.

♥ ♥ ♥

The Greatest Story I Ever TOLD YOU SO

Dad's dementia disappeared as quickly as it came and then we had another five days of behavioral bliss before Little Lex Lucifer showed up again. Ariana called so upset, "He went outside in the middle of the night with a hammer and just destroyed those two beautiful gardenia plants you bought. Everything's a mess because he tracked mud all through the house too. Then he lied that he didn't know what happened to them and swore that he hadn't done it."

"Oh yeah, another whodunit."

"I think we're going to have to lock him in at bedtime now."

"Okay, use the companion credit card I got you to buy a bell for above the back door, so in case you're taking a nap during the day you can hear if he goes out. Call a lock company to come put some dead bolts on and lock him in at night so you can sleep. Get some key locks put on the sliding glass doors and the windows, and then hide keys near each exit in case of an emergency and tell everyone but him where they are, including the neighbors."

I even had her put a double dead-bolt on her own bedroom door so he couldn't get into her things because he had thrown all her clothes out the window into the neighbor's yard. Then she came up with a brilliant idea. "Would it be okay if I put little peep-holes in the doors, so I can spy on him and he won't feel like I'm always in his face?"

I was so jealous that I hadn't come up with that *I Spy* idea myself. "You are not as dumb as I look, Ariana—yes, that's a fabulous idea."

Then, Dad started demanding the car keys *again*, saying his legs and eyes were "just fine." Ariana placated him and then one morning when he got out of bed he took a terrible fall. She rushed over to see if he was okay, but he was like "Jumpin' Jake Flash" and got up amazingly fast. Suddenly he was, Jake be nimble, Jake be quick, telling her that his reflexes were fine to drive. He got so angry that he'd fallen, he took his walker and threw it clear across the room, shattering Mom's lava lamp, causing hot oil and glass to splatter everywhere.

"Jake, *please* calm down!" Ariana pleaded. "Come on, let's sit down and calmly talk about your impulse to rage right now." With that, Action Jakeson took the walker again, raised it over his head and threw it as hard as he could, smashing it against the wall right next to her face. "Jake! Stop it now. You don't really want to go back into the hospital. Please think about what you're doing. I'm going to have to call Dr. Endure if you don't settle down right now!"

"I don't give a goddamn what you do, you fucking bitch. This is *my* house and I say what happens here!"

"OK, Jake, I know this is your house. I understand how frustrated you are right now. Oh, you know what? We have an appointment with your favorite doctor, Dr. Kiljoy, today. Why don't you get dressed and we'll go see her and Ray Steer—and then we can take a nice ride to get some lunch if you'd like to."

Hyde continued ranting but Ariana just ignored him and got Mom ready to go. Finally, he angrily consented and got into the car, spitting at her from the backseat as he called her nasty names. She secretly called me on her cell phone so I could hear every charming obscenity.

At Dr. Kiljoy's they went into an examination room and I was so happy when Horrible Hyde started pounding his fist, raging at *Ray*, that he could still drive. Ariana said Ray's eyebrows went straight up and his eyes got wider than those in a Keene painting. I could hear it all on the cellular and I was *thrilled* that Ray was finally witnessing a rage. It was one thing to be told about it, but seeing it *once* was worth two years of my begging him to believe me. In a moment Dr. Kiljoy would walk in and I listened in anticipation knowing that she would finally experience Horrible Hyde herself. The second she walked in Gentle Jekyll snapped back to greet her as Hyde disappeared into thin air. How can this be happening? I wanted to reach through the phone and *shake* Hyde out of him. She did her five minute exam as he exchanged pleasantries with her and then she left.

Then it wasn't five minutes later, back out in the waiting room, when Hyde was back throwing another tantrum and Ray had to be called to intervene. Dad insisted that the wheelchair they'd brought with them, that Mom had been sitting in the whole time, was not theirs all of a sudden. Ariana was making the next appointment when he suddenly took off pushing Mom down the hall and crashed her into the side of the door smashing her feet.

"Wow, get a pill into him right away, Ariana. I've *never* seen him like this," Ray said, completely shocked.

"Oh, Ray, you think this is bad? This is nothing. All you saw was a little pounding and a mildly bad attitude. When he's really bad, he's a hundred times worse than *this*."

I phoned Ray later, anxious to do a little, I TOLD YOU SO, that I had waited so long to do. "I'm so glad you finally saw a little glimpse of Horrible Hyde. Pretty interesting, huh?"

"Yeah, it's really scary. It's like he's a completely different person. How can he act like that?"

"Oh, it's a gift—he's amazingly talented. He's ready for Prime Time. I started dancing a little Flamenco. Somebody, please... bring me a rose.

"I see the danger you're talking about. When Ariana left the room, he expressed so much anger at her, cupping his hands and saying he could just *strangle* her."

"Oh nooo, I don't like to hear that. He choked me so I know he's capable of it. I'm *so* afraid he'll hurt her."

"Yeah, I'm going to call Dr. Endure and tell him about this."

Ariana said Dad spit at her from the backseat of the car all the way home, clapping his hands and laughing that he'd "out-smarted" her. "See, smarty pants, you can't do anything to me—Dr. Kiljoy likes me. She doesn't believe you, you fucking little bitch. And I'm going to get rid of *you* next. I don't want your fat-ass taking care of us anymore and I'm going to drive again too."

That night he got worse. Ariana phoned and asked me to try and talk some sense into him. "Dad, *please*—you have to calm down. Do you remember promising never to act like this again? Dr. Endure told you that you'd have to go into a home without Mom if you acted up again. Please don't make me put you in a home. Do you have any idea the stress you are putting on all of us? Ariana is about to quit, and I can't come back up there to help you. You're going to cry and beg to come home, but there won't be any way out."

"Oh that's just what you'd like, wouldn't you? Just put me away!"

"Dad, I love you, I always have, but you have dementia now and you don't think clearly sometimes. I know you *think* you are thinking clearly, but please believe me that you aren't."

"I'm thinking just fine. You're the one who isn't thinking of *me!*"

The next morning, Ariana came up with a brilliant plan. She told him to get dressed because they were going to the DMV. "Come on, hurry up, everybody UP, let's go. If they say you can drive, you can drive us home."

"Uhm... but I'm not sure I remember how to drive."

231

"Oh, don't worry, you'll remember, and I'll help you. I need you to be able to drive so you can go do errands for me. I have *lots* of work for you to do for me everyday—come on, let's go."

"But... I'm not sure I still can."

Mom chimed in, "You're a good driver, honey, you always have been. You've been *insisting* on driving for months now, making us all so miserable about it—so come on, let's go."

"But why do I have to go to the DMV, Ariana?"

"Well, try to think of it this way. I've been instructed to give you your pills everyday. Now, if I don't and then you have a heart attack, whose fault is it?"

"Yours!"

"Right. So now, I've been instructed *not* to give you the car keys. If I give them to you and you get in an accident, who's fault is it?"

"Yours," he nodded sadly.

"Right. So if you're going to keep demanding the car keys against my orders and be so nasty about it, I'd just as soon have the DMV tell me that you *can* drive and then it won't be *my* fault if you drive and get in a wreck. So come on, let's go right now. You said your eyes are good, your legs are good—I think you can drive just fine."

He exhaled and growled like a grizzly, hung his head, and then finally said softly, "No, I can't drive. My eyes and legs are real bad. It's too dangerous for me to drive anymore, Ariana—you just drive us everywhere."

Mom's jaw dropped wide open as she looked over at Ariana—completely flabbergasted. She looked back at Dad with the sternest evil eye, shook her furious finger at him and yelled, "Well... then we don't want to hear another *damn* word about it, honey, and I mean it now—*not another word*—TISK!"

♥ ♥ ♥

chapter♥fifteen

ACHY BREAKY HEART OF HEARTS

I t was all quiet on the western front for ten whole days again. "We're about to break the record again, but don't hold your breath!" I told Ariana. "His only bad behavior was when he made that huge mess eating the low-fat apple pie you baked for them." As she took a nap, he'd quietly taken his spoon to the center of it as it cooled and practically ate the whole thing.

"I know, that'll be so amazing. I haven't had to give him a pill to calm him down once. He's been so loving to Mom and helpful to me."

The next day Ariana told me that Dad was sitting on the edge of the bed asking her where he was. She talked calmly to him, assuring him that he was safe at home. He just kept looking around and saying that nothing looked familiar to him. She asked me to talk to him.

"Hi, Dad, how are you doing today?"

"Hi, honey. Oh… I'm just a little confused right now."

"I'm sorry, that must feel awful. Don't be afraid—you're at home with Mom and Ariana."

"Am I home, sweetheart?"

"Yes, Dad, trust Ariana. She'll show you around the house until something looks familiar, okay? It'll go away soon and you'll know where you are. It's just part of living so long and you're probably starting to get a little Alzheimer's. Almost everyone your age gets a bit of it, but hey, you're in good company, Ronald Reagan has it too. You'll feel better soon—rely on Ariana, okay?"

"Okay, I will. Gee, this is an awful way to live. Why are we still living, honey?" (Now there's the $64,000 question.)

"Well, I guess there's more for you to do in your life—more important *lessons* for you to learn. Apparently, God's not ready for you yet—heaven only knows and heaven can wait."

"Oh, yeah, well—maybe you're right, honey. So, how are you?"

"I'm fine, Dad—thanks for asking."

"Gee, I'm so glad you called, sweetheart—I feel a lot better just hearing your voice."

"Good, don't be afraid, okay? Rely on Ariana. I'll call you again tomorrow. I love you, Dad."

"I love you too, sweetheart—so much," he said softly.

"Who needs a heart when a heart can be bro-ken—ohhhh." Thank you, Tina.

Late that night, Ariana's desperate phone call woke me up. "Jackie, Dad's been completely out-of-control all evening, hallucinating and talking to people who aren't in the house. He and Mom are fighting and he keeps calling her nasty names. I was able to get a pill into him a couple of hours ago, but it hasn't calmed him down at all this time."

"Oh no. It's your decision, Ariana. Call 911 if you can't handle him and we'll *have* to get him placed in a home somehow."

"Oh, I just hate to have to do that now. He's been so good for so long this time and we've been making such great progress with his temper. I think it's the real dementia coming out this time because he's talking to your brother like he's right in front of him. He won't leave Mom alone, holding tight onto her arm and she got mad and screamed when he squeezed it too hard. I got her up, away from him, but he came out demanding she be with him. She didn't want to go back so I told him he's been squeezing the Charmin too hard and to go back to bed and *dream* about her."

"Oh that's a good one, Ariana. Do you think Mom is getting fed up with him yet? It'll be easier on her when we have to put him in a home if she's completely fed up with him."

"No way! That's her husband of fifty-seven years she always tells me, and she's standing by her man, just like Tammy Wynette."

The next morning Ariana called saying she was up all night with him and he never went to sleep. "Mom wants to talk to you."

"Hi, Mom, is Dad settling down yet?"

"No! He kept me up all night, talking to people he thinks are in the room. I don't know what's wrong with him."

"Well, he has dementia, probably a little Alzheimer's, Mom. We're trying some different medications to help him, but sometimes he'll act like that. He was really good for ten whole days, wasn't he?"

"Yeah, just like his old fun self, making us laugh, but then all of a sudden he acts so crazy—it's kinda scary."

"Do you want me to have him put in a nursing home, Mom?"

"Oh, gosh, honey. I hate to think of him having to go to one of those places all by himself. No, no, Ariana and I will keep trying to calm him down ourselves. We'll get him to behave himself."

"Okay, but if you get fed up, just let me know. If he hurts you or Ariana, I'll have to do it anyway you know."

"Oh, I know, honey... I know. I hope it doesn't come to that. I love you so much, sweetheart, and always remember—so does your father."

Inhale... and hold it... *("and every now and then I fall apaaart.")* and blabber it out all over everything—again.

♥♥♥

Unwanted: Dead or Alive

The next day Horrific Hyde was worse. Ariana could hear him swearing as he tried to open a bottle of aspirin with a butter knife. She asked if she could help and he got so frustrated he slammed the bottle on the counter, shattering it as the pills flew everywhere. He defied her and put a whole handful of pills in his mouth and swallowed them without any water. Ewww. Then he shoved her against the oven and hit her in the chest. She ran into her room and phoned me. "OK, Ariana, that's it! Call 911 right now. I will not tolerate him hitting you. That butter knife could be in your chest right now."

"Oh, I'm okay. I'll just let him calm down and make him think I'm calling the cops." As she told me the saga I could hear him pounding on her door, yelling for her to come out and give him some aspirin.

"I don't have any aspirin in here, Jake. You took a whole handful already. Go lie down now—I'm very upset. You hit me and I don't want to talk to you. Go to bed and maybe I'll talk to you later."

Then we heard him take a fall and he cried major alligator tears *screaming* for help. She watched through the peep-hole and it was all an act. "It's just a manipulation, Ariana. He'll get up in a few minutes."

"Oh, I know. He pulls the falling routine all the time for attention."

Sure enough, when she didn't come out, Humpty Dumpty got up and was back to pounding on her door. Mom was yelling at him to "stop that swearing, shut up, and come back to bed right now!" Oh yeah. I was trying to help Ariana cope and she sounded like she was handling it pretty well, but little Gary was there and I was terribly worried about how all this would affect him. She convinced me that Gary understood that the old man was just acting like a bratty little boy again. "Jackie, I'm just going to ignore him and eventually he'll go lie down." He kept pounding and kicking her door as hard as he could for a solid half hour as we talked, and then all of a sudden she screamed, "OH MY GOD, Jackie—he's broken down my door!"

"Call 911, Ariana! PLEASE call the poli...!" The line went dead and I was beyond a basket case waiting for her to call me back. *Please*, God, don't let him hurt her or Gary. Please, please, Reanne, MaryAnne, help her! I couldn't believe that my biggest fear might be coming to pass that very instant. Please, please, nooooo.

The next ten minutes seemed like ten hours as I bit off all my fingernails. Finally she called back exasperated. When he'd gotten in her room he wouldn't let her out, blocking the doorway with his body like a madman. She called 911 and they got there real quick because they could hear him threatening her in the background. As usual, as soon as the cops arrived Gentle Jekyll reappeared saying that Ariana had taken his aspirin away from him and wouldn't help him. They saw the busted door and the shattered aspirin bottle and got him ready to go. He knew he'd crossed the line and didn't put up much of a fight.

I was listening to the whole thing on the open line and then he wanted to talk to me. He begged me to tell the cops not to take him, but I calmly explained that we had warned him so many times but now it was too late. He spewed some swear words at me and yelled, "My daughter doesn't give a goddamn about me," as he threw the phone down on the counter as hard as he could.

The female officer got on the line and was kind to console me, saying that she understood what I was going through as she'd been through so much craziness with her own grandfather. "We see this type of thing all the time," I heard—*again*. Then the Mod Squad called the ambulance and Ariana made it clear that he had to be taken to Dr. Endure's psychiatric hospital even though it was out of their jurisdiction. Pleading worked and they finally agreed to take him directly there.

I was surprised when Ariana told me that Mom was actually okay with it all. I talked to her and she sounded like she'd had it with his rages too. "I kept telling him that this was going to happen, but you know your father—no one can ever tell him anything." Yep.

236

Ariana said she'd call the hospital to make sure they didn't have any more *glitches* and transfer Dad to the wrong hospital again. Huge grateful inhale… (thank God Ariana was safe—thank you, thank you) and slowly release it all the way out—again.

Two and a half hours later Ariana called me in a panic. "Jackie, you're *not* going to believe this. I just phoned the hospital and they said that Dad's been released already!"

"Whaaaat?"

"Yes, I just called there and the nurse said the paperwork shows that he's been released already and that somebody must have come to pick him up. Jackie, I screamed at her that there is *nobody* to come pick him up but *me*. They have absolutely no idea where he is. I described him and she said that he just wasn't there anymore—he left already."

How-how-how could this possibly be happening? I was about to go off the deep end, but of course—there wouldn't be any water in the pool. I just could not believe the incompetence. I should write a book. *Glitch Rage: or, Take This Medical System and Shove It… Please!* "OK, Ariana, call the Keystone Kops and the amateur ambulance company and find out what in the world happened."

"Jackie, I *did* already, but they say it's out of their jurisdiction now. Should I pack up Mom and Gary and drive down there and start looking for Dad on the streets?"

"Um… no, you have to stay there in case someone calls about him. I'll see what I can do from here. Call the police department down there and describe Dad wandering around the streets of San Francisco in his coveralls like Walter Brennan in *The Real McCoys*."

Ohmygoshagain—Dad's picture was going to be on a milk carton. Ariana and I spent the next thirty minutes in pure agony. I called the hospital and asked for the hospital director, as high up as I could get. After several lengthy explanations and *interminable* holds in-between (during which I bit off all my cuticles), I finally got a laisse-faire response. "Oh, yeah… Jake? No, he hasn't been released."

Did I hear wrong? Instead of *released*, maybe she said *deceased?* Oh no, he was there, fine and dandy. I guess they were looking for Waldo. I hung up so exhausted, wondering when the network execs were finally going to pull the plug on this terrible soap opera I was under contract to star in every single day: *The Guiding Glitch.*

♥ ♥ ♥

Bound on Broadway

They held him overnight in the hospital and the next day I could not believe that Dr. Endure was back to believing my father's "*very different, very* convincing," rendition of the aspirin story. Silly me, but of course—it was opening night. My lock jaw was back as I realized that Jake Barrymore had stepped onto the stage, found his key light, and done a stellar performance of *A Maniac For All Seasons* for his captive audience. How could I forget—the play's the thing. Oh yeah, he was gonna win a Tony for this one. A star is born. Encore! Encore!

Endure said, "Your father explained that his legs were hurting him real bad and he was trying to open the aspirin bottle and he got mad because Ariana took it away from him. He admits that he gave her a *little* push to get out of his way and she got upset and went in her room. Then she wouldn't come out to give him any aspirin and his legs were burning and the pain was just unbearable apparently. So, he was softly knocking on her door asking for her help, but he solemnly *swears* up and down, on his *life*, that he did *not* break it down. Frankly, he's so unsteady on his feet, he can barely walk and has to use a wheelchair— so I don't know how he could have *possibly* busted down a door."

Well, since I had recently taken the Lorena Bobbitt correspondence course, I remained calm as I gave Dr. Endure pep talk No. 2, which I'm sure he translated into my threatening to pulverize his precious peepee. I informed him of the fact that I was on the phone with Ariana and had heard the whole horrible episode in THX Dolby Stereo myself. I assured him that Dad's *Ironsides* impersonation was Academy Award winning and that he walked just fine at home. Ariana was *furious* and couldn't believe that Dr. Endure had doubted her word again—wanting to make him sing with the sopranos herself. SNIP-SNIP!

Finally, sounding so exhausted with it all (poor baby), Endure asked, "Well, what's your final answer then? Do you want to give him another chance and take him home again, or do you just want to go ahead and put him in a nursing home—and be done with him?"

"Here's my final answer: YES, we need to place him in a home right *now*. I'm terrified that he's really going to hurt someone," I said as I added Dr. Endure's name in big BOLD black ink on the long list of recipients of the movie—*The Doctor*.

♥ ♥ ♥

What a Long Strange Trip It's Been

"Jackie, you know, Mom is a completely different person without your father here. You won't believe what I got her to do," Ariana said. "It took her a really long time, and I just watched and encouraged her, but she was able to put the side rail on her bed down, get up, go to the pottie by *herself*, pull up her pants, wash her hands, get back into bed, put on her night cap, and pull the covers up over her! I asked her why she doesn't do that for me when Dad is here and she said that he won't let her. She's getting stronger now and I see that she can do a lot more than he lets her do. She wants to be up with me reading her *People* magazine and I've got her hooked on *all* the talk shows now, watching *Rosie, Ricki, Leeza* and *Sally* with me—and she *loves* it!"

"Oh my gosh—that's great!"

"I'm going to take her out for some fun before he gets back and intimidates her again. We're going to play bingo today at the senior center and then tomorrow night, I'll bundle her up and take her in the wheelchair and we'll go trick or treating for Halloween with Gary. I think she'll really have a good time."

A week of sanity went by while my father was in the psychiatric hospital. Dr. Endure had filed the conservatorship papers and I asked him to explain all the ramifications to me so I understood how it all worked. His response completely knocked me out. "I don't know anything about it—I just sign the paperwork."

Geeeese, I'm gonna go out on a limb here, but shouldn't he know all about it or at least have the interest to find out what it means when he signs paperwork to have people put away for the rest of their lives? I bet even Doc Hollywood would have found out.

Then the hospital discharge planner located a long-term, geriatric psychiatric hospital close by—and lo and behold, Dr. Endure was even one of the shrinks there. They would work on behavior modification with Dad—reward and punishment basics. If he were good, he'd get privileges. If not, he wouldn't. The first two weeks, no visitation. He'd be there for a thirty day trial to see if he could be helped or if he'd have to be placed permanently. If he was good, he could go home for visits. Ariana would be able to bring him in and out depending on his behavior. I kept thinking—if only he'd had some behavior modification therapy to control his impulses sixty, seventy, eighty years ago. This was really going to be interesting to see if they could teach a very old dog new tricks, and if there could really be a taming of the shrewd—*or*, if he was really incapable of controlling his rages because of the dementia. I couldn't wait to find out.

Ariana called, "I just talked to Dr. Endure and he asked if you've thought about letting Dad come home again or not. I told him that we've both agonized over it, but you're afraid for our safety and think that if we don't place him now, we'll just have to go through it again soon. I said that we're not sure what he's capable of doing and that the violence is definitely getting worse with the dementia. Then he said sarcastically, 'Well, I'm glad to see she has some compassion and empathy for her own father!' Jackie, I couldn't believe he said that—what in the world does he think you've been doing all this time?"

I was *astonished* that he thought I didn't love my father. How could he think *that* after all the blood, sweat and tears I'd shed trying to help him? "Boy, that really hurts me so deeply, I just can't tell you. I guess it's because he's only seen slightly demented, sweet gentle Jekyll and can't imagine how he could be so different. I'm sure Dad has charmed him to death and convinced him that *I'm* the mentally imbalanced one, just like he did with Dr. Kiljoy's office. Ray was shocked when he finally saw the tip of the iceberg. I hate to admit this because it's so darn pathetic, but it'll be the happiest day of my life when Dr. Endure actually experiences Horrible Hyde himself."

"I understand, Jackie, really I do. Ummm... I wasn't going to tell you this part and make you feel worse, but I think you should know who Dr. Endure really is. He said nastily, 'Well, when she gets old, she's going to be *just* like her father.' Jackie, believe me, you'll *never* be like your father—look at all the friends you have who love you and how much you care about everyone and help them."

A lightening chill shot up and down my surgically altered spine. I *prayed* that I would never turn out to be like my father. I was so dismayed at how utterly unprofessional it was for a doctor to say something like that. "Wow, that's so unbelievably hurtful, Ariana. I guess I should ask him if he'd give up his life completely for nine and a half months to go take care of his disabled parents without a day off—and then be consumed with their care every single day of his life long-distance. I have no doubt that if Dad were *his* father, he'd have locked him up and thrown the key away—a *very* long time ago."

♥ ♥ ♥

Hyde Risk Behavior

We were all set for Dad to go into the psychiatric facility for thirty days to see if he could be helped or if we'd have to place him there permanently. Dr. Endure had signed the papers to get the temporary "LPS Conservatorship" in place. Then, just as my blood pressure was coming down, the other slipper dropped right on my head. (CLUNK) I got an early morning call the day Dad was to be transferred to the psychiatric facility. "We've reviewed your father's case and we've decided we will *not* take him into our facility. Even though he has been a model patient while he's been in the hospital, his records indicate that he has 'labile' moods. Therefore, we cannot take the risk with our other patients if he's capable of any type of violence." WHAT?

I *pleaded... begged... cried... bribed...* and did everything I could think of to get them to reconsider, but it was no use. Oh-oh, not good— I was starting to understand the fine art of "going postal." How on earth could this be happening? It's a *psychiatric* hospital for heaven sakes. HELLO. You'd think they'd have dealt with combative individuals maybe just once or twice before, huh? Then the discharge planner called and coldly informed me that there were no other places to put my father and we'd have to bring him home right away. I let them know that I would be suing them BIG TIME if he came home and hurt anyone. Well, I guess I can kiss off getting a free lunch from them for my birthday.

Ariana and I were so upset and found ourselves back to square one. We were on the phone all day frantically trying to find someplace else to put him. The places I had found previously were booked solid. "OK, Ariana, we're going to do this ourselves, just like everything else. Get out the yellow pages and call around, but don't give these places any details. Just find out *if* they have a lock-up unit. Just be vague and say that you're checking out facilities in the area for the future placement of your grandfather. When you find one that meets our needs, I'll call and lie through my teeth, telling them that I have a 'sweetheart patient with money to burn' who needs to be placed right now. We'll just get him in *someplace* and then the Conservatorship will go forward, and we can buy some time to figure out what to do."

While Ariana ran around looking at the places that met our criteria, she had her mother stay with Mom. We found a few but it was worse than Laughlin, Nevada on a Fourth of July weekend: NO VACANCY.

We couldn't find any facility that had availability right then, even for a *model* patient who would help with bedpans.

Dr. Endure told Ariana he was too busy to meet her at the hospital when she picked up Dad. I was so proud of her when she flat out told him that she refused to pick Dad up, unless he were there to read Jekyll & Hyde the riot act again in front of her. "I don't want Jake to know that the reason he is coming home is because *they* won't take him there. Then he'll think he can keep getting out of it every time. I want him to think he's coming home because *I'm* allowing him to come home. Maybe that way he'll have more respect for me and believe that I have the power to actually put him away when I tell him that."

Ariana called that evening and I asked, "How'd it go? Did Dad cry and *'beg of you'* to believe him that he'll never yell at anyone ever again, so help him God?"

"Nooo, I was so surprised, Jackie. He barely said a word. Dr. Endure gave him the stern talk and threatened him again about his outbursts and he just said, 'Okay, fine, let's go.' It doesn't seem like there's any remorse anymore, he's getting used to it now. I don't know—I predict another rage in a few days."

"Oh *no*. I thought this two week stint would scare him real good and we'd at least get a couple weeks of good behavior out of him."

"I doubt it, we'll see. Mom was real happy to see him though. She said she wanted a high-ball when we got home so I made her a real weak one. Jackie, it was really something. She sat at the table with your father, lifted her glass to toast him and said, 'I love you, Jake,' and then she downed her drink like a sailor. Then they went to bed cuddling and kissing all night." My heart strings were twanged again. Yeah, in spite of everything, theirs was a true love story (and even though he was always saying "sorry"), it would probably go on—from here to eternity.

It seemed like I had already been through an eternity to get to the point we were at now. I related the saga to the conservator assigned by the State, and that Ariana expected Dad to be back in the psychiatric ward again soon. I was caught off guard to hear the warm heart of the government employee. "It's a terrible dilemma you've been through, but it's a lot more common than you think." (Geemeneeze—if I hear that *one* more time.) "Tell you what I'll do. I'll make an exception and put the 'T-Con' (Temporary Conservatorship) in my desk and if you have to bring your father in again within thirty days we can pick it up and continue the investigation so you won't have to start all over again.

If it's after that, there's nothing I can do and you'll have to start from scratch at day one. To lock someone up against their will you have to have an LPS Conservatorship—there's just no way around it."

I told Ariana, "Necessity is the mother of invention. Do you know what that means?"

"I think so. It means I'm gonna open up a Combative Dementia Care Home and get rich because there are lot of people out there like Dad with no place to go."

"You are beyond brilliant. We're going to have to take matters into our own hands and figure this out together, just like everything else."

"Okey-dokey, you can count on me."

I made a huge stink to Dr. Endure about wanting the *strongest* drug made to calm Ivan the Terrible down. He gave Ariana a prescription for a much stronger anti-psychotic. Ariana said that the three nurses at the desk looked up and *gasped* in horror when they heard what Dr. Endure was prescribing for their "sweetest patient of all time." This was the drug they give the most "out-of-control" inmates in prison to calm them down. I looked it up and yeah, it's strong all right— absolutely perfect. I had less than zero tolerance left. I couldn't wait for the next screaming soliloquy of the Sterile Cuckoo to try it.

Next, I bought a book on conservatorships and read it, making a list of questions. Then, I located the best legal eagle I could find, a geriatric conservatorship attorney near my parents, and got ready. If Dad were good for thirty days we'd lose the State Conservatorship guy, but I'd be ready to go forward with a "Probate Conservatorship" privately. The next time he was performing, "Springtime For Hitler on Heroin," and Ariana had him hauled off, I'd be ready to go into action. I needed a diagnosis of "dementia" from the psychiatrist to have the attorney file papers in my parents' county. There would be a forty-five day investigation. Then I would need to attend the court hearing to try to prove to the judge that my father needed to be placed in a home against his will. It would probably cost two to three thousand dollars.

A friend told me that the Alzheimer's Association did testing through the universities to help diagnose the elderly with symptoms like Dad's. I instructed Ariana to call them and find out where we could take him to see if they could get a clearer diagnosis. We'd provide the two previous CAT scans which had shown a "normal" amount for dementia for a man his age. With their expertise, I hoped they'd be able to evaluate how serious the dementia really was.

Dad had only been home for two days when Ariana called saying that he was being very mean to Mom again. "He didn't think I was home and I just watched through the peep-hole to see how he treated Mom when he thought I wasn't here. He called her a nasty name and gave her a little push to get her to walk faster to the table. Your mother yelled at him that if he ever called her that again, she'd kill him! Boy, you shudda seen his face drop when I came out of my room and he realized that I was home. He instantly turned sweeter than his Captain Crunch. Mom was so mad at him, so I got her away from him but now he's being completely horrible to both of us. I want to try the new stronger anti-psychotic, but I wanted to check with you first."

"You have my permission, honey. Give Snidley Whiplash one and let's just see how potent it is—I can't *wait* to find out."

"WOW!" she said when she called me a couple of hours later. "That stuff knocked him on his butt real fast. Nothing has ever worked that quickly. He's out like a light, snoring up a storm and Mom and I are up having a good ol' time watching our favorite shows—*Maurey, Montel* and *Jerry* we're rooting for the girls to beat up the guys again."

"Oh my gosh, well… it probably helps her get her aggression out because she'd probably like to beat the crap out of Dad herself right now. Wait, I've got it—maybe I can get us *all* booked on a talk show and we can duke it out on national television together."

"Oh my *goodness*, Jackie—what an image!"

♥ ♥ ♥

Born to Be Just a Wild and Crazy Guy

Joyous Jekyll came back for a few more days and then he made "cereal" for Mom by pouring milk over garlic salad croutons. Then he stood over the washing machine naked, doing laundry without any clothes in the machine. Then he headed toward Mom with the "good" scissors to cut her necklace off because he couldn't unhook it. Then he stuck a half gallon of milk in the freezer and in the middle of the night Ariana caught him at the stove with the plastic container in a frying pan, trying to "thaw out" the milk. Then he left a half gallon of frozen milk on Mom's pride and joy dining-room credenza all night and just destroyed the beautiful gloss finish. I had Ariana put a big doily and a vase over it so Mom wouldn't see it, because if she did— she really *would* kill him. (Hmmm... the perfect crime—they'd never put *her* in jail.) Kidding! Geeeese.

Then he hid Mom's nightie and told Ariana that he didn't know where it was. To be convincing he spent an hour looking for it with her. Ariana finally found it hidden in the back of his closet along with the missing stapler and the pencil sharpener. Then he admitted he had put them there for safe keeping. I got nauseous wondering if poor Camellia may have really been innocent. Where are those quarters!

The next night Ariana phoned exasperated, "He's been at it *again*. The police just left."

"Oh no! Did he hit you again, honey? Did they take him away?"

"Oh nooo, he called the police on *me*."

"Whaaaaat?" OK, somebody, please... bring me a pacemaker.

"Yeah, I was sound asleep when all of a sudden he started yelling for me from the kitchen table. I ran out there thinking something awful had happened and he started accusing me of having a party in my room. I told him that Gary and I were asleep and there was no party. I was afraid to let him in there if he was going to be a madman in front of Gary. He wouldn't believe me and he tried to call the police, but he kept mis-dialing so he handed me the phone demanding that I call the police—on *myself!* I got 911 on the line for him and then he said, 'There's a woman having a party here in my house and I want her removed. No, you can't talk to her. What? OK-OK, here Ariana, talk to them or they won't come get you.'"

"Ohhh my Goddd. I don't know why his escapades still shock me. What did Barnaby Jones say, honey?"

"I told them what was happening and to please come help me with him. They're getting quite a file on him now. Two cops came out right away and they were really great with him. They showed him the room and that it was just Gary sleeping. Then they talked to him for a real long time about how lucky he was to be at home and have us to take care of him. They asked me if I wanted them to call an ambulance to have him taken to the hospital again, but then Dad suddenly just said that he was sorry for bothering them, thanked them both for coming, and slithered off to bed leaving us sitting there. I got their names and they told me to call for them personally if I had anymore trouble with him and they'd be right out with an ambulance. I showed them the little peep-holes I put in and they were really impressed, saying what a good idea they are. They said they 'see this kind of thing all the time' and know how hard it is to deal with."

"Oh my gosh, Ariana. I'm so sorry. It's never a dull moment, is it?"

The next morning, my Godfather, Bo, called to tell me that my darling Godmother, Shelly, had just passed away. It really hit me hard, and I was terribly worried about Bo and all the stress on him. They'd had the most beautiful fifty-seven year marriage (a true love story, that *never* needed to be sorry) and I knew that statistically one usually follows the other. I just couldn't bear the thought of losing Bo too. Soon after, Ariana called and I cried as I told her the sad news. She gasped, "Wow, Jackie, your mother woke up this morning crying that Shelly had just died. I told her, 'Nooo, I'm sure she's still doing fine,' but she *insisted* and I couldn't get her to calm down. Wow, this gives me the chills—your mother must be psychic."

"I think WOW is a little bit of an understatement. More than psychic—Mom must have a red DSL hot line to the other side."

Then, that night the phone rang at two AM and if *I* had been psychic I wouldn't have answered the phone. OK, what bad news was about to befall me next? Sure enough, Horrific Hyde was spewing again. "I need some money!" he demanded.

"Hi, Dad. Okay, what would you like to buy at two in the morning?"

"I gotta have the trees trimmed and I want to get my hair cut too."

"Okay, no problem. Don't worry—I'll send Ariana some extra money so you can have those things done right away, okay?"

"Goddamn it, I want my own money! That fucking bitch won't give it to me if you send it to her. I don't want her to know every goddamn thing I do. I'm going to take care of her too—you watch. She's going to be real sorry for all she's done to me. You send it to me, do you hear me? I mean it—you send it or else! You send it right now in a brown envelope and I'll go sit outside and wait for the goddamn mailman." (Good idea, J.P.—go out and sit there for about four days and wait for the pony express.) I was getting nervous about where Tina was, since she was on duty that night.

"Okay fine, Dad, no problem, I will. Where's Tina?"

"Who? There's nobody here."

I took some deep breaths and tried to practice my Zen meditation. "Oh, I'm sure Tina's sleeping there tonight. Why don't you knock softly on her door—it's very late." Poor Tina came to the phone wondering what was going on. She assured me that he'd been on very good behavior all evening since she had gotten there when Ariana left. She calmed him down and he finally agreed to go back to bed. A few hours later I needed a defibrillator when the phone rang again.

"Where's my goddamn money? It hasn't come yet!"

"I promise I sent you some extra money already. Go to bed now, okay? The check's in the mail." (...and the bats are in the belfry.)

He spewed a few more insults and then slammed the phone down with, "OK, you better have, goddamn it, or you're gonna be sorry!"

I couldn't sleep the rest of the night. Ariana arrived at eight AM to relieve Tina and all hell apparently broke lose as I got a pandemonium call from Ariana. "Jackie, I'm going to give him another one of the stronger pills. He's completely out-of-control, screaming and throwing things all over the house like a madman. I just wanted you to know."

I was so completely exhausted from crying about Shelly and being awakened all night, I was completely ambivalent, well... yes and no. *("It don't matter to me.")* "No problem, honey. It worked the first time without any side effects—go for it. You don't have to check with me each time—just use it on King Kong whenever you need to. Just remember to get Fay Wray out of the way. I trust your judgement." I was, however, wishing she'd pour the whole bottle down Bela Lugosi's thick throat after she used a little bamboo under his fingernails. Guilt be GONE! I flopped back onto my pillow, pulled the covers over my head, and finally fell back asleep, thinking all would be fine, but nooooo. At ten AM he called again, screaming at the top of his lungs.

"What the hell kind of daughter are you—you've never done anything for me, you goddamn whore! You're gonna be real sorry too!" He went on and on spewing persecutions at me, my brother, my mother and basically the entire world. I felt my Zen evaporate into thin air and I suddenly *snapped* and completely lost all control, as I *exploded* and screamed back at him in a rage that rivaled his own.

"I can't take anymore of this! I was there for nine months and endured you choking me, throwing me out of the house, saying horrible threatening things to me, and I still stayed there and helped you. And this is how you repay me? Is this what you want for me after working so hard to put me through college? To end up being consumed with having to take care of you every single day of my life? I handle everything for you, it's a huge job. You're a demented old man and I've done everything I can to help you and keep you in your home, but

I don't want to do it anymore. What about me? You have Mom, Ariana and Tina there with you. Who's here for me? You're not here for me. All you do is give me grief. I can't take this stress *anymore*," I screamed hysterically and then I slammed the phone down.

A few minutes later he called, "Honey, I'm so sorry, let me talk to you, please, I'm sorry." NOT AGAIN! Jekyll was back, but I was beyond exhausted and too worn out to hear one more fleeting apology. For me, the bell was tolling, "Give me liberty or give me death."

"Nooooo!" I screamed as I slammed the phone down again.

Five minutes went by as I cried into my pillow. (I *really* have to get some waterproof mascara.) I felt like I was falling into the deep abyss of a bottomless snake pit and the pendulum was headed straight for me. Oh-oh, not good—I was starting to understand Billy-Jo McCalister.

Then I started worrying about Ariana, thinking the worst. Just the day before she'd found Mom's rolling pin, hidden behind a couch cushion next to her door. What was he planning to do—clobber her over the head with it? Ariana had gotten rid of that lethal weapon, but who knew what else he was capable of. God, please don't let anything happen to Mom or Ariana. Then the phone rang again and my father was back to being completely normal.

"Can I talk to you, sweetheart? Please, *I beg of you.* I'm worried about you, honey."

"Nooooo! Where's Ariana?" I screamed at him.

"Oh, she's just walking in the door right now. Here, Ariana, please talk to Jackie. I'm sorry, I really upset her. You gotta help her, honey. See if you can calm her down—she sounds *real* bad." I couldn't believe how completely sane he sounded.

Ariana had gone to the store as the drug had put him to sleep, and they were both snoring up a storm when she left. We couldn't believe it—he was so darn strong he must have become immune to it already, as it didn't even work on him for two hours this time. I wondered if he had just hidden it under his tongue and fooled her. I sobbed to Ariana that he was destroying me and to take me off the speed-dial. "Scare the crap out of him and tell him I'm done and he can take care of everything himself. Tell him I don't want anymore responsibility and Tina and you are quitting too."

"Okay, don't worry, get some rest. I'll handle everything. Rely on me." Poor Ariana—now she had *my* mental health to worry about.

She called later to check on me. "Wow, you won't believe your father. He's been crying really hard all day (so join the club), hitting #8 on the speed-dial, trying to call you *over* and *over.* I told him you took your phone off the hook and that you don't want to talk to any of us. I've never seen him cry this hard. He just keeps saying it's all his fault and how much he loves you. He must have tried to call you a hundred times. Mom just sits there shaking her head "tisk-ing" him and scolding him that his own son won't talk to him—and now his own daughter won't either because he's been so awful to you both."

"Good! I want him miserable, just like I am. Is Mom okay?"

"Oh yeah, I whispered to her what's going on so she doesn't worry and I think she's actually enjoying letting him have it too. She and I are really punishing him *bad.* I told him that he's pushed you to the brink and that you're washing your hands of him, and that Tina and I are quitting because we've had it with him too. I told him that the State will come in and put them in separate homes. Then he went into the kitchen and when I asked him what he was doing he said, 'Looking for a knife so I can kill myself.'"

"Oh, geeeese—did you offer to sharpen one for him?"

"Yeah, really. I sat down with him and we had a real serious talk about his behavior *again.* Jackie, he really loves you—I can promise you that. He cried so hard as he told me all about when you were a little girl and how cute and smart you were and how much he adored you and still does. Then he told me about all the things you did like the oil paintings—and the time you put firecrackers in the middle of big globs of oil paint and you blew a hole in the canvas and he said, 'Honey, let me get you some stronger masonite.' Then he loved helping you make blow-up paintings in the middle of the street until the police came."

"Yeah," I sniffled softly.

"Then he told me how you made hippie beads and sold them standing on the corner of Haight-Ashbury and that you made so much money. And then he told me how proud they were that you were the first one to go to college and how excited they were when you landed such big important jobs. He just sobbed in between beaming about you and your accomplishments. Then he told me that you taught film and photography at lots of big colleges and then about all the famous people you photographed and all the TV shows and movies you worked on. Oh, and then all the rock & roll groups you photographed for the *Midnight Special* TV show. He just went on and on. And then he told me how worried he was when you took a year off and traveled all over Europe by yourself, and about the time you almost drowned scuba diving. Gee, you never told me all this. Believe me, you should never doubt that deep down he really loves you. And I'll guarantee you something else—he *really* loves your brother too. He just sobbed talking about his son. I know him pretty well now and this was real."

"Oh, thank you so much, Ariana—thank you, thank you." I was a squishy marshmallow—*again.*

"Then he started playing 'follow the leader' chasing me around the house for hours, kissing me all over on my arms and face and hugging me, holding onto my shirt, begging me not to leave him. He kept saying how much he loves Tina and me and that we're like *family* to him."

"Gee, now there's an honor and a privilege ya want. Look how well Mr. Kissey treats his *family.*"

"Oh, he'll be back to calling me a 'bitch' in a few days. Boy, Jackie, it's impossible for a family member to do this type of work. It's hard on me, but I couldn't do it if he were my father. Look how strong of a person you are to go through all of this. Anyone else would have cracked a long time ago. Don't worry, okay? You just relax and rely on me. Oh, you know what else? I can't believe that the medicine didn't work this time. Maybe he tricked me and really didn't swallow it. I think I'm going to have to check under his tongue from now on. Gosh, he's so darn strong, I wish I could give him a shot of something to calm him down when he's bouncing off the walls." Hmmm, tequila or cyanide? Now, how did the plot to *Arsenic and Old Lace* go?

"Thanks *again*, Ariana. You have no idea how grateful I am for all you've done. You are such an angel to stay and put up with all of this. I'm just so sick and tired of it all—I just can't stand it any longer. I don't want to talk to him anymore, it's too hard on me. Don't put me back on the speed-dial. I don't want E.T. Senior to phone home. I'm not sure who I'm becoming but I'm definitely not myself anymore. I'm getting kinda scared because I'm starting to have rages myself."

"Oh don't worry, you just need a little break. I can handle him. Get some rest and then you'll be back to yourself—I'm sure of it."

I hung up so exhausted, glanced in the mirror and caught my sad reflection. "Mirror mirror on the wall, I am my father—after all."

Noooooo, anything but that!

♥♥♥

chapter sixteen

TO BE DEMENTED OR DECEPTIVE?
THAT WAS THE QUESTION

Silence was golden while I had no contact with my father, giving me the time to focus on Oprah's most valuable lesson of remembering my own spirit. I had a lot of life ahead of me and I knew my parents would never want me to be so unhappy. I had a responsibility to myself to make sure my own life fulfilled all the advantages they had worked so hard to give me.

As I analyzed the situation, I realized that the only way I was going to be able to cope with this responsibility long-term was to figure out a way to not let my emotions overwhelm me. I needed to be able to shift my perspective at *will* and become emotionally detached while still operating from a place of calm compassion. I knew I had to practice and "train" my brain using repetitive mental gymnastics to create *automatic* responses so that they would eventually become normal thinking for me. I knew my mind was like a computer that had to be programmed with positive thoughts in order to get positive behavior. I had to eliminate my doubts and fears, become addicted to positive thinking and be able to immediately cancel all negativity. If I *thought* negatively, I would *behave* negatively. Or, as Mom always said, "Garbage in—garbage out."

My biggest job was to work on me and I tackled it with positive message flash cards posted everywhere I looked: on the walls, in the drawers, in my car, on the phones, in the shower, in the refrigerator, in the microwave—that *constantly* reminded me of where I wanted to be emotionally. I became very aware of my thinking processes and when I noticed my mind going down a negative path, I immediately yelled, "CANCEL!" and pulled out my lists of positive messages and read them *over* and *over* until I got back on a positive track. I was quite pleased with myself, which made me feel even better, because it started making a huge difference—immediately. (*Or*, as Mom would say, "Pick yourself up, dust yourself off, and start all over again.")

Then… the *best* news. Ariana and I were just thrilled when the Alzheimer's Association accepted Dad in for a complete evaluation. We filled out a detailed questionnaire about his behaviors over the phone and then they did every test imaginable on him. The day of the diagnosis, Ariana had her son, Gary, sit with Mom and Dad just outside the glass meeting room while she was in with several doctors. When Ariana saw Dad try to escape with Mom, pushing her down the hall in her wheelchair, little Gary went into action. She rushed out to hear her five-year-old say, "Jake, if you're a good boy and sit here like you're s'posed to, I'll buy you a cookie outta that machine over there. I got a whole dollar in my pocket!" How cute is that? I called him later and raved about what a great help he was to his mommy and me.

After much testing and thorough evaluation, Dad was diagnosed with "multi-infarct vascular dementia." They only diagnose "probable Alzheimer's" (another type of dementia) when all other possible causes have been ruled out. They said that Alzheimer's cannot be definitively diagnosed with 100% accuracy until the brain tissue is examined under a microscope at autopsy, but they can be 80-90% sure. Since 50% of all persons over the age of eighty-five get Alzheimer's and he had so many of the symptoms, they felt that he probably had it as a secondary dementia.

The Alzheimer's Association was so *fantastic*, spending time helping me understand that Dad's brain was damaged in the frontal lobe, the area that controls short-term memory, judgement, logic, and *impulse* control. Ah-ha! It may have been damaged for a quite sometime, causing his flash-fire outbursts when he'd get mad. It was so comforting to finally be told what was happening to him.

They recommended that we try a drug called "Aricept" for Dad's memory loss. It took several months but then Ariana and I realized that Dad's memory was noticeably better. Since Mom had short-term memory loss and vascular dementia too, we put her on it and her memory also improved dramatically. Ariana was thrilled to no longer have to play the torturous *Twenty Question* quiz game every hour of wakefulness anymore. (Exelon is excellent for memory loss also.)

They stressed the extreme importance of Adult Day Care and helped us get my parents enrolled. It was a long process but it turned out to be well worth the wait. Prior to going, Dad fought Ariana about it for days, saying he would, "not go, NO, nope, not going, forget it," and he refused to take a shower or change his filthy coveralls for over a week. On the first visit he was completely repulsive and tried to sabotage it. The staff kept trying to keep him separated from Mom because he wouldn't leave her alone, holding on to her and touching her inappropriately.

Then, he threw his lunch on the floor in a raging temper tantrum and when that didn't make them let Mom be with him, he went into the bathroom and tried to escape. When he couldn't get out he came out of the bathroom with his coveralls unzipped exposing himself. *Then*, he even messed in his own pants and threw another swearing tantrum when they made him sit away from everyone because he smelled so bad. Four hours later when Ariana arrived to pick them up, all the social workers were completely exhausted with him and had already had quite enough of stinky Hyde the Hun.

"I'm sorry, Ariana. Jake is completely disruptive and we cannot allow him here. He will not be able to come back. His dementia is very bad and he's just not capable of controlling himself. Mariel is the sweetest person and her mind is still quite good, so we'd love to have her as often as possible."

Ariana begged and pleaded for them to give nasty Nanook of the North one more chance. She promised that his manipulations would stop and that he would be scrubbed up and on very good behavior by the next day. They were *very* skeptical, insisting that he could not control himself because of the dementia. We *roared*, knowing that he was quite in control of much of his manipulative behavior. No-no-no… demented does *not* mean stupid.

Ariana read Dad the riot act all night long. "Jake, you are not going to ruin this for Mariel—period! She's going whether you like it or not. We've waited three months to get into this place—so you can behave and go too, or you're going to be stuck with me while Mom has fun at school. There is no negotiating! Now get in and take a shower and I mean it, right NOW!" He ranted and raved but finally got in. When Ariana checked on him he was just sitting in there *fuming* mad, with his arms crossed, letting the water run over him.

"Jackie, I put on yellow rubber gloves and got a soapy washcloth and scrubbed your father from head to toe, and I do mean every inch. He spit and swore at me the whole time, but I don't care—he is *not* ruining what we worked so hard for. It's going to do Mom a world of good to be around other people. She already made a new friend today and she loves it there—and it's going to do *me* a world of good to have a little break."

"Oh yes, I think it's going to do ALL of us a world of good."

Well... it was completely amazing when the next morning Gentle Jekyll was back, singing a sweeter smelling tune. "Jackie, you won't believe it. Your father got up and let me help him get dressed in a nice pair of pants and a shirt for the first time since I've been here. When we got to the Day Care the social workers could not *believe* that he was even the same person. He participated in all the activities, left Mom alone, ate all his lunch, played the games, did the exercises, made a birdhouse, told stories, sang, and even charmed them all when he danced a waltz!"

"Oh my GOSH!" (*Uncontrollable* dementia my derriere!)

"Jackie, Mom was so happy today. I clipped her orchids and made her a corsage and she told everyone how her orchids finally bloomed. Then when I picked them up, I asked her, 'Doesn't Jake look great in his nice clothes, Mariel?' She put her index finger to her lips and said, 'Shhh, don't remind him. He'll be right back in those damn coveralls that I've hated for fifty-seven years!' Jackie, I was dying."

Pretty soon Dad became completely gung-ho on the Day Care and couldn't wait to go, waking Ariana up in the middle of the night asking if it was time to get up to go yet. We were so thrilled that he stopped protesting and actually started to enjoy it.

Then suddenly his temperament changed and it was, "Oh, Ariana, someone took a real bad fall over there today. We better not go back." Uh-huh. Ariana checked—just another tall tale. The next day when Ariana went to pick them up, she asked Mom how her day was.

Dad quickly answered for her, "She doesn't like it there anymore. Everyone is too old—she doesn't want to go back."

Mom piped up, "Well, I do *so* want to go back—I love going there." She looked at Ariana, mad as hell and said, "He's just an *asshole*, Ariana." We roared over that one. Later that night as Ariana was putting them to bed, Dad tried to convince her again that Mom didn't want to go back to Day Care. Mom's jaw dropped and she raised her hand and bonked Dad upside the head. "I don't care what you say—I'M GOING, aren't I, Ariana?"

Dad was so shocked he just rolled over, "Ohh-k, gee whiz!"

Ariana and I loved that Mom was finally starting to assert herself. Hey, what's bad for the golden goose is going to be *really* bad for the golden gander. Before Ariana went to bed that night, she gave them another pep talk about the Day Care the next day. "And now Mariel, I don't want to come in here and see any bruises or black eyes on Jake in the morning!" Mom started to laugh, then Dad started to laugh as he rolled back over to cuddle Mom, and then they all had a good ol' golden goose and gander giggle.

♥ ♥ ♥

How to Earn a Ph.D. at Home

Mom always said, "God never gives us more than we can handle." Okay, then there *must* be a real long-term solution to this, and by Jake, I was going to "put my thinking cap on" and find it. When even a *psychiatric* hospital rejected my father, I realized that I was back to having to solve everything myself. During his evaluation there the hospital staff had explained to me many of the behavior modification techniques they would use. I had heard of these methods of reward and punishment working on problem children and difficult teenagers, so I thought well, *maybe* I could teach them to Ariana to try on Dad. I'd have her implement my experimental course in "Elder Psychology 101" as I made up the curriculum as we went along.

I felt certain that what my father needed was to have Ariana be completely *consistent* with him one hundred percent of the time. If I were to hire her now, I'd get her a white medical lab coat and a stethoscope to give her even more authority. *My* biggest job was to strengthen her reserves and help shift her perception of the ongoing turmoil into one of a great learning opportunity. We both had to see Dad as an interesting *challenge* instead of a nightmare.

I taught Ariana how to administer "tough love" and not be swayed by my father's words, only his actions. When he behaved badly, first she used loving compassion, telling him how much she understood how upset he was. "Oh Jake, I'm sorry you're so frustrated right now. I understand—let's sit down and talk about it." *Sometimes* this calm approach would catch him off guard, not having anyone to argue with. By allowing him to calm down, giving him the feeling of being in control and making some of his own decisions, it helped him to feel less frustrated. I told her that accomplishing a *task* (like getting dressed or combing his hair) wasn't as important as making him feel more in charge of his life. A shower now or a shower later, eating now or later, giving him choices to pick from instead of yes or no questions, helped him feel more secure and in control of things.

But, if he didn't calm down with empathy, she'd give him three stern warnings and then there would *always* be a specific consequence that she followed through with, every single time. I had her use a calm tone of voice and a firm confident stance as defined limits were set and there were no idle threats. She was as consistent as Tiger Woods with her follow through as she took away privileges like dessert, being with Mom, watching television, or going to Day Care. She gave him penalty "time-outs" and refused to speak to him after her third warning. "One more time, Jake, and I'm calling Dr. Endure." After four times in the psychiatric hospital, that threat finally worked because he did *not* want to go back there again. Once while she was punishing him by keeping him home from Day Care, she drove him to a nursing home, took him on a tour of it, and told him that he was headed there, without Mom, if he didn't behave better. He shaped up real fast.

When she'd call exasperated with him, I'd point out that this latest tantrum was giving her more practice to see which of her new techniques would work the best. Several times a day we'd discuss the best ways to handle each mini crisis and many times her ideas were nothing short of brilliant. It was really something. For the first time in his life, my father was getting the *real* behavioral therapy that he should have gotten as a very young man—from a young woman with more smarts than all the so-called "professionals" we had been to.

I had spent over nine torturous months with my parents and it had already been another nine months since Ariana first met the infamous Jekyll & Hyde. It seemed like nine lives later to me. What a slow and arduous process, but as she started systematically using these new reward and punishment methods, my father *finally* started to abdicate to her authority. Without any caregiving experience, she was helping me change the course of my parent's lives, as well as my own.

He always wanted to know what time something was supposed to happen and would drive Ariana nuts with his constant harping, and then be furious if it didn't happen on the dot. She was able to stop the obsession by never telling him exactly what time she would do something. She switched to always being vague and relaxed about time frames. "Oh, sometime today. It'll happen when it happens and remember—you're not allowed to ask me about it." He *eventually* learned that "time" was off-limits. He got to where he'd shrug and know to just drop it. By keeping the daily schedule as consistent as possible so he would not get confused, she got him to relax and trust how she would handle things. Eventually he learned to just go with the flow of the day and not be so upset by any changes.

We were delighted—the progress was slow but sure with fewer and fewer setbacks. It became clear that these behavior modification techniques, in combination with the right medications, were finally starting to produce significant changes in his behavior. When he was good, she rewarded and praised him with loving attention, giving him the hugs and affection that he loved. As rewards she would offer little gifts, making him special dinners and treats, always reinforcing that it was because of his good behavior. She'd rave about how proud of him she was and spend more time with him, getting him to talk about his career or asking his advice. She encouraged him to talk about his childhood, and he shared more about his life with her than I had ever heard him express to anyone. I'd have her ask him about the war, the depression, specific events of his lifetime, and it made him feel good to tell her his stories. It was another win-win because it gave Ariana insight into history that she didn't have any knowledge of.

The family tradition of the "contract agreement" still worked well. One day when he played opossum, not wanting to go to Day Care, she let him negotiate a floating monthly *Elder Ferris Bueller's Day Off* when he'd get to stay home in bed. They wrote up a contract together, Mom witnessed it, and it was posted next to his bed. Then Ariana said she doubted if he was *really* going to keep his word. Dad yelled, "Well... I bet ya I do!" And—he did.

Another time, Mom had to stay home from Day Care because of a bad cough, but Ariana made Dad go anyway, despite his very loud protests. Once there, he suddenly had horrible pains in his legs and couldn't walk. The worried staff got him a wheelchair and babied him for hours. Then he started his Academy Award performance getting extremely sick, turning clammy white, falling, and saying he didn't know where he was. Playing it safe, the Day Care phoned Ariana insisting that she come take him to see Dr. Kiljoy right away. Uh-huh. They wheeled him out to the car and were worried that they couldn't lift him into it. Ariana just looked at him and commanded, "Get in the car, Jake." With that, he was miraculously cured and happily jumped right in. Aaaad let's inhale… (dementia?… or deception?… or both?) aaaand change that perspective before you go mad… and release.

She drove him straight to the emergency room while he insisted that he was suddenly much better and should just go home to bed with Mom. At the last minute she headed for home, letting him know that she wasn't buying his latest act. She took Mom away from him, putting her in the hospital bed. He threw a tantrum. She turned her back on him, put her hands over her ears and drowned him out with, "Jake, if you aren't in your bed on the count of three, I'm calling Dr. Endure and you're going to the psychiatric hospital for a two week attitude adjustment!" Lickety-split—he was back in the bed. Then she made him stay there for his meals and even made him use the portable urinal. No TV, no Mom, no walking, minimal communication. She kept telling him that if he was too sick to go to Day Care, he was too sick to get out of bed for *anything*. Well… by that night—he was *begging* to go to Day Care the next day. God Bless Ariana—*again!*

Ariana reinforced how lucky he was to have a daughter to take care them, who was willing to do what I had done. Deep down, I knew that he really loved me and didn't even realize the depth of the devastation he had caused me. Then, when he finally started to *really* thank me, I knew it had all been worth the unbelievable struggle. He began to say, "We love you so much, sweetheart," at the end of every conversation and I hung up and shed buckets of joy every time. *("Time heals all wounds they say, and I should know.")*

After much experimentation with numerous types, combinations and dosages of drugs, we discovered that one and a *half* milligrams of the anti-psychotic, with an anti-anxiety/anti-depressant, and Exelon for memory, produced the most consistent results at his current level of dementia. In *combination* with the behavior modification, we charted tangible proof on our calendars that we were finally on the right track.

As he learned to trust and let go of control, we were able to stop all the *heavy* psyche medications. So much of the really bizarre behavior stopped and we realized that certain medications had actually caused some of the craziness. His own stubborn nastiness and unwillingness to let anyone help him had forced us to use stronger medications to try to control him, which had only made his eccentric behaviors worse.

It was amazing that my father was starting his life over at nearly eighty-five years old. He was now better at controlling his temper (because there was always a serious *consequence*) than he had ever been in his entire life, even with the dementia. I thought Ariana and I should teach combative care classes and definitely get honorary Ph.D.'s in psychology—we'd sure earned them. I marveled that Amazing Ariana, who with no experience in elder care and only *one* year of high school, was more effective at controlling my father than all the doctors, nurses, therapists, social workers, and drugs we had tried—put together.

As you can imagine, I was so indebted to Ariana that I wanted to give her something in return. She'd had such a rough life and since her formal education was so lacking, I began discreetly mentoring her, teaching her something almost everyday. Then I'd quiz her to make sure she got it and I always enjoyed seeing how smart she was. Whenever there were educational programs on TV, I'd encourage her to watch them with me long-distance. "Turn on *Oprah*, Ariana. Dr. Phill McGraw is on and you're going to learn a lot about psychology and family relationships today, and tomorrow we'll watch Dr. John Gray."

"Jackie, you're so smart and educated, and you know so much about so many things, you should try to get on your friend, Regis' quiz show—I bet you'd be a millionaire!"

"Oh, thanks for the vote of confidence, honey, but no, I'm sure I've already used up all my lifelines—twice."

It warmed my heart as I began to recognize a change in Ariana. She was so proud of herself to be handling such a difficult job so well. I raved about the great job she was doing as she learned to successfully handle each situation, helping to build her self esteem. She learned so much about elder care that she started getting offers to talk about how to manage difficult elders and help others. I encouraged her, "You are the *only* person in the world to *ever* control Dad. Think what you could do with a 'normal' difficult elder."

If I could have bought Ariana a college education I would have, but at least I was able to get her a computer so she could learn the internet and e-mail. She was so terrified of it that it stayed in the box for months until I finally convinced her to tackle it. "You're not supposed to know how to use it. No one knows how to do anything at first. Look at all you've learned about how to handle Dad that you didn't know last year." Needless to say she became a "webmaster" telling me about all these incredible sites she found everyday and all the free stuff she got delivered. She even taught little Gary how to play with it. I realized that we had both been blessed to know each other. It was truly a win-win relationship that we had created. Getting to know Amazing Ariana has been a big part of the silver-lining to this unbelievable experience.

In the same way, the relationship with my brother had steadily improved, unfortunately—his health had not. He was now recovering from open heart surgery, and since I couldn't be with him I thought giving him a computer would help keep us in touch. For his birthday I had Ariana bring him one and she showed him all the internet tricks she had learned. He got completely hooked on it and I was so pleased that it gave him something fun to do. We e-mailed several times a week and at the end of his e-mails he always said, "I love you." You know I needed a tissue every single time.

Ariana called all my parents' friends and relatives regularly and let Mom talk as long as she wanted to. She'd make Dad stay in bed so Mom wouldn't be intimidated and just hang up quickly. Amazingly, he learned not to say a word about it if he wanted dessert. On lucid Sundays Ariana would take them to visit the friends that Dad had cut off over the years and Mom loved being able to see everyone again. Ariana gave Dad strict rules about his behavior when they went out because he'd just want to hurry hurry hurry and get back to home to bed. "If you sit there and make us uncomfortable and keep bugging us to go home the whole time, you're not going to get to go with us next week." Not having any other option, he started being his most charming self to all the friends he had alienated so long ago, and then he actually started to enjoy seeing everyone again too.

I had Ariana take them to see Mom's best friend, Gineva, and they all had such a lovely time laughing and reminiscing about the old days. Then it wasn't a month later when her daughter called me with the sad news that Gineva had passed away that morning. She didn't want to upset Mom and wanted me to decide if we would tell her. I hadn't even decided yet when I got a call from Ariana. "Mom is *insisting* that she got a letter from Gineva today and that something is very wrong because she repeated herself in the letter and Mom said that it is so unlike Gineva to repeat herself. She said, 'I'm sure Gineva has just died, Ariana.' Jackie, this is getting too spooky. First your Godmother and now Gineva. How could she know these things?"

"Wow. You know, I think it's actually quite comforting. Think of it as more proof that there really must be *something* beyond this physical life."

Then Dad started to get attached to Ariana's boyfriend, Lee, waking Ariana up in the middle of the night to ask what time Lee was coming over to watch sports with him. Lee would take the opposing team, rub Dad's head for luck, and then do back-flips and make him laugh when his team would score. He did so much to help out and I was very grateful to him too. He'd wash and wax Dad's car, and then take Dad and little Gary out to get their haircuts—boys day out.

Lee baby-sat Dad while Ariana took Mom to see Jeremy and Carrie every now and then. Dad was sad that he couldn't go along, but he learned not to argue about it. He'd say, "Please tell Jeremy I'm sorry for all I've done and that I love him very much." I was so happy that Mom got to see her son regularly without any repercussion. Jeremy was happy about it too, and I realized the emotional healing that had taken place. When they'd come home, Dad would ask her, "Did you have a nice day with Jeremy and Carrie, honey? Good, I'm glad, sweetheart."

My parents' dementia continued to surface intermittently and many times humorously. One day out of the blue Dad told everyone that he had a part-time job taking care of Clark Gable's horses. Mom was so excited and confirmed it, asking Ariana to take them shopping for hay. Then, Mom was convinced that I was making a movie that she was going to be in. When Dad's dementia caused fear, Ariana was able to sit with him and make him feel secure. She helped him understand that it was just his dementia and it would go away soon and not to worry so much about it. He finally trusted what she told him and instead of lashing out, he learned to accept that he just wasn't thinking clearly at that moment. He got to the point where he'd shake his head, laugh about it, and go lie down next to Mom and say, "Looks like my goddamn dementia's back again."

One morning at breakfast Dad announced that he had sold Mom's Mustang to Clive next door for thousands of dollars.

"What!" Mom said, "you better not have—that's *my* car. And you better not touch my dining-room set either!"

"No, Jake, look—the car's still there," Ariana told him. "Maybe you dreamed that, but I know you didn't sell it. Mom would kill ya."

"No? Are you sure? Hmmm, I coulda swore I did—but I'm glad I didn't if you didn't want me to, Mommy," he said kissing her. "Guess I'm just having a little more of my dementia again—oh well."

My obvious new theme song became, *"What a difference a year makes,"* because my parents had been happily attending Senior Day Care regularly for over twelve months. Long before I'd had several friends recommend it, but I remember thinking that it wouldn't be of much value and that my parents would never get out of bed to go *there*. Until I spoke with the Alzheimer's Association my impression of Day Care was that of a glorified nursing home. They helped me understand how important it was to give my parents something to do outside of being in bed—waiting to die.

Even though my parents were still together and in their own home, it was impossible for Ariana to supply enough daily stimulation. No one was more surprised than I when they became such shining success stories at the Day Care, progressing so dramatically in their behavior and strength. I started to tell everyone I knew who was struggling to manage their elderly parents about the *tremendous* value of Day Care. I smiled each time I heard the same reluctance: "They would never go *there*, Jacqueline." I realized that the negative stereotype of Day Care needed a major PR campaign.

Since we were making such great strides, I encouraged the Day Care staff not to let Dad slide with bad behavior there. When he'd act up they would separate him from Mom. That was the worst thing that could happen to him, so he got progressively better at controlling himself there too. Of course, he learned which social workers he could manipulate and which ones he couldn't. He'd snow each new worker until they'd finally get wise, always telling me that he was "quite the character." Really?

I loved that they enjoyed so many different activities at the Day Care: bingo and games, cooking, arts and crafts, singing, discussion groups, movies, exercise, a men's group for Dad, and a women's group for Mom. The center also scheduled regular visits with children and pets for them to interact with. They did Mom's nails regularly and the podiatrist would also come by. Ariana sent me the greeting cards they'd make for me and I'd shed tears every time. I realized that it was as hard and time consuming for me to raise my parents—as it must have been for them to raise me.

I called the Day Care staff frequently to thank the social workers who spent so much time working with them and making their lives worth living. "What's my mother doing at the moment?"

"Oh, she's really enjoying herself right now—she's painting a pretty picture and let's see... it looks like a green meadow with blooming flowers, a waterfall, and a great big rainbow in the sky."

I smiled, "Yes, that's one of her favorite places—and what's my father doing?"

"Oh, he's watching her and making her laugh. They're the cutest couple we've ever had—always holding hands and kissing."

Then, another transformation. I could *not* believe it when I heard that Dad's new best friend was a black man and they enjoyed being together and laughing. One day Dad came home from Day Care and as Ariana helped him off the shuttle he emphatically declared, "I have a dream!" The movie about Martin Luther King, Jr. that day had apparently left quite an impression. He said, "What a *great* man— I didn't know all that about him."

That night I called my father and we actually had a meaningful conversation about the turn of the century. Out of curiosity I asked him what he thought the greatest accomplishment of the century was since he had lived through most of it. I was so stunned when he said without missing a beat, "When they got the whites and the blacks to accept each other." It was totally amazing—his life-long bigotry was fading away too. I guess he forgot that he used to be prejudiced.

Ariana solved the shower arguments by telling Dad that he smelled bad and that it reflected badly on her if he wasn't clean. "It makes people think I'm not doing a good job of taking care of you, Jake. That really hurts my feelings." When he'd get in the shower and just sit in there mad with the water running over him, all she'd have to do was get out the yellow rubber gloves and *snap* them on.

"OK-OK, I'll wash!" he'd yell as he started scrubbing.

My mother continued to get stronger physically and emotionally, surprising the doctors who said not to expect her to survive her heart attack thirteen years before, or recover from her near-death infection two years earlier. I realized that with the proper care she was better than she'd been since her heart attack. She continued to assert herself, and with Ariana as her backup, Dad finally learned to let her have her way for the first time in her life. Ariana and I loved it every time she spoke up for what *she* wanted to do. Most of the time her wishes were simply to be with my father, as he was being so sweet and loving to her again—*most* of the time.

One day Ariana called teary-eyed to tell me what she'd overheard Dad say. "Mariel, I want you to know that I love you from the bottom of my heart and I always have." Mom said the same thing back to him and then they couldn't stop cuddling. For their fifty-ninth anniversary, they told me all they wanted to do was stay in bed and cuddle.

Ariana called, "Oh my gosh, they're *so* lovey-dovey in there today. You'd think they took some love potion number 9 or something. It's kiss-kiss-kiss and cuddle-cuddle-cuddle. They're acting like newlyweds!"

I smiled—yes, they were happier together in their eighties than they had been for years. I had such a warm glow knowing that all my efforts to keep them together in the final phase of their lives was really my true reward, and consider it to date—the biggest accomplishment of my life.

Ariana and I were exhilarated when we celebrated a solid year and a half without a *major* rage or police intervention. It was absolutely amazing that we had finally succeeded in controlling my father's raging temper for the first time in his life. Don't get me wrong, Hyde still stuck his ugly head out *regularly* to play, *Who's the Boss?*—but each time Ariana knew what to do. If he didn't calm down with compassion, then three stern warnings, she'd leave him sitting there with no one to fight with, *every* time. She'd go in her room and close the door. Ten minutes later she'd stick her head out, "Are you ready to talk nicely yet?"

"NOO!"

"Okay, let me know when you are." Ten minutes later she'd open the door and ask the same question. This could go on for an hour or two before he'd finally give up. *Eventually*, he learned that there was no benefit in it, screaming and yelling did *not* work—period. Since he knew he couldn't win with intimidation, he started giving up on the first time she stuck her head out. He didn't like the punishments he got *every* single time, and he learned that he could get much more from her if he behaved nicely, and so—he did. *Or*, as Mom would put it, "You can catch more flies with honey than vinegar—tisk!"

Then there was the time he got mad and took all the canned goods out of the pantry and threw them into the family room demanding that Ariana pick them up. She calmly stepped over everything and told him he would not be getting dessert that night unless he cleaned up his mess. He nastily refused so she put up a big chart and everyday he refused she marked down another big X for no dessert. She calmly hummed and vacuumed around everything for days. After watching Mom get mouth watering strawberry pie with a scoop of his favorite vanilla ice cream, he finally relented, apologized and helped put everything away. Ah-ha, reward and punishment—what a concept!

The visual charting technique worked well for all his bad behaviors. Whenever he was bad, even at Day Care, Ariana would announce that he had just lost another day of dessert and would mark it down on the big chart right in front of him. She held firm every single time and *eventually* he learned that to get dessert, he would have to behave, and so—he did.

Ariana's insight became so keen that she learned to distinguish between the true dementia and his life-long deceptive manipulations and when both were in play at the same time. We saw time and again that when he misinterpreted what was happening, it caused fear, and that translated into anger and lashing out. She remained calm and in control as she evaluated which technique was needed at the moment. Yes, there were still those occasional times when calming medication was needed, but she rarely had to resort to them because she knew how to handle him so well.

When he'd fire her and demand that she "get the hell out" she'd calmly say, "The only person going anywhere is *you*. Now get up and get dressed to go to Day Care or the ambulance will be here to take you to the hospital—which would you prefer?" He'd grumble and swear a blue streak as he got ready, but then later—he'd come home smiling again.

I was in absolute awe at how far we had come with him. Between the behavior modification that she did at home and what they did at Day Care, my father finally learned to control the raging temper that had continually shattered our dysfunctional family for more than fifty-nine years! I kept thinking how different our lives could have been had my mother been able to use these methods and stand up to him before Jeremy and I were so damaged by his volatile temper. What if all three of us had just walked away *every* single time he started his screaming tirades and left him sitting there pounding the kitchen table by himself.

Even though I had maneuvered around all the "elephants" in my path and all the pieces of the elder care puzzle had finally come together (Ariana, a correct diagnosis, the right medications, behavior modification, Day Care, and my own perceptual shift), I knew I still had an episode or two of *Senior Daktari* ahead of me. When the phone would ring late at night my heart would pound, expecting to hear that one of my parents had just passed away. I kept a check list handy for every scenario that might happen which prepared me for the inevitable: How would I deal with the grief from one when the other one goes? What if Ariana couldn't handle them any longer? Where were the best nursing homes? How would I transport them to a home near me? What did I need to know about funerals? How would I sell their home and get rid of all their stuff? And most importantly—what would I do with Mom's dining-room set?

By being as prepared as I could and surrendering what will be to the universe, I allowed myself to savor the joyous moments of my parents' last picture show. Rather than focusing on their disabling conditions, I shifted my perspective from grief and sorrow to one of celebration of their long life together that had created and molded me. I dismissed the feelings of anger at my responsibility and embraced the enormous pride I felt in my determined will and perseverance—and I treasured my own authentic power (that I had inherited and learned from my father), that had made their lives so much better at the end.

And wasn't it something—without knowing it, once again my parents were there for me, giving me a new path, a new passion in life, to do something so meaningful that I had never dreamed of doing. The self-confidence they had always instilled in me allowed me to write my first book, that may help countless others cope while they learn to manage their elderly loved ones. Yes, it was clear, there was a reason for all that I had gone through, and the silver-lining that Linda had promised me—was coming to pass.

♥♥♥

Ahhh, Hindsight—It's Always 20/20, Barbara

If this gut-wrenching experience has taught me anything, it has been this painful lesson: My parents would have surely deteriorated and died if I hadn't been able to persevere and turn things around. It was only by chance that the timing was such that I was able to devote an inordinate amount of time, tears and energy to solve the endless crisis. If I had still been working, or married...with children, it would not have been possible. But how many other families are facing similar circumstances who do not have the luxury of the time and resources I had? What about all those who live in rural areas with even fewer professionals to turn to? Even sadder and more alarming, how many elders will have to face their final years alone and isolated? It became apparent that far too many elders waste away too soon, and the main reason is clearly the amount and quality of care, or lack of it. For those who do have family members or others willing to care for them, how will these caregivers overcome the tremendous financial and emotional drain?

Without planning it, I had become the poster child for handling difficult elders, learning everything I never wanted to know about elder care but was afraid to ask. Friends started calling me, and then their friends called, seeking my advice about how to manage their elderly loved ones, particularly the behavioral issues. It drove home the reality that our life-long character traits just follow us right into old age—often getting intensified and distorted, particularly with the onset of dementia. I nodded in recognition when I read about the "more-so" theory of aging: Whoever we are as young adults, we will become "more so" that way as we grow older. Conversely, I heard many sad stories about how a sweet and loving mother had suddenly turned into a crotchety Cruella DeVil.

As I continually heard the same *overwhelming* frustrations that I had gone through, I realized that what I had learned could help so many others. After hearing my experience and advice, people would often ask what I would do differently, if I could get in a Time Machine and turn back the clock given what I know now. Well... it wouldn't take me nine and a half months or even nine and a half *weeks* to make significant progress. Fasten your seat belts again, because this time— it would be a *much* faster ride.

First and foremost, I would have bought Long-Term Care Insurance when my parents were still healthy. It is the most important link in estate planning. I encouraged everyone I knew to look into it and plan ahead and not be caught unprepared like I was. Had I done this, I could have saved myself a small fortune, not to mention my sanity.

What I didn't understand (and most people I talk to don't either) is that Medicare and regular health insurance do *not* cover caregivers to come *into* the home, nor do they cover the costs of an assisted living or nursing home. Once a patient has stopped improving or levels off and is released from the hospital, you're on your own to pay for their care. This is a *huge* expense. Long-Term Care Insurance would have covered skilled caregivers in my parents' home when my mother came home from the hospital. Yes, I would have needed an endless stream of them, but at least they would have been covered by the insurance. And later, if I have to place my parent(s) in a nursing home, the LTC insurance would have covered it. The alternative is bleak. Your parents have to *literally* become destitute before the government's Medicaid program will help with financial aid—but only if they go into a nursing home. You're on your own to pay for custodial care to keep them at home.

The list is long of all the things that I would now do differently—starting with calling Adult Protective Services when I arrived and saw their home in that deplorable condition and experienced my father's first illogical rage. By being on record with them from the outset, I'd be able to prove his inability to care for Mom right away. I'd have *them* tell him that the house had to be cleaned immediately and that he *had* to have a caregiver, or Mom would never be able to come home. *I* wouldn't have to be the bad guy—they would.

I'd start "tough love" behavior modification on him from the first minute I got there, being consistent and following through with *every* threat. If he was on good behavior, he'd get love and attention—but if he wasn't, I'd give him three warnings, refuse to speak to him and walk away immediately if the behavior did not stop. I'd understand how important it is to never *ever* reward bad behavior. I'd know not to raise my voice and let my emotions get the better of me during his insults—and I'd know to develop a protective shield that his nastiness would bounce off of.

I'd understand that a person doesn't go from normal to demented overnight, that it's a long process, and that at times he *was* capable of normal thinking—but when the dementia surfaced, he wasn't. My compassion would return because I'd understand that dementia is intermittent, it comes and goes. If what he said or did seemed illogical or irrational, big flag—IT WAS! Ohhh, the dementia's back again—don't get upset by what he's doing. He's terribly frustrated and he's grasping at anything he can to hold onto control—let it go, let it go.

I'd realize that life had become so frightening and confusing for him that he would pull out everything he had, from a lifetime of tried and true manipulative behaviors, to try to hold on to some feeling of security. By understanding that at times he just wasn't *capable* of rational thinking, I'd reinforce my own better judgement of what needed to be done. My frustration level would be reduced because I'd know to stop trying to use logic to win my arguments—and I'd know to use distraction instead. My perception of the crisis would shift from being overwhelmed to meeting a complex medical challenge, which would help me become emotionally detached and not so hurt.

I'd hire a geriatric conservatorship attorney and start the legal probate conservatorship process immediately, which would scare him into behaving better right away. I'd *go* to the police department and make as many friends as possible, as high up as I could, so that every time I'd call they'd know what was going on—and I'd "5150" him *every* single time he got even mildly violent. Even with intermittent dementia, he'd learn much faster that he couldn't get away with violence and I'd be building my case much sooner. Then, once he was in the legal system, I'd *demand* (by threatening the psychiatrist with a lawsuit if I had to) that they "5250" him for two weeks of observation. The dementia would eventually surface again and they could see what I was talking about.

I'd find the best social workers and I'd *demand* help while creating a paper trail with them, the doctors, and the police—documenting details of his behaviors. I'd get copies of his medical records and have them reviewed by a dementia specialist if I couldn't get my father to physically go there. I'd keep a daily journal of all his behaviors to help the doctors evaluate him. I'd get Kiljoy to write a "prescription" to go to the Alzheimer's Association which would make him more agreeable about going there. Then, getting a CAT scan done of his brain on a *newer* machine would produce the "dementia" diagnosis much sooner.

By keeping a hidden mini tape recorder in my pocket at all times and secretly recording his rages, I'd get help with medications much sooner, while avoiding being treated like the "unbalanced" one. Nanny-cams are now much more affordable and I'd get the rages on videotape immediately to prove my case to whoever I had to.

I'd find a *geriatric* psychiatrist and demand the proper medications with the least side effects as well as the most appropriate medication to help improve his cognitive abilities. (Aricept and Exelon.) Next, I'd lock up all his medications and find out if any might be causing adverse side effects. Then, I'd detox him off the narcotic pain pills that he took for "pain" because he really didn't need anything that strong.

Then I'd have the DMV call him in for an eye exam and have *them* take his license away so I wouldn't have to be the villain who took his last pleasure in life away from him. I'd be very sympathetic, saying how sorry I was that he could no longer drive and assure him that I'd arrange for alternate transportation. The Club would still be on the steering wheel at all times to make sure he couldn't drive.

Then, as soon as my mother was strong enough, I'd get them enrolled in Senior Day Care to give them a life outside of lying in bed all day, day after day, waiting to die. And then, *most* importantly, I'd clone Ariana—she's one in a million!

I'd know to make flash cards of all the good things my father had ever done for me and all the bad things that had happened to him in his life. I'd know to refer to these lists every time he got nasty to pull myself back to compassion. Then I'd find a caregiver support group which would help me cope and not feel so alone. By hearing how others were handling their frustrations, I'd gain more insight, ideas and strength. Many caregiving organizations offer weekend retreats for caregivers, supplying alternate helpers so the primary caregiver can get away and have a much-needed break.

Last but not least, I'd understand that the extreme range of conflicting emotions that I was experiencing were completely shame-free and normal. I'd ridden a roller coaster from love and honor to hate and disdain, followed by tremendous guilt and sorrow, as I struggled to stay on track and care for my parents. This time the emotional difference would be that the ride would be much less terrifying, because I would *understand* what was actually happening.

Isn't it something? My heart-wrenching experience has finally turned into a mission possible. Everything I have gone through can now become blessings to all those struggling with their elderly loved ones. More than anything I have ever done, I am committed to making a significant difference for all the people who are facing the overwhelming responsibility of elder care—and particularly to those managing a difficult elder or handling a heartbreaking case of combative elder rage.

Along the way, I hope I've made you laugh, helped you feel less alone, taught you much—and I hope I've helped you cope!

"That's my story and I'm stuck with it."

♥ ♥ ♥

This story is far from over. The continuing saga of Mariel, Jake, and the little gang of rascals, will be updated regularly on my website. You can give welcomed comments about *Elder Rage* and link to other valuable sites. A calendar of my upcoming appearances and speaking engagements is also posted. I'd love to hear from you.

Please log on to www.ElderRage.com

♥♥♥

Behavior Modification Guidelines

Everyone is unique, so the methods that work on one elder may not necessarily work on another. Some elders are mildly difficult and others are very challenging. The range in the dementia and memory loss varies tremendously also. If the dementia is mild, you will have periods of normalcy when you can implement new behaviors. If the dementia is advanced and short-term memory is severely damaged, reasoning is not going to work. In that case, when bad behavior occurs, it's better to look for a physical problem, such as pain, that may be making them lash out. Urinary tract infections (UTI's) are quite common in the elderly and can cause aggression. For a severely demented person who cannot learn new behaviors, use of behavior *management* (making them feel safe and comfortable) may be all you can do. Attempting logic may make them even more agitated.

Once all medical issues have been diagnosed and properly treated you will have a better chance of handling the behavioral issues. As hard as it is, you must accept that your parent may not be who they once were. The most important thing you can do is to shift your perspective to thinking of them as a puzzle, a project, a challenge to figure out. With enough practice, you will know when the dementia is present versus their lifetime behavior patterns that have gotten exaggerated and distorted. It's a learning process for you to be able to control your own emotions and find out what works best to manage each situation.

Behavior modification techniques should be tried whenever the dementia has not progressed to where their ability to learn has been lost. The Alzheimer's Association has tests that can measure the degree of the dementia. Once you begin these techniques, being *one hundred* percent consistent is one of the most important things you can do to manage a difficult or combative person. Also, keeping their daily schedule of rising, eating times and bedtime as consistent as possible will help avoid disappointment, frustration and confusion.

A combative elderly adult can be very much like an unmanageable child who needs strict boundaries of acceptable behavior. When you say you will do something, positive or negative, it is essential that you follow through *every* time to establish new routine behaviors and trust.

A reward cannot be an empty bribe just to get them to do what you want. Conversely, if you say you will take something away as punishment, you *must* take it away.

The following sections include behavior modification techniques along with suggestions for dialogue. Rewards and punishments have to be carefully considered and be appropriate for each situation.

When a Difficult Elder Displays Good Behavior
Reinforce by rewarding immediately with:

1. **Verbal Praise:** Say how proud you are of their specific positive behavior, happily raving about how well they're doing. *"I'm so proud of how nice you were to everyone today... I just love it when you're so cheerful and agreeable... You've been such a pleasure to be around that it makes me want to spend more time with you... I really appreciate your efforts to cut back on your complaining when I know you aren't feeling that well."*

2. **Loving Physical Affection:** Give warm hugs, kisses, gentle touch, massage or special grooming as you continue to verbally praise their positive behavior. This may be very difficult for families that have not been physically demonstrative in the past. Start with small gestures that you feel comfortable with. You may be surprised at how good it is for both of you. *"For being so good, I'm going to fix your hair in a special way today... I'm going to give you a foot massage because you've been such a pleasure to be around... Let's get our nails done together because it's fun to be with you when you're behaving this way."(As you say these things, try giving a gentle touch or a kiss on the cheek.)*

3. **Edible Treats:** Offer a special food or drink, or an outing to a favorite restaurant. Sometimes giving them something as simple as a favorite piece of candy as a reward can work. Emphasize that they are getting this treat because of their good behavior. It may be best to reserve dessert for rewards, and only after a healthy meal. *"I'm going to make you a special dessert tonight because you were so nice to all of us today... Even though you didn't want to go out today, I'm so proud of you for not arguing, so I'm going to fix you your favorite dinner and a special dessert."*

4. **Special Activity:** Enjoy a special television program together, visit a friend, go to the park; take in a movie, a play, a concert, a museum, a sporting event; play a game; do a craft. Again, emphasize that they are getting this reward because of their good behavior. *"I'm so happy with how you've been behaving, I'm going to get some tickets to a ballgame and take you out for a fun day... You've been so agreeable today, I want to take you to visit your best friend... I've enjoyed your company so much today, let me take you shopping for something special."*

5. **Special Attention:** Spend quality time engaging them in positive conversation, asking about their life experiences. Reminisce about years past. Give empathy and sincere understanding to their stories, even after the ump-teenth time. Assure them of your continued help and support. Create a sense of power and control by giving them choices and allowing them to persist in harmless activities. Quit arguing over things that are not important. Ask them for their advice with your own problems. This will help them feel needed and not like a burden. *"Let's get out the old photo albums and play your favorite music today... What do you remember about the day Pearl Harbor was bombed?... Where were you when the astronauts landed on the moon?... Where did you go on your honeymoon?... Would you like to go grocery shopping before we go to the barber or after?"*

6. **Gold Stars Charts:** Use big visible reward charts to track good behavior with gold stars or check marks. This might be demeaning and unnecessary for the mildly difficult individual, but very useful with a severely combative elder who may respond well to seeing their visual progress. When a pre-determined number of stars is reached, give a specific reward that they have been working toward. Start with small goals. If their behavior is good for three days in a row, reward them. Keep increasing the number of days needed to get the higher reward. *"Everyday that you have good behavior, you'll get a gold star on your chart... We'll put a check mark on this large wall calendar so you can see how well you're doing at controlling your temper... As soon as you have three good days in a row, then we'll go visit any friend you'd like to see... You've earned three gold stars so I'm going to get you some of your favorite ice cream."*

When a Difficult Elder Displays Negative Behavior
Reinforce by responding immediately with:

1. **Verbal Commands:** Remain calm and do not show that their bad behavior is upsetting you. They may persist just to get you riled up and create drama. You will command more respect if you exhibit a calm self-confidence. Speak calmly and slowly using direct eye contact and a firm body stance. Use short, simple sentences. Start using a technique called "if—then" statements, focusing on the positive outcome they will get if good behavior resumes. *If* you do this—*then* I will do that. Give choices of positive things they can pick from if they stop the bad behavior. *"If you will calm down—then we can play a game or watch a movie. Which would you prefer?... If you behave yourself and get dressed now—then I'll take you to the park or shopping today... If you stop screaming—then I will be happy to help you."*

   If these positive methods don't work, try to redirect their attention to something else. Distract them with an object, television, music, food, anything to get their mind off their current frustration. *"Oh, look at this letter we just got from your sister... Do you think the clothes are dry yet?... Is it time to take the dog for a walk?"*

   If distraction doesn't work, then you may need to resort to threatening with a *specific* consequence. Once you use a negative threat, you must follow through EVERY time. Make no idle threats or you will not be believed the next time. *"If you don't stop pounding your fist—then I'm going to stop speaking to you... If you don't stop throwing things right now—then I'm going to leave the room... If you don't take a shower soon—then we will not go visit your friend tonight."*

2. **Time-Outs:** If the situation escalates, calmly announce a ten to twenty minute cool-down period before the issue can be discussed further. Use the silent treatment, refusing to talk to them for the specified amount of time. If the heated argument resumes after the time-out, immediately call for a longer time-out and leave the room. You may need to repeat this several times. Make sure that the person can be left alone safely and that the time period is reasonable. *"You need a ten minute 'time-out' to calm down and*

275

think about your behavior... I'm very upset with you and I'm not going to speak to you for fifteen minutes... If you do not stop spitting—then I am leaving the room to give you twenty minutes to settle down... When you start behaving nicely—I will return."

3. **Three Strikes:** Another method is the "Third Time Is The Limit" rule. When the patient becomes uncooperative or combative, try to gain control by announcing that you are going to give them three warnings. With the first warning, be sure to use compassion, reasoning and compromise. If they continue to persist, give them a second warning while indicating that the issue is now closed. Let them know that if they push to a third warning there will be a specific punishment. You must take a specific action *every* time you reach your third warning. Eventually they will learn that by your second warning you mean business. *"This is your first warning to stop yelling. I'm sorry, I understand that you are very frustrated with everything right now. I want to help you but I can't if you keep screaming at me. I'm sure we can work this out... OK, this is your second warning now. Please stop yelling. I am not going to listen to you any longer. Think hard about what is going to happen if I get to my third warning. If you yell at me one more time—then this game of checkers is over... OK, this is your third warning and I will not tolerate your behavior any longer. I am putting the game away."* On your third warning, you MUST follow through with everything you have said you would do.

4. **Shame:** In conjunction with the other techniques, if the patient is aware enough, you can incorporate a tone in your voice that indicates how disappointed you are with their bad behavior. Calmly point out how shameful their actions are and how hurtful their behavior is. Tell them they should be ashamed of how childish they are acting. Getting teary-eyed yourself and displaying your own hurt feelings (real or acted) may bring on an apology. Once an apology is offered, kindly accept it and move on. *"You should be so embarrassed for acting this way, especially around your grandchildren... I'm so hurt that you could treat me this way, especially in front of your friends... You're acting like a spoiled child right now and I know you really don't want to behave this way... Your foul language is disgraceful. Stop it now, or I'm leaving you by yourself."*

5. **Remove Specific Privileges/Charts:** By removing privileges the patient will learn that there are immediate consequences to their actions. Depending on the severity of the behavior, respond by removing a favorite dessert, drink, TV, attention, communication or enjoyable activities. Use of a large calendar/chart can be very helpful by announcing that they have lost another day of dessert because of their bad behavior. *" OK, I'm marking the chart with another X so you won't get any dessert tonight because you've been so mean to us today... Your behavior is deplorable and you haven't calmed down, so we're not going to play bingo tonight... I've warned you about throwing things. If you throw that again, you will not get to see your friend today... Stop threatening me or I'm leaving. Do you really want me to leave right now?"*

6. **Call the Police:** It is very important that you respond to *any* violence, no matter how slight, as soon as it occurs. Don't listen to apologies, excuses or pleas for forgiveness. Resist being taken in by any change in their demeanor. Violence cannot be tolerated at any level or it will occur again. When the police arrive they will access the situation and determine if there is enough cause to remove the person. It can be a very difficult experience to see your loved one taken into custody, but it can actually be a blessing in disguise in the long run. They will learn that you will not tolerate any violent acts, and having a police report will help your credibility with the doctors. You will be building a case for filing a "Conservatorship" should it get to that point. They will be taken to a psychiatric hospital for evaluation and you'll finally be able to get a psychiatrist involved, whether your loved one wants one or not. You may have to go through this a few times to finally get control over an extremely rebellious person.

It will be of tremendous help if you go in person to the police department and explain your situation to high ranking officials. In addition, develop rapport with as many of the responding officers as possible. If the police are familiar with your situation, you will receive better cooperation each time you have to call. *"OK, that's it! You know the rules. I've told you over and over that I will never tolerate your being violent... You have pushed and hit me and now I'm calling the police. There is no further discussion or negotiation."*

How Do I Handle My Elderly Loved One Who:

1. *Wants all my time and attention?*

   Set reasonable but strict limits of when you can be available and when you can't. Never allow yourself to be manipulated. If you *never* give in to demands, your parent will learn that moaning and groaning doesn't work and will *eventually* stop trying. If you give in to extreme begging, they will continue to push harder and harder, knowing that you will eventually cave in.

   Always use an answering machine to screen your calls and never pick up and respond if your parent is being nasty or negative. When they ask for your help in a more reasonable way, respond positively to reinforce the good behavior, telling them how proud of them you are and how much you appreciate the way they have approached you this time.

   Getting your loved one involved in activities will be the best thing for both of you. Call information to locate the nearest "Area Agency on Aging" office to find the Senior Centers and Senior Day Care Centers nearby, and learn about enrollment and schedules. It may take a lot of coaxing and compassion to get your parent to step out of their comfort zone of being at home and to consent to go to Day Care where they don't know anyone. Remember that any type of change can be extremely frightening for elders. The Day Care professionals are very familiar with this problem and will help you. Ask one of the administrators to call and talk to your parent a few times to develop a relationship.

   Take your parent out for lunch and when they are in a good mood, casually stop by the Day Care to say hello to that administrator. Have an appointment set up so you can take a tour, meet the other seniors and staff, and reduce some of the anxiety. Encourage your loved one to attend no matter how much they protest. They may hate it at first, saying that everyone is too old, it's too much effort, or they just don't like it—but don't give up. Eventually they'll make new friends and look forward to all the activities. The pressure on you to entertain them will be drastically reduced.

If they cannot physically attend a Senior Center, you can hire a companion to come in and visit with them on a regular basis. This person can read to them, watch a movie, take them out for a walk or a ride, play a game, or talk about the old days, etc.

Call your local public libraries to find out about their volunteer programs. These volunteers can be very helpful by bringing printed books, audio books, movies and travel videos to the home regularly. These deliveries also provide a visitor whom your parent may enjoy talking with. Call the Eldercare Locator (800-677-1116) to find other programs for the elderly in your area.

2. *Makes constant unreasonable demands?*

Focus on the positive things you *can* do for your parent and don't emphasize the things that you can't. If you continue to eventually give in to their extreme demands these behaviors will get worse. Assertively set your boundaries of what you will and won't do ahead of time and stand firm, giving sympathy and empathy where appropriate. Don't let your better judgement be swayed by your sense of responsibility. If their demand strikes you as illogical or irrational, BIG FLAG—it is! If the bad behavior stops, give positive reinforcement by acknowledging their ability to control their conduct. You may want to give a specific reward to further encourage them. If the bad behavior continues, give three warnings, use the silent treatment, then walk away.

3. *Is inflexible, critical and negative?*

First, use empathy and sympathy within reasonable limits. Your parent may just need a hug or kiss at the moment and be too embarrassed to ask for the affection they crave. Instead of arguing, agree with them about how terrible something is for a short moaning session. Practice using positive phrases like, *"I'm sorry you're feeling so lousy... What can we do to cheer you up?... Let's put on some uplifting music and talk about good things."* Resolve within yourself not to let their negative energy and insulting comments get to you. Focus on anything positive that they say, redirecting their attention to change the subject.

If the negativity continues after you've tried repeatedly to change the subject, tell them that you will not engage in anymore negative conversation for the day. Their "negativity quotient" is used up. If you allow it to go on, giving too much sympathy, you are teaching them that the more they complain, the more attention they will get. Don't be an enabler.

Never respond positively to *any* negative behavior. For example, if your loved one screams at you to hand them something, do not do it until you are asked properly. Never respond to any demanding orders, telling them that you will be happy to accommodate their request if asked nicely. If the bad behavior continues, give three warnings, use the silent treatment, and then walk away.

4. *Complains about real or imagined physical symptoms?*

Set a time limit for these health "complaint" sessions. Listen, be sympathetic, offer solutions. Then, declare the complaint time over and divert their attention to a different topic or activity. If the moaning and groaning doesn't stop, give three warnings, use the silent treatment, then walk away.

Try a simple test to see if any of their symptoms might be psycho-somatic. The next time they complain of a minor ache or pain, quickly put a vitamin pill in their mouth, pretending the pill is an aspirin or pain pill. See if the mysterious pain immediately goes away. Don't tell them that their pains are not real, but privately let their doctor know what you discover.

Together, write down their symptoms in order of what bothers them the most. When you go to the doctor, see which symptoms they actually end up complaining about. Have the doctor address each issue, take notes, and cross each item off the list as they are reviewed. If your loved one is embarrassed to complain to the doctor, take charge and make sure the doctor knows all symptoms including: sleep, appetite, energy changes, memory problems, alterations in mood, inability to do basic things, incontinence, depression, anxiety and anger. Speak with the doctor in private if necessary.

Frequently bring all medications (prescriptions and all over the counter vitamins, etc.) to the doctor's to make sure there are no interactions. When a new medicine is prescribed, ask if any specific foods and alcohol should be avoided while taking this drug. Should this drug be taken with or without food? Should this drug be taken at a certain time of day? Is it all right to continue normal activities, such as driving? All drugs have side effects, and can interact with each other and produce further complications.

Get a lock box for their medications if you have any suspicions that they are not being taking appropriately. Hide a spare key someplace in their home in case you forget or lose your key, or if someone else has to give the medications if you cannot get there.

5. *Exhibits bizarre behavior and uses inappropriate/foul language?*

Bizarre or unusual behavior that is out of character is one of the first signs of dementia. Be aware and don't dismiss these early warnings signals. Seeking help at this early stage will greatly help your loved one and reduce your frustrations.

You can still set your limits of acceptable behavior. Correct them every time inappropriate behavior occurs and when foul or embarrassing language is used. Never resort to bad language yourself as that just perpetuates it. Keep your temper under control, or walk away until you can regain it.

Role playing can be used to teach appropriate behavior. Make it simple with specific dialogue showing them the proper way to ask for your help. *"I'd appreciate it if you could hand me the television remote... I'm glad you came to see me today... Could I please have a glass of milk?"*

If you are being verbally abused *("I hate you... I never want to see you again.")* never respond. Don't let your emotions get the better of you. Change your perception and don't escalate the problem into a screaming match or expect a rational discussion. When you are being called offensive names, do not respond. Acknowledge them only when you are being called by you correct name. Give three warnings, use the silent treatment, walk away immediately if the behavior does not stop.

6. *Has become suspicious and paranoid?*

Don't make light of it, argue, or tell them that their fears are irrational. Calmly acknowledge how awful it must be to feel that way and assure them you don't think they are crazy. Make them feel safe, loved, and assure them of your continued support. Report these symptoms with specific examples to their doctor immediately. If you get an unconcerned attitude from their doctor that it's just part of the aging process, *insist* on taking them to a geriatric psychiatrist for evaluation. With the proper medication, these fears can be greatly reduced.

7. *Is experiencing increasing levels of memory loss?*

Call the Alzheimer's Association and find out where you can take your loved one for evaluation. They are the experts at this—don't waste time with doctors who are not. Inquire about the drugs: Aricept and Exelon, and if they recommend Vitamin E therapy.

Make large "direction" signs and place them all over their house with specific easy-to-follow instructions. *"Brush Your Teeth... Turn Off Stove... Keep Door Locked."* Get a large wall calendar so that they can check off the days. To help insure that medications are not forgotten or doubled, make a chart that they can check off each time they take their pills. An erasable board can work well too. It will help them remember people if you label pictures of everyone they know and put them up where they will see them. (The larger the better.) For their telephone, get one that has one-button dialing with a photo and name of the person next to the number. The use of lists, tape recorders, crossword puzzles, trivia and computer games can help exercise the memory also.

8. *Makes up silly lies, exaggerates and cries wolf?*

These may all be efforts to get attention and sympathy. Understand that these actions are desperate attempts to hold onto power or a need for assurance of your continued support. They may also be craving physical affection and don't know how to ask for it. When you recognize an obvious lie, carefully evaluate the motive behind it. Don't get hooked into confronting them on unimportant issues. Instead, switch your perspective and let these tall tales roll off your back. Even though they are exasperating, you don't want to become a victim yourself. It takes two to play a game, so just don't play it.

There are times, however, when some of their attempts to control the situation cannot be overlooked. When these behaviors are constant and disruptive try behavior modification. Never respond with positive action to what you know is a manipulative lie or the lying will persist. Calmly let them know that you're aware that they are just trying to get more attention and that you will not let it upset you. Set strict limits of what you will and won't tolerate and let them know that you cannot be manipulated.

9. *Prefers to stay in bed or do nothing—"waiting to die"?*

This could be an ulterior motive to get more attention, or it may be a sign of depression. Carefully evaluate what's going on. Drop in unexpectedly a few times and observe their level of activity. If you suspect depression, ask their doctor to prescribe an anti-depressant. There is such a wide range of effective medications available today that there may be no need for them to suffer.

Then, get your parent enrolled in Senior Day Care to create a life outside of lying in bed all day. They have to have something to look forward to, friends to see, varied activities to do. You cannot supply all this stimulation yourself day after day. Go with them a few times, have lunch and introduce them to everyone to encourage the making of new friends. Additionally, many centers have a shuttle service to pick them up and bring them home.

If your parent is a "Sundowner" who wants to sleep all day and be up all night, there are a few things you can do to alter this pattern. In the morning, open all the windows and drapes to let in fresh air and sunlight; make lots of noise by turning on the radio and television, running the vacuum cleaner, dishwasher, etc.; plan activities, exercise and visitors. Getting an hour or two of sunlight daily can help regulate their circadian rhythm. Ask your doctor about Melatonin that may help them sleep at night. Make sure they are not getting any caffeine from coffee or chocolate in the evening. Also, have their doctor regularly review *all* of their medications to see if any may be causing daytime drowsiness. If possible, switch them to be taken at night.

10. *Refuses to allow a cleaning person into their home?*

If you arrive to find their home in a deplorable condition, don't rush to clean it. First, call Adult Protective Services and have them "drop in" to examine the condition of the home. Their report will automatically go to the local police department, so you will be visited by a police officer soon too. This puts you on record with them in case you need to prove that your parent can no longer take proper care of things. Have APS say that the home must be cleaned immediately for health and safety reasons. This way, you aren't the bad guy, making changes your loved one doesn't want.

11. *Gets furious if something doesn't happen at a specific time?*

Avoid telling them a definite time of when you will do something, or when something will happen. Give a broad window, be vague, and say that you will try to handle their request soon. Never commit to a specific time because they may tend to obsess over it. This way, it will be a pleasant thing to tell them that you have accomplished what they asked for, rather than disappointing them that you didn't have time. Don't lock yourself into a time frame that you may not be able to meet. You will build their trust if you don't have to disappoint them.

12. *Gets mad when told "No" they can't do something?*

Avoid responding with a flat-out "No" to their request. Let them know that you have considered the issue and understand their viewpoint, but explain that it's not a good idea right now. Indicate that maybe next time, or at a later date, you will be able to handle their request. Cheerfully distract their attention to something else more positive. Most of the time, they will completely forget about this request and have a different one by the next day.

Just like some children, the more some elders are told "No" they can't do something, the more they will keep fighting to do it. It can become a test of wills for power and control. In some instances, it may be best to just let them have their way (if there is no danger). Usually they will come to the conclusion on their own that it really wasn't such a good idea after all.

13. *Wants to eat constantly or only wants to eat the same thing?*

Keep the meal schedule as regular as possible and set a limit of three meals a day. Keep only healthy snacks available between meals. Serving the last meal as late as possible in the evening will keep them from wanting another meal later on. Have their doctor tell them how important good nutrition is. This desire to eat more than they should may indicate a compulsion that might be controlled with medication. The compulsion to excessively smoke and drink alcohol may be helped by medication as well.

14. *Refuses to take showers and change their underclothes?*

Remind them that cleanliness is important for their health and how much better they will feel after a refreshing shower. They may not realize that they smell and letting them know that it's embarrassing to be out with them, because of their offensive odor, can help you get them to bathe sooner. Tell them that if they are dirty, it reflects badly on you and your care. Telling them that it hurts your feelings for people to think that they are not being well cared for will usually result in them wanting to get cleaned up more often.

You may want to try bribes with the "If—Then" method. *"If you will take a shower—then I will make you your favorite dessert tonight... If you change your underclothes—then we can watch that television program you like... If you will let me wash your hair today—then we can go to the birthday party."* There are also rinseless shampoos for the disabled that are helpful between hair washing days. Just massage it into dry hair and that's it.

As soon as they agree to shower regularly, you can try the homemade "contract" technique. Help them write up what they are willing to do, have everyone sign it, and post it in their room. This will reinforce their commitment of what they have promised. With severely demented patients, you might keep several pictures handy of persons or objects to use as bribes. For example, a photo of a family member who is visiting that day, or a magazine picture of a treat. Additionally, you can show them an actual piece of candy and continue offering it as a bribe until the task is completed. The key is to find what works and use them again and again.

15. *Is a danger on the road but refuses to give up driving?*

This is a serious problem that cannot be overlooked and is usually one of the most difficult hurdles to overcome. Have a doctor that your loved one trusts check their eyes. Confidentially ask the physician for a letter that states that the patient is no longer capable of driving. A copy of this letter should also be sent to the DMV requesting that their license be taken away. This process may take several weeks.

If the situation is critical, contact the DMV immediately. They are experts at handling this problem. Someone will call your loved one requiring them to come in for a "routine" eye exam right away. If the DMV ends up taking the license away, be very sympathetic, saying how sorry you are that this has happened. This way, you're not the horrible person who took away their last pleasure in life. Assure them you will arrange for them to be taken wherever they need to go. Look into alternative transportation (inexpensive transportation specifically for seniors is available in many areas) so your loved one does not feel trapped at home. Get the car keys away from them and if you fear they may still try to drive, put "The Club" on the steering wheel.

16. *Needs but refuses to allow any caregiving help in the home?*

Keep in mind that any kind of change is very frightening for many elders and fear of the unknown can be greatly intensified. Have their doctor give them a "prescription" to get a caregiver. Ask the doctor to sternly advise them that they must have some help in their home or some legal action may have to be taken.

You can also have a caregiver agency send an administrator to help convince your parent how much easier things would be if someone came in to help them. Assure your loved one that you will monitor this person to make sure they do things properly.

If that doesn't work, contact Adult Protective Services to send a social worker to talk to your parent. Their report automatically goes to the local police department so you will be visited by an officer soon. A uniformed police officer may be enough to help convince your parent of the seriousness of the situation.

Decide if you want to hire a caregiving agency (which is more expensive, but the workers are usually supervised and bonded), or if you want to find someone on your own (which will require a lot more on-going supervision.). Ask if the agency is bonded and if it is a member of any state or national home care organization. Call to check them out. Ask for references of families who have a caregiver supplied by the agency right now. Call to see how happy they are with the service. Some agencies will do extensive background checks, drug screenings, others will not. Inquire as to *exactly* what background checks have been done on the person you are thinking of hiring from an agency and get everything in writing. If they will not put this information in writing, they probably have not done background checks. If you have Long-Term Care Insurance, be sure that the agency will take direct payment from the LTC company. In any case, it's extremely advisable to pack up valuables and remove all temptations from caregivers who come into the home.

As you begin interviewing caregivers, involve your parent in the process. Obtain an Application For Employment form from your local stationery store which will list the questions you can legally ask. Together, make a list of the non-negotiable qualities you want in your caregiver. Don't waste time interviewing applicants in person who do not meet your minimum requirements over the phone. For example: Do they have a *valid* driver's license? Will they give out their social security number so you can pay taxes properly? Do they live close by? Do they have adequate eldercare experience? Will they give you checkable references? Do they speak, read and write your language at a reasonable level? Do they have any objection to being fingerprinted? Have they ever been arrested or convicted? Will they sign a waiver to have a background check run on them? If you get a lot of hesitancy or refusal, save yourself the time of interviewing in person.

Get as many references as possible and check them. Talk to previous employers, families they have cared for, co-workers, landlords, neighbors, relatives and friends. Find out if they have been reliable, punctual, what duties they have performed and if there were any problems. By visiting the applicant in their own home, you will immediately see their level of cleanliness and organization. This is the level you can expect to see in your parent's home.

If you still want to feel assured further, you can do some background checking. It is illegal for the police to run a check on an individual unless there is probable cause of an outstanding warrant for an arrest. You can call the Trust Line (800) 822-8490 to check your caregiver for a criminal record. For $124 they will send you a fingerprinting kit. (The act of photographing and fingerprinting a caregiver can be enough to scare off any who may have a criminal record.) Ask to utilize the "Live Scan" computerized system to get results in three weeks versus the regular method that requires one to two months. In addition, they will check with the FBI for high misdemeanors and felonies nationally, but unfortunately, this takes three to four months.

You can also hire a private investigation firm, but be sure to ask: Are they checking in the county, state or nationwide? What types of crimes do they search for? How many years back do they check? They can check public records on: real estate, social security, DMV, taxes, etc. You can do some of this yourself by searching your county's public records.

Once you hire a caregiver, write down all their responsibilities. This should be done with everyone present so that it is very clear what will and won't be expected. Allow for expansion of this list as your loved one's health deteriorates.

You may be surprised by the amount of work caring for your elderly loved one requires. Some of these tasks may include: Toileting, diapering, bathing, brushing and flossing teeth, fixing hair, shaving, soaking feet, applying ointments and moisturizers, cleaning wax out of ears, applying make up, trimming nails, dressing, cooking, serving, feeding, administering medications, housekeeping, laundry, shopping, running errands, answering phone calls, keeping medical and dental appointments, providing social interaction, chauffeuring, monitoring medical devices, and providing emotional support.

Recognize that you may be expecting your caregiver to be a "psychologist," asking them to tolerate a difficult patient who can be uncooperative, hostile, manipulative and maybe even physically combative. Be sensitive to the many needs of your caregiver and overlook minor mistakes and allow for a learning curve.

Once the caregiving begins, your parent may make unreasonable demands. Therefore, a written list will assure the caregiver of their real responsibilities. Since most elders respect authority, if you give your caregiver a white medical lab coat, it may influence the most rebellious patient to behave better. When complaining about the caregiver inevitably begins, don't automatically defend the caregiver to your parent and get into a heated argument. Assure them that you will get to the bottom of the problem.

You may want to consider installing a nanny-cam, so you can see for yourself what is happening. A 3/8" wide camera lens can be installed in a lamp, clock radio, smoke detector, Kleenex box, phone, or just about anywhere. It shows a 90 degree angle of the room and will transmit to a VCR. If the complaints are well founded, report to the agency or take appropriate action on your own. If the complaints are superficial, strengthen the caregiver's resiliency about how to handle their difficult patient. Make it very clear to everyone that your parent does not have the power to fire the caregiver, or you'll go through this many times. Be sure to place a block of all 976 and international calls on the phone, and don't forget to ask for a copy of their car insurance in case your loved one is travelling in their car.

17. *Can no longer take proper care of their bills and finances?*

Convincing your parent that they need help with their finances may be very difficult so plan ahead. One solution is to get your parent a "companion" credit card, with a low limit, added on to your own credit card account. This way you will get the bill and they don't have to carry cash around that may get lost or stolen.

The most critical issue is to obtain a *Durable* Power of Attorney which will give you the legal authority to handle your loved ones financial and health matters. This contract should be drawn up by an "Elder Law" attorney (check the yellow pages) who will be familiar with all the current laws. Make sure it is *Durable*, meaning if your parent becomes incapacitated and can no longer make decisions, you will be able to. (Be sure to also have one drawn up for yourself, just in case something happens to you.) Your parent must be of sound mind when signing their finances over to you or you could be in legal trouble down the road. If the dementia is already severe, contact an "Elder Law" attorney immediately. This is another reason to have the earliest stages of dementia documented.

18. ***Refuses to see any other doctor but is not getting adequate care?***

If you are not happy with the care your loved one is getting, speak up and do not be intimidated. Doctors are just very busy people who may respond better if you are assertive and proactive in bringing to their attention the importance of a situation.

If that doesn't work, DO NOT SETTLE. The National Academy of Sciences (NAS) published a book in 2000: *To Err Is Human: Building a Safer Health System* which reported that some 7,000 patients die every year because of medication errors. That's more than die from workplace injuries. And even more alarming, the NAS estimates that at least 44,000 and perhaps as many as 98,000 people die in hospitals each year as a result of medical errors. That's more than die from automobile accidents, breast cancer, or AIDS—three causes that receive far more public attention. Additionally, many researchers feel that these numbers are probably *under* reported!

Remember, you are the client and you can fire your doctor and demand another one. Always get a second opinion on important issues such as surgery. Getting the right doctor can make all the difference in solving the myriad of health problems that an elderly person may have. Look for one who has a special interest in treating older adults. If you are with an HMO, contact the customer relations department, list your complaints and demand a new primary care physician if you are not happy with the one you have. Then contact the nearest Health Insurance Consumer Advocacy Program (HICAP) for additional help.

For the elderly, changing to an unfamiliar physician can be very unsettling. To help get around this, you can ask for copies of their medical records (this may require a Durable Power of Attorney). Take the records to another doctor yourself, even if you can't get your loved one to go. Ask this doctor to phone your loved one and try to establish a trusting relationship, convincing them to come in for an appointment. With the right tone, their fear of the unknown may be greatly reduced. With a little encouragement from a caring professional, your loved one may consent to go.

19. *Needs to see a psychiatrist but absolutely refuses to go?*

Modern medicine has made tremendous advancements in treating mood disorders. Drug therapy could make a significant difference in how they feels. A *psychologist* cannot prescribe medication, so be sure to find a *geriatric psychiatrist* as they will be experienced at diagnosing elderly behavioral symptoms. Usually this will require a referral from your primary care physician.

If your parent is suffering from depression you can have your family physician talk with your parent about how these feelings are nothing to be ashamed of and how unnecessary it is to suffer nowadays. The doctor should make light of seeing a psychiatrist and assure your loved one that they are not going crazy or losing their mind. Ask the doctor to write a "prescription" to see a geriatric psychiatrist, and suggest that he "rave" about how much this doctor has helped so many of his patients who are just like your parent.

Another way to get a behavioral specialist/psychiatrist involved is to ask your family physician to casually write a "prescription" to see the Alzheimer's Association, saying that it is "just a precaution" to rule it out. The Alzheimer's Association will be of tremendous value, helping you get your loved one tested for all types of dementia (Alzheimer's is just one type). They are the specialists in evaluating and diagnosing complex elderly behavioral symptoms. Getting an accurate diagnosis will help your loved one get proper treatment, and help *you* cope with their behaviors. Also, if you eventually have to get a "Conservatorship" to have your loved one placed in a home against their will, a diagnosis of dementia may be needed.

Another idea is to create a project out of making a cassette tape recording of all your parent's memories, an audio autobiography of their life. This will be nice for you to have after they pass away, and also useful for a psychiatrist to listen to if you cannot get your loved one to go in person. You can guide the questions and help with the recording so the doctor can hear what is really going on.

Another way to get them to the psychiatrist is to not tell them where they are going. Have the appointment set up and after going out for an enjoyable lunch or activity, pretend you have an errand and drive to the doctor's office. Say casually, "Oh, here's where that doctor's office is that I was telling you about. Let's see if we can make an appointment." Check in and then tell your parent that the doctor had a cancellation and would very much like to meet them right now.

20. *Acts completely normal and charming in front of others?*

Socially adjusted elder ragers will rarely show their "Hyde" side to anyone outside the family. No matter what horrors you describe, most doctors refuse to give out medications for conditions they don't see. Save yourself a lot of time and aggravation by keeping a small tape recorder hidden in your pocket, ready to go when the next behavioral problem occurs. Also, be sure to take pictures of the results of any violence such as broken objects and bruises. If that doesn't convince the doctors, install a nanny-cam to get the rages on tape as soon as possible. This is becoming more common and affordable. This can help convince doctors of *exactly* how bad the real behavior is and help you get the medications.

21. *Fakes illness at the Day Care to avoid staying?*

If your loved one starts to fake illness to keep from going to Day Care, explain to the staff about the possibility of manipulative behaviors. Unfortunately, they will not be able to tell if this time your loved one is acting or not, and they cannot afford to be held liable in case your parent really does become seriously ill.

When you pick up your parent act very concerned and tell them you are taking them straight to the emergency room and observe if their condition changes immediately. Continue driving there and if they beg to just go home, saying they are suddenly much better, begin behavior modification guidelines. Make them go to bed and don't allow them to get up for anything. If they are too sick to go to Day Care, they are too sick to get up and walk around the house. After a day or two of nothing but bed rest, they will probably be begging to go back to the Day Care. Also, audio plus *video* baby monitors are now very affordable, so your caregiver can observe what the real behavior is.

22. *Is driving me crazy as I try to deal with all their problems?*

Set reasonable but strict limits of your involvement and ask for *specific* help from family and friends. Set a schedule of who will do what/when with everyone involved. Contact your local Area Agency on Aging and see what resources are available near you. The more people you can bounce your frustrations off of—the more chances that solutions will present themselves. Getting support for yourself will surely help your stress level. Get into a support group because once you realize that so many others are going through the same problems, you won't feel so alone and you'll learn valuable tips about how to handle each mini crisis.

It's so hard to do but you have to change how you feel about the situation to keep your own stress level in check. You have to change your perspective. Shift your viewpoint from being in a "nightmare" to having an interesting "challenge" that you will overcome. If you can think of your loved one as a patient your perspective will change, and so will your stress level. This will help you detach emotionally so that their hurtful comments and deterioration will be less painful. Try to find some shred of humor in the absurdity of the moment. *Refuse* to let what they say rile you as they are not themselves. Take the high road, forgive them for getting old, and try to have compassion for the loss of their ability to think clearly.

Focus on the good things they have done for you. It may be helpful to make a list of treasured memories that you can refer to in your darkest moments. Remember the good that you have seen in them in the past. Also, make a list of all the bad things that have happened to them. Examine their life and try to understand what has molded them into who they are. Understanding what has pushed them this far will give you a deeper level of patience and compassion.

When you notice your tone of voice getting irritable or mean, recognize that you need to walk away immediately and regroup. De-stress yourself regularly, using deep breathing, stretching, meditation, and any relaxation methods that work for you. Take a calming bath, get a massage, take a walk, do some aerobics, listen to music or motivational cassette tapes. Give yourself positive affirmations because what you are doing is not easy and many would just walk away. Realize that you are doing the right thing and program yourself with positive thoughts.

Do some writing, such as keeping a journal, to purge and clarify your feelings. Keep a "Gratitude Journal" (Oprah swears by this method) of everything you have to be thankful for in your life and read it several times a day. You may find it helpful to make flash cards or your own cassette tape to remind yourself of all the positive things your loved one has done for you. When you're in the thick of it, you probably won't be able to recall one thing. By having these resources handy, when you need to be reminded most, they can help bring you back to compassion.

Realize that your parent is feeling terrible about their life. They're losing many of their friends and family and directly facing mortality. They are losing all sense of power and control over their life as well as their health: sight, hearing, mobility, bodily functions, energy, and well-being. And then, on top of all that, they have to be told what to do by a younger person, usually the *child* whom they raised, sacrificed and did so much for. Walk a mile with their walker and imagine how awful it must be and remember—you'll be old someday too. Plan for good Karma!

23. *Has pushed me to feelings of resentment and guilt?*

Know that you are not alone and that the extreme range of emotions you are having are normal. The primary caregiver is usually the most hated, manipulated and burdened. Who could possibly feel love when you are being put through so much? You have been slowly poisoned by their increasingly bad behaviors. Don't beat yourself up for having normal reactions to such a difficult situation. If you find yourself about to cross the line and become abusive, step back immediately and seek help right away.

You have to work hard now to shift your perspective of the situation to a higher plane so that your anger will subside and your compassion will return. Step back for a moment and ask yourself how you would be acting if you were in their place. Remember that your loved one is sick and their illness is what is causing them to be this way. Hate the illness, not the person.

It is a slow process to learn how to cope with a loved one's decline. Take it one day at a time and be patient with yourself—you are learning something new. You will feel so much better when you learn how to not let your buttons get pushed. Your loved one will eventually pass away and you don't want to have any guilt that you should have been more patient and learned to behave differently.

24. *Cannot be reasoned with when they go into an illogical rage?*

Your parent may have frontal lobe dementia which affects impulse control. Their flash-fire reactions may be uncontrollable. Do not try to argue, reason or use logic with them right now. They are not thinking rationally and they are not the person they used to be. This can be very difficult if you've always seen them as being very rational and now you have to witness their decline.

Realize that they are fighting to hold onto any kind of power and control, and they are very scared. Their inhibitions are raw, self control mechanisms may be gone, allowing them to say and do things that they formerly would have never done. Their brain damaging dementia is short-circuiting their ability to think clearly. If their actions seem outrageous, ridiculous, irrational and unfounded, don't second guess yourself, they are! Immediately understand that they are very ill and let the insults roll off you. Validate their frustrated feelings, telling them you understand how awful they must feel at the moment. Try to give them some sense of control over their life by offering choices of things they *can* do. Sympathize as much as you can. Remember, behind the rage is usually tremendous fear and frustration.

Try to divert their attention to something positive. If they do not calm down, begin behavior modification techniques: give three warnings, the silent treatment, and then walk away. If they have previously been in a psychiatric hospital for evaluation, remind them that they don't want to go back there. After they calm down, taking them for a visit of a nursing home may be a good reminder of how lucky they are to be living where they are.

It will be helpful to create a paper trail in case you eventually have to prove your case to a judge. Keep a detailed calendar notebook, recording each rage or inappropriate/bizarre behavior and send updates to social workers, doctors and police regularly. Note the time of day, the environment, the weather, the people present, what they ate, and check to see if any medications have been changed. Look closely for anything that might be different and try to determine what may have caused the behavior: Could there have been a misinterpretation of something that triggered fear? Is there too much stimuli? Some elders may not be able to filter out a lot of noise or activities and can become confused and overwhelmed. Is there any physical pain present? Urinary tract infections (UTI's) are common in the elderly and can make anyone irritable. Look behind the surface of the rage and try to piece it together. This will help you understand your parent better, help you avoid future rages, and help their psychiatrist evaluate proper treatment.

25. *Is completely unmanageable and needs to be placed in a home?*

When all else has failed you may have to resort to legal means. Look in the yellow pages under "Attorneys—Elder Law," and only hire a specialist who knows the current laws. You will need to start the legal process of a Conservatorship. A Durable Power of Attorney may not be enough if your parent is fighting your decision and if they appear normal to the doctors. This process could take several months.

Make sure you select a home that has a "combative care unit" and that they have experience with difficult patients. Don't mention the negative behavior or the home will suddenly be completely booked-up. These places don't want difficult, combative patients in their facility and who can blame them? If your parent becomes completely unmanageable while at the facility, sedation will be tried, but if they continue to disrupt everyone and there isn't a lock-up unit, you may be asked to take your loved one home.

Organize an intervention with all the members of your family to be with you as you explain where your loved one is going to live. Assure them of your continued love and frequent visitation. This may be one of the hardest things you'll ever do, so surround yourself with as much support as possible.

Long-Term Care Insurance

This is the only type of insurance that will provide for care *in* the home as well as in assisted living/nursing homes. Medicare and health insurance does *not* pay for long-term care. The average annual cost of caring for a person who needs long-term care is between $40,000-$70,000. There are three ways to pay for long-term care:

1. Pay for in-home caregivers and assisted living/nursing homes out of pocket. This is expensive and can often deplete a family's life savings.

2. Meet a very specific poverty level and qualify for government assistance through the Medicaid program. Unfortunately, options become very limited because a patient can only be placed in a nursing home that accepts Medicaid. The government program for low income elders does not cover caregivers in the home. Furthermore, it is illegal to transfer assets to anyone in order to be eligible for Medicaid. Upon application, the review process may warrant an examination of bank records for the last 36 months.

3. Buy Long-Term Care Insurance. This is the best way to cover the costs of caring for someone who may need long-term care. This type of insurance will help protect your family's assets from the rising cost of caring for your loved one. It must be bought while the person is still healthy and before illness strikes.

Make sure that the coverage is comprehensive: it covers all levels of care *in* the home as well as at an assisted living/nursing facility. Be sure to check into compounded or simple interest inflation protection. It should cover respite care and allow you to hire caregivers from an agency or privately. Refuse exclusions for psychiatric conditions and be sure that it pays for home care co-ordination. Some policies cover the cost of Adult Day Care programs. You may want to consider a "Partnership Plan" that partners with your state of residency, allowing for retention of assets without having to spend-down to be eligible for Medicaid after your LTC insurance policy expires.

GE Financial (800) 456-3399   www.gecapital.com
John Hancock (800) 543-6415   www.jhancock.com
Transamerica (800) 227-3740   www.transamerica.com

Ten Warning Signs of Alzheimer's Disease

Reprinted with permission of the Alzheimer's Association of Orange County.

1. *Recent memory loss that affects job skills.*

   It's normal to occasionally forget assignments, colleagues' names, or a business associate's telephone number and remember them later. Those with dementia, such a Alzheimer's disease, may forget things more often, and not remember them later.

2. *Difficulty performing familiar tasks.*

   Busy people can be so distracted from time to time that they may leave the carrots on the stove and only remember to serve them at the end of the meal. People with Alzheimer's disease could prepare a meal and not only forget to serve it, but also forget they made it.

3. *Problems with language.*

   Everyone has trouble finding the right word sometimes, but a person with Alzheimer's disease may forget simple words or substitute inappropriate words, making his or her sentence incomprehensible.

4. *Disorientation of time and place.*

   It's normal to forget the day of the week or your destination for a moment. But people with Alzheimer's disease can become lost on their own street, not knowing where they are, how they got there or how to get back home.

5. *Poor or decreased judgment.*

   People can become so immersed in an activity that they temporarily forget the child they're watching. People with Alzheimer's disease could forget entirely the child under their care. They may also dress inappropriately, wearing several shirts or blouses.

6. *Problems with abstract thinking.*

Balancing a checkbook may be disconcerting when the task is more complicated than usual. Someone with Alzheimer's disease could forget completely what the numbers are and what needs to be done with them.

7. *Misplacing things.*

Anyone can temporarily misplace a wallet or keys. A person with Alzheimer's disease may put things in inappropriate places: an iron in the freezer, or a wristwatch in the sugar bowl.

8. *Changes in mood or behavior.*

Everyone becomes sad or moody from time to time. Someone with Alzheimer's disease can exhibit rapid mood swings from calm to tears to anger for no apparent reason.

9. *Changes in personality.*

People's personalities ordinarily change somewhat with age. But a person with Alzheimer's disease can change drastically, becoming extremely confused, suspicious, or fearful.

10. *Loss of initiative.*

It's normal to tire of housework, business activities, or social obligations, but most people regain their initiative. The person with Alzheimer's disease may become very passive and require cues and prompting to become involved.

HOW IS ALZHEIMER'S DIAGNOSED?

There is no single diagnostic test for Alzheimer's Disease. Instead, AD is diagnosed by comparing a series of test results and exams including: a thorough medical history, assessment of mental status, physical exam, neurological exam, lab tests including an EEG and brain scan, such as a CT, MRI, PET, or SPECT, psychiatric and other exams. A diagnosis of Alzheimer's disease through this evaluation is considered 80-90% accurate. The only way to be absolutely certain is through an autopsy.

Three Stages of Alzheimer's Disease

Reprinted with permission from Lisa Gwyther, *Care of Alzheimer's Patients: A Manual For Nursing Home Staff*, 1985. Published by American Health Care Association and the Alzheimer's Association.

1. **First Stage:** two to four years, leading up to and including diagnosis.

   - Recent memory loss begins to affect everyday activities, and if working, job performance.

   - Unable to remember what they were just told to do.

   - Confusion about places—gets lost going to and from familiar places and misplaces and loses things.

   - Loses spontaneity—spark or zest for life, seems disinterested.

   - Loses initiative—can't start anything.

   - Mood and personality changes—becomes anxious about their symptoms, withdraws from others.

   - Has poor judgement, makes poor decisions.

   - Requires more time to perform and accomplish routine tasks, unable to organize, plan things and follow through.

   - Has difficulty handling money, paying bills.

2. **Second Stage:** two to ten years after diagnosis. (longest stage)

   - Has increased memory loss and confusion along with shorter attention span.

   - Has problems recognizing close friends and/or family.

   - Makes repetitive statements and/or movements.

   - Becomes restless, especially in late afternoon and night, may wander.

   - Experiences occasional muscle twitching or jerking motions.

   - Has difficulty with perceptual-motor problems, is unable to get onto a chair easily and may be unable to set the table.

- Has difficulty expressing thoughts, finding the right words and will often make up stories to fill in the blanks.

- Finds reading, writing, and working with numbers difficult.

- May become suspicious, irritable, fidgety, silly, and subject to mood swings, especially tears.

- Loses impulse control; sloppy; may not want to or afraid to bathe; may undress in public; may forget table manners.

- Has weight fluctuation, usually gains and loses weight; big appetite for junk food and other people's food; will forget when the last meal was eaten and gradually loses interest in food.

- May see or hear things that are not there and will be convinced they are real.

- Often gets fixed ideas about something that is not real or true; repeats things over and over.

- Generally requires full-time supervision.

3. **Terminal Stage:** one to three years.

- Can't recognize family or self in mirror; talks to own image.

- Will lose weight even when a balanced diet is given.

- Has very little ability to provide any self-care such as bathing, dressing, eating, and toileting.

- Loses the ability to communicate with words; may groan, scream, or make strange grunting sounds.

- May put everything in the mouth or touch everything. May suck on things.

- Loses control of bowel and bladder functions.

- May experience seizures, difficulty swallowing, skin breakdown, and infection as a generalized debilitation occurs.

- Will become totally dependent and will sleep more; gradually body functions decline until death.

Startling Statistics

- An estimated 43% of Americans age 65 or older will spend time in a nursing home. 1

- By 2012, 75% of Americans over age 65 will require long-term care. 2

- Nursing home costs are high, between $40,000 to $70,000 per year, depending on where you live. The average length of stay in a nursing home is 2.5 years. 3

- Long-term care costs are rising at 6% annually. 4

- 73% of Americans incorrectly believe that Medicare is the primary funding source for most older persons' long-term care costs. 5

- In 1999, over 25 million Americans provided 80 percent of the home care to ailing or vulnerable family members. 6

- Average life expectancy at the turn of the century was 47. In 1999, average life expectancy was 73.7 for males and 79.3 for females. 7

- In 2000, there were 34 million Americans over the age of 65. By 2025, there will be 62 million. That's almost double in 25 years. 8

- In 1999, there were 76 million Baby Boomers. In 2000, 50% of Americans were 50 or older. 9

- One out of three will have their life affected by some form of dementia, either in themselves or a loved one. 10

- More than 4 million Americans have Alzheimer's disease. More than 19 million say they have a family member with the disease. By 2050, 14 million people in the U.S. are estimated to have AD. 10

- The annual cost of Alzheimer's care in the U.S. is now at least $100 *billion* and will soar to at least $375 *billion* by mid-century, overwhelming our health care system and bankrupting Medicare and Medicaid. 10

- Alzheimer's disease does not happen overnight. It begins to attack the brain 10 or 20 years before the first symptoms appear. Patients will live an average of 8 to 20 years after the first symptoms. 10

- More than 75% of those afflicted live at home. The estimated annual value of this informal care system is $196 *billion*. Spouses who are suffering from the strain of caregiving are 63% more likely to die than other spouses of the same age. 10

- Health insurance and Medicare do not pay for the long-term care that most patients require. Long-term Care Insurance must be purchased before the onset of the illness. 10

- Alzheimer's disease is costing American business over $33 *billion* a year, largely due (79%) to the lost productivity from absenteeism of employees who care for ailing family members. 10

- Nearly one out of every four U.S. house-holds (23% or 22.4 million households) is involved in caregiving to persons aged 50 or over. 11

- Between 10.3 and 14.7 million Americans age 18 and over are afflicted with adult-onset brain disorders. 12

- The average woman can expect to spend 17 years caring for a child and 18 years caring for an elderly parent. 13

Sources

1. *New England Journal of Medicine*, 1997
2. *Tribune Media Services*, February, 1997
3. *Fortune Magazine*, October, 1996
4. *American College of CLU & ChFC*, 1996
5. *National Council on Aging/John Hancock LTC Survey*, 1997
6. *AARP*, 1999
7. *The World Almanac and Book of Facts*, 1999
8. *Statistical Abstract of the United States*, 118th Edition, 1998
9. *Brain Fitness* by Robert Goldman, M.D., DO, Ph.D., 1998
10. The Alzheimer's Association, 2000
11. National Alliance for Caregiving and AARP. *National Survey*, June, 1997
12. Family Caregiver Alliance, 1996
13. The Long-Term Care Campaign, 1993. *Women and Long Term Care*. Washington, DC

Other Diseases That Act Like Alzheimer's

Reprinted with permission of the Alzheimer's Association of Orange County.

Many conditions can cause dementia. Dementia related to depression, drug interaction, thyroid and other problems may be reversible if detected early. It is important to identify the actual cause in order to receive proper care.

Alzheimer's disease is the leading cause of dementia. Some of the other diseases that cause dementia are:

1. **Creutzfeldt-Jakob Disease (CJD):** A rare, fatal brain disease caused by infection.

2. **Multi-infarct Dementia (MID):** Also known as vascular dementia. Results from brain damage caused by multiple strokes (infarcts) within the brain.

3. **Normal Pressure Hydrocephalus (NPH):** A rare disease caused by an obstruction in the flow of spinal fluid.

4. **Picks Disease:** A rare brain disease that closely resembles Alzheimer's, with personality changes and disorientation that may precede memory loss.

5. **Parkinson's Disease:** A disease affecting control of muscle activity, resulting in tremors, stiffness and speech impediment. In late stages, dementia can occur.

6. **Lewy Body Disease:** A disease, recognized only in recent years, in which the symptoms are a combination of Alzheimer's disease and Parkinson's disease.

7. **Huntington's Disease:** A hereditary disorder characterized by irregular movements of the limbs and facial muscles, a decline in thinking ability and personality changes.

8. **Depression:** A psychiatric condition in which many severely depressed persons also display symptoms of memory loss. Depression can often be reversed with treatment.

Epilog

When I finished writing my book, I happened to read an article in the *Alzheimer's Association Newsletter* by Dr. Rodman Shankle, on handling aggressive behavior in the elderly. I couldn't believe it—a doctor who *really* understood what I had gone through. I contacted him and asked if he would be interested in reviewing my manuscript. I was elated when he wanted to endorse it and even contribute a final chapter about handling aggression in dementia. I was grinning ear to ear—I guess I had some karma coming.

Dr. Shankle co-founded the UC Irvine Alzheimer's Center, and from 1988 to 1997 served as its medical director. He has established a community based dementia program that specializes in the diagnosis, management and treatment of Alzheimer's disease and other causes of dementia. He has discovered new treatments for dementia-related behavioral problems, and has diagnosed and managed over 5,000 persons with dementia, creating screening tools that will anonymously and confidentially detect the earliest stages of dementia with over 90% accuracy.

Dr. Shankle's amazing website (http://www.mccare.com) is designed for at-home, on-line early detection of the various types of dementia. With this information, you can help your parent's doctor be more accurate with an early diagnosis which will enable you to get the right medications and the most appropriate help.

If only I had met Dr. Shankle when I first realized that my father was not thinking clearly—but then, I'd never have written this book to share with all of you. I am forever grateful for his guidance and continuous words of encouragement. His chapter makes a significant contribution to expanding this book into a complete guide to handling aggressive elders.

Contact Dr. Shankle
(949) 723-4106   rshankle@mccare.com

<u>Education</u>
M.D., Brown University, 1983
Statistical Training, Harvard University, 1979
M.S., Biomedical Statistics, U.S.C., 1978
B.S., Stanford University, 1977

A Physician's Guide
to Treating Aggression in Dementia

By Rodman Shankle, MS, MD

I have successfully helped many families in crisis with a relative who has become uncontrollably aggressive. Correctly diagnosing and treating aggression in dementia is a challenging task for many doctors to deal with effectively. After reading Jacqueline's riveting story, I knew her book would help many people, and that a chapter explaining how to properly diagnose and treat this most difficult aspect of dementia could provide a useful resource for families and their physicians. This chapter is written to help you and your doctor work together to find the most appropriate treatment for managing aggression in your loved one.

Aggression in verbal, sexual or physical form is extremely common in moderate to severely demented persons. An unfortunate reality of our current understanding of the medical treatment of virtually all behavioral problems related to the progression of Alzheimer's disease and other causes of dementia is that there is very little in the way of well controlled clinical trials to guide our selection of the best treatments. Where such information exists, I have included it as references at the end of this appendix. Where such information does not exist, I have relied on an understanding of the basic and clinical research on aggressive behavior in animals and humans, combined with pharmacological knowledge of potentially useful medications, plus personal experience in treating over 4,000 demented patients, most of whom developed behavioral problems at some point during their dementia.

As with any physician, the sample of patients I have treated is biased by many factors such as geography and demographic makeup of the region I serve. Another physician's experience with their sample of demented persons may therefore differ from my own. However, since humans are more like each other than they are different, it is likely that there will be many similarities among the demented patients I have treated and those treated by other physicians. The recommendations in this appendix should therefore be generally useful, but must be tempered by the treating physician's judgment and knowledge of the individual patient's condition.

Definition of Normal Aggression

Aggression is a normal human behavior that serves an evolutionary purpose: to promote survival of individuals under adverse circumstances. Normal aggressive behavior is done in socially appropriate ways. When the *context* of the aggressive behavior is considered socially inappropriate, aggression becomes a concern.

Examples of Normal Aggression

Normal aggressive behavior is useful in a variety of situations: parents protecting their children, soldiers protecting their country, children playing sports, students taking exams, and working to improve a product.

Types of Abnormal Aggression

Abnormal aggressive behavior can take physical, verbal or sexual forms. Physical or sexual aggression is more common in men, while verbal aggression is more common in women.

Examples of Abnormal Aggression

A grandfather attacks his three-year-old granddaughter because he mistakes her for an intruder; he strikes out at a caregiver when they help him bathe, dress, or brush his teeth. Violent behavior is of great concern to caregivers, but it can be successfully managed if the conditions under which it is most likely to occur are properly identified.

Natural Course of Aggression in Dementia

Aggression is a common behavioral abnormality seen in Alzheimer's disease and other forms of dementia, particularly during the moderate to severe stages. Aggressive behavior due to the progression of the dementia itself (see Causes) can spontaneously resolve on its own over the course of six months to 3 years, presumably due to continued changes in the brain's pathways regulating aggression. Therefore, medications used to treat aggression can be tapered on a trial basis every six months.

Because dementia usually produces gradually progressive damage to the brain, abnormal aggressive behavior usually starts with a few isolated episodes, followed by more frequent and severe aggressive outbursts over time. This point emphasizes the value of periodic screening for the first signs of aggression and other common behavioral problems in a demented person. If treatment is started early, serious problems can be avoided (see Screening).

Types of Aggressive Behavior

1) Territorial Aggression

Territorial aggression occurs when an individual's boundaries are crossed, and is commonly seen among individuals defending their family, their property, their business, or when someone invades their "personal space". The aggressive behavior is defensive, with a goal of discouraging those trying to invade their "territory". In dementia, persons requiring assistance with dressing, bathing, toileting, etc., may perceive that their "territory" is being invaded and inappropriately respond to defend themselves by lashing out at the perceived invader.

2) Male-to-Male Aggression

Aggression between males is common and consists of ritualized responses to establish dominance. When a young male challenges a senior male, the elder male may respond by "putting the young whippersnapper in his place".

3) Aggression Induced by Fear

Any situation perceived as threatening, such as a new caregiver or the belief that one's spouse is having an affair, can trigger aggressive behavior. In dementia, persons may see or hear things incorrectly, and respond to protect themselves. One patient misinterpreted the bough of her tree swaying in the wind outside their kitchen window as someone trying to get into the house. She repeatedly called 911 until she was properly treated.

4) Aggression Induced by Aggravating Stimuli

Frustrating situations, such as being unable to fix something or unable to respond to an unfair situation, can make people irritable and become more easily upset. Also, chronic pain can make people more likely to "blow up" at seemingly minor provocation. In dementia, frustration followed by aggression can result from a variety of situations. Some sources of aggravation or frustration in dementia include being unable to do what one had been able to do in the past; sources of pain that can not be explained to others; or the *sensory deprivation* that occurs from sitting at home all day doing little to nothing.

The Nine Major Causes of Aggressive Behavior

Aggressive behavior can normally occur in the context of territorial behavior, interaction between males, and fearful or aggravating situations. In dementia, *abnormal* aggressive behavior is largely due to misinterpretation of events. The most common reasons that events are misinterpreted by demented persons, resulting in inappropriate aggressive behavior, can be summarized as:

1) Infection

Infection produces aggression by increasing confusion or discomfort. Urinary tract infections, sometimes from improper hygiene, are particularly common. Pneumonia, sometimes from food inadvertently going down the airway, also occurs when swallowing incoordination develops in the severe stages of the dementia.

2) Head Injury

Head Injury can produce aggressive behavior by: 1) bleeding in the brain (subdural hematoma), 2) pain, or 3) direct damage to the brain. Head injury due to falling often occurs in moderate to severe dementia when persons develop body incoordination or problems interpreting what they see.

3) Pain

Aggressive behavior can result from poorly controlled illnesses such as arthritis, headache or nerve pain, as well as from injuries related to incoordination in the moderate to severely demented patient.

4) Worsening of an Illness

Worsening of an illness can also produce aggression by increasing confusion or discomfort, which can occur when a person does not take their medications properly or can not do the behaviors necessary to control the illness.

5) Development of a New Illness

Development of a new illness can also produce aggression by increasing confusion or discomfort. Hypertension, osteoporosis, cancer, stroke, heart disease, and diabetes are all common disorders of the elderly that should be considered as possible causes of aggressive behavior.

6) Changes in the Environment or People in the Environment

Environmental changes can increase disorientation or misinterpretations and evoke fear-induced aggressive behavior. When moving to a new place to live, taking a trip, or having a new assistant come into the person's life, it may be wise to use an anti-aggression medication starting two weeks before, and continuing the medication (see Treatment) as long as needed (usually about one month). This strategy may avoid a catastrophe.

7) Changes in Sleep

Changes in sleeping pattern are common as the dementia progresses. An impaired sleep-wake cycle can increase confusion and increase the potential for aggressive behavior. (Think about the last time you had a sleepless night, and how irritable you were the next day). There are several major causes of an impaired sleep-wake cycle. One cause is reduced melatonin levels. In Alzheimer's disease, melatonin levels can be up to five times lower than age-matched control subjects (Liu et al., 1999), which suggests that supplemental melatonin may be very helpful in restoring a normal sleep-wake cycle.

Another cause of altered sleep is inadequate exposure to sunlight, particularly in the morning. An hour of sunlight exposure helps normalize the melatonin cycle, which controls when we feel sleepy. Another cause of impaired sleep is inadequate exercise, which should be done in the daytime. Finally, because body temperature, sunlight exposure and melatonin cycles are all intertwined, a hot bath in the evening for about 20 minutes may help restore a normal sleep pattern.

8) Changes in Medication

Medication must always be considered as a potential *cause* of aggressive behavior. The usual situation is that a medication's dose is changed or a medication is added or withdrawn, causing aggressive behavior to develop. The aggression can be related to either increased confusion or altered levels of a brain neurotransmitter involved in the control of aggressive behavior (See Neurophysiology).

9) Progression of the Dementia Itself

When the progression of the dementia damages brain areas that control aggressive behavior (See Neuroanatomy), abnormal aggressive behavior can develop. A diagnosis of aggression due to disease progression is largely a diagnosis of exclusion, and should not be made until the other possibilities discussed have been considered. Some of the brain areas that regulate aggressive behavior also control social behavior, so it is possible that social behavioral interventions, such as Adult Day Care or structured activities with a companion, may also reduce the aggressive behavior. If not, then a re-balancing of the brain chemistry through medication is needed (see Treatment).

The Potential for *Violent* Aggressive Behavior

The potential for violent aggressive behavior is a serious concern that can be addressed by the exemplary research of Jonathon Pincus (1999). He has studied murderers and found three common elements that characterize a dangerously violent individual: 1) a past history of being abused physically or sexually, 2) paranoia, and 3) brain damage. All three elements must be present to identify a dangerously violent person. In dementia, some level of brain damage is always present. Paranoia is characterized by an unreasonable suspiciousness or misinterpretation of surrounding events or circumstances. Paranoid delusions are a common feature of moderate to severe dementia, which usually occurs two to six years after the first dementia symptoms. Pincus' study is very helpful because it means that, even if a demented person has brain damage and is paranoid, they are unlikely to become violent or dangerous to others (even though they may be aggressive) unless the demented person has a history of being physically or sexually abused.

Medications That Can Increase or Decrease Aggression

1) Medications That Can Produce Confusion
Medications which can *increase* confusion include:
  a) The benzodiazepines (diazepam, lorazepam, alprazolam, temazepam, oxazepam, and flurazepam).
  b) Tricyclic anti-depressants (e.g., amitryptaline and imipramine).
  c) Non-selective dopamine antagonists (anti-psychotics) such as thiothixene, haloperidol, chlorpromazine, loxapine, and sometimes risperidone.
  d) Anti-tremor agents such as benztropine and trihexyphenidyl.

e) Anti-histamines such as diphendydramine.

f) Anti-incontinence agents such as hyoscyamine, oxybutynin, and tolterodine.

2) Medications That Usually Reduce Aggressive Behavior

Medications that increase the level of serotonin can reduce aggressive behavior (sertraline, bupropion, venlafaxine, fluoxetine, paroxetine, fluvoxamine, citalopram, buspirone, and trazodone.) In addition, medications that reduce the response of certain receptors to the brain transmitter, norepinephrine, reduce aggression (clonidine, an alpha-2 receptor blocker, and propranolol, a beta receptor blocker). Unfortunately, these facts are not commonly known in the medical community, and these agents may not be considered as the treatment of choice for aggressive behavior.

3) Anti-psychotic Medications

The anti-psychotic medications are often used inappropriately as the treatment of choice for aggressive behavior. The situation under which anti-psychotics *are* an appropriate treatment is when the patient has aggression plus psychosis (hallucinations: seeing, hearing, feeling, or tasting something that is not there; or delusions: *e.g.*, thinking and fearing that someone is trying to harm them). In this case, treating the psychosis will also treat the aggression if the aggression has resulted from the psychosis. However, in the absence of psychosis, there is very little evidence that anti-psychotics directly reduce aggression. Rather, non-selective anti-psychotics (See Dopamine Receptor Blockers) slow down movement, which may reduce aggression by making a person parkinsonian ("zombie-like" with various combinations of reduced movements, rigidity, loss of balance or falling, short shuffling footsteps, and tremor at rest).

4) Medications That Can Paradoxically Produce Aggression

Interestingly, medications that increase the brain's inhibitory transmitter, GABA (which usually reduces brain activity and "tranquilizes" people), can help reduce aggression in *some* patients. Sometimes, however, these GABA agents can paradoxically *increase* aggression. A possible explanation for this phenomenon is that Alzheimer's disease selectively damages brain neurons that produce excitation while leaving the neurons that produce inhibition relatively undamaged.

Thus, the Alzheimer's disease brain has relatively much more inhibition than a normal brain, which can make an individual more inhibited, stifled, or constrained than they are normally. Giving such individuals medications that increase GABA shifts the balance of excitation-to-inhibition even further in the direction of inhibition. This shift can increase confusion and fear in an already impaired individual, and may account for the paradoxical *increase* in aggression and lashing out that can occur when given GABA medications. Medications acting primarily on GABA are best used for the treatment of emergency situations in which the aggressive behavior must be stopped immediately by sedating the person.

5) Anti-convulsants

Besides the benzodiazepines, a paradoxical increase in aggression can also occur with anti-convulsants, such as valproic acid or gabapentin. However, the anti-convulsants do not appear to produce increased confusion as frequently as do the benzodiazepines, and therefore may be a useful therapeutic alternative for aggressive behavior.

6) Acetylcholine Receptor Blockers

Medications such as anti-incontinent agents or tricyclic anti-depressants, reduce acetylcholine in certain areas of the brain (lateral hypothalamus, lateral or dorsal amygdala) reduce aggressive behavior in some patients. Again, paradoxically, demented patients given such drugs often show *increased* aggressive behavior. This is because the levels of acetylcholine in Alzheimer's disease brains are already so markedly reduced that further reductions are likely to produce confusion, which increases the likelihood of aggression. The lowered levels of acetylcholine in the brains of Alzheimer's patients also explains why they do not develop aggression when given agents that *increase* acetylcholine, such as donepezil and tacrine which are the currently approved drugs for managing memory loss in Alzheimer's disease.

Diagnosis of the Cause of Aggression

The setting for evaluating and treating abnormal aggressive behavior is best done where the aggressive behavior typically occurs. However, if abnormal aggressive behavior is not detected in its early stages, there may be a crisis that requires the individual to be hospitalized to prevent them from hurting themselves or others. The disadvantage of this hospitalization is that the abnormal aggressive behavior may re-appear when the demented person returns to the environment originally associated with the aggressive behavior. Therefore, assessment in the early stages of aggressive behavior is beneficial for everyone.

Demented persons who are paranoid and have a history of being abused sexually or physically while growing up have a greater potential for *violent* aggressive behavior and should be treated in a geriatric psychiatry unit.

Aggression Evaluation Steps to Determine the Best Treatment

1) Take a history to identify whether an infection, injury, source of pain, sleep disorder, worsening of an existing illness, development of a new illness, change in environment, or medication change could explain the aggressive behavior.

2) Inquire whether the person was sexually or physically abused while growing up and if they are currently having paranoid delusions to determine if they have a greater risk for violent aggressive behavior.

3) Determine if any other behavioral problems have developed along with or prior to the aggressive behavior.

4) Identify if there are any consistent triggers for the aggressive behavior, such as interaction with a particular person, a particular time of day, a particular room or view, or a particular activity.

5) If infection is likely:

   a) Get a urinalysis and a complete blood count.

   b) If pneumonia is suspected, get a chest xray.

6) If injury is likely:

   a) Examine for sources of pain and take x-rays of suspicious areas.

   b) Evaluate changes in alertness and, if there is a suspicion of head injury, get a CT scan of the head.

7) If worsening of an existing illness is likely, assess the illness and measure the degree of change.

8) If a new illness is suspected, do appropriate tests, such as a CT scan of the head for a stroke, an electrocardiogram for a heart condition, a fasting blood glucose for diabetes, a blood pressure measurement for hypertension, etc.

9) If a sleep disorder is suspected, an evaluation by a neurologist specialized in sleep disorders may be advisable. However, first establish the following information. Get a record of:

   a) When the person sleeps.

   b) How long they sleep.

   c) What wakes them up.

   d) How long it takes them to go back to sleep.

   e) What they take to go back to sleep.

   f) If they snore or stop breathing for periods of time.

   g) If daytime exercise helps them sleep at night.

   h) If an hour of sunlight in the morning helps them sleep at night.

   i) If a hot bath in the evening helps them sleep at night.

   j) Their morning and evening melatonin levels or their morning body temperature hourly for three hours after they awake.

10) Look for changes in the environment or for new persons in the demented person's life. Examine whether there is a clear relation between the change and the aggressive behavior.

11) Look for medications that have been added or stopped, or doses that have changed. Examine whether the change could be the source of increased confusion or aggression directly (See Causes).

If any of the above potential causes are present, then they should be treated, and the effect on the aggressive behavior monitored by use of a daily chart measuring time, place and circumstances of the aggressive behavior. If none of the above have occurred or if treatment of any identified factors do not resolve the aggression, then it is likely that the dementia is progressing and causing the problem. Note that this diagnosis is made after excluding other possibilities.

Screening

Periodic screening to detect abnormal aggression as well as other behavioral problems associated with dementia increases the chance that evaluation can be done without having to transfer the patient to a more secured setting. Screening at home involves periodically (every one to three months) checking to see if any of the common behavioral problems associated with dementia have occurred. Dementia-associated behavioral problems include:

1) Tremor: A frequent, rhythmic shaking of the hands or some other part of the body.

2) Rigidity: Reduced movement or a stiff appearance of the body.

3) Slowed Movements: Such as when performing tasks or speaking.

4) Falling: Not due to a bad hip, leg, foot or arthritis.

5) Difficulty Walking.

6) Unable to Walk.

7) Loss of Balance: Not due to a bad hip, leg, foot or arthritis.

8) Masked Face: A fairly constant, blank stare on the face with reduced eye-blinking.

9) Visual Hallucinations: Seeing things that are not present.

10) Auditory Hallucinations: Hearing conversations, voices, or sounds that are not present.

11) Paranoid Delusions: An unreasonable fear of people stealing things, plotting behind their back or some other unwarranted suspicion.

12) Impaired Judgement: In handling situations or social circumstances they would normally have handled well.

13) Disinhibition: A marked change in social restraint, like behaving inappropriately in public.

14) Euphoria: Inappropriately joking, being humorous or laughing in situations where previously they would not have done so.

15) Apathy: Loss of interest or motivation in doing things they enjoy.

16) Marked decline in Activities: In the activities they usually do.

17) Verbal Aggression: Abusing or scaring others by using foul, nasty, threatening, frightening or cruel language.

18) Physical Aggression: Abusing or scaring others by hitting them, or throwing them, or throwing or damaging things.

19) Sexual Aggression: Abusing or scaring others by inappropriate, unwanted or persistent sexual displays or behaviors.

20) Agitation: Very nervous or anxious behavior, such as excessively worrying, fidgeting, getting up and down, or wringing hands.

21) Pacing: Excessively walking or moving about without leaving the premises. The person may appear distressed or have a sense of urgency about them.

22) Wandering: "Escaping", leaving the house or premises, when not supposed to or without realizing what they are doing.

23) Depression: A sad or pessimistic mood that persists for weeks.

24) Weight Loss: A noticeable, unintentional loss in weight.

25) Weight Gain: A noticeable, unintentional increase in weight.

26) Insomnia: Unable to fall or stay asleep at night.

27) Impaired Wakefulness: Drowsiness or difficulty staying alert during their usual waking hours.

28) Mutism: A marked reduction in how much they usually spoke.

29) Perseveration: Inability to stop doing or saying one thing and shift to doing or saying something else. Example: someone who keeps picking up their fork when they mean to pick up their knife.

30) Apraxia: Forgetting how to do things or having increased difficulty in doing them, such as brush teeth, put on clothes, cook, pay bills, operate a car or other tasks/hobbies they typically did.

31) Urinary Incontinence: Inability to hold urine until getting to the toilet.

32) Urinary Tract Infection: of the kidney, bladder, or ureter.

33) Inappropriate Urination or Defecation: Urinating or moving bowels in inappropriate locations such as on plants, carpets, corners, etc.

34) Trouble Swallowing: food or liquids.

35) Seizures or Epilepsy.

36) Myoclonus: Sudden and brief body or limb jerks, lasting seconds or less, with no loss of consciousness. It can occur while sleeping.

Prevention

Although it is not common to think of prevention when one already has a disease, it is good sense to do things that will *prevent complications* of a disease, just as when a person with diabetes controls their blood glucose to prevent loss of vision or sensation, stroke and kidney dysfunction. The keys to preventing aggressive behavior involve doing things that assist the function of the brain areas that control aggression (See Neuroanatomy). Treating other behavioral problems as soon as they first appear will reduce the risk of aggression developing as a consequence of these problems. Since altered serotonin and norepinephrine transmitter activity is most closely correlated with aggression, any alterations in these neurotransmitters can warn of impending aggressive behavior. Symptoms indicating that a change has occurred in these neurotransmitters include depression, anxiety, and altered sleep/wake cycle activity.

Disturbed sleep/wake cycle activity commonly occurs in mild to severely demented persons (Pat-Horenczyk et al., 1998), but is not necessarily disturbed in normal aging adults on no medications (Zeitzer et al., 1999). In Alzheimer's disease, there can be marked reductions in brain melatonin, the hormone that regulates the sleep/wake cycle. Since melatonin is derived from serotonin, an altered sleep/wake cycle can be a warning signal that aggressive behavior may appear due to low serotonin levels as well as impaired sleep.

Getting at least one hour of sunlight a day helps maintain the sleep/wake cycle (Gross, Gysin, 1996). Also, exercise may help maintain the sleep/wake cycle (Partonen et al, 1998). Finally, because free radicals can produce oxidative brain damage, which may contribute to the progression of dementia, supplementing with melatonin (a very potent anti-oxidant) is not harmful and can be quite helpful. The exact dose will vary from 200 micrograms to 9 mg taken one hour before bedtime, depending upon what dose helps the patient sleep.

By providing increased daily structure through programmed activities (Adult Day Care, family activities, or professional companions), you are assisting the patient's frontal and temporal lobes, making it possible for them to engage in activities they otherwise could not do. The increased number of activities that the patient can successfully participate in significantly reduces frustration, which in turn reduces aggressive outbursts.

Neuroanatomy of Aggression

There are many areas of the brain involved in the production and regulation of aggression. In dementia, the areas most often affected that produce aggressive behavior are the orbito-frontal lobe, the temporal lobe, and the limbic system. These areas determine how appropriate a behavioral response is to a particular event. When any of these brain areas are damaged, responses can be either too impulsive, too emotional, or too out of context.

Other types of aggressive behavior, which do not appear to be in response to any particular stimulus, may arise from damage to brain structures below the cortex, such as the hypothalamus, amygdala, brainstem or other subcortical nuclei. These types of aggressive behaviors are usually sudden outbursts that seem to appear out of nowhere and have a very simple, highly repetitive nature about them. Fear, hunger or sexual desires may trigger them. They are unplanned and target the nearest individual or object available, and can consist of screaming, spitting, pounding, kicking, biting, scratching, humping, or throwing.

It is useful to distinguish these types of aggressive behavior from those types that appear to involve an inappropriate response to interaction with a human or a misperception of something in the environment. The sexually- and hunger-driven types of aggression may be more responsive to medications that block the response of alpha-2 receptors to norepinephrine such as clonidine, or to anti-testosterone medications such as medroxyprogesterone.

Neurophysiology of Aggression

The primary neurotransmitters involved in the cortical control of aggressive behavior are serotonin and norepinephrine. This is why the most useful drugs for treating aggression are usually those that modulate serotonin or norepinephrine (See Medications). The serotonin receptor most closely associated with control of aggression is the 5HT1a subtype, while the norepinephrine receptors most closely associated with aggression control are the alpha-2 and beta subtypes.

Dopamine does not appear to play a major role in aggression control. It does, however, indirectly affect aggressive behavior by reducing physical activity and altering how we perceive objects or events (useful if a patient is hallucinating or delusional). Therefore, a dopamine receptor blocker can help an overly aggressive person by reducing their activity (which is fine so long as their movement is not too reduced). Dopamine receptor blockers can also help patients whose aggression results from hallucinations (misinterpreting a shadow of a tree for an intruder) or delusions (convinced that people are stealing things from them).

Testosterone controls the level of irritability and the display of aggressive behavior in males. Males who easily become impatient, frustrated or irritated, or are more dominant have higher testosterone levels. Testosterone can be reduced by medications that act at the 5HT1a serotonin receptor, such as buspirone, and a recently developed anti-aggression agent, Eltoprazine (not currently available in the USA). Since these agents have much fewer side effects than medroxyprogesterone, it is advisable to try them first in persons with elevated testosterone levels and aggressive behavior.

Treatment of Aggression

The treatment of abnormal aggressive behavior depends upon its cause. Infections are treated with antibiotics. Injuries are treated directly. Pain is relieved. A worsening illness is managed better. A new illness is diagnosed and treated. An offending medication is removed or adjusted. Environmental and people factors are evaluated and adjusted. Sleep is normalized. Dementia progression is managed behaviorally and, if necessary, medically. Obviously, evaluation to identify the offending cause of aggression will result in greater treatment success.

Behavioral Treatment of Aggression

A structured daily schedule provides a number of benefits towards reducing aggression and other behavioral problems associated with dementia. Structure removes the need for the person to remember what they should be doing, and can provide physical exercise, socialization, and exposure to sunlight. Structure takes advantage of the fact that motor skills or procedures are best maintained and learned in demented persons when there is little variation of time, place, persons involved, and activity performed (Dick et al., 1995, 1996).

Adult Day Activity Centers provide many of these benefits. For those demented individuals who have been "loners" most of their life, a variant of this would be to provide structured activities with a single companion. It usually takes two weeks to one month of doing the structured activities before the demented person begins to accept and enjoy doing them. One should not make the mistake of letting the person with the dementia decide after a few visits whether they want to engage in the program, anymore than you would have let your child decide whether they wanted to go to school. Quite often, demented persons simply do not have the capacity to reason what is best for them (and for you and the family).

Medications to Treat Aggression

Once it is decided to use medication to control aggressive behavior, there are several useful points to keep in mind with regard to selecting the appropriate medicine.

1) If the aggressive patient also has delusions (thought misperceptions) or hallucinations (sensory misperceptions), then an anti-psychotic agent should be tried first.

   a) Patients who are extremely overactive may be tried on a non-selective dopamine blocker such as haloperidol, loxapine or risperidone.

   b) Patients who are not extremely overactive should be tried on a selective dopamine blocker. The only two currently available are olanzapine and quetiapine.

   c) Propranolol and other beta receptor blockers can lower the total dose of anti-psychotic medication required as well as add their own anti-aggression effect.

   d) Valproic acid can lower the total dose of anti-psychotic drug as well as stabilize mood and itself reduce aggression.

   e) The non-selective dopamine receptor blockers can lower serotonin levels, so that it may be necessary to add a serotonin medication, such as an SSRI (Selective Serotonin Reuptake Inhibitor).

2) If the aggressive patient does not have delusions or hallucinations,

    a) then aggression can be treated with a medication that regulates serotonin or norepinephrine levels.

        i) Patients who are having difficulty sleeping may benefit from trazodone, paroxetine or venlafaxine at bedtime.

        ii) Patients who are not having difficulty sleeping may benefit from bupropion, sertraline, citalopram, fluoxetine, or buspirone in the morning.

        iii) For quicker response (within a few days), it may be desirable to use propranolol (or a selective beta blocker (metoprolol) if propranolol is not indicated) which can be adjusted to a total daily dose of 10-90 mg over one week. Adjustments of 10-30 mg can be made every two to three days if necessary to a final dose of 10-30 mg two to three times daily. This may give the serotonin medication enough time to take effect as they sometimes take up to two weeks once the right dose is identified.

    b) If these medications do not work, then second line agents include clonidine, valproic acid and gabapentin. Donepezil can also be tried although it is likely that patients will already be on these medications if they have Alzheimer's disease. The dosage of Aricept may be increased by 5 to 10 mg not faster than every two weeks to as high as 20 mg at bedtime. Although 10 mg per day is the recommended maximal dose of Aricept, 20 mg can usually be safely tried without side effects if there is no response at lower doses.

    c) Before resorting to third line medications, the possibility that the person may have delusions or hallucinations should be reconsidered. If the possibility exists, then either selective or non-selective dopamine receptor blockers should be tried according to the guidelines above. Third line medications include lithium and medroxyprogesterone.

3) If the aggressive patient does not have delusions or hallucinations but does have agitation or anxiety (see Screening), then aggression can be treated with a medication that reduces anxiety.

a) While the primary medications used for anxiety in non-demented patients are the benzodiazepines (See Medications), these medications can increase confusion and aggression. Therefore, it is useful to first try propranolol, buspirone or paroxetine.

    i) Propranolol can work very quickly and be adjusted every three days to a maximum daily dose of 10 to 90 mg (Shankle et al., 1995). These doses are far below those typically used in other types of patients, such as schizophrenics, but they work in many demented patients. I have some patients whose aggression has been controlled for years on such low doses of propranolol, whose aggression returns within a few days if propranolol is stopped. When propranolol or a selective beta receptor blocker works, it has the advantage of fast action and no side effects (at these low doses).

    ii) Buspirone can take weeks to months to become effective and the exact dose is quite variable (10 to 60 mg per day). propranolol is therefore often given to deal with the acute episodes of anxiety or aggression, while gradually increasing buspirone every other week to control anxiety and aggression on a long term basis.

    iii) Paroxetine, in doses of 10 to 40 mg given at bedtime, takes about two weeks to control anxiety and aggression, although partial effects may be seen within one week.

b) For managing acute anxiety or aggression, if the beta receptor blockers fail, then one can consider giving either an anti-convulsant (valproic acid or gabapentin), an anti-psychotic or a benzodiazepine on an as needed basis to control severe episodes.

4) If the aggressive person does not have delusions or hallucinations, but does have depression, then aggression can be treated with an anti-depressant that modulates serotonin and/or norepinephrine levels. This includes all of the SSRIs (see below) as well as trazodone. [Desyrel]. Note that paroxetine [Paxil], an atypical SSRI used for panic disorder and obsessive compulsive behavior, may be less effective than other SSRIs for treating aggression.

Anti-Aggression Medications Grouped by Their Site of Action

1) Serotonin Receptor Medications

An area in the brainstem called the "median raphe nuclei" is the primary source of serotonin, which is transmitted to serotonin receptors throughout the brain. Animal and human studies show that lowered serotonin levels directly evoke aggressive behavior.

The most common serotonin medications are the class of anti-depressants called the Selective Serotonin Reuptake Inhibitors (**SSRIs**). An older tricyclic anti-depressant, trazodone, also has high serotonin activity with relatively few side effects (some patients, however, can develop a tilt to their walking). These medications have not been extensively studied in the treatment of aggression in dementia, but the available studies indicate they are effective. The SSRI medications that can be given in the daytime include sertraline, bupropion, fluoxetine, citalopram, buspirone, and sometimes venlafaxine. The medications that should be given at bedtime include trazodone, fluvoxamine, paroxetine, and sometimes venlafaxine (when it induces drowsiness). At the dose given, these medications take about two weeks to exert their full effect, but some effect can be noted within 3 to 5 days.

These medications should be started at the smallest available dose and adjusted once a week. In more critical situations, the starting dosage can be larger and adjustments made every three days, with the understanding that the dose may need reduction once control is achieved.

2) Norepinephrine Receptor Medications

Medications that block the beta receptor of the neurotransmitter, norepinephrine, have been extensively used for psychiatric disorders such as schizophrenia and anxiety, but have been relatively unused in dementia. In these psychiatric disorders, large doses (200 mg/day or more) are typically used.

In dementia, one can successfully use much smaller doses of beta receptor blockers. For example, propranolol, a beta receptor blocker often used in hypertension and some forms of heart disease, has been shown to be effective in treating aggressive behavior in demented persons at total daily doses between 10 and 90 mg, given in two or three divided doses. Because of their short duration of action, aggression improves within three days of an effective dose. One can adjust propranolol every three days to achieve faster control of aggressive behavior, which may be useful while waiting for a serotonin drug to become effective. These doses are usually well below the dose range at which side effects from propranolol occur (slowed heart rate, reduced blood pressure, depression, and confusion). For those who can not take propranolol because of congestive heart failure, diabetes, bronchitis or other problems, a more selective beta blocker, such as metoprolol may be helpful. It is interesting to note that concert musicians who suffer from stage fright often take 10 mg of propranolol before performing; critics consistently rate their performances on propranolol as better.

3) Dopamine Receptor Blockers

Although not primarily categorized as anti-aggression medication, drugs that block dopamine receptors (also known as neuroleptics or anti-psychotics), are frequently used to treat aggression. *Non-selective* dopamine receptor blockers, such as haloperidol, thiothixene, and even risperidone (to a lesser degree) reduce aggression by inhibiting movement and reducing hallucinations or delusional thinking. These non-selective dopamine receptor blockers can be very effective in treating aggression when its primary cause is a hallucination (seeing, hearing, feeling or tasting something that frightens them) or delusion (thinking that someone is trying to harm them). However, since *non-selective* anti-psychotics also inhibit movement, people can develop unacceptable side effects of parkinsonism (rigidity, mask-like face with reduced blinking and "staring", short, shuffling steps when walking, mumbling speech and slowed body movements). Sometimes, slowing a person down who is excessively physically active can be a good thing, so that non-selective dopamine blockers are useful in persons with hallucinations or delusions, aggression and excessive motor activity.

Selective dopamine receptor blockers currently include quetiapine and olanzapine. These medications usually do not produce parkinsonian symptoms. However, they can cause weight gain, which can be very disturbing to some patients. They are quite useful when the patient has delusions or hallucinations, aggression, but is not excessively physically active. Typically, safe total daily dosages are 2.5 to 7.5 mg at bedtime for olanzapine and 25 to 100 mg for quetiapine. Olanzapine is usually given once at bedtime; quetiapine can be tried initially once a day, but may need to be given twice a day if aggression appears at the end of the day or evening.

In summary, dopamine receptor blockers do not act on aggression directly, but rather act on hallucinations or delusions, which can be the primary cause of aggressive behavior. Unless delusions or hallucinations are present, dopamine receptor blockers should not be the first choice in treating aggressive behavior. Serotonin- or norepinephrine-modulating medications should be the treatment of choice.

4) GABA Receptor Medications

The most frequently misused medications for aggression are the benzodiazepine family, which include lorazepam, oxazepam, diazepam, temazepam, alprazolam, clonazepam and flurazepam. As previously mentioned, these drugs can increase aggressive behavior by increasing confusion. Because benzodiazepines usually become ineffective after one month of daily use, they are not useful for long-term treatment of aggression., and should be reserved for emergencies, when it is necessary to sedate an actively aggressive person. A similar problem exists with zolpidem.

5) Anti-convulsants

Anti-convulsants, such as valproic acid, carbamazepine, gabapentin, topiramate, lamotrigine, and phenytoin have complex actions in the brain, which may sometimes help treat aggression. Anti-convulsants are usually a second line of defense after other medications have been tried. Part of their action is inhibitory (GABA), but they do not develop tolerance like the benzodiazepines. They can, however, increase confusion, especially at higher doses. They appear to be helpful, particularly when there is a mood disorder (depression and/or mania) or psychosis associated with the aggressive behavior. Valproic acid, for example, can improve mood disorders (particularly mania) as well as psychosis, thus lowering the required dose of an anti-psychotic. Sometimes, valproic acid will acceptably control these symptoms without an anti-psychotic. These drugs usually take about one week to reach their full effect, but can demonstrate noticeable effects within three days.

6) Anti-Testosterone Medications

Medications that reduce testosterone may reduce aggressive behavior in patients with relatively high testosterone levels. However, it is now being recognized that elderly men have a risk for testosterone deficiency. It has also been recently discovered that testosterone can improve nonverbal and verbal skills in testosterone deficient elderly males. Testosterone therapy will probably be tried more often, particularly in demented men. Whether we will see an increase in aggressive behavior in such persons remains to be seen.

Aggressive behavior that is related to elevated brain testosterone has a very primitive appearance, such as putting plants or other objects into the mouth, or engaging in indiscriminate sexual activity with other persons or objects. In this case, the aggression may respond to anti-testosterone medication, such as medroxyprogesterone. Such medications, however, have many potential side effects and should be considered only as a last resort. Before starting such a drug, it is wise to measure the testosterone level to see if it is actually elevated.

Conclusion

Aggression is only considered to be a problem when it is displayed in the wrong social context. The brain damage that occurs in dementia such as Alzheimer's disease results in aggressive behavior out of context particularly during moderate to severe dementia. There are many causes of aggressive behavior in demented persons that need to be considered, identified and treated before attributing aggressive behavior to "dementia progression". Behavioral approaches to treating aggressive behavior should usually be tried first, although they may be ineffective without some medication. In considering which medications to select for the treatment of aggressive behavior, one needs to consider the other medications the person is taking as well as the other behavioral problems that co-exist with the aggressive behavior. By doing so, the best medical treatment can be selected and the aggressive behavior reduced.

Only rarely is it necessary to place a person in an institutional facility to control aggressive behavior. However, if they have dementia plus a childhood history of being physically or sexually abused plus paranoid delusions, then they have a much higher risk for being violent, and temporary institutionalization should be done until the aggressive behavior is controlled.

Periodically checking for the first appearance of behavioral problems associated with dementia allows problems to be detected, diagnosed and properly treated in their earliest stages. Such a screening approach for dementia-associated behavioral problems could have helped avoid some of the catastrophes Jacqueline and many others have experienced in taking care of demented persons.

Notice

The indications and dosages of drugs recommended in this book have been developed according to the best available information in the medical literature at this time, as well as based on Dr. Shankle's experience in treating demented patients with aggression and other behavioral problems for over 12 years. Due to the paucity of controlled clinical trials for the treatment of aggression and other behavioral problems related to dementia, the medications described do not necessarily have specific approval by the Food and Drug Administration for the treatment of these dementia-related problems. The package insert for each drug should be consulted for use and dosage as approved by the FDA. Because standards for usage change, it is advisable to keep abreast of revised recommendations, particularly those concerning new drugs.

References

Dick, M.B., Nielson, K.A., Beth, R.E., Shankle, W.R., and Cotman, C.W. Acquisition and Long-Term Retention of a Fine Motor Skill in Alzheimer's Disease. Brain and Cognition, 1995;29:294-306.

Dick, M.B., Shankle, W.R., Beth, R.E., Dick-Muehlke, C., Cotman, C.W., and Keane, M.L. Acquisition and Long-Term Retention of a Gross Motor Skill in Alzheimer's Disease Patients Under Constant and Varied Practice Conditions. Journal of Gerontology: Psychological Sciences, 1996;51B:103-111.

Gross F, Gysin F. Phototherapy in psychiatry: clinical update and review of indications. Encephale, 1996;22:143-8.

Liu RY, Zhou JN, van Heerikhuize J, Hofman MA, Swaab DF. Decreased melatonin levels in postmortem cerebrospinal fluid in relation to aging, Alzheimer's disease, and apolipoprotein E-epsilon 4/4 genotype. J Clin Endocrinol Metab, 1999;84:323-7.

Partonen T, Lappamaki S, Hurme J, Lonnqvist J. Randomized trial of physical exercise alone or combined with bright light on mood and health-related quality of life. Psychol Med., 1998;28:1359-64.

Pat-Horenczyk R, Klauber MR, Shochat T, Ancoli-Israel S. Hourly profiles of sleep and wakefulness in severely versus mild-moderately demented nursing home patients. Aging (Milano), 1998;10:308-15.

Pincus JH. Aggression, Criminality and the Frontal Lobes. In The Human Frontal Lobes, eds. Miller BL, Cummings JL. Guilford Press, New York, 1999:547-556.

Shankle, W.R., Nielson, K.A., and Cotman, C.W. Low-Dose Propranolol Reduces Aggression and Agitation Resembling that Associated with Orbitofrontal Dysfunction in Elderly Demented Patients. Alzheimer Disease and Associated Disorders, 1995; 9:233-237.

Zeitzer JM, Daniels JE, Duffy JF, Klerman EB, Shanahan TL, Dijk DJ, Czeisler CA. Do plasma melatonin concentrations decline with age? Am J Med, 1999;107:432-6.

Valuable Resources

AAA Foundation for Traffic Safety (55+ self exam test)
800-305-7233
www.aaafts.org

AARP Legal Hotline (American Association of Retired Persons)
800-424-3410
www.aarp.org

Accent on Information (Accent on Living: Ideas for home accessibility)
309-378-2961
www.accentonliving@aol.com

Access to Recreation Catalogue (Exercise equipment for the disabled)
800-634-4351
www.accesstr.com

AdaptAbility: Products for Independent Living
800-243-9232
www.ssww.com

Adult Day Care Referrals (National Council on the Aging)
800-424-9046
www.ncoa.org

AgeNet.com (Examines concerns for the elderly)

Aging Network Services (Linkage to private geriatric care managers)
301-657-4329
www.agingnets.com

Alzheimer's Disease and Related Disorders Association
800-272-3900
www.alz.org

Alzheimer's Disease Education & Referral Center (Clinical trials)
800-438-4380
www.alzheimers.org

Alzheimer's Information
www.ec-online.net

American Association for Geriatric Psychiatry
301-654-7850
www.aagpgpa.org

American Association of Homes and Services for the Aging
202-783-2242
www.aahsa.org

American Health Care Association (Referrals to care facilities)
202-842-4444
www.ahca.org

American Medical Association
800-621-8335
www.ama-assn.org

American Occupational Therapy Association (Health & Rehabilitation)
301-652-2682
www.aota.org

American Physical Therapy Association
703-684-2782
www.apta.org

American Psychiatric Association (Fact sheets on aging)
202-682-6000
www.psych.org

American Psychiatric Nurses Association
202-857-1133
www.apna.com

American Psychological Association (State referrals)
800-374-2721
www.apa.org

American Society on Aging
www.asaging.org

American Speech-Language-Hearing Association
800-638-8255
www.asha.org

America's House Call Network (Long-term care)
www.housecall.com

Area Agency on Aging (Eldercare Locator: referrals)
800-677-1116
www.n4A.org

Assisted Living Federation of America (State referrals)
703-691-8100
www.alfa.org

AT&T Accessible Communication Products Center (Catalogue)
888-708-0874
www.telephones.att.com

Better Hearing Institute (Free booklets on hearing loss)
888-432-7435
www.betterhearing.org

Caregiver91.com (Local and regional resources)

Caregiverzone.com (Resources for caregivers and seniors)

Caregiving.com (Monthly newsletter)
847-823-0639

Children of Aging Parents (Counseling and referrals to caregivers)
800-227-7294
www.careguide.com

Choice in Dying (Forms for Living Wills and Durable Power of Attorney)
800-989-9455 (Telephone crisis counseling)
www.choices.org

Disability resources on the internet
www.disability.com

Eldercare Locator (Provides referrals to local Area Agencies on Aging)
800-677-1116
www.n4A.org

Elderweb.com (Eldercare resources)
309-451-3319

Electric Mobility Catalogue (Electric scooters and power chairs)
800-662-4548
www.electricmobility.com

Enhanced Vision Systems
800-440-9476
www.enhancedvision.com

Family Caregiver Alliance (Support for caregivers)
800-445-8106
www.caregiver.org

Funeral and Memorial Societies of America
800-765-0107
www.funerals.org

Grief Recovery Helpline
800-445-4808
www.grief-recovery.com

Healthandage.com (Foundation for Gerontology)

Health Insurance Association of America (Guide for Long-Term Care)
800-879-4422   202-824-1600
www.hiaa.org

Hemlock Society USA (Right-to-die advocacy group)
800-247-7421
www.hemlock.org

Homecare America
877-SHOP-HCA
www.homecareamerica.com

Hospice Education Institute (Referrals for the terminally ill)
800-331-1620
www.hospiceworld.org

Hospice Helpline (Referrals for the terminally ill)
800-658-8898
www.nho.org

Independent Living Aids Catalogue (Low vision aids)
800-537-2118
www.independentliving.com

Institute of Gerontology
www.iog.wayne.edu

Institute for Successful Aging (Coaching, Training, Research)
206-523-5640
www.fullpotential.com/jwg/isa

Lighthouse International Catalogue (Low vision aids, talking products)
800-829-0500
www.lighthouse.org

Long-Term Care
www.housecall.com

LS&S Group Catalogue (Low vision aids, hearing impaired products)
800-468-4789
www.lssgroup.com

Meals on Wheels Foundation (Meals to homebound persons)
616-531-9909
www.mealsonwheels.org

Medicaid (Health Care Financing Administration)
410-786-3000
www.hcfa.gov

Medic Alert (Medical identification bracelets and necklaces)
800-825-3785
www.medicalert.org

Medicare Hotline (Will let you know what expenses are covered)
800-638-6833
www.medicare.gov

NAHB Research Center (How to retrofit homes for the disabled)
301-249-4000
www.nahbrc.org

National Academy of Elder Law Attorneys (Free brochure)
520-881-4005
www.naela.org (Local referrals)

National Adult Day Services Association (NADSA)
202-479-6682
www.ncoa.org/nadsa/

National Alliance for Caregiving (Education for caregivers)
301-718-8444
www.caregiving.org

National Alliance for the Mentally Ill (Referrals to support groups)
800-950-6264
www.nami.org

National Association of Area Agencies on Aging (NAAAA)
800-677-1116 (Eldercare Locator)
www.aoa.dhhs.gov

National Association for Continence
800-252-3337
www.nafc.org

National Association for Home Care (Referrals to local providers)
202-547-7424
www.nahc.org

National Association of Professional Geriatric Care Managers
520-881-8008
www.caremanager.org

National Association of Social Workers (Membership organization)
800-638-6799
www.socialworkers.org

National Citizens Coalition for Nursing Home Reform (Referrals)
202-332-2275
www.nccnhr.org

National Council on the Aging (NCOA)
800-424-9046
www.ncoa.org

National Domestic Abuse Line
800-799-SAFE
www.ndvh.org

National Eldercare Referral Systems (Nursing home reports)
800-571-1918
www.nursinghomereports.com

National Family Caregivers Association
800-896-3650
www.nfcacares.org

National Federation of Interfaith Volunteer Caregivers
800-350-7438
www.nfivc.org

National Foundation for Depressive Illness
800-248-4381

National Health Information Center (Referrals)
800-336-4797
www.nhic-nt.health.org

National Hospice Organization (Referrals to services for the terminally ill)
800-338-8619
www.nho.org

National Institute on Aging Information Center
800-222-2225
www.nih.gov/nia/

National Institutes of Health
www.nih.gov

National Institute of Mental Health (Clinical trials)
301-443-4513
www.nimh.nih.gov

National Institute of Neurological Disorders and Stroke
800-352-9424
www.ninds.nih.gov

National Mental Health Association
800-969-6642
www.nmha.org

National Organization for Rare Disorders
800-999-6673
www.rarediseases.org

National Osteoporosis Foundation
800-223-9994
www.nof.org

National Safety Council (Course for elderly drivers)
800-621-6244
www.nsc.org

National Senior Citizens Education and Research Center
301-578-8800
www.nscerc.org

National Senior Citizens Law Center
202-289-6976
www.nsclc.org

National Stroke Association
800-787-6537
www.stroke.org

New Lifestyles (Area guide to senior residences and care options)
800-869-9549
www.newlifestyles.com

Ombudsman Program (Counseling and Advocacy in California)
800-231-4024 (Crisis line for seniors in long-term care facilities)
www.aging.state.ca.us

People's Medical Society (Patient Advocacy and Information)
610-770-1670
www.peoplesmed.org

Pharmaceutical Research and Manufacturers of America
202-835-3400
www.phrma.org

PharmInfo Net (Medication information)
www.pharminfo.com/pin_hp.html

Sears Home Health Care Catalogue
800-326-1750
www.sears.com

Self Care Catalog: Tools for Healthy Living
800-345-3371
www.selfcare.com

Senior Advisors Network (Free financial counseling for Southern CA)
800-640-5626

Senior Alternatives (Retirement communities)
www.senioralternatives.com

Senior.com (Information for seniors)

Senior Corps Hotline (Volunteer programs: Foster Grandparents,
Senior Companion Program, Retired Senior Program)
800-424-8867
www.seniorcorps.org

Senior Law Home Page
www.seniorlaw.com:80

Senior Options (Nationwide guide to senior services)
www.senioroptions.com

Senior Sites (Senior housing, healthcare and services)
www.seniorsites.com

Seniors-site (Non-profit senior housing)
www.senior-infosite.com

Smith & Nephew Catalogue (Rehabilitation products)
800-558-8633
www.easy-living.com

Social Security Administration (For direct deposit of SS checks)
800-772-1213
www.ssa.gov

Terra Nova Films (Videos on caring for elders)
773-881-8491
www.terranova.org

Trust Line (Background criminal checks in California)
800-822-8490
www.trustline.org

United Way of America (Referrals to community care programs)
800-892-2757
www.unitedway.org

U.S. Administration on Aging
202-619-0724
www.aoa.dhhs.gov

Visiting Nurse Association of America (VNAA)
800-426-2547
www.vnaa.org

Volunteers of America, Inc.
800-899-0089
www.voa.org

Well Spouse Foundation (Association of spousal caregivers)
800-838-0879
www.wellspouse.org

Widowed Persons Service (AARP)
202-434-2277
www.aarp.org

Yes, I Can, Inc. (Help in finding accessible products)
800-FON I CAN
www.yesican.com

Recommended Reading

Amarnick, C. *Don't Put Me In A Nursing Home!*
Deerfield Beach, Fl: Garrett Publishing, Inc., 1996

Amen, Daniel. *Change Your Brain, Change Your Life: The Breakthrough Program for Conquering Anxiety, Depression, Obsessiveness, Anger and Impulsiveness.* New York: Times Books, 2000

Astor, Bart. *The Baby Boomer's Guide to Caring for Aging Parents.* New York: Macmillan Spectrum, 1998

Beard, Patricia. *Good Daughters: Loving Our Mothers as They Age.* New York: Warner Books, 1999

Berman, Claire. *Caring for Yourself While Caring for Your Aging Parents.* New York: Henry Holt & Co., 1997

Bloomfield, Harold. *Making Peace With Your Past.* New York: HarperCollins, 2000

Bradshaw, John. *The Family: A New Way of Creating Solid Self Esteem.* Deerfield Beach, FL: Health Communications, 1996

Brandt, Avrence L. *Caregiver's Reprieve: A Guide to Emotional Survival When You're Caring for Someone You Love.* San Luis Obispo, CA: Impact Publishing, 1997

Buckingham, R.W. *When Living Alone Means Living At Risk: A Guide For Caregivers and Families.* Buffalo, NY: Prometheus Books, 1994

Caldwell, Marianne Dickerman. *Gone Without A Trace.* Forest Knolls, CA: Elderbooks, 1995

Cassidy, T.M. *Eldercare: What To Look For, What To Look Out For!* Liberty Corners, NJ: New Horizon Press, 1997

Chearney, L.A. *Visits: Caring For An Aging Parent: Reflections and Advice.* New York: Three Rivers Press, 1998

Combs, Linda. *The Long Goodbye and Beyond: Coping With Alzheimer's.* Wilsonville, OR: Book Partners, 1999

Cooper, Joan Hunter. *Fourteen Friends Guide to Eldercaring.* New York: Capital Books, 1999

Davenport, Gloria. *Working With Toxic Older Adults: A Guide to Coping With Difficult Elders.* New York: Springer Publishing, 1999

Dowling, James R., and Nancy L. Mace. *Keeping Busy: A Handbook of Activities for Persons With Dementia.* Baltimore, MD: The Johns Hopkins University Press, 1995

Evans, Patricia. *The Verbally Abusive Relationship: How to Recognize it and How to Respond.* Holbrook, MA: Adams Media, 1996

Feil, Naomi. *The Validation Breakthrough: Simple Techniques for Communicating With People With Alzheimer's-Type Dementia.* Baltimore, MD: Health Professions Press, 1993

Ferrin, Kelly. *What's Age Got To Do With It?* San Diego, CA: Alti Publishing, 1999

Forward, Susan. *Toxic Parents: Overcoming Their Hurtful Legacy and Reclaiming Your Life.* New York: Bantam Books, 1989

Forward, Susan, and Donna Frazier. *Emotional Blackmail: When the People in Your Life Use Fear, Obligation and Guilt to Manipulate You.* New York: HarperCollins, 1998

Friel, John C., and Linda Friel. *An Adult Child's Guide to What's Normal.* Deerfield, FL: Health Communications, 1990

Goldoftas, Lisa, and Carolyn Farren. *The Conservatorship Book.* Berkeley, CA: Nolo Press, 1997

Gould, Jean. *Dutiful Daughters: Caring for Our Parents as They Grow Old.* Seattle, WA: Seal Press, Feminist Pub, 1999

Gray-Davidson, Frena. *The Alzheimer's' Sourcebook for Caregivers: A Practical Guide for Getting Through the Day.* Los Angeles: Lowell House, 1999

Greenberg, V.E. *Respecting Your Limits When Caring For Aging Parents.* San Francisco: Jossey-Bass Publishers, 1998

Gwyther, Lisa and T. Patrick Toal. *Pressure Points: Alzheimer's and Anger.* Durham, NC: Duke University Medical Center, 2000

Ilardo, Joseph. *As Parents Age: A Psychological and Practical Guide.* Acton, MA: VanderWyk & Burnham, 1998

Kingsmill, S., and B. Schlesinger. *The Family Squeeze: Surviving the Sandwich Generation.* Toronto: University of Toronto Press, 1998

Kuhn, Betty. *What to Do When Mom Moves In: Ideas to Make it Easier.* Wilsonville, OR: Book Partners, 1999

Lebow, Grace H., and Barbara Kane. *Coping With Your Difficult Older Parent: A Guide for Stressed-Out Children.* New York: Avon Books, 1999

Lee, Anita Jones, and Melanie Callender. *The Complete Guide to Eldercare.* Hauppauge, NY: Barrons Educational Series, 1998

Levin, Nora Jean. *How to Care for Your Parents: A Practical Guide to Eldercare.* New York: W.W. Norton, 1997

Loverde, Joy. *The Complete Eldercare Planner: Where to Start, Which Questions to Ask, and How to Find Help.* New York: Times Books, 2000

Mace, Nancy L., and Peter Rabins. *The 36-Hour Day: A Guide to Caring for Persons with Alzheimer's Disease, Related Dementing Illnesses and Memory Loss in Later Life.* Baltimore, MD: The John Hopkins University Press, 1999

Martin, Laurence M. *The Nursing Home Decision: Easing the Transition For Everyone.* New York: John Wiley and Sons, 1999

McFarlane, Rodger, and Philip Bashe. *The Complete Bedside Companion.* New York: Simon & Schuster, 1998

McIlwain, H., and D. Bruce. *My Parent My Turn.* Nashville, TN: Broadman & Holman, 1995

Molloy, William. *Caring For Your Parents in Their Senior Years: A Guide For Grown-Up Children.* Willowdale, Ontario: Firefly Books, 1998

Morris, Virginia. *How to Care For Aging Parents.* New York: Workman Publishing, 1996

Morse, Sarah, and Donna Quinn Robbins. *Moving Mom and Dad*. Petaluma, CA: Lanier Publishing, 1998

Pipher, Mary. *Another Country: Navigating the Emotional Terrain of Our Elders*. New York: Riverhead Books, 2000

Ross, Sandra. *Pitching In: When Your Elderly Parents Need Help*. Laguna Niguel, CA: Creative Opportunities, 1999

Rubenson, Ellen B. *When Aging Parents Can't Live Alone: A Practical Family Guide*. Lincolnwood, IL: NTC/Contemporary Publishing, 2000

Schiff, Harriet Sarnoff. *How Did I Become My Parent's Parent?* New York: Penguin Books, 1997

Schomp, Virginia. *The Aging Parent Handbook; The Baby Boomer Dilemma; How to Take Care of Your Loved Ones*. New York. HarperCollins, 1997

Scileppi, K.P. *Caring For The Parents Who Cared For You: What To Do When An Aging Parent Needs You*. Secaucus, NJ: Carol Publishing Group, 1996

Simon, George K. *In Sheep's Clothing: Understanding and Dealing With Manipulative People*. Little Rock, AR: A.J. Christopher, 1996

Volicer, Ladislav, and Lisa Bloom-Charette. *Enhancing the Quality of Life in Advanced Dementia*. New York: Brunner/Mazel, 1999

Whybrow, R. *Caring For Elderly Parents*. New York: The Crossroad Publishing Co., 1996

Williams, G.B., and P. Kay. *The Caregiver's Manual: A Guide To Helping The Elderly And Infirm*. Secaucus, NJ: Carol Publishing Group, 1995

Wold, L.F., and A.F. Anderson. *Family Realities: Helping Aging Parents, Closing The Family Home, Dividing Family Possessions, Putting Affairs In Order*. Vista, CA: Harmony House, 1998

Young, Ellen P. *Between Two Worlds: Special Moments of Alzheimer's and Dementia*. Buffalo, NY: Prometheus Books, 1999

Zgola, Jitka M. *Care That Works: A Relationship Approach to Persons With Dementia*. Baltimore, MD: The Johns Hopkins University Press, 1999

Contact the Author

Jacqueline Marcell

Is available to speak about Elder Care at your: Company, Business Association, Community Center, Conference or Special Event, Health-Care Facility, or Radio/Television Program. She also does individual counseling.

Impressive Press

(949) 975-1012

www.ElderRage.com

jmarcell@elderrage.com

Quick Order Form

Fax   (949) 975-1013 *(Tear out and fax this form)*
Phone   (949) 975-1012 *(Have your credit card ready)*
Internet   www.ElderRage.com
                 e-mail: impressivepress@home.com
Mail   Send this form with a check, or your credit card info to:
                 Impressive Press
                 25 Via Lucca, Suite J-333
                 Irvine, California 92612-0604

Please send _____ copies of the Impressive Press book:

Elder Rage By Jacqueline Marcell

Company _____

Name _____

Address _____

City _____ **St** _____ **Zip** _____ - _____

Phone (_____) _____

E-mail _____

CA Sales Tax Add 7.75% for books shipped within California
Example: One book: 19.95 + 1.55 Sales Tax = $21.50 *(plus* shipping)

Shipping *US*: Add $4 for the first book and $2 for each additional
International: Add $9 for the first and $5 for each additional (estimate)

Total $_____ ❑ Check enclosed *(Sorry, no COD)*

To Order by Credit Card *(Please check one)*

     ❑ Visa   ❑ American Express   ❑ MasterCard

Name on Card _____

Account Number _____

Expiration Date _____ / _____

Signature _____

Comments _____

Quick Order Form

Fax   (949) 975-1013 *(Tear out and fax this form)*
Phone   (949) 975-1012 *(Have your credit card ready)*
Internet www.ElderRage.com
             e-mail: impressivepress@home.com
Mail   Send this form with a check, or your credit card info to:
             Impressive Press
             25 Via Lucca, Suite J-333
             Irvine, California 92612-0604

Please send _____ copies of the Impressive Press book:

Elder Rage By Jacqueline Marcell

Company _____

Name _____

Address _____

City _____ **St** _____ **Zip** _____ - ____

Phone (____) _____

E-mail _____

CA Sales Tax Add 7.75% for books shipped within California
Example: One book: 19.95 + 1.55 Sales Tax = $21.50 *(plus* shipping)

Shipping *US*: Add $4 for the first book and $2 for each additional
International: Add $9 for the first and $5 for each additional (estimate)

Total $_____ ❑ Check enclosed *(Sorry, no COD)*

To Order by Credit Card *(Please check one)*

❑ Visa   ❑ American Express   ❑ MasterCard

Name on Card _____

Account Number _____

Expiration Date _____ / _____

Signature _____

Comments _____

Quick Order Form

Fax	(949) 975-1013 *(Tear out and fax this form)*
Phone	(949) 975-1012 *(Have your credit card ready)*
Internet	www.ElderRage.com
	e-mail: impressivepress@home.com
Mail	Send this form with a check, or your credit card info to:
	Impressive Press
	25 Via Lucca, Suite J-333
	Irvine, California 92612-0604

Please send _____ copies of the Impressive Press book:

Elder Rage By Jacqueline Marcell

Company _____

Name _____

Address _____

City _____ **St** _____ **Zip** _____ - _____

Phone (_____ **)** _____

E-mail _____

CA Sales Tax Add 7.75% for books shipped within California
Example: One book: 19.95 + 1.55 Sales Tax = $21.50 (*plus* shipping)

Shipping *US*: Add $4 for the first book and $2 for each additional
International: Add $9 for the first and $5 for each additional (estimate)

Total $_____ ❑ Check enclosed *(Sorry, no COD)*

To Order by Credit Card *(Please check one)*

❑ Visa   ❑ American Express   ❑ MasterCard

Name on Card _____

Account Number _____

Expiration Date _____ **/** _____

Signature _____

Comments _____